Philosophy in the Ancient World

Philosophy in the Ancient World

An Introduction

JAMES A. ARIETI

WITH ILLUSTRATIONS BY
DAVID M. GIBSON

ROWMAN & LITTLEFIELD PUBLISHERS, INC.

Lanham • Boulder • New York • Toronto • Oxford

ROWMAN & LITTLEFIELD PUBLISHERS, INC.

Published in the United States of America
by Rowman & Littlefield Publishers, Inc.
A wholly owned subsidiary of The Rowman & Littlefield Publishing Group, Inc.
4501 Forbes Boulevard, Suite 200, Lanham, Maryland 20706
www.rowmanlittlefield.com

PO Box 317
Oxford
OX2 9RU, UK

British Library Cataloguing in Publication Information Available

Library of Congress Cataloging-in-Publication Data

Arieti, James A.
  Philosophy in the ancient world : an introduction / James A. Arieti ; with illustrations by
David M. Gibson.
      p. cm.
  Includes bibliographical references and index.
  ISBN 0-7425-3328-X (cloth : alk. paper) — ISBN 0-7425-3329-8 (pbk. : alk. paper)
  1. Philosophy, Ancient.   I. Title.
  B171.A68 2004
  180—dc22   2004018830

Printed in the United States of America

⊗™ The paper used in this publication meets the minimum requirements of American National
Standard for Information Sciences—Permanence of Paper for Printed Library Materials, ANSI/NISO
Z39.48-1992.

For my friends Mary and Eugene Donovan

ἰητρὸς γὰρ ἀνὴρ πολλῶν ἀντάξιος ἄλλων

—Homer

CONTENTS

ILLUSTRATIONS

PREFACE

Of course there is no substitute, none at all, for reading the ancient philosophers in the original Latin and Greek. As Don Quixote said, reading a translation is like looking at the back of a tapestry.[1] Still, reading their works, or what remains of them, in translation is the next best way to understand their thought. Why, then, this book, which is not a collection of the ancient works either in the original languages or in translation but a general introduction to the subject in *English*?

For the same reason that while there is no substitute for seeing original works of art, there is still something to be gained from reading the museum notes as we wander among the paintings. And for the same reason that we benefit from the information provided about the music at a concert we are about to hear. The notes inform us about the rivalries and goals and other influences of the artist, the culture in which the works were created, the patrons and opponents. This information very often enhances our appreciation, and while no sane person would wish to read the museum or concert notes instead of experiencing the artworks themselves, all the same, it is beneficial to have these secondary materials.

Well, what else can I say? If you read only the works written by the ancient thinkers, just as if you only *heard* the music by Mozart, you might not realize that they actually led human lives. Just as children are sometimes astonished to discover that their parents were young once, dashing perhaps, and sometimes foolish, sometimes even in love, so it comes as a shock to discover that the ancient philosophers are not simply the sources of obscure pronouncements or knotty arguments or enchanting dialogues

---

1. Miguel de Cervantes, *Don Quixote*, pt. II, chap. 62. These are the exact words: *el traducir de una lengua en otra, como no sea de las reinasde las lenguas, griega y latina, es como quien mira los tapices flamencos por el reves*: "translating from one language to another, unless it be from the queens of languages, Greek and Latin, is like looking at the wrong side of Flemish tapestries." No doubt Cervantes intended it as a sign of the profound madness of his hero that he made an exception for Greek and Latin.

but panting human beings who suffered, as we all do, from complex psyches and traumatic historical circumstances—for, as Don Quixote also says, life is a veil of tears. This book aims to show the humanity of the philosophers and to examine their thought as the product of human minds. It aims at a brief intellectual history from Homer to Boethius, from about 800 B.C.E. to about 500 C.E., a period of thirteen hundred years, nearly half the entire time that written works have existed in Europe.

It is of course self-evident that all human beings, to a large degree, are shaped by the cultures in which they live. But it is apparent, too, that great thinkers are not simply spokespersons for their cultures; somehow they transcend those cultures and address matters of universal significance. Their greatness is confirmed by the test of time, the standard by which we may consider great works that have been praised by many people, in many lands, in many times. Such works are universal, or as close to it as humanly possible. From studying these thinkers in the context of their times and the other contemporaneous intellectual work, it might be possible to understand the process of achieving greatness, and such understanding might encourage further achievement.

This book, then, is not meant in any way to be a substitute for reading the ancient philosophers themselves. It should be read along with them. The first chapters will lay out a context for the origin of philosophy—what it was in Greek art, poetry, and character that may have influenced the remarkable experiment of examining the world through reason. Later, the chapters on tragedy and rhetoric will describe the targets at whom philosophers were aiming their powerful arguments—even some literary giants whose works have passed the test of time summa cum laude had philosopher-enemies. Subsequent chapters will look at the changes that affected intellectual developments when the great empires of the Hellenistic Age, especially Rome, replaced the culturally rich city-state in which philosophy was born. The last chapters will examine the challenges created by the encounter of pagan philosophy with Judaism and Christianity. Throughout, this book will attempt to identify which parts of a philosopher's thought are narrowly appropriate only to his own era, which are universal, and which simultaneously both narrow and universal.

ACKNOWLEDGMENTS

I should like to acknowledge those who helped me to think about the ancient world—and about everything else, too. Even if I haven't gotten it right, I'm still grateful. First, I should like to thank my teachers four decades ago when I was an undergraduate at Grinnell College, Hippocrates G. Apostle, William S. Cobb, John M. Crossett, and William T. McKibben. Next, I should like to thank my teachers at Stanford University, Mark Edwards, Brooks Otis, Lionel Pearson, T. B. L. Webster, and my dissertation director, Antony E. Raubitschek. As I have grown old, my appreciation of how much I learned from these individuals has steadily become deeper.

I am most grateful to my old friend and classmate David M. Gibson, who generously contributed his time and talent to drawing the illustrations for this book, and to my former student Austin Stracke, who painstakingly prepared the map of philosophers.

I am grateful also to my daughter Ruth Sophia Arieti and to my colleague Diana Rhoads, who read the entire manuscript and made numerous corrections and suggestions; to Marc Hight and Patrick Wilson, who read parts of the manuscript and also made numerous corrections and suggestions; to Brian Burns and Richard McClintock, who helped with preparing the illustrations for publication; to Jane Holland for secretarial assistance; and to Gerry Randall, who helped me to track down all sorts of material through interlibrary loan. And, of course, I am grateful, as always, to my wife Barbara for her encouragement and patience. Finally, I should like to record my gratitude to Hampden-Sydney College, which granted me two summer fellowships to work on this project.

This book is much better than it would have been without the individuals named here. For all the defects that remain, if you believe that everything is determined genetically, you may blame my mother and father; or, if you believe that everything results from the environment, you may blame the circumstances of the planet during the last few years; or, if you believe in original sin, you may blame the fall of Adam; or, if following Plato, you believe that all error comes either from ignorance or physical disability, you may blame my ignorance or physical decrepitude. But, if you follow my advice and the main line of ancient Western philosophy—which attributes responsibility to individuals—you will appropriately blame me.

James A. Arieti
Hampden-Sydney, Virginia
August, 2004

Though Aristotle claimed that a human being reaches his intellectual peak at age forty-nine (*Rhetoric* 1390b9), chronologists reckon a person's flowering—his *floruit*—at about age forty. The mists of time have made the precise reckoning of chronology quite difficult. Sometimes, when a birth year is not known, a floruit can be estimated on the basis of what is known about an individual's career. When this information too is uncertain, the floruit is shown below with a question mark. Most of the dates here are those in the *Oxford Classical Dictionary* (3rd ed., 1996). For the sake of putting all the thinkers on more or less the same time line, those whose dates are well established are given a floruit at age forty, and the order of listing is by year of floruit.

Thinker	Birthplace	Floruit	Dates	Contribution
Hesiod	Ascra	700	fl. 700 (?)	Didactic poetry
Solon	Athens	600	600 (?)	Lawmaker in Athens
Thales	Miletus	584	624–546	First philosopher
Anaximander	Miletus	570	610–540	Principle of the boundless
Anaximenes	Miletus	546	fl. 546	Air as material principle
Pythagoras	Samos	520	fl. 520 (?)	Theories of mathematics and music
Xenophanes	Colophon	530	fl. 530 (?)	Critic of his contemporaries
Heraclitus	Ephesus	500	fl. 500	Theory of perpetual change
Parmenides	Elea	500	fl. 500	Theory of unity and of perpetual constancy
Aeschylus	Eleusis	485	525–456	Tragic playwright of *Oresteia*
Zeno	Elea	464	fl. 464	Paradoxes in support of Parmenides
Anaxagoras	Clazomenae	460	fl. 460	Theory that world arises from Mind
Sophocles	Colonus	456	496–406	Tragic playwright of *Oedipus*
Empedocles	Acragas	453	fl. 453	Theory of four elements
Euripides	Athens	445	485–406	Tragic playwright of Socratic topics
Gorgias	Leontini	445	485–380	Rhetorician and theoretician of rhetoric

Thinker	Birthplace	Floruit	Dates	Contribution
Protagoras	Abdera	445	fl. 445	Relativist: "Man is the measure of all things"
Herodotus	Halicarnassus	440	fl. 440	First Greek historian
Melissus	Samos	440	fl. 440	Theory of a *finite* Parmenidean One
Leucippus	Miletus (?)	430	fl. 430 (?)	With Democritus, founded atomic theory
Socrates	Athens	429	469–399	Inspirational figure in philosophy
Hippocrates	Cos	429	469–399	Father of medicine
Democritus	Abdera	420	fl. 420	Founder of atomic theory
Thucydides	Athens	420	fl. 420	Historian of Peloponnesian Wars
Antisthenes	Athens	406	446–366	Founded school of Cynics
Plato	Athens	389	429–327	Doctrine of ideas
Xenophon	Athens	388	428–354	Writer of Socratic reminiscences
Diogenes (Cynic)	Sinope	364	404–323	Famously snapped at the powerful
Aristotle	Stagira	344	384–322	Comprehensive philosophy on many topics
Theophrastus	Lesbos	330	370–288	Student of Aristotle, botanist
Xenocrates	Chalcedon	330	fl. 330	Headed Academy
Crates	Thebes	328	368–288	Enthusiastic cynic, extolled the "natural life"
Epicurus	Samos	301	341–270	Turns atomism into comprehensive system
Euclid	Alexandria	300	fl. 300	Geometer
Zeno	Citium	295	335–263	Founds Stoic School
Apollonius	Perga	275	fl. 275	Established geocentric model of universe
Aristarchus	Samos	275	fl. 275	Mathematician, introduced theory of epicycles
Polemon	Athens	274	314–269	Convert to philosophy, headed Academy
Colotes	Lampascus	270	310–260	Enthusiastic follower of Epicurus
Herophilus	Chalcedon	270	fl. 270	Physiologist who identified body functions
Erasistratus	Ceos	260	fl. 260	Physiologist who studied nervous system
Archimedes	Syracuse	247	287–212	Innovative mathematician
Chrysippus	Cilicia	240	280–207	Turns Stoicism into comprehensive system
Sextus Empiricus	unknown	200	fl. 200 (?)	Developed skepticism
Hipparchus	Nicaea	165	fl. 165	Developer of spherical geometry
Posidonius	Apamea	95	135–50	Stoic polymath

Thinker	Birthplace	Floruit	Dates	Contribution
Cicero	Arpinum	66	106–43	Eclectic writer on Hellenistic philosophies
Philo	Alexandria	10 C.E.	30 B.C.E.–45 C.E.	Father of theology, reconciled Bible and Plato
Seneca	Corduba	36 C.E.	4 B.C.E.–65 C.E.	Stoic author and martyr to philosophy
Pliny the Elder	Comum	63	23–79	Prolific author of *Natural History*
Epictetus	Hierapolis	95	55–135	Stoic ex-slave, authored *Enchiridion*
Ptolemy	Alexandria	135	fl. 135 (?)	Astronomer, established geocentric model
Marcus Aurelius	unknown	161	121–180	Stoic Roman emperor, authored *Meditations*
Galen	Pergamum	169	129–199	Prolific medical writer with philosophic bent
Minucius Felix	unknown	240	fl. 240	Used philosophy to convert to Christianity
Plotinus	Lycopolis	244	204–270	Founder of Neoplatonism
Diogenes	Oenoanda	250	fl. 2nd c.	Enthusiastic, and rich, Epicurean
Mani	Persia	256	216–276	Founder of Manichaeism
Porphyry	Tyre	274	234–305	Student and preserver of Plotinus's thought
Arius	Libya	300	260–336	Taught that God the Son is not equal to God the Father
Diogenes Laertius	unknown	325	fl. 325 (?)	Author of *Lives of the Philosophers*
Basil	Caesarea	370	330–379	Christian who saw benefit in Greek culture
Augustine	Thagaste	394	354–430	Prolific writer on Christian philosophy
Boethius	Rome	520	480–524	Author of *Consolation of Philosophy*, planned to reconcile Aristotle and Plato
Simplicius	Cilicia	530	fl. 530	Commentator on Aristotle

BRITAIN

PELAGIUS
fl. 380 c.e.

ARPINUM

CICERO
106–43 b.c.e.

STAG...

ARIS...
384–32...

COMUM
(CISALPINE GAUL)

PLINY THE ELDER
23–79 c.e.

NICAEA

HIPPARCHUS
fl. 165 b.c.e.

ROME

MARCUS AURELIUS
121–180 c.e.

ELEA

PARMENIDES
fl. 500 b.c.e.
ZENO
fl. 464 b.c.e.

THEBES

CRATES
368–288 b.c.e.

CORDUBA
(CORDOBA, MODERN SPAIN)

SENECA
4 b.c.e.–65 c.e.

**LOCATION
UNKNOWN**

SEXTUS EMPIRICUS
fl. 200 b.c.e.?

TACITUS
56–118 c.e.?

MARCUS AURELIUS
121–180 c.e.

MINUCIUS FELIX
fl. 200–240 c.e.

DIOGENES LAERTIUS
fl. 325 c.e.?

BOETHIUS
480–524 c.e.

THAGASTE
*(SOUTH AHRAS,
MODERN ALGERIA)*

AUGUSTINE
354–430 c.e.

ASCRA

HESIOD
fl. 700 b.c.e.?

ELEUSIS

AESCHYLUS
525–456 b.c.e.

ELIS

PYRRHO
360–275 b.c.e.

ACRAGAS

EMPEDOCLES
fl. 453 b.c.e.

LEONTINI

GORGIAS
485–380 b.c.e.

ATHENS

SOLON
fl. 600 b.c.e.?

EURIPIDES
485–406 b.c.e.

SOCRATES
469–399 b.c.e.

ANTISTHENES
446–366 b.c.e.

PLATO
429–347 b.c.e.

XENOPHON
428–354 b.c.e.

THUCYDIDES
fl. 420 b.c.e.

POLEMON
314–269 b.c.e.

COLON...

SOPHOCL...
496–406 b.c...

SYRACUSE

ARCHIMEDES
287–212 b.c.e.

CYRENE

ARISTIPPUS
435–360 b.c.e.

100 km

0   100 Miles

BDERA

MOCRITUS
l. 420 B.C.E.

OTAGORAS
l. 445 B.C.E.

ASSUS

CLEANTHES
301–232 B.C.E.

CHALCEDON

XENOCRATES
fl. 330 B.C.E.?

HEROPHILUS
fl. 270 B.C.E.

SINOPE

DIOGENES THE CYNIC
404–323 B.C.E.

LAMPASCUS

COLOTES
310–260 B.C.E.

ERESOS
(LESBOS)

THEOPHRASTUS
370–288 B.C.E.

CLAZOMENAE

ANAXAGORAS
fl. 460 B.C.E.

CAESAREA

BASIL
330–379 C.E.

PERGAMUM

GALEN
129–199 C.E.

COLOPHON

XENOPHANES
fl. 520 B.C.E.?

CILICIA

CHRYSIPPUS
280–207 B.C.E.

SIMPLICIUS
530 C.E.

HIERAPOLIS

EPICTETUS
55–135 C.E.

EPHESUS

HERACLITUS
fl. 500 B.C.E.

APAMEA

POSIDONIUS
135–50 B.C.E.

PERGA

APOLLONIUS
fl. 275 B.C.E.

OENOANDA

DIOGENES OF
OENOANDA
2nd c. C.E.

CITIUM

ZENO
THE STOIC
335–263 B.C.E.

MILETUS

ANAXIMANDER
610–540 B.C.E.

ANAXIMENES
fl. 546 B.C.E.

THALES
fl. 480 B.C.E.?

LEUCIPPUS
fl. 430 B.C.E.?

TYRE

PORPHYRY
234–305 C.E.

SAMOS

PYTHAGORAS
fl. 520 B.C.E.?

MELISSUS
fl. 440 B.C.E.

EPICURUS
341–270 B.C.E.

ARISTARCHUS
fl. 275 B.C.E.

COS

HIPPOCRATES
469–399 B.C.E.

HALICARNASSUS

HERODOTUS
fl. 440 B.C.E.

PERSIA

MANI
216–276 C.E.

OS

RATUS
B.C.E.

CNIDUS

EUDOXUS
fl. 350 B.C.E.

RHODES

POSIDONIUS
135–51 B.C.E.

ALEXANDRIA

EUCLID
fl. 300 B.C.E.

PHILO
30 B.C.E.–45 C.E.

PTOLEMY
fl. 135 C.E.?

LIBYA

ARIUS
260–336 C.E.

LYCOPOLIS
(EGYPT)

PLOTINUS
204–270 C.E.

CHAPTER 1

A World Ready for Philosophy

I. Why Ancient Philosophy

Why, you ask, are there no flute girls in Scythia? An obscure ancient thinker named Anacharsis explained that there are no flute girls in Scythia because this cold region has no vines. A famous ancient thinker, Aristotle, objected that Anacharsis's explanation omits these critical steps that connect cause to conclusion:[1] it is a fact of nature that Scythia is without vines; if there are no vines, there are no grapes; if there are no grapes, there is no wine; if there is no wine, there are no drinking parties; if there are no drinking parties, there is no singing; and if there is no singing, there are no flute girls. Anacharsis, you'll want to know, was also interested in the theory of leisure and not just in flute girls. He said that we seek leisure for the sake of exertion. Aristotle fleshed out this thought too: to exert oneself for the sake of leisure would be silly, for leisure is a form of relaxation, and we need relaxation because we cannot always be working; relaxation, he concluded, is not a goal; it is sought for the sake of activity.[2] This Aristotle, who was interested in everything, including the activities of babies, tells us who invented the baby rattle and why:[3] it was Archytas of Tarentum, and he invented the toy to amuse infants so that they would not go around the house breaking things.

These are all examples of the philosophic mind, the kind of mind that goes hunting for *why*: *Why* are there no flute girls in Scythia? *Why* do we seek leisure? *Why* was the rattle invented? It begins with the facts of nature itself—say, the absence of vines in Scythia; it then follows up the effects of those facts as they relate to human nature. The philosophic mind seeks knowledge by reasoning.

Yet a contemporary person with a philosophical disposition and a personal set of *why's* might wonder, *why* on earth would anybody in his right mind take up *ancient* philosophy? "Ancient philosophy!" he might exclaim. "Why, isn't it in the same class as alchemy or cave-painting or oxen pulling plows? Who cares about flute girls in Scythia, anyway! Why should anyone use up a part of his precious leisure thinking about the strange notions of dead men who lived around the Mediterranean Sea more than two and a half millennia ago? Better to move on to the world of now."

Figure 1.   Flute Girl

Flute girls, who also worked as prostitutes, were a regular feature of Greek drinking parties. Indeed, for the Greeks, flute girls and drinking parties were as natural a combination as birthday cakes and candles for us. Plato frequently mentions flutes and flute girls in his dialogues. In the *Gorgias,* flute playing is named as an activity productive of no benefit other than pleasure. In the *Symposium,* a word that means *drinking party,* both wine and its "natural" accompaniment—flute girls—are ironically banished so that a discussion concerning *eros* (sexual desire) might take place with only sober men present.

The question of why engage in any activity is not one to pass over flippantly, and it is not self-evident that ancient philosophy is worth our time. If, in a sense, "we are what we eat," in a deeper sense, we are *what we think.* Is thinking about ancient philosophy good for us, and, if so, how? A smart consumer looks at the nutritional label on a product's packaging. What is the nutritional data for ancient philosophy?

Another ancient thinker, much more famous than Anacharsis and more famous than even Aristotle—Socrates—is reputed to have declared, "The unexamined life is not worth living." Socrates meant that we ought to philosophize on everything we do, even on engaging in philosophy. Against this declaration are the words of Sophocles' Jocasta, "Take life as it comes; don't examine it; it might get you into trouble; 'tis folly to be wise." Which of the two is right? Well, if you're the sort of person who goes to a modern movie theater complex where twenty or more different movies are playing, and you leave up to some operation of chance which one you're going to see—in other words, if you agree with Jocasta—you may skip this section. But if you read movie reviews or take advice from your friends because you want to increase the likelihood of spending a valuable two hours—if you agree with Socrates—perhaps this section will offer a justification of the subject.

There are five reasons to take up the story of ancient philosophy: 1) it's a whale of a good yarn; 2) it enables us to see whole schools of philosophy from beginning to end and to examine their life cycle, why they rise and fall and fade away; 3) it enables us, without anger or prejudice, to reflect on the philosophical views themselves, for without close involvement or a stake in the issues, we can be objective in a way that we can't about the controversies of our own time; 4) it provides us a glimpse of the human soul's adventure in understanding and thus helps us to know our own nature; and 5) it very often provides us with knowledge of truth, and such knowledge is our greatest possession, good for its own sake, good for the sake of our activities, and good for the sake of the things we make. We shall take these up these reasons in ascending order of importance.

(1) Far from leading cloistered lives in ivory towers with only mildewed books as companions, the philosophers of the ancient world lived amidst the swirl and din of their fellow humans. Their quest for understanding set them apart for special suffering, and from the mockery of the first philosopher we know of, Thales of Miletus, to the miserable execution of Boethius at the end of antiquity, their stories excite our imagination and stir our sympathy or disdain. The story of *human* philosophy is inseparable from the story of human beings—and in particular of human beings whose lives were complicated because of the pursuit of wisdom. If tales of seafarers and pirates and knights absorb our attention, so too the tales of these pioneers of thought. And the tales of the philosophers' courage in seeking knowledge despite tyrannical oppressors, in maintaining an equanimity of mind amidst persecution, in finding internal strength while their bodies were subjected to the indignities of imprisonment—these are stories to inspire us.

(2) The schools of Pythagoras, Plato, Aristotle, the Stoics, and the Epicureans once enjoyed the esteem we give Harvard or the Institute for

Advanced Study at Princeton. Why did these schools rise from insignificance, enjoy a golden moment in the sun (a moment that sometimes, as in the case of Plato's school, lasted hundreds of years!), and then fade? What factors account for the differing degrees of longevity? How intimately are the personalities and eccentricities of their founders bound to the ultimate disposition of the schools? There is a tidiness to the examination of institutions when we can survey the whole course of their lives, when we can trace the causes of their rise and fall. One great advantage of the history of *ancient* Greece and Rome is that it is over, so that we can look at the whole civilizations from beginning to end and assess the follies and genius of all sides. The schools of ancient philosophy also offer this advantage.

(3) Closely related is the fact that the concepts the ancients developed are largely free from contemporary controversies. One can evaluate Plato's theory of forms without the passions of partisanship. Moreover, ancient philosophy arose long before the faiths of the biblical world arrived in Europe, and so it experienced seven centuries of development before it became embroiled in the challenges that those faiths present. A partisan Christian like Augustine will take this fact as a lamentable defect in philosophy, and he confesses that were it not for the absence in Neoplatonism of the doctrine of the Incarnation, he would happily have been a Neoplatonist. But this freedom from assumptions based on faith allowed philosophy to develop its issues with a pure clarity and, when the challenge of biblical religion did present itself, enabled philosophy to become a major force in the theology that resulted from trying to apply the rules of reason to the God of the Bible.

(4) The first who endeavored to understand the world were pioneers in the use of their minds. Without the technical instruments we take for granted, the first philosophers sought to comprehend man, nature, and the universe with only their unaided senses and the power of thought. They did not even have as a tool the science of formal logic. The discovery that nature is orderly and that the order often appears in numbered patterns was a startling breakthrough. So too were the insights that language has a structure with consistent parts of speech and a syntax; that health and disease obey regular laws; that triangles, no matter how varied, share universal qualities; that some kinds of sequential claims are more persuasive than others—in short, that thought can open a window to reality. When we

think how hard it is to find what we are looking for even when we know what we are looking for, we see how much more difficult it must have been for the first thinkers, who had to come up with the questions, devise the methods of inquiry, and then determine whether the answers were plausible. The story of ancient philosophy is the story of this pioneering work. It is a story of the possibilities inherent in human nature.

(5) Finally, in a great many subjects ancient philosophy hit the mark of truth. To be sure, in some matters it did miss the mark and miss it notoriously: the world is not made only of water, men do not have more teeth than women, the number four is not itself morally just. How and why it went so gloriously wrong is in itself fascinating, yet no one would wish to spend much time on even a fascinating story of error. Nay, one should spend time with Greek and Roman philosophy because in a number of fundamental and abiding matters its success was magnificently triumphant: in ethics, in logic, in mathematics, in metaphysics, many of the accomplishments of the ancients are still vital, evocative, and valid.

6

II. Qualities of the Greek Mind Conducive to Philosophy

Why did what we call philosophy originate in the Hellenic world rather than elsewhere? To begin to answer this question, let us compare a brief passage from Genesis with one from Homer's *Iliad*. In each a divinity is speaking to a human being. In the biblical passage, God for the first time addresses the man (later identified as Adam) whom he has just created:

> And the Lord God commanded the man, saying: Of every tree of the garden thou mayest freely eat; but of the tree of the knowledge of good and evil, thou shalt not eat of it; for in the day that thou eatest thereof thou shalt surely die.[4]

The passage from the Bible occurs in the context of chapter 2 of Genesis, where the text is providing details about the creation of man and woman. God has breathed into the nostrils of the man and has made him a living being. But the creation of the man is not yet complete, for he needs to be made a *moral* being, that is, a being with some kind of code of conduct, and this step comes in the form of the commandment not to eat from the Tree of the Knowledge of Good and Evil. God's words are phrased as a command, not as advice: the mood of the verb is imperative. The consequence of violating the command is death. We must thus assume that Adam understood the words of the commandment, all the words, including *knowledge, good, evil,* and *die.* For God to give a commandment not fully understood would hardly have been fair. Such an act would be akin to giving the reader a commandment in an undeciphered ancient language and threatening death for not fulfilling it. Adam's immediate response is not recorded, and the story quickly goes on to the next subject, God's judgment that it was "not good for the man to be alone."

Contrast this passage with one from Homer's *Iliad,* where a god, Athena, speaks to a human, here Achilles, for the first time in the poem. The context is King Agamemnon's consummate and despicable arrogance toward Achilles. At Troy, the Greek army has been suffering a terrible plague, and Achilles has consulted a seer to ascertain its cause. The seer has revealed that Apollo has sent the plague because he is angry at Agamemnon, the commander in chief of the allied Greeks, for kidnapping the daughter of one of the god's priests and then refusing to ransom her to her father. Under pressure, Agamemnon has agreed to return the captive girl but has demanded Achilles' prize. Agamemnon wants the prize in order to show that he is more powerful than Achilles. This sort of haughty action, done not for the sake of gain but simply for the sake of showing superiority over someone else, is what the Greeks called *hubris.* Achilles, the greatest of the warriors at Troy, is enflamed at Agamemnon's outrageous demand and prepares to take his sword out of its sheath to slay the king. At this moment, the goddess Athena comes to him. Athena says,

> I have come down to stay your anger—but will you be persuaded by me?—from the sky; and the goddess of the white arms Hera sent me, who loves both of you equally in her heart and cares for you. Come then, do not take your sword in your hand, keep clear of the fighting, though indeed with words you may abuse him, and it will be that way. And this also will I tell you and it will be a thing accomplished. Some day three times over such shining gifts shall be given you by reason of this outrage. Hold your hand then, and obey us.[5]

7

Where the Hebrew God commands, the Greek deity seeks to persuade.[6] This is a key difference in the two cultures. The three religions that developed from the Bible all require obedience. In Judaism, obedience takes the form of following the commandments; in Christianity, of accepting various claims of faith; and in Islam, of submission to God's will as mediated by Mohammed. An ancient Greek, however, even when directly addressed by his gods, had to be *persuaded*.

What is persuasion? It is a process by which one individual induces another to assent to a proposition as a result of some kind of a demonstration or argument. In the present case, Achilles is persuaded by Athena's appeal to Hera's love and by the promise of the future benefits of yielding to Agamemnon's will.

Throughout the *Iliad*, we see warriors meeting in council and attempting to persuade one another of their views. The Homeric ideal is twofold and is summarized in the mission of Achilles' boyhood tutor: to educate Achilles to become a speaker of words and a doer of deeds.[7] The ability to speak well (that is, to be a "speaker of words") was interpreted by later Greeks as intellectual eminence, as distinct from the quality of doing deeds, which was interpreted as excellence in practical matters. In the *Iliad*, intellectual eminence is exemplified by Odysseus, Phoenix, and Nestor, who excel in council. Thus, at the very beginning of Greek literary culture we find an appreciation of mental acuity.

In the Homeric educational ideal we may observe another pervasive quality of the Greek character: the ordering and ranking of all aspects of human life. The ideal human being combines the contemplative and practical lives, but are the two lives equal, or, if one is superior, which carries away the prize? This question occupied many ancient thinkers. In a lost play by Euripides, *Antiope*, there was a scene in which Antiope's sons Amphion and Zethus represented the differing values of the contemplative and practical lives. In the end of that play, the god Hermes predicted that Amphion's skill in the gifts of the Muses would build the walls of Thebes. Thus, by the intervention of gods, the contemplative life prevailed—the operations of which are, according to myth, the province of the Muses. In Plato and Aristotle the debate takes the form of whether the best kind of human being (who, of course, is a philosopher) ought to engage in the practical affairs of his community or separate himself from the community in order to devote himself to study. In Roman times it was Cicero who perhaps best embodied both kinds of lives, for he served as consul of the Roman Republic, was preeminent in rhetoric, and wrote treatises on philosophy. In modern times, one form that the same debate takes is whether the federal government should provide funding for pure (that is, *contemplative*) as well as for applied (that is, *practical*) research. This Greek tendency to divide and sort things out in a ranking order took a multitude of forms: the assigning of the arts to the nine Muses, the division of the classical virtues into four, the Platonic separation of the soul into three parts, the classification of the basic types of regimes into three or six, the sorting of the kinds of causes into four, the distinction between appearance and reality, and so on and on. Exactly how reality ought to be chopped up is, of course, a fundamental problem that is often taken up in ancient philosophy.[8]

In the respect afforded skill in debate we may observe two closely related features of the Greek mind: its love of competition and its dutiful attention to making sure that the reward of competition, victory (in Greek, *niké*—often represented as the winged goddess Victory), went to the right person. In the *Iliad*, the warriors fought primarily for their own glory, a glory measured by a quantitative standard; that is, the more prizes a man brought home, the greater his glory.[9] When Agamemnon offers Achilles boundless gifts to lure him back into battle, the offer is a tangible acknowledgment of Achilles' superior merits and of the Greek army's dire need.

Competition manifested itself in every activity of life. In the *Odyssey*, for example, even when Nausicaa and her companions simply wash clothes, they make a contest out of the activity.[10] Training for athletic games was a major feature of education, and the competitions themselves were so important that the response to even major calamities might be suspended until the conclusion of the games. Xenophon reports, for example, that Sparta delayed reacting to her disastrous defeat in the Battle of Leuctra until the festival of the Gymnopaidiai could be completed as usual.[11] Competition was encouraged among soldiers, and when battles were over, prizes were awarded to the best fighters. The Greeks debated even the choice of the happiest and second happiest of human beings, as Herodotus reports in his *History of the Persian Wars*.[12] The practice of Socratic dialectic—a struggle to discover truth by producing a consistent argument without contradictions—is inherently competitive. For those who have witnessed it

9

Figure 2.   Niké (Victory)
Niké is usually depicted as winged. Wings are symbolic of lofty ascent and evoke the majestic soaring of victorious eagles. Wings are also a symbol of flightiness—of speedily transient comings and goings. As a winged bee flits from flower to flower or a winged bird from branch to branch, never alighting very long in one place, so winged Victory does not dally in a single place: a victor who wins a prize today will lose it tomorrow. The concept of the transitory nature of success or of happiness or of victory is called the "principle of vicissitude." The consequences of not remembering it, always bad, represent a constant motif in classical literature.

in actual practice, far from inducing somnolence, a dialectical exchange becomes as riveting as a cross-examination during a trial. The courtroom trial itself arose out of the Greek mind and is another way its competitive character showed itself.

As we shall see, the ancients did not uniformly praise competitiveness. They did not all believe, like Adam Smith, that "an invisible hand" directs competition to a public good. One early thinker, Xenophanes, complained that the whole practice of ranking was flawed, that athletes were given far too much praise and thinkers like himself far too little. In Thucydides' *History of the Peloponnesian War*, some Athenians acknowledged that other cities criticize Athens for its competitive streak, especially as it was expressed in an addiction to lawsuits. But Athenians saw virtue in the litigiousness, for the alternative to lawsuits, they said, was vigilante violence.[13] The complaint made by some who conversed with Socrates that philosophical arguments were a competitive spectator sport rather than a serious pursuit of truth is somewhat validated in Tacitus's description of Nero's pastimes, one of which was to watch philosophers wrangle pointlessly.[14]

The competitiveness of the Greeks is a feature also of their deities. In the elegant mythology of the poets, the various gods contend with one another for status with both Zeus and human beings. For example, in the rivalry over who would be the patron deity of Athens, Poseidon and Athena each performed miracles for the good of the inhabitants. Poseidon, god of the sea and of the horse, produced a spring of salt water and a horse for the citizens; Athena produced an olive tree. In a decision implicit with future theological debates, the people themselves chose Athena, goddess of wisdom (a choice that perhaps also shows the rank of intelligence over that of power).[15] Another example of competition among divinities occurs in Euripides' play *Hippolytus*, where Aphrodite, the goddess of sex, has destroyed Hippolytus because of her rage at being ignored by him. Artemis, the goddess of virginity—Aphrodite's rival—swears to take vengeance on someone dear to Aphrodite. As we shall see, these sorts of religious ideas will come under the critical scrutiny of philosophers.

From the beginning of philosophy, competitiveness remained vigorous, as thinkers contended to present the best argument. At first, part of the competition involved *implying* that the positions of the others were weak, mistaken, or absurd. This implication came about when a subsequent thinker put forth a more comprehensive claim or a claim that pointedly dealt with a defect in his predecessor's position. Later thinkers directly attacked the work of others. To observers, this latter competitiveness often appeared as obnoxious squabbling, and a reputation for disputatious quibbling greatly tarnished the luster of philosophers.[16]

Some people, perhaps influenced by the sardonic remark of Edward Gibbon that to the philosophers of Rome all religions were equally false,[17] tend to think of philosophers as remote from religion and as excluding divinities from explanations of reality. In fact, most philosophers, at least ancient ones, struggled to define or illustrate the place of the gods in the operation of the universe. Starting with the first philosophical thinkers, the divine lies at the heart of their reflection. Philosophers lived in communities and were affected by the religious ambience of their surroundings. They were aware of the differences in beliefs about the gods from community to community—and this awareness stimulated philosophical reflection.

These features of the Greek mind—an esteem for excellence in debate, a need to be persuaded rather than commanded, a tendency toward hierarchical ordering, and a thoroughgoing competitiveness in every facet of life—provided the fertile ground in which the seeds of philosophy took root. One might truly point out that all people in all times and all places share these characteristics to a greater or lesser degree. Nevertheless, these are enduring and pervasive qualities of the Greek ethos, and though the ground might have been fertile elsewhere as well, it was in Greece where the seeds happened to fall and philosophy happened to be born. How that occurred we shall take up a little later.

III. Before Philosophy: Homer and Hesiod

The most important poet in the classical world was Homer. A distant second was Hesiod (note the hierarchical ranking). Perhaps, given their importance to the ancient world, it would be appropriate to say a few words about why their poems are significant and about the philosophical issues implicit in them. The next two sections will look at these issues and then consider why, though these poems contain philosophical issues, they are not themselves *philosophy* and will conclude with a few comments on literary genre since to a large extent our concept of genre defines what we consider to be philosophy.

A. HOMER

The *Iliad* announces its topic in the opening line: the Muse is to sing about the *menis* of Achilles, a word sometimes translated as *rage*, sometimes, as *anger*. Well, is the poem's subject the *anger* of Achilles or his *rage*? The Greek word may be translated both ways, but the emotions designated by the terms are quite different, and how people understand the word will influence their interpretation of the poem. Aristotle defines *anger* as the painful emotion directed at an individual whom we believe to have treated us unjustly.[18] It is therefore a rational response, for it depends on a sense of justice. *Rage*, on the other hand, though it may exhibit similar symptoms, is not based on justice, nor does it seek justice. It is simply an unreflective desire to retaliate for an injury. In reading the *Iliad* one will have to decide whether Achilles' response is anger or rage or whether it begins, say, with an anger that somehow undergoes a transformation into rage. This is an important question in the poem, and how one answers it will affect how one evaluates the critical decisions Achilles makes throughout the actions of the poem. The understanding of the word *menis* goes to the heart of the philosophical practice of definition.

There are a multitude of other philosophical questions implicit in the poem. When Agamemnon seizes Achilles' prize, Achilles withdraws from battle and prays to Zeus, king of the gods, that he grant the Trojans success on the battlefield. Zeus fulfills this prayer. The Greek generals send ambassadors to Achilles to urge him to return to the fight, and they convey Agamemnon's offer of gifts magnificent in quality and quantity. But Achilles refuses to return to the war and rejects the proffered gifts, boldly declaring that there is no such thing as honor since the reward is the same for the cowardly and the courageous. To understand the significance of Achilles' decision here, we must recall that honor was the preeminent value of the Homeric warriors, and acquiring it was their principal motive in joining the expeditionary force to Troy. This honor, as we have said, was quantitative: the more prizes and booty a man acquired, the more he was esteemed by others and the more highly he thought of himself. When Achilles denies the value of honor, he is repudiating the values of his fellow Greeks and stands physically apart and spiritually alienated from them, no longer judging himself, or them, by quantity of prizes. Later in the poem, when Achilles' friend Patroclus dies, Achilles realizes that it was his own foolish anger (or rage) that kept him from battle, and he senses that he alone bears the responsibility for his friend's death. This sense of personal responsibility, this sense of guilt, is something wholly new in the *Iliad* and in ancient Greek culture: it is the birth of the internal standard of self-judgment that we later call *conscience.* In the rest of the *Iliad,* we watch as Achilles endeavors to expiate this guilt. Since his guilt is very great—Achilles knows he has caused the death of his friend and of many other dear companions—he wishes to punish himself by death. As he learns from his goddess mother, he cannot die except by killing Hector—for it is fated that Achilles' death will follow swiftly on Hector's. Achilles thus understands that in order to die he must first kill Hector. Homer beautifully represents this symbolic suicide by the motif of Achilles' armor. When Achilles allows Patroclus to go into battle instead of going himself, Achilles lends his armor to Patroclus so that he might be mistaken for Achilles and thus frighten the Trojans. Hector, upon slaying Patroclus, strips that armor and puts it on himself. Since it is now Hector who resembles Achilles, there is a metaphorical reinforcement of the idea that Achilles is the one responsible for killing his friend. When Achilles finally fights Hector, it looks as though he is fighting himself, and, in a figurative sense, he is. But when Hector is slain and Achilles does not die at once, he tries, in effect, to kill Hector over and over again, attempting to destroy the Trojan's body by dragging it behind a chariot. By the final book of the poem, when Hector's father comes to Achilles to ransom his son's body, Achilles has already learned from Patroclus's ghost that a human being is not completely dead until he is buried. In a moving scene with much reflection on human sorrow, Achilles gives up the body of Hector to Priam for burial. There are perhaps various motives for the return of the body, but prominent among them must be Achilles' belief that when Hector is buried and thus fully dead, he, Achilles, will be able to die and thereby expiate his guilt. The poem ends with the Trojans' burial of Hector. The last line of the poem, "Such was the burial of Hector, breaker of horses," implies that now that Hector is completely dead, Achilles is as good as dead too.

14

While this particular thematic summary of the *Iliad* has followed one general interpretation of the poem, it should be clear that the poem contains a vast assortment of prompts for philosophical inquiry.[19] Among the questions the poem raises are the nature and value of honor; the nature of a hero and of a heroic action; whether the standard of behavior should be established by others or by oneself and the related question of whether values are relative or grounded in absolutes; whether foreknowledge has any appreciable effect on decision making; whether humans are responsible for their actions or whether, because they simply carry out the wishes of the gods, responsibility lies with the gods; whether Achilles, for all his irrational cruelty, nevertheless exhibits heroic behavior beyond excellence as a killing machine, and, if so, how? In addition (and not included in the thematic summary given earlier) are questions concerning the war itself: whether it is worthwhile to fight to restore the unfaithful Helen to her husband; whether deceit is permissible in war; whether one should act on the basis of dreams, which might be true or false; whether a "battle of champions" is a rational way of settling a dispute and whether such a battle has any possibility of success; how one copes with rage and the inevitable horrors of war. And of course there are the associated questions having to do with debate: why are some speakers more successful at persuasion than others, and what is it about Nestor in particular that accounts for his uncanny success, while others, like Hector's wife Andromache and Agamemnon, fail?[20]

B. HESIOD

Hesiod was the second most important poet of the archaic period in Greece, the period that immediately preceded the era in which philosophy began. His two major works are the *Works and Days*, a didactic poem detailing how to manage one's work for maximum profitability, and the *Theogony*, an account of the coming into being of the gods and the world.

Works and Days begins as Hesiod tries, by means of myths, to educate his brother Perses. In each myth Hesiod explains the present condition of humankind in order to persuade Perses to face up to the human condition, to change his way of life, and to settle their dispute over their father's estate. There are, Hesiod avers, *two* kinds of strife, a bad kind, which fosters wars and destruction, and a good kind, which stirs people to quit their idleness as they watch their neighbors growing rich from work. Hesiod offers alternative explanations for why the world will not sustain idleness: the myth of Pandora, a woman who took a lid off a jar, letting plagues and woes fly out, and the myth of the five ages, in which humans went from a long-ago Golden Age life without sorrow, disease, and old age to the present Iron Age, in which life is full of toil and violence. He encourages Perses to pursue virtue and justice and concludes this section of the poem by calling on the lords to stop their bribe-eating since justice and prosperity require an honest legal apparatus. Hesiod proceeds to the longer second part of the poem, where he lays out the best times of the year for performing the various jobs that provide an honest livelihood. The great lesson of the poem is that if one studies nature and sows and reaps and sails at the right time of year, prosperity is most likely to follow: the critical moment, he teaches, is best in all things.

Hesiod's lesson about the importance of understanding nature and its regular patterns for the sake of acquiring wealth laid the groundwork for the intellectual effort known as natural philosophy—the attempt to comprehend the physical order of the world. Important also for later inquiry was the attempt to locate the origin of evil. To be sure, the various myths of Pandora and of the five ages are not very satisfying to a rational mind, and they appear to be only tangentially connected to their point, yet they challenge the unsatisfied to produce better explanations and in this way too perhaps served as a catalyst for philosophical reflections.

IV. Why Homer and Hesiod Are Not Philosophy

The question of who is and who is not a philosopher perhaps strikes us today as properly belonging to a comic routine. Yet before the words *philosophy* or *philosopher* came into being, how could anyone know that he was a philosopher? The root of the word *philosophy* does not appear in Greek before the fifth century B.C.E.[21] In an ancient anecdote, Pythagoras is said to have been the first to call himself a *philosopher*.[22] Pythagoras had to explain to Leon, the prince of Phlius (a town in the Peloponnese), that a philosopher was "one who was eager for wisdom." But what of Thales and Xenophanes and the other thinkers who lived before Pythagoras invented the term? What did *they* think they were doing?

The question is complicated because of the means by which the ancient thinkers conveyed their thought. Thales, Xenophanes, Heraclitus, Parmenides, and most of the other thinkers who preceded Herodotus, if they wrote at all, wrote in verse. Plato, who comes after Herodotus, Thucydides, and some other prose writers, composed what Aristotle called "Socratic Conversations"[23] but we call "dialogues." Some of these are written like plays, without any stage directions except for the names of the speakers preceding their lines. Others are written more in the manner of novels, with speakers indicated by such terms as "I said" or "Socrates asked" or "he responded while laughing."

In our age, a postmodern critic might declare, "Let us not categorize this or that as philosophy or as any other genre, for if we do, we will inhibit the natural and genuine response of the reader." And he might add, "If someone wants to understand Homer as a philosopher, let him; if someone wants to think of Einstein as a poet, let him do so." The ancients themselves, however, would not have been friendly to this postmodern view. For them, a work was not a sort of Rorschach inkblot, to which any kind of response is proper because it shows something about the one who experiences the inkblot. The psychologist who administers the Rorschach inkblot is interested primarily in the patient, not in the inkblot; the ancients were interested primarily in the inkblot, the works themselves, and not in the patient, the reader. Aristotle himself takes up the question of how to treat the ancient thinkers. He writes,

> It is the way with people to tack on "poet" to the name of a meter, and talk of elegiac poets and epic poets, thinking that they call them poets not by reason of the imitative nature of their work, but by reason of the meter they write in. Even if a theory of medicine or physical philosophy be put forth in a metrical form, it is usual to describe the writer in this way; Homer and Empedocles, however, have really nothing in common apart from their meter; so that, if one is to be called a poet, the other should be termed a physicist rather than a poet.[24]

The Greek word for genre is *eidos*, which we translate by a term like *genus*, with its attendant notion of *species*. But the Greek word means basically a "look," that is, what we mean when we say of an object that it does not have the same "look" as another object we are comparing to it. Behind the whole notion lies the sensory awareness that things either look alike or do not; and if they look alike, they can be treated and responded to in similar ways.

Two questions arise here: 1) Are these classifications, these genres, real—that is, do they have a verifiable existence? 2) Whether they do or not, are they useful in any way to our dealing with, our reacting and responding to, any particular concrete example of the category? The first question is the kind that philosophy classifies as "metaphysical" and is of great interest in the history of philosophy, for it involves such problems as whether ideas

17

have an independent existence.[25] This matter will be taken up later in this book.[26] The second question, whether such genres are useful, will be taken up presently.

We might start with the fact that language itself classifies. For example, the word *rose* is a category and says that the thing we call a rose is distinct from every other kind of object in the universe. All language rests on the very practical assumption that everything is what it is and not another thing. Metaphorically we may assert that A is B, that a girl is a rose, but we do not act literally on that basis, not unless we are insane. Now the usefulness of a knowledge of genre for readers *before* they read derives from a universal feature of human nature, namely, the desire to know beforehand what an experience is like in order to act properly, that is, to act in accordance with its nature and in this way not violate or spoil the experience. Knowing the genre to which a given work belongs enables readers to organize their responses, just as knowing whether one is to attend a wedding or a funeral enables one to organize the appropriate attire.

Now if it is a good thing to know what a thing is like, with as much precision as the nature of the thing will allow, so that we can respond to it correctly, then it is clear that we ought to respond to it in accordance with its nature. For example, we expect to find sugar sweet, to find summer hot, to find water wet. In any given case, we may find a person who experiences one of these and does not respond as expected; but we do not regard such a case as typical or right. If it is 110 degrees in the shade and somebody says he is cold, we may accept the fact that he is cold—though many of us would probably not believe him—but we do not regard his response as normal or correct. So, too, if one of our friends reads the *Oedipus Rex* and thinks it a comedy, the funniest thing he ever read, we may defend his right to have his opinion, but we do not regard his opinion as being worth anything. There are such things as stock responses, and there ought to be. As C. S. Lewis is reputed to have said, "What we need is more stock responses."[27]

Why then do we distinguish Homer and Hesiod as *poets* and Thales and Parmenides—who thought about what the world was made of and whether motion was logically possible—as *philosophers*—a distinction that these individuals could not themselves have made? The best answer is that of Aristotle quoted previously: it is the judgment that content is more essential to genre than form. Though the story that Homer tells is *philo-*

sophical, that is, evocative of universal questions and suggestive of universal truths, it is first and foremost a *story*; that is, it describes a situation without explicitly analyzing or explaining it. The truths that it teaches must be abstracted from the story by a conscious effort of a rational mind. And these truths will be meaningful to us if they are relevant and applicable to the objective and psychic world in which we live. Hesiod perhaps would be a little closer to philosophy than Homer, for the stories he tells are told to be appreciated not for their own sake but for the sake of some explanatory point. For example, the stories of Pandora and of the five ages are told to explain the unpleasant necessity of working for a livelihood.

As we shall discover as we look at the first thinkers known as "philosophers," difficulties arise because they use poetic language, with the ambiguities that such language involves. Later thinkers aimed at reducing ambiguity to a minimum, and it was expressly to reduce ambiguity and improve clarity that technical vocabulary and logic were developed.

V. Other Conditions Affecting the Birth of Philosophy

A. THE *POLIS*

Because the kind of community—the *polis*—in which the early Greek philosophers lived is very different from what we know today, a brief description of the *polis* would perhaps be useful. The word is generally translated as "city-state," but elaboration is necessary. Some insight into the nature of the *polis* can be gleaned from the following paragraph from Thucydides' *History of the Peloponnesian War*:

> The Thirty Years' Truce, which was entered into after the conquest of Euboea, lasted fourteen years. In the fifteenth, in the forty-eighth year of the priestess-ship of Chryseis at Argos, during the ephorate of Aenesias at Sparta, in the last month but two of the archonship of Pythodorus at Athens, six months after the battle of Potidaea, and just at the beginning of spring, a Theban force a little over three hundred strong, under the command of their *boeotarchs*, Pythangelus, son of Phyleides, and Diemporus, son of Onetorides, about the first watch of the night, made an armed entry into Plataea, a town of Boeotia in alliance with Athens. The

gates were opened to them by a Plataean called Naucleides, who, with his party, had invited them in, meaning to put to death citizens of the opposite party, bring over the city to Thebes, and thus obtain power for themselves.[28]

Thucydides endeavors to explain exactly when an armed force from Thebes attacked Plataea, a neighboring city about nine miles away. Why does not Thucydides simply state the hour, day, month, and year? The answer of course is that he cannot, for all the Greek *poleis* (the plural of *polis*) measure time differently, giving their months different names and different numbers of days, beginning their years in different seasons, and marking the years by different significant milestones. Thus Argos kept track of time by the years of its priestess-ship (as if we were to keep time by saying "the third year of the papacy of Pius VI" or "the fifth year of the papacy of John Paul II"). Sparta kept track of time by the office of ephorate and Athens by the names of the archons. The Battle of Potidaea helped set the exact year for those unfamiliar with the various record-keeping mechanisms of these three cities, and the season rendered the time somewhat meaningful in yet another way.

The laborious complexity in specifying the time of the Theban invasion results from the insularity of the different *poleis*. Each *polis* was, for the most part, quite isolated from its immediate neighbors and much more so from *poleis* farther away. Each had, in addition to its own system of timekeeping, its own weights and measures, its own currency (once money was invented in the sixth century B.C.E.), its own legal system and constitution, its own cuisine, its own customs concerning marriage and child rearing and education, its own locally important deities and religious rituals, its own holidays, and its own dialect and pronunciation of the Greek language. Traveling from one *polis* to another, culturally, would have been like going from Albania to England in the period before globalization.

For a greater sense of a *polis*, one must imagine living in a small city of perhaps ten thousand male citizens and their female relations, with a somewhat larger number of slaves, many of whom would have been concubines. In this city virtually all music and other entertainment would have been homegrown, and, apart from the most famous poets like Homer and Hesiod, other poets would have been unfamiliar. Life would have revolved around daily rituals involving the deities of the city and the surrounding countryside (where "surrounding" means walkable in no more than a day or two). Benjamin Franklin describes in his autobiography how, as a young lad, he moved from Boston to Philadelphia, where he found his familiar bread wholly unknown, a situation that would have been typical of ancient Greece at large:

> Then I walk'd up the Street, gazing about, till near the Market House I met a Boy with Bread. I had made many a Meal on Bread, and inquiring where he got it, I went immediately to the Baker's he directed me to in second Street; and ask'd for a Bisket, intending such as we had in Boston, but they it seems were not made in Philadelphia, then I ask'd for a three penny Loaf, and was told they had none such: so not considering or knowing the Difference of Money and the greater Cheapness nor the Names of his Bread, I bad him give me three penny worth of any sort. He gave me accordingly three great Puffy Rolls. I was surpriz'd at the Quantity, but took it, and having no room in my Pockets, walk'd off with a Roll under each Arm, and eating the other.[29]

Every ancient polis similarly would have had its own recipe for making bread and virtually everything else, and, like the young Franklin, the inhabitants of one *polis* would have found the bread of another quite alien.

The inhabitants of a *polis* might spend their entire lives in their city's territory except—as in Socrates' case—when participating in military expeditions. The insularity of the *polis* was both symbolized and actually enforced by its walls, which afforded protection from wild animals and human enemies. The terrain of Greece contributed to the insularity, for rough mountains that rise quite precipitously rendered travel from one city to another an arduous process by land and, given the primitive condition of sailing vessels, a dangerous and tortuous process by sea.

The last sentence in the passage from Thucydides reveals a darker side of this type of community. Though the Thebans are mortal enemies of Plataea, the gates of Plataea are opened by a Plataean, Naucleides, "who, with his [political] party, had invited them in, meaning to put to death citizens of the opposite party, bring over the city to Thebes, and thus obtain power for themselves." So intense was Naucleides' hatred for his fellow Plataeans of the other political party, and so deep his desire for

21

power, that he was willing to kill the members of the other party and turn his city over to the enemy.

If a *polis* promoted fellowship and a deep sense of participation, it also promoted intensely felt feelings about the good for the community (to put it generously) and stimulated an ambition for power not restrained by any bounds of decency. If a man hated his fellow citizens, where could he go? Self-exile meant leaving for an alien environment, where one would be a cultural ignoramus, untutored in the idiom and a stranger to the customs and rituals the adoptive city took for granted. The possible choices were, alas, only too clear, and too often, especially in times of stress, citizens resorted to civil conflict.[30]

How and whether life in *poleis* was conducive to philosophizing is a matter on which we may speculate. Perhaps active participation in community affairs, with the concomitant need for skill in persuasion, sharpened men's wits. Perhaps one stimulating feature of *poleis* was the fact that there was so much variety among them since each had its own constitution and culture, even when only a few miles distant from others. Perhaps this multiplicity of constitutions and cultures, combined with the Greek spirit of competitiveness, prompted people to reflect on which culture or system was best and why; on whether all cultures were equally the result of arbitrary convention or whether some were more directly drawn from human nature itself; why, if other social animals, like bees, have separate but still identical types of organization, human beings organize themselves in many various ways. Indeed, political philosophy seems to have arisen from just these reflections. Finally, perhaps by a process akin to Darwinian natural selection, the multiplicity allowed an environment where productive and creative ideas could flourish.

Later, toward the middle of the fourth century B.C.E., when travel became somewhat easier and, more significantly, when the Greeks were united against Macedonia, and a little later still, when they were conquered and brought together under Macedonian rule, this local outlook changed, and people began to think of themselves as part of a larger community, indeed, as citizens even of the world and of the universe. The breaking up of the *polis* and its replacement with the *cosmo*-polis, the world-state, as exemplified first by Alexander's empire and then by Rome's, is a major chapter in the story of philosophy in the ancient world.

B. ARCHITECTURE AND ART

Ancient thinkers found themselves in a world adorned with great art. Enough works have survived into modern times to give us a sufficient hint of the underlying cultural values that contributed to the development of philosophy. The discussion here will not deal with the art on pottery and other domestic items but will be limited to the monumental buildings that represent a significant civic and financial investment and the sculptures that adorned them, for these are more likely to reflect the collective public values of the people.

When one observes a Greek temple, several features present themselves. Seen from a distance, the structures loom large and breathtaking. As sailors passed Cape Sounion and looked upward at the Temple of Poseidon in its splendid natural setting high on a cliff over the sea, the building would have appeared as a distinctly *human* creation that arose from a human sense of proportion and form. What is true of this Greek temple is true of all: there is no attempt to blend the structure into harmony with nature, none of the attempt that we find in the works of Frank Lloyd Wright to conform the structure's shape to setting. Indeed, just the opposite seems to be the aim: to impose a work of the human mind, with its ordered simplicity, symmetry, and unnatural geometry—that is, pure, regular shapes not found in nature—on the wild and untamed land. The massive Parthenon and Propylaea on the Athenian Acropolis, the Temple of Concord in Agrigentum, the Temple of Poseidon at Paestum, the Temple of Aphaia on Aegina, and perhaps, startlingly, even today, the Temple of Apollo at Bassae, which emerges in a high plateau surrounded by towering mountains—all declare to nature that human intellect has left its mark.

The basic measure of a Greek temple was the diameter of the lower columns, which was used to determine the number and height of the columns. The measure depended on the frieze to be sculpted, for the frieze would determine whether the spacing of the columns would be uniform or whether there would be some variation.[31] The temple is an entirely artificial creation: its right angles, peaked roofs, and rectangular terrace of three steps all assert the force of consciously numbered proportion.

Just as the art that adorns innumerable churches shows the same scenes over and over again—stories in the life of Jesus and tales of the various saints—so the art in Greek temples showed the same themes repeatedly,

Figure 3. Sounion
In Lord Byron's verse, "Sounion's marbled steep,/ Where nothing save the waves and I may hear our mutual murmurs sweep," is the rocky headland that rises nearly 200 feet above the sea. Here stands a majestic temple of Poseidon, to whom sailors prayed for safety as they left Athens for the eastern Aegean Sea and to whom they offered thanks when they returned safely home.

perhaps with even less variation than the art in churches. These themes include the wars between the Lapiths and Centaurs, between the Greeks and Amazons, between the Greeks and Trojans, and between the gods and the giants.

What was so important in these stories to induce the Greeks to repeat them on their temples? Let us look first at the myths that involve human victories. The Lapiths, a mountain tribe in Thessaly (the area of Greece just north of Boeotia), were human descendents of Apollo, the god of reason. When the Lapith king Perithous was to marry a woman named Hippodameia (whose name means "horse-taming"), he invited centaurs, creatures half man and half horse, to the wedding. At the wedding feast, the centaurs became drunk and tried to carry off some Lapith women but were defeated. In the temple friezes portraying the battle, the Lapiths, even when wounded or about to be raped, show expressions of complete serenity. One meaning of this art appears to be that a full possession of one's passions—the virtue of self-control (*sophrosyne* in Greek)—is what sets humans, and especially Greeks, apart from the half-human, half-bestial

Figure 4. Forms Imposed on Nature

Pure geometric shapes are not found in natural landscapes, and the imposition of them in Greek monumental architecture is a deliberate attempt to contrast the structures that result from human intelligence with those found in the craggy mountain ranges and uneven valleys. "This contrast of the natural and the devised is at the heart of Greek religious architecture. It heralds both the separateness of human achievement from the dark ancient forces of the land and the propitiation of these divinely controlled forces through the act of building" (Spiro Kostof, *A History of Architecture: Settings and Rituals* [New York and Oxford: Oxford University Press, 1985], 124).

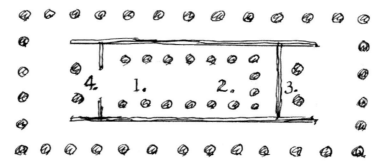

Figure 5. Temple Diagram

Though the precise proportions changed over the centuries, the basic form of a Greek temple is constant: a central rectangular room (*naós*: 1) at the far end of which (2) stood the statue of the god, with porches at both ends, one of which enclosed a room (*opisthódomos*: 3) for the sacred vessels, the other (*prónaos*: 4) of which led to the *naós*. The *naós* was surrounded by rows of columns that supported a roof. The width of a temple was half its length. In the classical period the columns along each side was double the number at each end plus one. As shown in this drawing, the Temple of Hephaistos, which overlooks the agora of Athens, has thirteen columns on the sides, six at the ends.

Capital →

Column
8 x capital
4.6 x diameter

Figure 6.   Temple Proportions
In the sixth century, the height of a column was 4.5 to 5 times its lower diameter and 8 times the height of the capital. But as the ideal human proportions became lankier, so did those of columns, and by the fifth century the height of a column was 5.5 times its lower diameter and 12 times the height of the capital (Spiro Kostof, *A History of Architecture: Settings and Rituals* [New York and Oxford: Oxford University Press, 1985], 125). That there is a natural proportion seems a characteristic of ancient thought. Polyclitus, a sculptor of the latter part of the fifth century B.C.E., claimed that the proportions of an ideal male could be calculated on the basis of his index finger. Underlying the idea of proportion is that the universe is a *cosmos*, a thing of beauty (of which, for the Greeks, order is a requirement).

centaurs. Important too in the story is that the battle occurred just when the centaurs were violating a respectable marriage between a king and a royal princess (for Hippodameia was the daughter of King Oenomaus, ruler of the area that included Olympia). Perhaps nothing so distinguishes humans from beasts as marriage, which stamps the sexual union—a basic animal function—with the mark of human mind—the placing of limits, controls, and order on nature. In defeating the centaurs, the Lapiths exhibited self-mastery. In upholding the legitimacy of marriage, they were doing exactly what temple architecture itself does, subjugating brute forces to the human mind.

The battle of the Greeks and the Amazons depicts essentially the same mastery of mind over wild nature. The Amazons were a tribe of women who did not permit any men in their country. To continue their existence, which of course could not be done without males, once a year they went to mate with men from a neighboring tribe. Male children who resulted from these matings were put to death, while female children were brought up by their mothers, who cut off their daughters' right breast so that it would not interfere when the girls were shooting a bow or throwing a spear (the name *Amazon* was believed in ancient times to be derived from the words for "without a breast"). The story depicted in the temple art depicts one of Heracles' twelve labors, the quest for the girdle of the queen of the Amazons, Hippolyte (whose name means "horse-loosing"). Accompanied by his friend Theseus, Heracles successfully carried off the girdle. But Theseus carried off Hippolyte's sister, too, an act that provoked the Amazons to undertake an invasion of Attica, during which the sister died fighting alongside Theseus.[32] The defeat of the Amazons shows the victory of the forces of order over the wild impulses of barbarians, the suppression of improper sexual unions, and, in the Greek mind,[33] the enforcement of woman's proper place in the hierarchy of the world.[34]

Scenes depicting the Trojan War reflected the same themes of order and marriage, for the Greeks fought for the restoration of Helen to her lawful husband Menelaus. According to the myth, the Trojan prince Paris was met by the goddesses Hera, Athena, and Aphrodite and asked to judge the most beautiful. Each offered a bribe, and Paris chose the bribe of Aphrodite—possession of the most sexually alluring woman ever, whether she was married to someone else or not—rather than the bribes of Hera (power) or of Athena (wisdom). Paris chose a sexual union in conformity with the wild force of nature rather than political or intellectual supremacy. In temple architecture, the Greek victory over the Trojans symbolizes once again the power of mind over this uncontrolled impulse of nature.

Finally, the battle between the gods of Zeus's generation and the giants, a conflict known as the Gigantomachy (literally, *battle with Giants*), represents the confirmation of the rule of justice and order that is established by Zeus's generation of gods. The Giants are the children of Gaia (Earth), born from the drops of blood that fell to the ground when Cronus castrated his father Ouranus. The Giants were urged by their mother to attack the Olympians, but they lost the battle and were imprisoned or killed. The power of Zeus firmly established, his principal duties are to dispense justice and to preserve destiny (*moira*), that is, to see to it that each thing fulfills its nature. The universe can therefore be a place of order and civilization. Again, the art depicts the subjugation of irrational forces to order and law.

Greek sculpture of nonmythological subjects shows the same control over nature. The sculpture of the archaic period (850–500) is marked by calmly controlled physical poses, much in the Egyptian style, and suggest minds in control of the bodies in which they dwell. Male nudes are sexually calm, and their bodies show relaxed muscles. Later, in the classical period (480–350), sculptures become much more realistic in terms of the bodily poses. Muscles are strained, and the flesh seems almost to breathe, but the same profound self-control is still present, though now it is confined to the facial expressions. Perhaps the classical emphasis is on the self-control of one's psyche: no matter the pain the body of a man might be suffering, his soul shows the unruffled serenity of idealized Olympian gods.

The underlying principle that a human mind can overcome the mysterious and powerful forces of nature is the fire that fuels the philosophic mind. Of course, humans present a paradox that will be very much a focus of the ancient philosophers: on the one hand, human reason, along with the order it imposes, is quite apart from "nature, red in tooth and claw"; on the other hand, humans, along with the reason that distinguishes them, are as much a part of nature as animals. Perhaps the first thinkers who were to be called *philosophers* hoped that just as a rational mind could turn cold, hard, raw stone into beautiful and useful shapes so it could subdue the rest of nature. A few rules of proportion and harmony alone could exert the supremacy of mind.

In conclusion, let us look at the two similar names that figured in the myths of the Lapiths and of the Amazons. The Greek princess was *Hippodameia*, "Horse-taming." The Amazon queen was *Hippolyte*, "Horse-looser." By nature a flight animal that runs from any perceived danger, the horse is difficult to tame but nevertheless capable of being tamed (that is, of being made obedient to reasoned human commands). The Greek woman's name suggests control over this naturally wild but potentially tame animal; the Amazon woman's name suggests the animal in its untamed wildness. The Greek world, from its archaic beginnings, celebrated and venerated mind. This love of mind proved the fertile soil in which philosophy could take root.

Figure 7. Self-Control
One feature of classical Greek art is the outward depiction of the soul's inner calm. We find this calm in Greeks, but animals or barbarians (i.e., non-Greeks) are depicted with grimaces and other expressions of pain. Johann Joachim Winckelmann (1717–1768), one of the founders of art history as a discipline, wrote that Greek art captured a spirit superior to what was found in nature: "The most eminent characteristic of Greek works is a noble simplicity and sedate grandeur in gesture and expression. As the bottom of the sea lies peaceful beneath a foaming surface, a great soul lies sedate beneath the strife of passions in Greek figures" (*Reflections on the Painting and Sculpture of the Greeks*, 1755).

VI. How and Where Philosophy Began

Iris is the goddess of rainbows and the messenger of the gods. How beautiful the ancient myth that makes her the daughter of Thaumas (*Wonder* in Greek)![35] For what is more evocative of our sense of wonder than a rainbow? So many colors in an arc curving majestically and hanging in the sky. Sometimes a fainter second and even third rainbow appear above. It is difficult—nay, impossible—not to rejoice in and wonder at rainbows. In a fine passage, Plato shows Socrates exclaiming to a young man who has just confessed his wonder at a certain philosophical problem, "This sense of wonder is the mark of the philosopher. Philosophy indeed has no other origin, and he was a good genealogist who made Iris the daughter of Thaumas."[36]

Aristotle agrees with his master Plato but adds details about the beginning of philosophy:

> It is because of wondering that men began to philosophize and do so now. First, they wondered at the difficulties close at hand; then, advancing little by little, they discussed difficulties also about greater matters, for example, about the changing attributes of the Moon and of the Sun and of the stars, and about the generation of the universe. Now a man who is perplexed and wonders considers himself ignorant (whereas a lover of myth, too is in a sense a philosopher, for myth is composed of wonders), so if they philosophized in order to avoid ignorance, it is evident that they pursued science in order to understand and not in order to use it for something else. This is confirmed by what happened; for it was when almost all the necessities of life were supplied, both for comfort and activity, that such thinking began to be sought. Clearly, then, we do not seek this science for any other need; but just as a man is said to be free if he exists for his own sake and not for the sake of somebody else, so this alone of all the sciences is free, for only this science exists for its own sake.[37]

If philosophy began in Miletus, it would confirm Aristotle's assertion that leisure for reflection was available only after people had the necessities of life. In the sixth century B.C.E., Miletus was the wealthiest city in the Greek world. Located at the mouth of the fertile valley of the Maeander River, it was the port for trade with southern Phrygia. It had four harbors, one of which was very large. Though Miletus traded with Egypt, trade with cities on the Black Sea was a much greater source of wealth. Miletus virtually monopolized this trade, and she founded more than sixty colonies along the Hellespont and coast of the Black Sea, among them the famous cities of Abydus, Cyzicus, and Sinope. As a reprisal for her leadership in the Ionian Revolt against Persian rule in 500, the Persians under King Darius stormed and sacked the city. The Athenian tragedian Phrynichus produced a historical play about this disaster, *The Fall of Miletus*. Herodotus reports that the play had so demoralizing an effect on the Athenians that it was banned from ever being performed again and the playwright fined. Miletus, at that time of its destruction, was what Athens would become: the cultural center of the Hellenic world.

No one knows exactly how philosophy came into being. Perhaps as a port city, Miletus was a fertile ground, for, with people coming from and going to different places, there was the opportunity for bandying ideas in cross-cultural conversations. Of course, ports in antiquity, like wealthy modern ports, offered bored sailors more opportunities for vice than coffeehouses (or their ancient equivalent) offered intellectuals opportunities for philosophical discourse. Even if a port like Miletus was a stimulating locale and therefore a fertile place for the birth of science,[38] there remains the question of why it was Miletus and not one of the hundreds of other wealthy ancient port cities.

Of course, that philosophy began in Miletus and not elsewhere may be largely, even entirely, a result of chance. Similar conditions surely existed in other places. One might as well ask why the inventor of the electric light was born in Milan, Ohio, and not in Cleveland. Genius can develop anywhere, even in obscure and remote places. With so many variables, the exact causes for why things arise in particular places is probably impossible to ascertain.

VII. The Branches of Philosophy

Organizing knowledge, departmentalizing research, is so familiar to us that we do not think that anyone ever invented the idea. For us, the four academic divisions of knowledge—humanities, social sciences, natural sciences, and a miscellaneous collection of everything else—are enshrined in the catalogues of every liberal arts college in the Western world. Under them are grouped the various subdivisions. In the natural sciences we find physics, chemistry, and biology; in the humanities, philosophy, literature, and art; in the social sciences, politics, economics, and psychology; and in miscellaneous, communication and library science.

Most universities, in the interests of egalitarian uniformity, consider all classes in every subject to be on an equal plane, every hour of academic credit equal to every other hour. Aristotle, however, a pioneer in organizing the various sciences and disciplines into groups,[39] would have ranked them in a hierarchy, and his hierarchy would have been based on the significance of the subject matter or on its relationship to the material that depends on it. For example, he says that theology, because of its magisterial subject—immovable, eternal, and divine—is the first of the sciences, more significant even than mathematics. And he says that politics, though the most architectonic of the practical disciplines—since its objectives are greater and more complete than the objectives of other disciplines—nevertheless depends on a foundation of ethics, which should therefore be studied first.[40]

Philosophy refers to the practice of understanding the world through the faculty of reason. As thinkers discovered—or invented—boundaries in the subject matter on which they concentrated their thought, the various branches of philosophy began to emerge. Thus, as some applied their minds to understanding nature and the various things in the physical world, there arose the branches of learning that we call *physics, zoology, botany*, and *physiology*. As others reflected on reality and being, subjects hidden from the senses, there arose the branch we call *metaphysics*. As thinkers aimed their thought at other topics, the other branches arose: *logic*, from those who described (or invented) the system that governs the rules of reasoning; *ethics* and *politics*, from those who investigated how human beings should live individually and collectively; *rhetoric*, from those who sought the mechanisms of persuasion; *aesthetics*, from those who formulated the sensations, feelings, and thoughts of human beings as engendered in art; *epistemology*, from those who tried to uncover the nature of knowledge; and *psychology*, from those who examined functions of the soul (*psyche* in Greek) like imagination and sensation. In addition, philosophers worked on grammar, mathematics, medicine, city planning, astronomy, and many other fields that today we would not expect to find in a department of philosophy.

In the ancient world, thinkers, not yet constrained under the yoke of specialization, were free to wander from one field to another, and polymaths flourished throughout philosophy's first millennium, even during the age of Hellenistic specialization. We in the twenty-first century have all become polymaths, for, with a few keystrokes on a computer, we can link ourselves to databases all over the world and acquire information on any subject that ever passed through a human skull. Every now and then we need to pause to marvel at the achievements of those ancient scholars, who, in the most luxurious comfort they could dream of in their wildest fantasies, toiled with wax tablets in broiling or freezing dark libraries over unindexed scrolls scratched in a barely legible script.

In the next chapter we shall take a look at the first thinkers who came to be called *philosophers* and try to determine what is so magnificent about their accomplishment.

Discussion Questions

1. What sort of individuals might find the views of a philosopher, or philosophy in general, threatening? For a philosopher to be found threatening, does it matter whether he be dealing with the nature of the celestial bodies or with the best way to live or with the existence and nature of God? Are the different subject areas of philosophy menacing to different sorts of people?

2. One way the Greeks expressed the verb *to obey* was with a verb that means *to persuade oneself.* Is this an accurate depiction of obedience? If one "persuades oneself," is one really *obeying,* or is one either following an argument or acting in one's own best interests (say, obeying an order to avoid having to think for oneself or to avoid punishment)? Is it possible for human beings to engage in mindless, unthinking obedience? If so, and if such obedience is a virtue, is it fair to hold people responsible for what they do obediently? Are there occasions when blind obedience is clearly preferable to requiring a persuasive argument?

3. Throughout history, philosophy has been attacked for its argumentativeness. It has been accused of arguing for argument's (and not truth's) sake, of wasting time on superficial and irrelevant questions (a charge parodied as arguments about the number of angels that could dance on the point of a needle), and, perhaps most serious of all, of making the truly worse appear to be the better. Have you engaged in any sorts of arguments that really were guilty of these charges? Why did you do so? Does it undermine

the philosophic enterprise to engage in such arguments? Or do nascent philosophers engage in this sort of competitive play to hone their skills as future philosophers, just as young goats play by butting their heads in mock combat?

4. If you are about to take up a book and read it, how much information do you want to know about it? Do you want to know, for instance, that it is a novel and not a technical manual? If it is a novel, do you want to know that it is a mystery and not a romance? If it is a mystery, do you want to know that it will have a happy ending? How does the amount of prior information you have about the book affect (a) your willingness to read it and (b) the expectations you have about it? How limiting are the judgments you make of a book before reading it? What about movies? How much information do you need before you'll invest ten dollars and two hours in one?

5. Philosophy is said to deal with matters of *universal* significance. Yet any individual philosopher must come from a very particular place and live in a particular time. What challenges do you see for philosophers in trying to gaze on the universal while at the same time being wedded to the here and now?

34

6. Art traditionally has been called an "imitation of nature." But if art is a celebration of our triumphs, of our victory over the irrational forces, even over the irrational forces of nature, how then is it an imitation of nature? And if it is an imitation of nature, what sort of imitation is it? One type of imitation is impersonation, whereby an impersonator tries to capture the personality of a famous cultural figure. To what degree must an imitation resemble the subject itself in order to qualify as an impersonation? To what degree must they differ? How true to nature do we want our imitations to be? Why is there a variety of answers to this question?

7. What was the most important feature of the Greek character that led to the development of philosophy? Are there any elements in that character that delayed or distorted or hindered the development of philosophy? Which features of Greek character do you predict will be changed as a result of philosophy?

Notes

1. Aristotle, *Posterior Analytics* 78 b31. The steps provided here are in part suggested in the commentary of Hippocrates G. Apostle, *Aristotle's Posterior Analytics* (Grinnell, Iowa: Peripatetic Press, 1981), 142.

2. Aristotle, *Nicomachaean Ethics* 1176 b30–35.

3. Aristotle, *Politics* 1340 b27.

4. Genesis 2:16–17.

5. Homer, *Iliad*, trans. Richmond Lattimore (Chicago: University of Chicago Press, 1951), 1.206–214.

6. An epigram by the poet Simonides (92D), written to commemorate the Spartans who died at Thermopylae, lends insight into this Greek conception of persuasion:

> O stranger, report to the Lacedaemonians
> that we lie here persuading ourselves to obey their words.

Simonides, who came from one of the Greek islands and who lived with equal ease and familiarity in democratic Athens and in the feudal courts of Thessaly and Sicily, closes in the Greek with the word "persuading." The verb, here in participial form, is used in the middle voice and literally means "persuading ourselves in our own interest"; the verb comes to mean "obey," but it never has the sense that the English word conveys, of mere or even blind acceptance and fulfillment of orders. A Greek always had first to be persuaded, a process that for him meant to hear the arguments and then to make up his own mind. The epigram thus captures the Spartans' conscious and willing choice of death in behalf of their cause. The translation is the author's.

7. Homer, *Iliad* 9.443.

8. For example, the subject forms the content of Plato's dialogue *Sophist*. Aristotle, who discussed the matter often, is of course the consummate genius at formulating distinctions.

9. See James A. Arieti, "Achilles' Guilt," *The Classical Journal* 80 (1985): 193–203.

10. Homer, *Odyssey* 6.92.

11. Xenophon, *Hellenica* 6.4.16.

12. This is the famous conversation between Solon and Croesus about who was the happiest of men. The conversation anticipates a good deal of later Greek ethical reflection. See *Discourses on the First Book of Herodotus* (Lanham, Md.: Littlefield Adams Books, 1995), 44–53.

13. Thucydides, *History of the Peloponnesian War* 1.77.

14. Tacitus, *The Annals of Imperial Rome* 14.16.

15. One of the implied questions is whether human beings control the gods. Another is why the gods do not always agree; that is, can there be more than one divine way, and, if so, can there be more than one perfect way, or does divinity not equate with perfection?

16. Plato himself mocks this disputatiousness, which came to be called *eristic*, in his dialogue *Euthydemos*.

17. *The Decline and Fall of the Roman Empire,* Great Books of the Western World Edition (Chicago: Encyclopaedia Britannica, 1952), vol. 1, chap. 2.

18. Aristotle, *Rhetoric* 1378 a31–37. Aristotle distinguishes it from hateful rage in 1382 a1–19.

19. This interpretation of Homer's *Iliad* appears in a series of articles: "Achilles' Inquiry about Machaon: The Critical Moment in the *Iliad*," *The Classical Journal* 79 (1983–1984): 125–30; "Achilles' Guilt," *The Classical Journal* 80 (1985): 193–203; "Achilles' Alienation in *Iliad* 9," *The Classical Journal* 82 (1986): 1–27; and "Homer's Atê and Litae," *The Classical Journal* 84 (1988): 1–12.

20. The Greek traditions of philosophy, tragedy, history, and rhetoric will all deal with these questions.

21. Pierre Hadot, *What Is Ancient Philosophy?* trans. Michael Chase (Cambridge, Mass.: Harvard University Press, 2002), 9.

22. Diogenes Laertius, *Lives of Eminent Philosophers* 8.8. The anecdote is told also by Cicero, *Tusculum Disputations* 5.8.

23. Aristotle, *Poetics* 1447 a 30.

24. Aristotle, *Poetics* 1447 b 12–20, trans. Ingram Bywater, in *The Complete Works of Aristotle: The Revised Oxford Translation*, ed. J. Barnes (Princeton, N.J.: Princeton University Press, 1984).

25. See p. 177.

26. See chapter 18, pp. 348–49.

27. I heard this anecdote thirty years ago from my friend and colleague John M. Crossett, who was quoting from memory. I have not been able to track down the source.

28. Thucydides, *History of the Peloponnesian War*, trans. Richard Crawley, rev. and ed. Robert B. Strassler (New York: Free Press, 1996), 2.2. Subsequent quotations to Thucydides are from this translation.

29. Benjamin Franklin, *The Autobiography of Benjamin Franklin*, ed. Leonard W. Labaree et al. (New Haven, Conn.: Yale University Press, 1964), 75–76.

30. For a terrifying account of the civil conflict in Corcyra, which Thucydides says is representative of such conflicts throughout the Greek world, see *The History of the Peloponnesian War* 3.84. See the quotation of the contiguous passage on p. 144 of this book.

31. For details, see Spiro Kostof, *A History of Architecture: Settings and Rituals* (Oxford: Oxford University Press, 1985), 124–25.

32. The son of Theseus's union was Hippolytus, the subject of Euripides' play *Hippolytus*, a man who was so opposed to sex that he ignored worship of Aphrodite. Perhaps the moral was not that sex should be ignored but that it should be regulated. In Euripides' play, Hippolytus is the favorite of Artemis, the goddess of both chastity and marriage. Inasmuch as Hippolytus was chaste, perhaps he pleased Artemis but in avoiding sex, even marital sex, perhaps was not entirely her devotee.

33. The Greek world, like the rest of the world until the twentieth century, considered the good woman to be silent and unavailable to men, including male relatives, except for her husband. The more sexually ignorant she was, the more erotically appealing she was. For details on the representation of women, see Ellen D. Reeder, *Pandora: Women in Classical Greece* (Princeton, N.J.: Princeton University Press, 1995), 123.

34. Eva C. Keuls, *The Reign of the Phallus: Sexual Politics in Ancient Athens* (New York: Harper & Row, 1985), sees the victory over the Amazons as representing "the subduing of the rebellious female." In the Greek mind women were more instinctively natural and subject to natural passions, so in this sense, a victory over rebellious women, or women who were defying their place as women, would affirm the world order.

35. Hesiod, *Theogony* 266.

36. Plato, *Theaetetus* 155d.

37. *Metaphysics* 982 b12–28, trans. Hippocrates G. Apostle (Grinnell, Iowa: Peripatetic Press, 1979). Subsequent quotations of the *Metaphysics* are from this translation.

38. The terms *philosophy* and *science* are at this early time synonymous.

39. As he says, each area of knowledge marks off some area of reality to study in relation to the other areas (*Metaphysics* 1025 b8–10).

40. On theology, see *Metaphysics* 1025–1026 a32; on politics, see *Nicomachean Ethics* 1094 b8.

Select Bibliography

HOMER

Carter, Jane B., and Sarah P. Morris, eds. *The Ages of Homer*. Austin: University of Texas Press, 1995.
Clarke, Howard W. *The Art of the Odyssey*. Englewood Cliffs, N.J.: Prentice Hall, 1967.
Edwards, Mark. *Homer, Poet of the Iliad*. Baltimore: Johns Hopkins University Press, 1987.
Finley, M. I. *The World of Odysseus*. 2nd ed. Harmondsworth: Penguin, 1991.
Nagy, Gregory. *Homeric Question*. Austin: University of Texas Press, 1996.

HESIOD

Burn, A. R. *The World of Hesiod: A Study of the Greek Middle Ages, c. 900–700 B.C.* 2nd ed. New York: B. Blom, 1966.
Pucci, Pietro. *Hesiod and the Language of Poetry*. Baltimore: Johns Hopkins University Press, 1977.

ART AND ARCHAEOLOGY

Boardman, J., ed. *The Oxford History of Classical Art*. Oxford: Oxford University Press, 1993.
Pedley, J. G. *Greek Art and Archaeology*. London: Cassell, 1993.

Pollitt, J. J. *Art and Experience in Classical Greece.* Cambridge: Cambridge University Press, 1972.

Richter, G. M. A. *Handbook of Greek Art.* London: Phaidon, 1987.

Robertson, M. *A Shorter History of Greek Art.* Cambridge: Cambridge University Press, 1981.

Sparkes, B. A. *Greek Art.* Vol. 22 in *Greece & Rome* New Surveys in the Classics. Oxford: Classical Association/Oxford University Press, 1991.

Spivey, N. *Greek Art.* London: Phaidon, 1997.

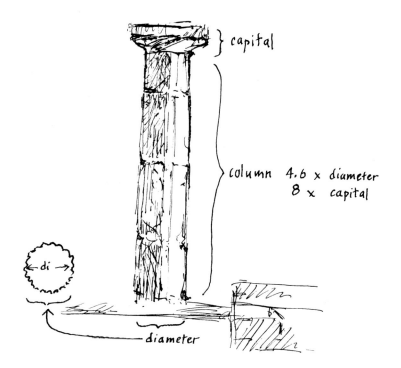

CHAPTER 2

Philosophy Begins

I. By What Name Shall We Call the Milesian Thinkers?

We call the first philosophers "Presocratics," but they could not have thought of themselves in this way. They could no more have conceived of themselves as *pre*-Socrates than Inca goldsmiths in 1300 C.E. could have thought of themselves as *pre*-Columbus. Nor could these Greek thinkers have thought of themselves as *philosophers*.[1] To call them "*presocratic*" is of course to make the work of Socrates the dividing line, a notion that had been given authority even before Cicero uttered his famous words that Socrates brought philosophy down from the sky and placed it in the houses and cities of men.[2] The division implies that before Socrates philosophy dealt with what the world and celestial bodies were made of and with logic and metaphysics. After Socrates, according to the formulation, philosophy was expanded to include a rational investigation of human ethics and the human soul.

Like so many things in the history of philosophy and—alas—in the history of everything else, the neat formulation is misleading and is itself a result of the prejudices and partisanship of its formulators. It is misleading because by *fiat* it takes *some* early thinkers who dealt with matters of physics and logic—Thales, Anaximander, and many others who came to be called "Presocratics"—and declares *them* to be philosophers. Others known for their wisdom—Solon and Protagoras and Gorgias—it omits or calls by the disparaging (to the callers) name of *Sophists*. This formulation probably began in the Academy of Plato, where Aristotle studied for twenty years, and it became so entrenched that it seems almost natural to historians of philosophy. We shall try here not to label the early thinkers as Presocratics. Instead, we shall take a look both at them and also at some thinkers who have not received this honorific epithet. We shall look at these latter partly for the learning that they offer and partly to examine how the men traditionally called *philosophers* responded to them.

Early thinkers referred to their own activity as *historie*, "inquiry," the same term Herodotus uses for his work about the Persian Wars. They also refer to their work as *sophia*, "wisdom." As we shall see, unlike Herodotus, who traveled and asked questions of the people he met, these thinkers both asked the questions and offered the answers, and if they offered any wisdom, it arose from their own genius, not from the minds of others.

Who, we might ask, was the intended audience for their inquiries or for their wisdom? To address this question, we might recall Aristotle's comment about Miletus, that it was a wealthy city in which the necessities of life were easily obtained. Thus people had time for leisure, and perhaps, as always, leisure delights in novelty. Perhaps the new kind of discussion about what the world was made of and how things were generated attracted enough of an audience to keep the activity alive. Perhaps it was just barely kept alive by the three Milesian thinkers with whom we are acquainted—Thales, Anaximander, and Anaximenes, whose careers cover a century (from about 625–525). Tradition claims that Anaximander was the pupil of Thales and Anaximenes the pupil of Anaximander. But the claim is probably misleading, first because it likely arises from the ancient Greek tendency to invent an orderly process for the sake of order[3] and, second because the term "pupil" is used anachronistically. If Anaximander, for example, heard the "wisdom" of Thales and thought that he could improve on it with his own wisdom, he is not what we would call a "pupil" in a sense familiar to contemporary education.

II. How Do We Know about the Early Thinkers?

Of the early thinkers from Miletus only one sentence has survived from antiquity, and this sentence, by Anaximander, was saved only because it was quoted in a compendium of early thought, and the compiler of the compendium had his own reasons for including this particular sentence. In other words, the information that we have, and that must perforce be included in this book, is mostly hearsay, second- or third- or fourthhand (or worse), tainted by the motives of the tellers, contaminated by faulty memory and incompletion, and embellished by a poetic art that tries to make a telling interesting, even at the expense of rigorous adherence to truth.

The direct statements of the early thinkers were preserved in fragmentary form by later writers who, of course, chose their quotations judiciously to make their own points. Often they sought to enhance the stature of their own work by an authoritative quotation from a venerable ancient. These quotations, because they are taken out of context and selected for a wholly particular and immediate motive, do not give a fair glimpse into the quoted thinker's body of work (if we can even refer to such work as a *body*—a term that suggests an organic coherence and system). Nor will the quotations necessarily be accurate, as those who quoted may have relied on memory or on texts that were corrupt.[4]

Our second source of information comes in summarizing statements by other writers, like Plato or Aristotle or Aristotle's favorite student Theophrastus, who, perhaps at his teacher's behest, compiled the compendium just referred to, *Teachings of the Naturalists* (the word translated as *Naturalists* is *physikoi*, "those who deal with *physis*," nature). Theophrastus's compendium has not itself survived, though it is so often referred to that a partial reconstruction has been attempted.[5] In the case of such innovative and brilliant geniuses as Plato and Aristotle, the motive for mentioning an earlier thinker is often to show how his work was incomplete or wrong, and the whole discussion is, in any case, shaped and construed through the system of the genius. Thus, for example, when Theophrastus was collecting the works of earlier thinkers, he probably possessed a list of questions that Aristotle had put together on what he considered to be the most important topics of philosophy. Theophrastus would then have gleaned from the earlier thinkers what he could find and have put down what he assumed were their thoughts about these topics. It is clear that the process would have been rife with opportunities for twisting the thought so as to fit the topic, as happened over and over again in the history of philosophy.[6] Entire subject areas that the early thinkers may have investigated, since they did not appear on Theophrastus's list, might have been entirely omitted as irrelevant or uninteresting. And subsequent discussions would been constricted by the controlling structure of the great masters and the limitations of knowledge engendered by earlier reports.

In short, then, a student of early Greek philosophy must be willing to devote his mind to an account that would not be admitted in an honest courtroom. Here there is no possibility of a verdict beyond a shadow of a

Figure 8.   Philosophers in Art

Aside from Socrates, who was ugly, all the philosophers of antiquity were exceedingly hand-some. Their unkempt hair and scraggly beards showed their disdain for the vanity that afflicted mere other men. Their brows were uniformly furrowed from the intensity of their deep thoughts. Their invariably penetrating eyes were capable of seeing through false appearances to the true reality, etc., etc. In actual fact, we don't know what the philosophers looked like, and the portraits that remain illustrate what the artists *thought* they should look like. You may attach the name of any philosopher (except Socrates) to this portrait.

doubt. Instead, everything is doubtful, and if any shape at all can be derived through the mist and fog of time and error and distortion, it is indistinct at best. Nevertheless, despite the incompleteness of what remains, a student of the history of Western thought can wonder at the questions that excited the contemplation of the early thinkers, and he can amuse his curiosity as he ponders their answers. This extraordinary quality of both the questions and the answers convinced the ancients themselves that an intellectual revolution had occurred.

III. The Thinkers from Miletus:
Thales, Anaximander, Anaximenes

A. THALES (624–546)

The most famous anecdote about Thales is told by Aristotle, who does not claim that it is true but says that it was told of Thales because of his reputation for wisdom. Aristotle writes,

> Thales was reproached for his poverty, which indicated that philosophy was of no benefit to man. But, the story goes, from his knowledge of astronomy he perceived, while it was still winter, the coming of a great harvest of olives in the coming season, and, having procured a small sum of money, he made a deposit for the use of all the olive presses of Miletus and Chios, which he rented for a low price since no one bid against him. When the harvest came and there was a sudden and simultaneous demand for the use of the presses, he let these at whatever price he wished and made a fortune, thus pointing out that philosophers can easily become wealthy if they wish but that wealth is not their main pursuit in life.[7]

We can pass over the obvious impossibility of the story—that summer's weather could be predicted on the basis of astronomical observations during winter (after all, modern meteorology, with information from satellites, cannot predict the weather even three days hence!). What is important is that Thales is portrayed as a man who showed the lesson of Hesiod's *Works and Days*: study nature, apply its lessons, and wealth will follow. More importantly in the present context, however, Thales illustrates *Aristotle's* lesson: the true man of philosophy is not interested in the practical applications of knowledge but in knowledge for its own sake.

A love of knowledge for its own sake or, perhaps better, of *understanding* for its own sake is what marks the thinkers from Miletus. It is often and accurately said that the radical change in Milesian thought is its freedom from mythology, that is, its search for explanations reflective of universal laws of nature. This freedom from religious explanation is a manifestation of an attempt to understand for the sole sake of understanding. If the god Poseidon is responsible for earthquakes, then it is to Poseidon that one can appeal for escape from their menace. But if, as Thales is reported to have said, earthquakes come about from the agitation of the water on which the earth floats,[8] then there is no god to whom one can appeal for safety. The knowledge about the cause of earthquakes would exist for its own sake, simply for the satisfaction of knowing the cause.[9]

Thales is most recognized for his claim, as Aristotle records it, that the material principle of all things is water.[10] Given the total absence of a scientific vocabulary on which to draw, including a general word for "matter" (for the distinction of matter and energy or of matter and spirit had not yet been drawn), Thales may have had in mind the changeable condition of water, that is, the fact that it can be transformed into either liquid, solid, or gas. Thus water may be a metaphor for the various forms of matter.[11] Alternatively, because life comes from water and because water is a major component of all living things, Thales may have meant the claim as a metaphor for the significance of water for life. Aristotle suggests that Thales came to his conclusion from "observing that all food is moist and that heat itself is generated from the moist and is kept alive by it (and that from which things are generated is the principle of all)."[12] As we shall see, the early thinkers tended to be extremely metaphorical in their discourse, even employing human ethical terms to describe physical forces (Empedocles, for example, speaks of "love" and "strife" as the elemental forces of nature[13]), and so there is always a danger of interpreting their remarks too literally. It seems unlikely that Thales would have been counted one of the Seven Sages of the ancient world if he had meant that everything, as we find it, is literally water, a claim that would have generated laughter or pity, according to the generosity of his hearers.

Thales also discusses soul (*psyche*). Aristotle writes that "Thales seems to have understood the soul as something in motion [kinetic]—if indeed he said that the stone has a soul because it moves iron."[14] Aristotle adds, "There are also some who say that the soul is blended in the whole [universe]; and it is perhaps from this view that Thales, too, thought that all things are full of gods."[15] These passages illustrate how in thinking about nature, Thales stretched the limits of his vocabulary in order to make his insights intelligible. He seemed to be suggesting that soul is the source of movement—a view most people share today, at least in some contexts. We see a motionless corpse and conclude that its soul has departed. We speak of a dead person's body as distinct from the person himself. We say, "So and So's body lies in state in the Rotunda" or "the child's

45

body was removed from the river." Perhaps Thales believed that the soul is a god because it causes things to move and that movement is the essence of being alive. Thus rivers, trees, winds, and celestial bodies are gods and are alive (unlike rocks) because they move and seem to have the faculty of self-motion. Independent self-motion is an exceedingly difficult concept and, in the history of philosophy, often has a divine cause. Aquinas's favorite proof for the existence of God, for example, depends on God as the self-moving cause of motion.[16] Here, at the beginning of the philosophical tradition, movement is the province of soul; all that seems to generate its own movement is alive in this sense and possessed of soul. As Aetius (a second-century C.E. compiler of the views of early philosophers) writes, "Thales said that the mind of the cosmos is god, and that the whole is ensouled and full of spirits, and that a moving [kinetic] divine power penetrates through the elemental moisture."[17]

Assuming that these attributed comments are accurate, Thales seems to have made two different claims about the gods. On the one hand, he seems to have said that souls are gods because they are self-moving. On

the other hand, he suggested that the mind of the cosmos, its systematic order, somehow penetrates the moisture and is a god. What is revolutionary in this thinking is the depersonalizing of the divine, the making of the divine both the intellectual framework for the world and the actual sustained perpetuation of that framework through the physical world. Thales defined "god" in a nonmythological way, as a physical force and as an intellectually comprehended pattern. Though he used the words *soul* and *god*—the language of religion—his thought was quite distinct from the religion of his contemporaries. There would be no altars, no sacrifices, no hymns to Thales' divinities, for they were not appropriate objects of prayer or ritual.

The day Thales first asked questions about the makeup of the world and proposed new solutions was one of the truly revolutionary moments in the history of the world. Another came when Thales made one of the first *quantitative* predictions of note: he is the first person we know of to predict successfully by mathematical means a total eclipse of the sun. Although this prediction was correct only to the nearest year, the historian Herodotus reports that the occurrence of the eclipse was significant enough to cause the Lydians and the Medes immediately to make peace after six years of war.[18] If the eclipse in question was indeed the one of 28 May 585 B.C.E., the anniversary of that day should perhaps be as well committed to our memory as the dates of the signing of the Declaration of Independence or the storming of the Bastille or the landing by Neil Armstrong on the moon.

B. ANAXIMANDER (610–546)

Perhaps Anaximander looked at Thales' conclusions and, in the Greek spirit of competition, thought to himself, "I can do better." His "better" is that the principle of the world is the *boundless* (*apeiron*), an undefined entity that can become anything and everything.

As we look around, we see that all the various things—rocks, trees, houses, rivers, stars—have names and natures that separate them from everything else. If each thing has a *fixed* nature, how is it possible for things to come into being or pass out of being or to change in any way? Anaximander's solution is that the underlying matter does not itself have the boundaries of a fixed nature; instead, all matter is rich in and full of potentialities: thus, rock can be formed into a house, water can dry up and become air, bread can be digested and become flesh. Where Thales' use of *water* was meant, perhaps, to imply the changeable nature of an underlying reality, Anaximander's term *boundless* is an improvement on the metaphor, for it cuts immediately to the core problem of change, that is, how one thing takes on a new set of properties to become something else.

The mechanism of change comes from a war between opposite forces, of which the four principal pairs are the hot and the cold and the wet and the dry. Perhaps Anaximander looked at the cycle of the year and saw that summer and winter were opposed to each other by time with the intervening seasons of spring and fall, when winds seemed to contend with each other and rain and sun competed for dominance. Or perhaps he saw that puddles dried up quickly under the heat of the sun or that water can extinguish fire. Or perhaps he saw that living flesh is warm, dead flesh, cold. In any case, his explanation is in terms of natural qualities, not in terms of gods. (It is important to keep in mind, however, that the term "natural qualities" could not as yet have occurred to Anaximander himself, for "nature" [*physis*] had not yet emerged as a separate concept.)

47

Attempting to improve on Thales' idea of the world as floating on water, Anaximander claimed that the world was shaped like one of the cylindrical slices of a temple column called a drum and that we live on the upper surface of it.[19] The depth of the cylinder, he says, is one-third its width. The earth stays in place because above and below and around it to the sides it is equally distant from the heavenly bodies. He arrives at this startlingly unintuitive conclusion by reflecting on the motion of the sun and by determining that the sun and other heavenly bodies revolve in a daily circular orbit around the earth. He speculates that the sun's course is twenty-seven times the diameter of the earth and that the moon's is eighteen times the diameter of the earth.[20] Though he does not give the course of the stars, perhaps it would be safe to assume a course nine times the diameter of the earth, so that the diameter of the earth, at three times its depth, would complete the orderly set of proportions.[21] The attribution of a mathematical ratio to the universe, the same kind of ratio that we observed in temple construction,[22] suggests that Anaximander is claiming, if vaguely, that an intelligible set of ordered rules governs the universe. This powerful notion is perhaps the forerunner of the idea that the universe embodies a beauty and hence is a *cosmos* (the Greek word for an ordered place operating according to law).

These ideas are supported by the only sentence of the Milesians actually quoted. The quotation comes in a sentence in which Simplicius, a sixth-century C.E. commentator on Aristotle, quotes from Theophrastus's compendium of earlier philosophy. Simplicius is summarizing Anaximander's idea that out of the "boundless"

> come all the heavens and all the worlds in them into being. And to the things that are their coming-into-being (*genesis*) and their destruction is [as Anaximander puts it] rather poetically, "according to their debt; you see they pay the penalty to each other for their injustice according to the assessment of time."[23]

Though the text is so difficult that Theophrastus himself perhaps prefers to quote it rather than risk misinterpreting it, with more boldness than Theophrastus, we may venture a guess as to its meaning. The language includes a metaphor from law courts, where debts are paid and contracts enforced. In Anaximander's view of the world, the various forces of dry, wet, hot, and cold transform the *boundless* into the various objects that we see in turn, as things are born and die and pass into different forms. As a just balance is achieved in a courtroom, when debtor becomes creditor, or in the give-and-take of commerce, so in the universe, in the give-and-take of competing forces, a balance akin to human justice occurs under the guidance of the controlling judge of time. If this, or anything like it, approximates the meaning behind Anaximander's metaphor, there would again be an assertion of reasoned law behind the apparent disorder of the universe. Is this an anthropomorphizing of the universe, a projecting onto the universe a human mind? Or is this a further development of Western science, which seeks to understand the fundamental laws hidden behind the diversity of what we see with our eyes? Or is it, perhaps, both?

C. ANAXIMENES (585–528)

The third of the Milesian thinkers, Anaximenes, proposed air as the principle of the world. As in the cases of Anaximander and Thales, no explicit criticism of predecessors survives, nor we do possess any second-hand comments about such criticism. But from the traditional accounts about Anaximenes, it is possible to speculate what his criticism might have been. One difficulty of such speculation is, of course, the impossibility of knowing where Anaximenes' vocabulary was metaphorical and where it was literal. If, on the one hand, Thales' *water* was a metaphor for matter because water could take on the shape of any container and could exist in gaseous, liquid, and solid states, it would seem difficult to find fault with *water* as the term for *matter*. If, on the other hand, we apply literalness to water as the actual substrate of the universe, then it is indeed difficult (nay, impossible) to see how water could transform itself into *everything*, especially into fire, which appears to be a polar opposite with no potential water in it at all. Perhaps—to carry the speculation a little further—Anaximenes anticipated the pervasive (if problematic) future practice of interpreters of philosophy and the Bible of taking some parts metaphorically and other parts literally.

Where water presented the apparently insoluble difficulty of transformation into or out of fire, air presented the advantage of invisibly taking on different forms in a way that could be actually perceived. We can feel air that is hot, cold, moist, or dry. Moreover, we can feel the wind blowing on our skin and then surmise that the same wind is invisibly whirling the dry leaves. Air, moreover, has as good a claim to be the source of living things as water, for air is the breath of life—without air, there is no life. Thus, like Anaximander's *unbounded* (*apeiron*), air has the quality of invisibility, but unlike the *unbounded*, there is actual evidence that it exists. It is a perceptible part of nature while at the same time it enjoys a place in the explanatory intellectual and invisible realm that is somehow "beyond nature," that is, in what later philosophy would call *metaphysics*.[24]

Anaximenes offered many other views. As a mechanism for the transformation of air into different substances he proposed processes of condensation and rarifaction: when air is condensed, it is cold; when it is relaxed, it is hot.[25] He suggested that air is a god,[26] perhaps because he saw it as including the faculty of self-motion. He claimed that the earth is flat and situated in the midst of air that surrounds it.[27] The range of his thinking was very extensive and included also discussions of earthquakes,[28] rainbows,[29] and lightning.[30]

IV. General Remarks on the Milesians

The Milesian thinkers found an audience that remembered and transmitted some of their views. Despite what may appear to us as the insufficiently self-critical naïveté of their teaching,[31] we may note several significant features. First, they were genuinely interested in knowledge for its own sake. Their speculative models on the principles that explained the world brought no practical advantages or encouraged any engineering marvels. Indeed, the view that the world rested on water or air or was shaped like a cylinder was about as likely to help one earn a living by farming as the view that the world began in what is called a Big Bang or that the universe is fourteen billion years old (give or take a couple of billion). Such information is simply and wholly a pure joy to human minds.

Second, these thinkers grappled with the vexing problem of how to express their thoughts when there was no preexisting vocabulary suitable to the task. Later thinkers would solve the problem by the expedient of inventing new terms that they would call "technical vocabulary" and others would call "jargon." The solution of the Milesians was to employ the language of metaphor. This solution, alas, generated a dilemma: how literally should the various metaphors be taken? This dilemma was to perplex later philosophy as well. For example, among those who study Plato we may observe a continual struggle to distinguish which parts of the Platonic writings are to be understood literally, which metaphorically, and which—if we might dare suggest—in both ways simultaneously.

Third, despite the traditional claim that gods are foreign to the work of philosophy, we find that the early thinkers attempted to include the divine in their formulations of reality. Like later thinkers, they tried to work out a reconciliation of their religious views with their views of nature. Thus Anaximenes, for example, did not reject gods; indeed, he thought that gods, like everything else, were made of air,[32] Thales, that everything was full of gods. Perhaps, as we have discussed, these thinkers were using *gods* as a metaphor for self-motion or were somehow attempting to account for a principle of self-motion. In the hunt for the ultimate origin of motion they would have been anticipating one of the fundamental and as yet unsolved problems of physics.[33]

51

Discussion Questions

1. To what extent is your thinking controlled by nomenclature? Is the phenomenon of nomenclature akin to that of genre? If "Shakespeare" were catalogued in libraries under "philosophers" and "Einstein" under "mathematicians," would you approach their writings differently from the way you do?

2. Aristotle claimed that philosophy could take place when people had leisure. A quick look around at contemporary culture (and perhaps the culture of all of history!) shows that philosophy is not the first, nay, not the fifth or sixth most sought after activity for leisure time. So while leisure may be a necessary condition for philosophy, it is clearly not a sufficient one. What else must there be?

3. In a great many cases the most we can know about a past event is quite limited. From examining what archaeologists call *realia*, things that were used in daily life—oil lamps, clothing, and so forth—we can, to some degree, tell what everyday life was like. But what can be learned through such artifacts about the inner life of ancient peoples is quite limited. What about the evidence in literary works? Even with all the distortions of language, is it

possible to gain insight into a people's mental life? Or does the possibility of distortion undercut the value of any deductions that can be drawn? In short, how does the knowledge of past peoples that is gained from the fragmentary literary remains stack up against the knowledge gained from artifacts?

4. Metaphor vastly increases the power of language. For example, here follows a list of ingredients that appears on a container of Häagen-Dazs vanilla ice cream:

> Rich, creamy, and totally indulgent, Häagen-Dazs vanilla ice cream is the pure combination of sweet cream and fragrant vanilla. Häagen-Dazs vanilla ice cream is all natural with no preservatives, artificial flavors, or colorings.

Now consider the possibility of reading the ingredients as a description of one's daughter or one's friend simply by substituting the person's name for "Häagen-Dazs vanilla ice cream." In what ways has communication been enhanced by reading the ingredients as metaphors for the person's qualities? What dangers are there if she takes the reading too seriously?

5. In word processing on computers, the terms *widow* and *orphan* have special meanings drawn by analogy with the literal meanings. According to the "Help" function in Microsoft Word, "A *widow* is the last line of a paragraph printed by itself at the top of a page. An *orphan* is the first line of a paragraph printed by itself at the bottom of a page." In a similar way, the terms *male* and *female* are used to distinguish various hardware fittings. Can Thales have been using the term *god* in a similarly metaphorical way? What are the advantages and disadvantages of such metaphors?

6. Did Anaximander deal satisfactorily with the problems left by Thales? Did Anaximenes successfully address the problems of both Thales and Anaximander? Why might each, at least at some point, have been satisfied with his own work? Can you imagine a conversation among the three in which they critiqued each other's thought?

7. Which of the Milesian thinkers seems to have made the greatest contribution to philosophy, and why? Before naming the thinker, be sure to list your criteria of philosophical greatness.

Notes

1. See chapter 1, pp. 16–19.

2. *Tusculum Disputations* 5.4.10.

3. We often see this ordering tendency. For example, the Greeks loved to find a coincidence in dates. Thus, according to the tradition, the battles of Artemisium and Thermopylae took place on the same day, as did the battles of Plataea and Mycale.

4. When in the dialogues Plato has a character quote from Homer's known texts or from those of other poets, we often find misquotations, some of which arise perhaps because of the frailty of memory, others because a subtle point can be made by a slight emendation to the established text.

5. This was done by A. Diels, *Doxographi Graeci* (Berlin: Typis et Impensis G. Reimeri, 1879).

6. For example, Simplicius writes in his *Commentaria*, "Theophrastus says that Xenophanes of Colophon, teacher of Parmenides, put forward the thesis of the unity and completeness of that-which-is [i.e., the cosmos]; but he adds that the thesis of Xenophanes does not belong in this context, since Xenophanes was speaking not of the cosmos, but of the unity and completeness of God" (quoted in Hermann Fränkel, *Early Greek Poetry and Philosophy*, trans. Moses Hadas and James Willis [Oxford: Oxford University Press, 1975], 259 n. 17). For an example of a medieval Jewish philosopher's attempt to find Aristotelian philosophy in the Psalms, see the discussion of Abraham Ibn Daud in James A. Arieti and Patrick A. Wilson, *The Scientific and the Divine: Conflict and Reconciliation from Ancient Greece to the Present* (Lanham, Md.: Rowman & Littlefield, 2003), 182–85.

7. Aristotle, *Politics*, trans. Hippocrates G. Apostle and Lloyd Gerson (Grinnell, Iowa: Peripatetic Press, 1986), 1259 a10–18.

8. The source is very late, Seneca's *Natural Questions* 3.14. Seneca is quoting an unnamed source.

9. Perhaps the knowledge that earthquakes arise from the movement of tectonic plates is similarly satisfying for its own sake since, as yet, there is nothing we can do to prevent earthquakes or predict them with an accuracy even approaching that with which we predict the weather.

10. Aristotle, *Metaphysics* 983b19 ff.

11. Aristotle himself will later use for matter the word *hyle*, which literally means "wood," presumably because as wood can be carved into many shapes, so matter can take on many forms.

12. Aristotle, *Metaphysics* 983b22.

13. See pp. 116–18.

14. Aristotle, *On the Soul*, trans. Hippocrates G. Apostle (Grinnell, Iowa: Peripatetic Press, 1981), 405a19. Subsequent quotations to *On the Soul* are from this translation.

15. Aristotle, *On the Soul* 411a7.

16. *Summa Theologica* Question 2, Article 3.

17. G. S. Kirk and J. E. Raven, *The Presocratic Philosophers* (Cambridge: Cambridge University Press, 1966), 95–96.

18. Herodotus, *The History* 1.74. With regard to reports of successful but isolated predictions, there is always the possibility of a selection effect in the reporting; that is, there could have been numerous eclipse predictions mathematically on a par with that of Thales but unsuccessful and hence unreported. Thales may just have gotten lucky.

19. Ps. Plutarch, *Stromateis* 2; Hippolytus, *Refutation of all Heresies* 1.6.3.

20. Hippolytus, *Refutation of all Heresies* 1.6.4–5.

21. Kirk and Raven, *The Presocratic Philosophers*, 136–37.

22. See pp. 25–26.

23. Simplicius, *Physics* 24. The translation is the author's.

24. *Metaphysics* is a term variously used. In general, it refers to the study of being as being. For example, animals, rocks, and ideas all have some form of being; metaphysics is the branch of philosophy that deals with the being itself, without dealing with the things that have the being.

25. Plutarch, *Moralia* 947f (DK 13 B1).

26. Cicero, *On the Nature of the Gods* 1.10.26.

27. Aristotle, *On the Sky* 294 b13 (DK 13 A20).

28. Aristotle, *Meteorology* 365 b 7.

29. Hippolytus, *Refutatio* 1.7.

30. Aetius 3.3.1–2, quoted in Kirk and Raven, *The Presocratic Philosophers*, 138.

31. And, of course, in fairness to these thinkers, we must keep in mind the very fragmentary nature of what remains of their work.

32. Augustine, *City of God* 8.2.

33. A modern form of the question would ask what initiated what is called the "Big Bang."

53

Select Bibliography

THE PRESOCRATICS

Barnes, Jonathan. *Early Greek Philosophy*. London: Penguin Books, 1987.

Furley, David. *The Greek Cosmologists*. Vol. 1. Cambridge: Cambridge University Press, 1987.

Hussey, Edward. *The Presocratics*. London: Duckworth, 1993.

Kirk, G. S., J. E. Raven, and M. Schofield, eds. *The Presocratic Philosophers*. 2nd ed. Cambridge: Cambridge University Press, 1983.

Long, A. A., ed. *The Cambridge Companion to Early Greek Philosophy*. Cambridge: Cambridge University Press, 1999.

McKirahan, Richard D., Jr. *Philosophy before Socrates*. Indianapolis: Hackett, 1994.

Mourelatos, Alexander P. D., ed. *The Presocratics: A Collection of Critical Essays*. Garden City, N.Y.: Anchor Doubleday, 1974.

THALES, ANAXIMANDER, ANAXIMENES

Kahn, C. H. *Anaximander and the Origins of Greek Cosmology*. New York: Columbia University Press, 1960.

CHAPTER 3

Philosophy Moves to Italy

55

I. Italy

According to Samuel Johnson, the purpose of travel is to go to Italy.[1] In the mid-sixth century, two important thinkers, Pythagoras and Xenophanes, achieved this goal. Pythagoras left his native island of Samos, in the eastern Aegean, and Xenophanes left Colophon, not far from Samos, on the coast of Ionia (modern Turkey). Given the ties a man had to his *polis*, what could have induced anyone to leave his part of the world and go far away?

During the second half of the sixth century, Persia, ruled by the mad Cambyses and the imperialist Darius, was the dominant rising power in the Western world. Southern Italy, where Pythagoras and Xenophanes immigrated, had been colonized by Greeks, was full of open spaces, and promised a level of freedom not available to Greeks living under the immediate Persian shadow.

Our principal source for the history of Pythagoras's native Samos is Herodotus, who tells about a long and vicious struggle for power by a number of tyrants and would-be tyrants. Samos's population suffered mass reprisals for insurrections and betrayals as these few selfish power-hungry men struggled to dominate the island.[2] It is not surprising that a resourceful and ambitious lad like Pythagoras might flee such a place to save his life and to pursue his fortune in a more promising environment.

II. Pythagoras

It is ironic that the man possessing one of the few ancient names familiar to most people today is himself unknown in any meaningful way. According to tradition, Pythagoras moved to Croton in southern Italy, where he founded a secret brotherhood. He was a dynamic, inspirational leader, renowned, if also mocked, for his learning. Since the secrets of the brotherhood were very well kept, very little is known for sure about it. What is known is that the brotherhood believed in the transmigration of souls, a process whereby souls did not die but returned in the bodies of animals or human beings. It was perhaps for this reason that Pythagoreans kept special dietary laws, abstaining from kidney beans (which, perhaps reminding them of embryos, were believed to contain the souls of the dead) and meat (which might turn out to have housed the souls of one's ancestors or friends). They cultivated the art of memory, requiring members to perform exercises such as recalling the previous day's activities and conversations with the greatest possible exactitude. Whether Pythagoras himself or someone else is responsible for the discoveries attributed to him is, for the most part, impossible to determine. Pythagoras was given all the credit. His followers treated him as something of a deity, not pronouncing his name but referring to him as "he himself" or as "the man." Among the legends associated with the Pythagorean brotherhood is the story of a certain Hippasus, who was allegedly put to death for having divulged the secret that the square root of 2 is irrational (that is, not able to be expressed as a ratio of integers). Although the story is probably false, it shows the reputation the Pythagoreans enjoyed for their secrecy and for their wish that the world actually be without what might be regarded as mathematical ugliness.

Like the Milesian thinkers whom we have considered, the Pythagoreans were looking for an underlying principle beyond what could be seen with the senses. They thought they had found this principle in mathematical order, the basis of which was number, for number gave everything proportion, shape, and quantity. Numbers in ancient times were presented as points forming geometric figures, and these figures were of great importance to the Pythagoreans, who derived fascinating arithmetical facts from them and also attributed to them imaginative moral and physical qualities.

Even numbers made symmetrical figures. In Greek, the word for "even numbers" (*artioi*) means *joined* and has a positive connotation of order and clarity. The number *four*, being doubly symmetrical, was for the Pythagoreans a perfect number and was identified with justice and law. They depicted the first four even numbers as follows:

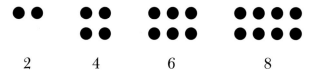

| 2 | 4 | 6 | 8 |

Odd numbers (*perittoi*, the word for *excessive*) were presented as points on a *gnomon* (from the likeness of the angle to that on a Babylonian sundial):

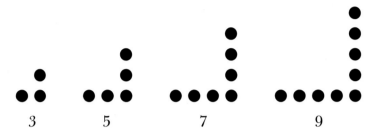

Triangular numbers were those that could be drawn in a triangular shape:

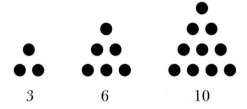

Of these, Pythagoreans were especially fond of 10, for ten is the sum of the first four numbers $(1 + 2 + 3 + 4 = 10)$ and yields a triangle with sides of four units. This number they called the *tetractys* (*fourness*), and it is reported that the *tetractys* was used in oaths.[3]

The Pythagoreans were so convinced that numbers and mathematical beauty ruled the universe that they constructed their model of the universe not on what they observed but on what they thought it should be. Since they wanted the number 10 to pervade the universe but the number of observed bodies added up to only 9 (earth, sun, moon, five planets, and the sphere of stars), the Pythagoreans added a mysterious invisible "counter earth" to round out an even ten.[4] Expressing a similar desire to conform physical material to their notions of number, the Pythagoreans, who originally were aware of only four of the five regular polyhedra—the tetrahedron, cube, octahedron, and icosahedron—and believed that these corresponded to the four elements fire, earth, air, and water,[5] when they learned of a fifth regular polyhedron—the dodecahedron—they added a mysterious fifth invisible element, *aether*, to the four.

One of the truly amazing discoveries made by the Pythagoreans was that musical harmony is based on mathematical proportions. Since all accomplishments were credited to Pythagoras, the story of the discovery gives him the leading role. One day, the story goes, he happened to hear the pleasing sounds produced by the clanging of a blacksmith's ham-mers.[6] The hammers turned out to have weights in 12, 9, 8, and 6 units, and from these numbers he derived the octave (12:6 = 2:1), the fifth (12:8 =9:6 =3:2), the fourth (12:9 =4:3), and the whole tone (9:8). He discovered as well that when the string of a lyre is halved in length while maintaining the same tension, the note played is increased by an octave. The significance of this discovery, which perhaps formed the basis of the whole Pythagorean confidence that the universe is based on number, is the uncovering of what had been hidden—this fact that hidden mathemat-ical ratios are the basis of perceptible harmony. Aristotle writes,

> Since of mathematical objects numbers are by nature first, and (a) [the Pythagoreans] seemed to observe in numbers, rather than in fire or earth or water, many likenesses to things, both existing and in generation (and so they regarded such and such an attribute of numbers as justice, such other as soul or intellect, another as opportunity, and similarly with al-most all of the others), and (b) they also observed numerical attributes and ratios in the objects of harmonics; since, then, all other things ap-peared in their nature to be likenesses of numbers, and numbers to be first in the whole of nature, they came to the belief that the elements of numbers are the elements of all things and that the whole heaven is a harmony and a number. And whatever facts in numbers and harmonies could be shown to be consistent with the attributes, the parts, and the whole system of arrangement of the heaven, these they collected and fit-ted into a system; and if there was a gap somewhere, they readily made additions in order to make their whole system connected.[7]

Thus music contributed to health;[8] thus the heavenly bodies moved harmoniously, creating the "music of the spheres."[9] Ethics, too, fell under the province of mathematics, for moral excellence was thought to be a kind of harmony, or a kind of squareness (as in our expression *fair and square*, in which *square* connotes moral goodness). Where Pythagorean ethical terms were strictly mathematical and where they were metaphori-cal is impossible to say, and the Pythagoreans themselves were probably uncertain on the matter. In early Greek thought numbers are not simply quantities but express qualities as well. We may note the same linguistic phenomenon in our own idiom, in which such terms as *obtuse, acute, odd,* and so forth have qualitative as well as mathematical meanings.

Unlike the Milesians, the Pythagoreans were deeply concerned with souls. Perhaps their belief in numbers contributed to a belief that the soul too is somehow connected to mathematics. When someone is thinking about number, the numbers or quantities are in a way distinct from what is being counted. The *five* in *five apples* is a notion distinct from the apples themselves. When one concentrates only on the numerical quantity, one leaves the particularity of, say, the specific apples and indeed leaves the particularity of his own life. In the intense focus on the pure quantity, as he is wholly focused in thought, he seems to be free of a body and has a sense of being purely soul. It is not difficult to see how some such process like this—a process that resembles Plato's description of the soul's glimpse of the World of Ideas[10]— might have inspired the Pythagoreans with the idea of a soul separate from the body that could commune with the eternal truths of mathematics.

Perhaps the Pythagoreans too early on became wedded to a faith that their mathematics could explain everything. As a result, too many ad hoc inventions had to be made to save the system. At any rate, the Pythagoreans faded from the scene at the end of the fourth century B.C.E., when mathematics was becoming less associated with the appendices of non-quantitative baggage.

III. Xenophanes

Xenophanes (570–478 B.C.E.) lived as an exile from about the age of twenty-five, when he left his native city of Colophon in Asia Minor. It is no wonder that he left home: he was an independent thinker and a cheerful critic of his culture's values. For example, he pointed out the rewards that come to someone who wins a victory in the Olympic Games—free board at public expense or a rich treasure—and protested that no athletic skill was as good as his wit. The victorious athlete does "not fatten the storehouses of the city."[11] Xenophanes could have addressed his lament as well today, for this particular habit has not changed: we reward our athletes—at least with earthly gold—far more than we do our scholars.

Xenophanes offered a biting criticism of the traditional conception of the gods. He wrote, "Homer and Hesiod attributed to the gods whatever is shameful and blameworthy in the eyes of men—stealing, adultery, and deceiving one another."[12] With considerable audacity, Xenophanes declared that the standard of the gods' character must not be tradition or even faith but moral purity. His statement goes beyond an attack on mere anthropomorphism (rendering the gods in human form). Xenophanes declared that for gods to behave in a way that we would frown on in human beings is incompatible with the essence of divinity and that therefore the poets are wrong in attributing such behavior to the gods. In other words, he asserted that we can make true claims about the divine based on standards discoverable by reason. The gods do not commit adultery, steal, or deceive because these actions are intrinsically wrong. He suggested, moreover, that the gods live according to a standard beyond their will. Adultery is not wrong because the gods declare it to be wrong; it is wrong, and the gods do not engage in it because it violates an objective standard. Thus the gods too are subject to law. They are, in a sense, less free than the king of Persia, whose will itself is the law. As Anaximenes had rendered the gods subject to the inexorable physical law that everything is air, so Xenophanes put universal moral law above any private divine prerogative.

In a series of three fragments, he exposed the fallacies in anthropomorphic thinking:

> But mortals consider that their gods are born and that they have clothes and speech and bodies like their own.
>
> Ethiopians say that their gods are snub-nosed and black; Thracians that theirs have light blue eyes and red hair.
>
> If cattle and horses and lions had hands, or were able to draw with their hands and do the works that men can do, horses would draw the forms of the gods like the horses, and cattle like cattle, and they would make their bodies such as they each had themselves.[13]

Here Xenophanes showed how human beings cannot help but think of their gods in terms of themselves. To make the point most satirically, he crossed the boundary that separates humans from other animals and said that nonhuman animals would make their gods look like themselves, just as we humans do.

In a great monotheistic insight, Xenophanes claimed that God must be wholly different both from the common conception of divinities and from men: "One god, greatest among gods as among men, not the equal of mortals in form or mind."[14] Xenophanes reasoned that it is as foolish to anthropomorphize a god in mental as in physical form. Whatever God is, he must be wholly different from mortals in all his characteristics and capabilities. Xenophanes described God's intellectual difference: "As a whole he sees, as a whole he perceives, as a whole he hears."[15] Whereas humans can see only parts, never wholes, God has utterly different capabilities. By using words evocative of our most intellectual sensory faculties—sight and hearing—Xenophanes stressed his deity's intelligence. In addition, "He remains forever in the same condition, changing not at all; it is not fitting for him to pursue now this and now that; with no effort, by the thought of his mind, he agitates all things."[16] Here Xenophanes' god seems quite unlike any god of Greek mythology. Xenophanes' God does not move, perhaps because movement implies a lack of completeness or perhaps a better and worse location; for Xenophanes, God must always be the same, always perfect. If he did pursue now this and now that, he would perhaps be less than perfect (for one pursues only what one lacks or desires; and if one lacks or desires anything, one is imperfect). The activity of Xenophanes' God is mental; he even moves things with his mind. The notion is perhaps not unlike that we find in Genesis, where God, saying "let there be light," creates by simple *fiat*. We should note that Xenophanes said that God agitates *all* things. The philosopher was not speaking of a local deity who serves only a part of the earth. He was speaking of one God for the entire cosmos.

Xenophanes extended his mockery of anthropo*morphism*—making a god like a human being—to anthropo*centrism*—the idea that human life is the focus of all the world: "If god had not caused yellow honey to be produced, people would pronounce figs so much sweeter."[17] We humans judge sweetness by what we ourselves experience, making the sweetest food with which we are familiar into the ideal, the standard of sweetness. If it happened that a less sweet food were the sweetest that we had, then that lower degree of sweetness would be the ideal. In short, we set up anthropocentric ideals, ideals relative to our experience and not to truth. This concept rejects the ubiquitous human practice of basing judgments on human experience. In ridiculing and rejecting anthropocentric standards, Xenophanes did not, however, go so far as to postulate an absolute grounded in a transcendent being.

Xenophanes' view of the arts departs from the tone of dismissal of certain human tendencies. In general, the ancients believed that gods revealed the arts to humans. Demeter gave the cultivation of grains; Dionysus gave wine making; Athena gave weaving. Mythological stories describe how the gods taught these arts. One implication of this view is that the various arts were given to mankind already whole, developed, and perfected. A consequence of this belief was a disinclination to try to improve the arts by inventiveness. After all, if a god has given an art, it must be perfect, and to attempt progress or development would be foolish, even impious. Xenophanes rejected this view of the gods: "Not all things in the beginning did the gods reveal to mortal men, but men by searching in time find out what is better."[18] Here, in the idea of "searching in time" lies the implication of our modern idea of progress. The arts of civilization did not come as the complete, wholly formed gift of the gods but have been worked out by human beings. If in his other writing Xenophanes had diminished humanity by taking away the commonness with the gods and the control of standards, here he gave humanity the power to progress and to develop the arts. Of course, attached to this power is an implied imperfection, for progress always aims at improvement, and the capacity for improvement implies a lack of perfection.

Xenophanes had little sympathy for the Pythagorean theories of the reincarnation and transmigration of souls. He mocked, "They say that once Pythagoras passed a puppy that was being maltreated. He took pity and spoke thus: 'Stop beating it, for it is the soul of a dear friend; I recognized the soul by its voice.'"[19] As was his method, Xenophanes exposed what he regarded as the silliness of a view by painting an extreme version of it. In this case, he seemed also to be mocking his friend, who has returned as a dog.

Xenophanes expressed unequivocally the limitations of human access to knowledge of the divine:

> No man has seen nor will anyone ever know the truth about the gods and all the things I speak of . . . but [mere] belief is fashioned over all things. All of him [God] sees, all of him thinks, all of him hears.[20]

Here we find the great difference between humans and God. Humans cannot see through to the truth of things. Trapped in humanity, trapped in

63

relativism—the notion that ideas are not always true but are conditioned by the times and places where people live—humans can judge only on the basis of themselves. How different is Xenophanes from the Greek poets, where the gods are merely more powerful and deathless humans! The gulf between human beings, who see and understand nothing clearly, and God, who has direct knowledge of everything, is very wide in Xenophanes.

Despite the brilliance of his insights, Xenophanes, unlike Pythagoras, seems to have had no followers and his deity no worshippers. Xenophanes did find support for his views a century later, in Plato, whose dialogue *Symposium* might be considered a complement to Xenophanes' attack on anthropomorphizing the gods. In the *Symposium*, Socrates and a diverse collection of his friends engage in an informal rhetorical contest in which each gives a speech describing and praising *Eros*, the god of sexual desire. What is most conspicuous in the dialogue is the way each draws a picture of the god that resembles the speaker. For example, a physician named Eryximachus describes *Eros* as a physician; a tragedian, Agathon, describes *Eros* as a dainty tragic poet like himself; and Socrates describes *Eros*—sexual desire—as a barefooted philosopher just like Socrates. It is probable that Plato was trying to expose the silliness of making a deity in the image of humans and particularly in the image of whoever is speaking (each making himself the god of sexual desire).

Though Xenophanes was not a systematic thinker and did not put forward an innovative theory of nature, he was nevertheless a revolutionary individual. In rejecting his own culture with its corrupt attitudes—the excessive veneration of athletes instead of the deserving wise, the relativism of cultural judgment, and the belief that the gods are laws unto themselves—and in substituting the idea that standards are objective and impose their own necessity, he was advocating a rational and philosophical approach to life. This commitment to objective rationality was to be highly influential in the development of philosophy.

Discussion Questions

1. The Pythagoreans made some genuine discoveries about music and mathematics, discoveries that gave them confidence that they had found the key to unlocking all the mysteries of nature. Can you think of other exam-

ples where excellence in one area deluded someone into thinking that he possessed excellence in other areas as well? Is overconfidence a danger that grows naturally out of success? What, if anything, can be done to guard against the dangers of success?

2. It seems a tendency of human beings to describe things that we do not know in terms of things that we do know. For example, when we hear a word in a muffled way, our minds usually clarify the word by refining it into a word we know. What happens on the small scale of words seems also to happen on a large scale in entire systems of thought. For example, someone might have a particular insight that explains something, say, that animals respond to pleasant stimuli and learn in this way; this insight then becomes the principle of an entire system, and everything that has to do with animals is somehow fitted, or made to fit, with this original insight. Or, say, someone has the insight that human beings are motivated by economic circumstances, and then this insight is developed into a system that explains everything as motivated by economic causes. Does this process seem to be inevitable, or can it somehow be avoided? Is there a generalizing tendency in human nature that tries to explain everything by a single principle or set of principles? Do we humans somehow feel more content the fewer the explanatory principles we need?

3. How would a cultural critic like Xenophanes have been tolerated by his contemporaries? How far are people able to tolerate views that stab at the heart of what they believe at the deepest levels? Do you think the manner in which the criticisms were made would have an effect on the level of toleration? How would you judge the manner of Xenophanes' criticisms?

4. Is it possible to find a religion that does not engage in some form of anthropomorphism? If there were such a religion, would it be very appealing? Why or why not?

Notes

1. Well, he *almost* put it this way. What he actually said (as reported by Boswell) was, "A man who has not been in Italy, is always conscious of an inferiority, from his not having seen what it is expected a man should see. The grand object of travelling is to see the shores of the Mediterranean" (*Boswell's Life of Johnson*, ed. George Birkbeck Hill [New York: Harper & Brothers, n.d.], 41–42).

2. Herodotus 3.139–149.

3. According to Iamblichus, *The Life of Pythagoras* (in the *Pythagorean Sourcebook and Library*, ed. Kenneth S. Guthrie [Grand Rapids, Mich.: Phanes Press, 1987], 95), this was the form of the oath:

I swear by the discoverer of the Tetraktys,
Which is the spring of all our wisdom,
The perennial root of Nature's fount.

4. Aristotle, *Metaphysics* 986a 10–12.

5. These, together with the fifth (the dodecahedron), are sometimes called "Platonic solids" because Plato, in his dialogue *Timaeus*, uses them to describe what the world is made of.

6. Iamblichus, *The Life of Pythagoras*, 86.

7. Aristotle, *Metaphysics* 985 b27–986 a8.

8. 58 D1, 164 (in H. Frankel, *Early Greek Poetry and Philosophy*, trans. M. Hadas and J. Willis [Oxford: Blackwell, 1975], 277).

9. Aristotle, *On the Heavens* 290 b12.

10. This notion will be taken up later in chapter 10, pp. 175–77.

11. Xenophanes, frag. 3.

12. Xenophanes, frag. 11.

13. Xenophanes, frags. 14, 16, and 15, trans. G. S. Kirk and J. E. Raven in *The Presocratic Philosophers* (Cambridge: Cambridge University Press, 1966).

14. Xenophanes, frag. 23.

15. Xenophanes, frag. 26.

16. Xenophanes, frag. 25.

17. Xenophanes, frag. 38.

18. Xenophanes, frag. 18.

19. Xenophanes, frag. 7.

20. Xenophanes, frags. 34 and 24, trans. Sarah Broadie in *The Cambridge Companion to Early Greek Philosophy*, ed. A. A. Long (Cambridge: Cambridge University Press, 1999).

Select Bibliography

For a general bibliography on the Presocratics, see the bibliography in chapter 2.

PYTHAGORAS

Kahn, C. H. "Pythagorean Philosophy before Plato." In *The Pre-Socratics: A Collection of Critical Essays*, edited by Alexander P. D. Mourelatos. Garden City, N.Y.: Anchor Doubleday, 1974.
——. *Pythagoras and the Pythagoreans: A Brief History*. Indianapolis: Hackett, 2001.

XENOPHANES

Lesher, J. H. *Xenophanes of Colophon: A Text and Translation with a Commentary*. Toronto: University of Toronto Press, 1992.

CHAPTER 4

The Turn of the Fifth Century: Heraclitus and Parmenides

67

I. The Turn of the Century

The Greek world could not know in 530 B.C.E. that it was about to begin two centuries of tumultuous change. The change would penetrate life intellectually, politically, materially, militarily, and artistically, and the West would be forever altered. What conditions so rich in potentiality existed at the turn of the fifth century?

The Persian autocracy loomed menacingly invincible. Cyrus had spread his empire from the edge of the Hellenic world on the Asian shore of the Aegean eastward all the way to the borders of India and from the Black Sea all the way south to the Indian Ocean. Cambyses, Cyrus's son and successor, had added the ancient and wealthy land of Egypt to the Persian Empire, and Darius, Cambyses' successor, having failed to conquer the cold and damp part of Europe then known as Scythia (the area vaguely bounded by the Danube and Don Rivers), was gazing greedily at

sunnier Greece. West of Greece lay Italy, where Rome was still an insignificant mote of a village but where in the south and in Sicily the Greek colonies were growing in power. In the eastern Aegean, the tyrant Polycrates ruled a thriving Samos, its naval fleet dominant, its ports prosperous, and its people, though crushed under the yoke of their oppressor, drinking fresh water delivered by a monumental public work, a tunnel three-quarters of a mile long through a mountain. On the Greek mainland, Sparta was the preeminent military power, and in the western Aegean, Aegina and Athens competed for maritime supremacy.

It was at this moment that two extraordinary thinkers came to prominence, Heraclitus in Ephesus, a city about twenty miles north of Miletus on the eastern shore of the Aegean, and Parmenides in Elea, a city on the front ankle of Italy. Their competing conceptions mirror their births at opposite ends of the Greek world.

II. Heraclitus

Heraclitus (fl. 500 B.C.E.), born to a noble family, had the right to an aristocratic title by the laws of heredity. With a contempt for status very rarely flattered with imitation, he gave up his title to his brother. According to traditional accounts, Heraclitus dedicated his treatise, which survives in fragments of no more than a few lines each, to the Temple of Artemis, evidence perhaps that the treatise was intended neither for posterity nor even for a human audience. It is just as well since Heraclitus believed that humans are incapable of understanding his rational explanations. He says about people,

> Of the *Logos* [Greek for *rational account*], which is as I describe it, men always prove to be uncomprehending, both before they have heard it and when once they have heard it. For although all things happen according to this *Logos*, men are like people of no experience, even when they experience such words and deeds as I explain, when I distinguish each thing according to its constitution and declare how it is; but the rest of men fail to notice what they do after they wake up just as they forget what they did when asleep.[1]

Famously wise predecessors were not spared this lack of confidence in his fellow humans: "Learning many things does not teach intelligence; if so it would have taught Hesiod and Pythagoras, and again Xenophanes and Hecataeus."[2] The claim that most people are incapable or unwilling to understand the truths of philosophy is common in the history of thought. From Heraclitus through Plato, through the Stoics, through the theologians of the Middle Ages and on, philosophers have distinguished the "few" who can understand from the "many" who cannot. Perhaps this distinction of the few and the many in other philosophers is a "coping mechanism" to help philosophers accept the fact that their work is not attractive to many people. In Heraclitus's case, the unattractiveness seems entirely justified by an opaqueness that won him the nickname of the "dark" or the "obscure." But where obscurity in some thinkers may be a cultivated affectation, in Heraclitus the obscurity is intimately connected with his thought, for his fundamental conceptions are that nature hides the truth and that underlying all reality is a clash of opposites. As he said, "Nature loves to hide herself."[3]

According to Heraclitus, the world consists of an oscillation between opposites that are in continuous flux. He wrote, "Living and dead are the same, and awake and asleep, and young and old, for the ones, turned over, become the others, and the others again, turning over, become the one."[4] And also, "The cold is heated, the hot cooled, the wet dried, and the arid drenched."[5] For Heraclitus nothing exists except the constant transformation of one thing into another. He declared, "You enter the same river, but other waters flow unto you."[6] Heraclitus elaborated his doctrine of opposites with the metaphor of a harmony, according to which different tensions on a string will produce a beautiful sound. Consider this pair of fragments:

> Things taken together are whole and not whole, something which is being brought together and brought apart, which is in tune and out of tune; out of all things there comes a unity, and out of a unity all things.
>
> They do not apprehend how being at variance it agrees with itself [literally, how being brought apart it is brought together with itself]: there is a back-stretched connexion as in the bow and the lyre.[7]

The principle of harmony, that things opposed to each other work together in a creative way, is one of Heraclitus's central metaphors for the world. Just as in music high notes and low notes, flats and sharps, long notes and short notes all collaborate to form a concordant whole, so too the various opposite forces and conditions of the world harmonize in forming a whole. This truth is apparent in our lives, where hunger and thirst, pain and pleasure, sleep and waking—all opposites—are necessary components of life and health. For Heraclitus there is not an underlying substance of which things are a form, no shapeless matter or *apeiron*, as Anaximander suggested. The world is made of opposites that continuously change into one another.

Heraclitus did not actually use the word *opposites*. His metaphor for this operation of the universe is *war*. Whereas for other people war is the god Ares (*Mars* in Latin), destroyer of all that is beautiful and dear, sacker of cities and ravager of fields, for Heraclitus war is what generates the creative pairing of opposites: "War is all-father and all-king, and he appoints some to be gods and others to be men; he made some to be slaves and others to be free."[8] As Werner Jaeger put it, "War thus becomes, in a way, Heraclitus's primary philosophical experience."[9] The underlying reality is a war, everlasting and all-pervasive, between the opposites of the universe. God, for Heraclitus, is what keeps the eternal war raging, God, who is himself a unity of opposites: "God is day-night, winter-summer, war-peace, fullness-hunger. . . . He changes his appearances, just as oil, when blended with perfumes, is named after the smell of each perfume." For Heraclitus the tension created by the oppositions *is* the world.[10] While men see some things as just, others as unjust, for God all is just: God sees the big picture and sees that the opposites are necessary for each other. It is, after all, sickness that makes health good, hunger that makes satiation good.[11]

Fire is associated with Heraclitus, and some think that he makes it the basic material principle of the world. But in Heraclitus "fire" is a metaphor for the principle of opposition of all things. Fire is destructive, of course, for it burns everything up. On the other hand, warmth, which comes from fire, is found in living and growing beings.[12] Fire seems a perfect metaphor for change since it constantly changes its shape. Indeed, in a brilliant metaphor that shows a modern economist's understanding of the nature of money as a medium of exchange—that is, a currency into which everything can be converted for the purpose of trade—he writes, "Everything is exchange for fire, and fire for everything, as gold is for merchandise and merchandise for gold."[13] Fire is responsible for souls, for souls vaporize from what is moist,[14] and the wisest and best souls are dry.[15] Moreover, souls participate in the process of cosmic change. Writing about souls, perhaps constituted of fire, Heraclitus says that "it is death to become water; for water it is death to become earth; from earth water comes into being; and from water, soul comes into being."[16] Soul thus seems to be greater than physical things, for "one could not discover the limits of the soul, even if one traveled by every path in order to do so; such is the depth of its meaning."[17] But physical things, even the sun, are limited: "the sun is the breadth of a man's foot."[18] Here Heraclitus's metaphor suggests that the size, and even the location, of physical objects, even of the sun, is finite relative to us. He wittily has us imagine a person lying on his back and blocking the sun with his foot. At one stroke, he has changed the location of the sun from above our heads to behind our feet and has shown how small it is. (And to block the sun with a foot instead of, say, a hand is perhaps a way of mocking it.) The soul, as he has said, has no boundaries, but the "Sun will not overstep *his* measure. If he did, the Furies, the ministers of Justice, would find him out."[19]

Soul for Heraclitus is capable of understanding the universe and, what is more, of living in accordance with the understanding.[20] The world is not relative, and the truths that Heraclitus has discovered are available to all who are awake—Heraclitus's metaphor for being intelligent.[21] This idea that human souls are capable of understanding the universe and of living in accordance with it and the associated idea that human souls and the universe contain the same cosmic fire are conceptions that will infiltrate the philosophy of the West. If all human souls are constituted of the same fire, then perhaps all humans are related as children of the same universe, citizens of the same city, brothers and sisters in the same family.

III. Parmenides (fl. 501–490)[22] and His Successors

A. PARMENIDES

As we have seen, the early thinkers discovered the problem of change, that is, how a thing could give up its nature and take on a new one. Their solutions suggested that matter was either one thing capable of undergoing transformations (so Thales, Anaximenes, and Heraclitus) or, at its most basic level, something undefined and therefore able to take on any form. Transformation, as Aristotle says,[23] is one of the types of motion, and if, as Heraclitus suggested, things are always being transformed into something else, they are always in motion. Heraclitus's most quoted statement expresses the impossibility of stepping into the same river twice,[24] a beautiful metaphor for the concept of the world's constant change. Because a river is always flowing, its waters always moving downstream, a moment after one has stepped into it, it is in a sense a different river.

Heraclitus would say that what is true of the river is true of everything physical. A tree, for example, is never in an absolutely fixed state, for its chemistry is dynamic: its sap flows up and down, its leaves emerge and then fall off or get nibbled by bugs or rustled in the wind. In short, the tree and its parts are never in a stable condition. How, then, can we say that we know the tree? Even if we knew all the properties and conditions of the tree at one moment, once that moment has passed, do we know the tree the following moment? Like trees, everything physical—animate or inanimate— is subject to aging, radioactive decay, bombardment by various kinds of waves, constant repositioning of its atoms and electrons, and so forth. In a word, everything is in a constant state of flux.

Yet if we speak of not stepping into *the river* twice, the river must have *some* recognizable identity, just as a tree does, despite a condition of constant change. When one looks out a window and sees the tree on which five years earlier he carved his initials, he *does* recognize the same tree. The initials are still there! Clearly there has been *something* that has remained the same since five years before, and so, like the river, the tree has an identity. It can be classified a *thing*, that is, something whose identity has remained the same, at least in some way, for a measurable amount of time. It is obvious that though there might be truth in Heraclitus's claims, those claims are not true without qualification.

At the other end of the spectrum of thought lies Parmenides, one of the most strikingly brilliant and provocative philosophers who ever lived.[25] Like Heraclitus, Parmenides is said to have come from a noble family and to have been wealthy. Unfortunately, like so much of ancient biography, details of his life may be more in accord with what the biographer thought *ought* to have been true than with any actual facts. In general, there may have been an assumption that anyone who could devote his life to philosophy had to be rich, for in Greek the word *study* is the word for *leisure* (from *schole*, from which derives our word *school*). Parmenides came from Elea, in southwest Italy, the same city where Xenophanes of Colophon ended up after a life of travels. Perhaps because he was from the same city, he is said to have been Xenophanes' student, but, again, such claims are dubious and are perhaps based more on a desire for such linkage than any actual linkage.

According to Parmenides, there is no change of any kind whatsoever; all apparent change is illusory. Parmenides' famous dictum captures this insight: "Whatever is, is; whatever is not, is not."[26] This simple expression of his philosophy belies its complexity.

73

What Parmenides means is that there is something called *being* and that whatever has being, is. All being is the same insofar as it is being. For example, a flea and a house can both be said to be, and with respect to their being they are identical. The same would be true for subatomic quarks, solar systems, galaxies, and everything else. All being, as being, is the same.

Parmenides' meaning becomes much harder to grasp when we consider the negative. When we say, for example, "I have no money," what is denoted by the concept "money" has no being; we cannot in a strict sense talk about or conceive nonexistent money or anything else that does not exist. Other sorts of negatives indicate similar cases of nonbeing. If we say, "The house is not green," "not-green" has no being, and hence no meaning, for the mind cannot grasp a concept of "not-green" any more than it can grasp a concept of the nonbeing of anything. If we imagine the house as blue, we are imagining blue rather than "not-green." "Not-green" in itself cannot be imagined. Even implicit negatives, Parmenides would argue, are impossible. For example, to say that something has begun is to say, implicitly, that at one time it was not and hence is to speak unintelligibly. According to Parmenides, minds can conceive only of things that have being.

Parmenides also denies the possibility of plurality. For to say that we have a plurality of items is to say that one thing is not or is not like another thing. But "is not" and "is not like" are negatives and hence unintelligible concepts. In the same way, the only permissible qualities are "all" and "full." For to be "thin" would imply "not fat," a negative, a form of nonbeing, which cannot exist. So there is only Being, which is expressed in the one-word sentence "Is." Among numbers there is only "one"; in time, there is only the eternal, which must be an unchanging single moment, and in space, only the full or universal. For Parmenides, Being is indivisible and homogeneous, like a perfect sphere.[27] This came to be known as the "Parmenidean One" or simply as the "One."

Parmenides' most famous application of this principle is to motion. To move means to go from a place where we are to a place where we are not. But "are not" cannot be; hence motion is impossible. In the end, we are left with a powerful logical argument that says that one thing cannot differ from another, that there can be no motion, and indeed that there can be no change of any kind whatsoever (for any change is a movement from what is to what-is-not). Although the argument seems manifestly absurd, for we can disprove it by moving—or seeming to move?—it is not so easy to point to any logical flaw. Parmenides leaves us with a universe that is an undifferentiated, unchanging, eternal sphere. This strange idea seems to be the conclusion of his book *Way of Truth*.

Here is how Parmenides himself summarizes his thought:

> Come now, and I will tell thee—and do thou hearken and carry my word away—the only ways of enquiry that can be thought of: the one way, that it *is* and cannot not-be, is the path of Persuasion, for it attends upon Truth; the other, that it *is-not* and needs must not-be, that I tell thee is a path altogether unthinkable. For thou couldst not know that which is-not (that is impossible) nor utter it; for the same thing can be thought as can be.[28]

The consequence of Parmenides' conclusions, of course, is that the world we live in, the world we think is real, cannot be real. One of Parmenides' disciples was Zeno, who conceived of the famous paradoxes showing that motion is impossible.[29]

Before Parmenides, thinkers employed deeply rich and evocative metaphors to express their ideas. A good deal of their thought, if interpreted literally, devolved into nonsense. The present attempt to describe their work in the most favorable light has sometimes squeezed sense out of the fragmentary thought by connecting the surviving quotations into a coherent picture. Even so, at many places the result has been disturbingly fuzzy. As mentioned, the ancients themselves called Heraclitus "The Obscure," not a term that philosophers in the West have considered a badge of honor. What Parmenides introduced is logic (from the Greek *logike*, pertaining to the rules for a rational account, *logos*)—adamantine, steely, uncompromising logic. The surviving fragments are the longest connected passages of any of the early thinkers and allow us to see the power of his thought. In the claim that "what is is and cannot not be," he rejects any accommodation to logical contradiction. This is a milestone in the history of philosophy, and forever afterward self-contradiction in argument will be taken as an infallible proof of error. Whatever is not known by uncontradictable reason, says Parmenides, is "opinion."[30] And when measured against the necessity of noncontradiction, the Milesians and all others who trust their senses are simply wrong. In celebrating the supremacy of reason, Parmenides discovered the road to truth.

One might wonder what was going through Parmenides' mind as he constructed his argument for the impossibility of motion, plurality, and qualities. Perhaps Parmenides thought himself as living in a dream, where what appeared to his senses was illusory. Or perhaps he had an uncanny ability to suspend disbelief in what would have appeared to him, as to us, to be actual distinctions among different things, actual motion, and the actual possibility of negative claims. In writing the *Way of Truth* he surely noticed that he was moving his pen, was writing different words, and was making negative claims, such as the claim that one *cannot* conceive of a negative claim. Yet the logic of his claims must have seemed insurmountable both to himself and to those who heard them. Perhaps one can, in the end, only stand in awe at such devotion to logical consistency.

B. ZENO AND MELISSUS

Parmenides' successors Zeno (fl. 464) and Melissus (fl. 440) carried on the work of their master and refined it in some important ways.[31] If the stories of their political lives are true, their nobility would have given their master a great deal of joy.[32] Zeno is said to have heroically defied a cruel tyrant by refusing to give up the names of his fellow conspirators, by instead claiming the tyrant's own friends as the conspirators. Finally, when pretending to have a secret to tell the tyrant, he grabbed the tyrant's ear with his teeth until the tyrant's guards stabbed him to death.[33] Melissus is said to have commanded a fleet that defeated Athens in a naval battle in 442, making possible Samos's freedom from the Athenian Empire.[34]

As a philosopher, Zeno is most well known for his famous paradoxes showing that motion is impossible. These were preserved by Aristotle, who was convinced that he alone had explained them.[35] Two examples are perhaps sufficient for indicating what Zeno had in mind. One paradox maintains that although a flying arrow appears to be in motion, it must really be at rest, for it is stationary at every (infinitesimally short) moment of its flight and is therefore stationary throughout its whole flight. The argument depends on the infinite divisibility of time, in which each moment is so infinitesimally brief as to be instantaneous and hence without movement. A second paradox states that it will be impossible to move from point A to point B, for before one arrives at B one must go to a point M that is halfway between A and B and before M to a point M_1 that is

Figure 9.   Zeno's Paradox: The Arrow
At every moment of its flight through the air, this arrow occupies a space that is equal to itself and no other place. When the arrow (or anything else) occupies a space equal to itself and no other place, it is not moving. If the arrow is not moving, it is at rest.

halfway between A and M and so on in smaller and smaller steps—so that one never actually moves from A to B even in an infinity of time.[36]

Aristotle thought that he discovered the solution to the paradoxes. He says that the distance from A to B and the time it takes to go from A to B are infinite in one respect and finite in another respect. On the one hand, the time and the distance are both finite if they are measured by units, say, fifty yards and twenty seconds. On the other hand, any continuum, whether of time or distance, is infinitely divisible. And to be infinitely divisible is different from being infinite in extent. A space that is finite in extent may be traversed in a finite amount of time even though it is infinitely divisible. Aristotle claims that Zeno goes wrong in saying that the distance is infinitely divisible into points while failing to add that moments are infinitely divisible in the same way.[37] One may question whether Aristotle did in fact solve the paradox, for motion may take place in time as well in space, and if time

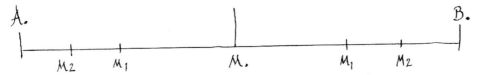

Figure 10.   Zeno's Paradox: The Impossibility of Motion
The paradox takes two forms, and it is not clear which Zeno intended: (1) To go from A to B, it is necessary first to arrive at the midpoint M. But to arrive at M, it is necessary first to arrive at M_1, and before arriving at M_1, it is necessary first to arrive at M_2, and so on to infinity. Since it is impossible to traverse an infinite number of parts in a finite time, it will be impossible to reach B. (2) To go from A to B, it is necessary first to arrive at the midpoint M. It is then necessary to arrive at M_1, which is the midpoint of MB. Then it is necessary to arrive at M_2, the midpoint of M_1B, and so on to infinity. Again, since is it impossible to traverse an infinite number of parts in a finite time, it will be impossible to reach B. (After H. G. Apostle, *Aristotle's Physics* [Bloomington, Ind., and London: Indiana University Press, 1969], 296).

is infinitely divisible, why would we not be stuck in a limitless extended moment? Zeno's paradoxes continue to perplex even into our times.[38]

Melissus's departure from Parmenidean orthodoxy was in the substitution of an *infinite* all-encompassing One for a *finite* all-encompassing One. For Parmenides the One had to be finite in order to be complete. But Melissus could not conceive of boundaries beyond which there would be void.[39] Perhaps he felt that the void, nonbeing, could not, on good Parmenidean grounds, exist, and so the universe had to be infinite.

The work of Parmenides was startlingly brilliant and rightly stirred up a tremendous reaction in the intellectual debate that characterizes the West. In the next two centuries Empedocles, Anaxagoras, Democritus, Plato, and Aristotle would all try to solve the riddles of the thinker from Elea. That finding the errors of Parmenides and his disciples would tax the genius of such eminent thinkers is a testimony to the brutal power of his new logic.

Discussion Questions

1. Is there anything in the geopolitical situation at the end of the sixth century that might have inspired the thought of Heraclitus and Parmenides, who saw change and sameness as the core principles of nature?

2. Heraclitus is known for his idea that everything flows (*panta rei*). If it is true that everything flows, how is it possible to know anything for longer than an instant? Are there any ways in which Heraclitus is right that everything changes? Are there any ways in which he is mistaken?

3. In what ways are Heraclitus's metaphors of fire and war appropriate for his thought? Are there ways in which the metaphors might also be misleading?

4. Parmenides' reasoning led to a conclusion that was absolutely inconsistent with experience. But how can seemingly sound reasoning be wrong? If you can find no defect in either the premises or the logical steps of an argument, are you bound to accept the conclusions? Does a firmly held and apparently reasonable belief trump a seemingly logical counterargument? If you can, compare the conclusions of Parmenides with some of the conclusions of quantum physics, which also seem to fly in the face of experience.

5. Why do you suppose that Zeno's paradoxes are so compelling? How do they present the conundrum of reconciling logic and experience?

6. Does the often-heard platitude "The more things change, the more they remain the same" fit the thought of Heraclitus or Parmenides, or both?

Notes

1. Heraclitus, frag. 1, trans. G. S. Kirk and J. E. Raven, *The Presocratic Philosophers* (Cambridge: Cambridge University Press, 1966). Subsequent quotations of Heraclitus are from this translation. For similar statements, see also frags. 17, 34, 56, 57, and 107.

2. Heraclitus, frag. 40.

3. Heraclitus, frag. 123.

4. Heraclitus, frag. B 88.

5. Heraclitus, frag. B126.

6. Heraclitus, frag. B12.

7. Heraclitus, frags. 10 and 51. Frag. 50 says, "Listening not to me but to the Logos, it is wise to agree that all things are one." The "one thing" is probably this principle of harmony or the principle of harmony "as an actual constituent of things, and in many respects . . . co-extensive with the primary cosmic constituent, fire" (G. S. Kirk and J. E. Raven, *The Presocratic Philosophers* [Cambridge: Cambridge University Press, 1966], 188).

8. Heraclitus, frag. 53.

9. Werner Jaeger, *The Theology of the Early Greek Philosophers* (New York: Oxford University Press, 1967), 118.

10. Heraclitus, frag. 67.

11. Heraclitus, frag. 111.

12. Heraclitus, frag. 30.

13. Heraclitus, frag. 90.

14. Heraclitus, frag. 12.

15. Heraclitus, frag. 118.

16. Heraclitus, frag. 36.

17. Heraclitus, frag. 45.

18. Heraclitus, frag. 3.

19. Heraclitus, frag. 94.

20. Heraclitus, frag. 2.

21. Heraclitus, frags. 113 and 89.

22. There is debate about Parmenides' dates. Diogenes Laertius (9.23) says that Parmenides flourished in the sixty-ninth Olympiad ($776 - 276 = 500$, where 776 is the year the Olympics began and 276 is sixty-nine times four, the number of years in each Olympiad). The confusion comes because in the *Theaetetus* (183e) and *Sophist* (217c) Plato writes that a young Socrates conversed with an old Parmenides. But given that Plato is notoriously imaginative when it comes to chronology (for example, in the *Menexenus* [245e] the character Socrates alludes to the Peace of Antalcidas, concluded ten years after the historic Socrates' death), I take it that Plato is inventing in the *Parmenides* a dramatic situation where Socrates can talk to the great thinker.

23. *Physics* 201a10–15.

24. Heraclitus, frag. 91.

25. Alfred North Whitehead, who said that all of Western philosophy consists of footnotes to Plato, would perhaps have been more accurate to have made the claim about Parmenides.

26. Parmenides, frag. 2.

27. Parmenides, frag. 8.

28. Parmenides, frag. 2, in Kirk and Raven, *The Presocratic Philosophers*.

29. See the next section on Parmenides' successors Zeno and Melissus.

30. Frags. 8, 51.

31. Zeno was from Elea, like Parmenides, and is said to have been his pupil. Certainly in this case Zeno carried on the work of his purported teacher. Melissus was from Samos and probably was born too late to have learned from Parmenides, but his work is Parmenidean, though his conclusions differ in some respects from those of Parmenides.

32. This would have been in stark contrast to Socrates' "pupil" Alcibiades, whose political life must have caused Socrates great pain.

33. Diogenes Laertius 9.26.

34. Diogenes Laertius 9.24.

35. The first is discussed and refuted in the *Physics* 233a2131, the others in 239 b4–240 a15.

36. This paradox is reminiscent of a joke about a beautiful woman, an engineer, and a mathematician. The beautiful woman says, "I am yours. Just walk over to me. But each step you take in my direction must be half the one before." The mathematician understands that under these conditions he will never reach her and gives up. The engineer, however, walks over to her and embraces her. The joke was undoubtedly invented by an engineer. It embodies the old conflict between pure and practical science or, in medieval terms, between superlunary metaphysics and sublunary reality.

37. Aristotle does not seem altogether pleased with his solution to the problem, which he gives in *Physics* 233 a21. He discusses its inadequacy at 263 a11. For a full discussion of the paradoxes, see J. A. Faris, *The Paradoxes of Zeno* (Brookfield, Vt.: Ashgate Publishing, 1996).

38. See, for example, V. C. Chappell, "Time and Zeno's Arrow," *Journal of Philosophy* 59 (1962): 197–213, and Hermann Fränkel, "Zeno of Elea's Attacks on Plurality," *American Journal of Philology* 63 (1942): 1–25, 193–206.

39. Melissus, frag. 5.

Select Bibliography

For a general bibliography on the Presocratics, see the bibliography in chapter 2.

HERACLITUS

Guthrie, W. K. C. "Flux and Logos in Heraclitus." In *The Pre-Socratics: Critical Essays*, edited by Alexander P. D. Mourelatos. Garden City, N.Y.: Anchor Press, 1974.

Kahn, C. H. *The Art and Thought of Heraclitus: An Edition of the Fragments with Translation and Commentary*. Cambridge: Cambridge University Press, 1979.

Kirk, G. S. "Natural Change in Heraclitus." In *The Pre-Socratics: Critical Essays*, edited by Alexander P. D. Mourelatos. Garden City, N.Y.: Anchor Press, 1974.

PARMENIDES

Curd, Patricia. *The Legacy of Parmenides: Eleatic Monism and Later Presocratic Thought*. Princeton, N.J.: Princeton University Press, 1998.

Gallop, D. *Parmenides of Elea: Fragments. A Text and Translation with an Introduction*. *Phoenix* Supplementary Volume 18 (1984).

Kingsley, P. *In the Dark Places of Wisdom*. Inverness, Calif.: Golden Sufi Center, 1999.

Mourelatos, Alexander P. D. *The Route of Parmenides: A Study in Word, Image, and Argument in the Fragments*. New Haven, Conn.: Yale University Press, 1970.

ZENO

Faris, J. A. *The Paradoxes of Zeno*. Brookfield, Vt.: Ashgate Publishing, 1996.

Salmoln, Wesley C. *Zeno's Paradoxes*. Indianapolis: Bobbs-Merrill, 1970.

The Persian Wars and Their Aftermath: Sophistry and Rhetoric

I. The Persian Wars

For most Greeks the war against Persia was a good war. It preserved their independence and showed just how magnificent were the virtues that had achieved the victory. The men who fought against Persia were hailed for the rest of their lives as "Marathon fighters," and even their children shined in the glory their fathers bequeathed them. The cities that had sided with the Persians or had remained neutral lived ignominiously with that choice. The war resulted in the political dominance of Athens in the Hellenic world, and, in consequence of the manifold genius of the Athenians, their political dominance brought cultural hegemony as well.

From the momentous time of Cyrus the Great, who had brought Persia to empire, Persia's growth, despite a few setbacks, was dynamic and steady. Darius, though he had failed to conquer the nomadic Scythians, nevertheless added Macedonia and Thrace to Persia's dominions. When Ionian Greeks, the Greeks living on the Asian shore of the Aegean, rebelled against Persia, Athens, the original colonizer of many of the Ionian cities, impetuously came to help them and, in a militarily foolish move, burned the wealthy Persian provincial capital of Sardis. In partial retribution, Persia destroyed Miletus, killing the men, enslaving the women and children, and razing the city to the ground. Darius is said to have had his servants remind him of the Athenians three times before every meal as he contemplated vengeance against Athens.[1]

In 490, Darius sent a fleet to Greece, which, after conquering the islands in the middle of the Aegean known as the Cyclades, conquered Euboea and prepared to engage the Athenians on the plain before Marathon, where, with a great advantage in cavalry, Persia could expect an easy victory. Only Plataea, a small town a few miles from Thebes, sent soldiers to reinforce the Athenians. The Spartans had promised help, but the moon was not quite right, they claimed, and so Sparta delayed. At Marathon, Athens operated under its peculiar law that each of ten generals held the overall command for one day in rotation. No action took place until Aristides, an Athenian noted for his virtue, yielded his day of command to Miltiades, thus setting an example for the other generals. In the ensuing battle, the Athenians, charging the Persians at a run, defeated them in a remarkable victory that produced fewer than two hundred casualties for the Athenians and over six thousand for the Persians. The surviving Persians fled to Persia.

Ten years later, Darius's son Xerxes carried on the campaign against Greece. Concluding that his father lost because the Persian forces had been insufficient, Xerxes collected an army of about two and a half million (if Herodotus can be believed), marched it across the Hellespont into Europe over a pontoon bridge, and dispatched a fleet across the sea to Europe. The Greeks, whose spies kept them informed of the massive force that was approaching, were understandably in a state of utter panic: Persia, a mighty empire with the world's most powerful military forces, was on the march against them. Those who "Medized," that is, gave the Persians symbolic earth and water in token of submission, could expect a relatively soft occupation, but those who refused to Medize faced enslavement or death.

Athens at this time had as one of its leaders a certain Themistocles, the main political rival of the famously virtuous Aristides. Where Aristides was preeminent in moral excellence, Themistocles was creatively resourceful and energetic. When silver had been discovered in Laurium, Athens had debated whether to distribute money to every citizen or to use the money for a common purpose—reinforcement of the fleet for possible engagement with Aegina, Athens's maritime rival. In what must be regarded as one of the world's great feats of persuasion, Themistocles convinced his fellow citizens to vote for the fleet.

The Persian army, marching south from Thessaly toward Athens, was delayed by three hundred heroic Spartans who fell at Thermopylae. The Athenians abandoned their city, the men boarding ships, the women and children deposited on the small island of Salamis, in the Saronic Gulf just off the coast of Attica. While the rest of the Greeks were certain that the safest strategy lay in building a defensive wall across the Isthmus of Corinth, Themistocles believed that victory lay in engaging the Persian fleet in the narrow strait off Salamis, where the vast numerical superiority of Persian ships would be a hindrance to their maneuverability. By various ingenious and devious machinations he succeeded in bringing about the battle there, and the ensuing Battle of Salamis proved one of the most significant naval victories in the history of the world.

The Persians were startled at their loss and feared for the safety of King Xerxes. Leaving behind a land army to redeem their honor, they retreated en masse to Persia. In the following year, at the Battle of Plataea,

Figure 11.   Wall across the Isthmus of Corinth
The Greeks opposed to Themistocles's plan to fight the Persians in the waters near Salamis wanted to build a wall across the isthmus of Corinth, as shown in the map above. They hoped that this wall would keep the Persians out of the Peloponnese.

this army suffered another loss to the numerically inferior Greeks, who were united under the command of Sparta. With this loss, the Persian assault on Europe was permanently abandoned.

It was clear that Athens had been the savior of Greece. Herodotus writes,

> At this point I am forced to declare an opinion that most people will find offensive; yet, because I think it true, I will not hold back. If the Athenians had taken fright at the approaching danger and had left their country, or even if they had not left it but had remained and surrendered to Xerxes, no one would have tried to oppose the King at sea. If there had been no opposition to Xerxes at sea, what happened on land would have been this: even if the Peloponnesians had drawn many walls across the Isthmus for their defense, the Lacedaemonians would have been betrayed by their allies, not because the allies chose to do so, but out of necessity as they were taken, city by city, by the fleet of the barbarian; thus the Lacedaemonians would have been isolated and, though isolated, would have done

deeds of the greatest valor and died nobly. That would have been what happened; or else they would, before this end, have seen that all the other Greeks had Medized and so themselves would have come to an agreement with Xerxes. In both these cases, all of Greece would have been subdued by the Persians. For I cannot see what value those walls drawn across the Isthmus would be, once the King was master by sea. So, as it stands now, a man who declares that the Athenians were the saviors of Greece would hit the very truth. For to whichever side they inclined, that was where the scale would come down. They chose that Greece should survive free, and it was they who awakened all the part of Greece that had not Medized, and it was they who, under Heaven, routed the King. Not even the dreadful oracles that came from Delphi, terrifying though they were, persuaded them to desert Greece; they stood their ground and withstood the invader when he came against their own country.[2]

To a very large extent, it was the general awareness of the debt owed Athens for its contribution to Greek freedom that induced the other Greeks to yield supremacy to Athens. And Athens lost no opportunity to remind the rest of the Greeks of the debt. But a moral debt loses its bite after a few decades, and by the end of the fifth century, when Athens was still harking on the memory of her heroism, the past glories rang hollow.[3]

The war brought about a number of important changes in the intellectual landscape. First, it showed the Athenians that their new democracy, a quite novel political arrangement, was capable of great actions. Under oligarchy and tyranny, Athens had been just one of a number of *poleis* of moderate power; under democracy, it had blossomed into prominence. Yet it was impossible for any conscious person living under pure democracy—a form of government in which the *entire* citizenry, not a representative group, is responsible for the government—not to recognize its inefficiency, ignorance, and susceptibility to sudden passion. Before, only a few statesmen had to concern themselves with legislation and administration; now, everyone was responsible for the laws and their execution. The question of how to run a regime became part of the discourse of politically active people and formed the seed of what developed into political philosophy. Though Plato later calls the first political thinkers by the derogatory name *sophists*, his view should not prejudice our investigation of the subject. Two of these sophists, Protagoras and Gorgias, were pioneers in making politics a subject of study.

As we have seen, the early thinkers were absorbed by the investigation of natural causality. After the Persian Wars, an interest in the theories of causality concerning human affairs arose, perhaps from reflection on what had occurred in the war and how only a few small changes in various actions might have brought about a very different outcome.[4] People now asked new questions: Why do old empires fall? Why do new ones arise? As there are laws that govern the transformations of inanimate physical objects, are there also laws governing human transformations? Do regimes and empires have a life cycle with predictable, regular patterns? How does chance or luck figure in human affairs? These questions dominate the thinking of the Athenian tragedians and of Herodotus, and they will recur in the philosophies of Plato, Aristotle, Stoics, and Epicureans.

The new form of government, democracy, validated by its success against Persia, brought to the fore the mechanism of persuasion. An ability to persuade had been admired at least from Homeric times, but now democracy revealed the urgency of acquiring it. An ability to persuade meant political power in assemblies, legal success in courtrooms, and the

esteem of one's fellow citizens. Good speakers became leaders, and perhaps for this reason the word in Greek for *speaker* (*rhetor*) is also the word for *politician*. A market developed for those who could teach the art of persuasion, and there was no shortage of teachers hawking their skills. Alert Greeks understood the double-edged nature of rhetoric, which could be used both to educate and to delude, and the resulting ambivalence toward rhetoric became a stimulating subject for philosophy.[5]

Perhaps more than anything else, the Persian Wars taught Greeks the practical advantages of the power of mind. The overwhelmingly numerous Persian menace had not been subdued by force; quite the contrary, the Greeks were a sparrow overcoming an eagle. The Greeks succeeded by the sheer power of intelligence. It had been the strategy of the brilliantly resourceful of Themistocles that defeated the Persian hordes. What mind could achieve for military excellence perhaps it could accomplish for other things as well. Thus it is no wonder that after the Persian Wars intensive intellectual effort was put into other areas that seemed susceptible to thought, among which were mathematics, medicine, and science as well as rhetoric and politics.

II. Rhetoric and Sophistry

Unlike the thinkers we have examined in earlier chapters, who were concerned with knowledge for its own sake, the sophists, for the most part, were concerned with knowledge for its practical benefits. Thus they reflected not on the origin of the universe or on what things were ultimately made of—questions of exclusively theoretical interest—but on questions of human life whose answers might provide clues for obtaining worldly success.

Very little remains of the actual words of the early sophists and inventors of rhetoric. Most of what we think we know comes from the accounts in Plato's dialogues and a few comments scattered here and there in other ancient authors. Unfortunately, learning about the sophists from Plato would be like learning about Franklin Roosevelt from what Barry Goldwater wrote or about Ronald Reagan from what George McGovern wrote. Still, through the fog of misrepresentation, accidental or deliberate, a few matters might be discerned. For example, one might be able to tell from Goldwater that Roosevelt was concerned with the well-being of people who had little money. But the story would be told from the point of view that since everything Roosevelt did sprang from a fundamentally erroneous view of human nature, the long-term consequences of his actions were more disastrous than beneficial. Thus, beyond a vague sort of awareness of the general issues, not much in the way of specific knowledge could be ascertained.[6] As Plato seems to have declared all-out war on the sophists, we need to be very cautious in accepting what he said about them.

In a monarchy or aristocracy based on descent, there was little need for oratorical skill; a blue blood could give orders and expect them to be obeyed. He did not have to persuade others that he should be the leader. But after the Persian Wars, in *poleis* with democratic constitutions, political skills were essential. Celebrity-sophists traveled throughout the Greek world, lecturing and offering education in the very political skills that would bring success. The greatest of these skills was "to be good at speaking."[7] This phrase, like "good lawyer," carries the same ambiguity in Greek as it does in English, and the ambiguity goes to the heart of the problem of sophistry. We know when we need "a good lawyer": it is when we're guilty but wish to be acquitted. Of course, no loving parents wish for their son or daughter to be "a good lawyer" in this sense. In the same way, "to be good at speaking" implies, on the one hand, an ability to manipulate the truth so as to persuade cunningly by appeals to emotion, displays of eloquence and verbal pyrotechnics, deception, and many other forms of bamboozlement. On the other hand, "to be good at speaking" also implies a desire to speak the truth plainly, without ornament, and without emotional appeals intended to distract or confuse. Very early on it became clear that a successful rhetorical ploy was to seem to be a plain speaker while subtly manipulating the hearers. Aristotle makes the Machiavellian observation that it is necessary for a speaker to conceal his art and to *seem* to be natural: men suspect artifice in speech the way they suspect doctored wine and think that the speaker is trying to trick them. Hence speakers try to persuade their audience that they are "just plain ordinary men."[8] A Latin proverb (*ars est celare artem*) says that art lies in concealing art.[9]

These problems, which first became apparent to the Greeks, have never been solved in the Western world. We can trace the periods when eloquence was admired, even worshipped, and can observe when it went out of favor and plain speaking came to the fore.[10] At the beginning of Plato's *Apology*, Socrates says that he was so overcome by the eloquence of his accusers that he almost believed them—and then he mordantly adds that he cannot compete with them in eloquence unless truth matters. In Euripides' *Medea*, Jason says that he will have to match his wife's speech with a rhetorical display of his own.[11] Where is sincerity when there is so great a consciousness of artistry?

Gorgias (483–376), a rhetorician from Leontini, in Sicily, was one of the sensational successes in the mid-fifth century. His prose exploited all the vices of which the highly inflective and highly syntactic Greek language was capable, including its natural tendency toward assonance, rhyme, balanced contrasting clauses, and subtle distinctions in similar words. Larue Van Hook has attempted to convey a sense of the Gorgianic style in an English translation of *The Encomium of Helen*, one paragraph of which is quoted here:

> But if by violence she [Helen] was defeated and unlawfully she was treated and to her injustice was meted, clearly her violator as a terrifier was importunate, while she, translated and violated, was unfortunate.

Therefore, the barbarian who verbally, legally, actually attempted the barbarous attempt, should meet with verbal accusation, legal reprobation, and actual condemnation. For Helen, who was violated, and from her fatherland separated, and from her friends segregated, should justly meet with commiseration rather than with defamation. For he was the victor and she was the victim. It is just, therefore, to sympathize with the latter and anathematize the former.[12]

Though contemporary taste finds this razzle-dazzle rather tiresome, the Greeks found it enchanting.[13] Gorgias had many imitators of his pyrotechnics, and Plato often delights in making fun of them.[14]

Among the questions the sophists raised was one that has come to be known as "the problem of convention and nature" (in Greek, the problem of *nomos* and *physis*). The problem is still with us and sometimes is referred to by the variant name of "the problem of nature/nurture." It is manifested in various ways.

One way concerns whether the reality that we understand around us is created by our minds or whether our minds understand reality as it actually is. Protagoras began one of his controversial works claiming that "Man is the measure of all things, of things that are that they are, and of things that are not that they are not."[15] The statement probably means that in the human world humans determine the various standards and limits. Plato, who has Socrates take Protagoras's statement to mean a total and pervasive relativism, where every individual man establishes his own standards of everything, pointedly caps his misrepresentation of Protagoras by declaring that "God is the measure of all things."[16] Of course, when the two statements are put side by side, what ancient would have been so bold as to prefer Protagoras's?

Another manifestation of the problem of nature and convention reflects the discovery by the early thinkers that the rules governing the human mind and the whole universe are fundamentally the same. For example, the Pythagoreans had claimed that the same rules of number that govern nature also govern human life. The sophists, however, saw the morality that was practiced as a human construct that differed starkly in different places. Justice meant not transgressing the laws of the state in which one lived as a citizen. And if the laws were different in different states, then what was just in one state was not just in another. They inquired into whether there was an underlying universal justice for all humans beings that arose out of their nature as human beings. One sophist, Antiphon (fl. fifth century B.C.E.), claimed in this revolutionary spirit that Greeks and barbarians have the same nature:

> This can be seen from the natural needs of all men. They can all satisfy them in the same way, and in these matters there is no distinction between Greeks and barbarians. We all breathe the same air through mouth and nose, and all eat with our hands.[17]

To live in a state one had to obey the laws made by men or at least "appear" to obey them. But the laws of *nature* had to be obeyed no matter what. The sophistic inquiries into what is natural to human beings—reason and kindness and trying to be like the gods and seeking knowledge and living in harmony with other people in a good state or, alternatively, getting as much as possible for oneself and giving in to temptations and seeking as much sensual pleasure as possible and surrendering to superstitious fancy—all these matters have stimulated philosophical discourse for millennia.

Closely related is the problem of civilization and the state. Is human social organization a result of nature, or is it somehow a defiance of nature? Does civilization arise from an agreement of people to live together for common benefits like protection and culture? And if it does, is such an agreement natural? And if it is natural, what kind of state most conforms to human nature? Is there a state in which human beings can best fulfill their nature? Are states living organisms, subject to diseases, as living organisms are, and, if so, do the diseases follow a natural progression, and can they be prevented or cured? Or is the notion of the state as an organism a metaphor that, when taken literally, presents more problems than insights? These are a few of the questions that were asked by the sophists. They invented the questions, invented the vocabulary for discussing them, and offered tentative answers.[18]

Fundamental to the work of the sophists and their claim to educate men for political life, indeed, fundamental to education generally, is the question of whether virtue can be taught, and if so, in what meaningful sense. Perhaps it is self-evident that flute playing or chariot driving are skills that can be passed on to other human beings. What about good-ness? Parents hope to train their children to be good people, yet their hope is frequently disappointed as apparently good parents have un-scrupulous children. If virtue can be taught, virtue would seem a kind of knowledge, like the knowledge of playing a flute, and would seem to be subject to rules. But if so, why do people argue about teaching virtue al-though they do not argue about flute playing?

And closely related to the question of whether virtue can be taught is the question of whether the faculty of speaking well can be taught. The very existence of manuals on rhetoric that articulate myriads of subtle dis-tinctions suggests that technique can in fact be taught. Yet there always re-mains the question of whether a knowledge of techniques can be trans-lated into creative skill. One might know very well what a metaphor is and even be able to analyze metaphors with great acumen without being able to invent a single one, just as one might be a fine *critic* of baseball without being able to pitch a ball or swing a bat. But if a knowledge of technique will not produce good speakers, why should one spend hard-earned drachmas paying Protagoras or Gorgias for lessons? Will studying with a good teacher guarantee that one becomes a good speaker? Or is it neces-sary to have talent? And if it is necessary to have talent, where does the tal-ent come from? If it comes from the gods, who needs expensive lessons?[19]

Like the Milesian thinkers, who recognized that the form in which we see things does not constitute their underlying reality, so the sophists and later thinkers were aware that what *seems* to be a good argument might not in actual fact be so. Yet persuasion works by convincing someone that a proposition is true, that is, by making a proposition *appear* to be true, whether in fact it is true or not. The art of persuasion—rhetoric—did not claim to use perfect arguments to achieve its goals. Aristotle, who perhaps wrote the best book on rhetoric, said that it is the counterpart of dialectic or logic,[20] and he defined the basic instrument of rhetoric, the en-thymeme, as a rhetorical syllogism, that is, a syllogism in which the prem-ises are merely probable.[21] Zeno of Citium (not to be confused with Zeno of Elea, whom we discussed in the previous chapter) compared logic to the closed fist, rhetoric to the open palm.[22] From Zeno's analogy we can deduce the special quality of rhetoric: it is like an insult, for a slap in the face, although it does not knock one down or out, stings and wounds the psyche more than does a blow from a fist. Rhetoric uses language to work on the emotions. One of the perennial charges against rhetoric is that it makes the worse argument *appear* the better. This is a severe charge, for it makes rhetoric guilty of deliberate fraud, and to teach others to be skilled at fraud would be like teaching them to be skilled at embezzlement or at being a "good" pickpocket or embezzler.

This general discussion will give an idea of the kinds of issues that the sophists raised in the mid-fifth century. Plato represents the sophists in an almost uniformly bad light, and the power of his prose has cast a permanent shadow on their achievements. If, however, we suspend our fondness of Plato, just for a while, we can perhaps give them part of their due and acknowledge that even Plato and his followers are in their debt, for the sophists raised issues of the utmost significance for understanding social life. Furthermore, they paved the way for education in the West by their commitment to developing intellects and by their faith that character and statesmanship could be taught.

The sophists were perhaps the first to revere language, *logos*, in its complex fullness. Protagoras is credited with having invented grammar by distinguishing the tenses of verbs and dividing discourse into questions, commands, wishes, and answers.[23] Prodicus of Ceos did additional work on the parts of speech and specialized in drawing distinctions between words.[24] To those who have studied grammar from their first days at school, the division of language into the parts of speech seems the most natural thing in the world, but the discovery that language is ordered must be hailed as one of the great insights in human history, akin to the mathematical discoveries of the Pythagoreans. If it is reason that distinguishes human beings from the other animals, and if language is the expression of reason, and if grammar is the structure of language, then grammar is nothing other than the study of human nature. Along with grammar, the sophists first inquired into the origin of language, and their opposing three theories—that it arose naturally from something inherent in humans or, conversely, that it is an artificial construct or, compromisingly, that it is somehow a mean between what is natural to humans and what is agreed on by convention—still find adherents.

Finally, we should note that the sophists were the first to be prosecuted by the state for their academic views. The first prosecutor was Athens, hailed in Pericles' Funeral Oration as "the school of Hellas." The first man we know of to be prosecuted was Protagoras himself, presumably for a book he read aloud at the home of the tragedian Euripides. The book was *On the Gods*, and the opening has been preserved by Diogenes Laertius:

> As to the gods, I have no means of knowing either that they exist or that they do not exist. For many are the obstacles that impede knowledge, both the obscurity of the question and the shortness of human life.[25]

One might think that Protagoras would have been more admired for his modesty than censured for his atheism. Protagoras's punishment was banishment from Athens, a punishment that certainly cut into his income since it deprived him of wealthy Athenians as students but perhaps not so terrible a punishment for a noncitizen who could make his way elsewhere in the world. The same city would later prosecute Socrates, who in Plato's *Apology* similarly made a modest claim—the claim that he knew only that he did not know anything. Socrates will suffer a punishment of execution by hemlock. Philosophers, throughout the history of the West, will often suffer a similar fate. In this way, the words of Pericles proved ominous in a way he surely did not intend.

93

Discussion Questions

1. If you had been in Athens in the decade before the Persian invasion, would *you* have been convinced by Themistocles to give up the chance for private wealth by building a common fleet? You probably think that you would have, but that's because you know what happened. Pretend that you were an opponent of Themistocles' policy. What arguments would you have used to urge a distribution of the new wealth to the citizenry?

2. Will the publication of Herodotus's judgment about Athens as the savior of Greece have endeared Athens to the rest of Greece or estranged her from it? Will it have given Athenians a sense of confidence or puffed them up with arrogant pride?

3. Aristotle says that improved techniques of smelting iron ore contributed to the rise of democratic constitutions in Greece. He argues that when more people became able to afford armor (because of the reduction in the cost of

iron), fighting was no longer the sole prerogative of the rich nobility, and there consequently arose a demand for broader participation in the working of government. Can you think of other ways in which technological improvement, intellectual innovation, and political life are related?

4. Most people respond at a deep emotional level to eloquence. Beautiful words are quoted in times of sadness, in moments when inspiration is required, on a thousand different occasions. But what, if anything, distinguishes eloquence from manipulation? Sly, crafty speakers are usually suspect. Are eloquent speakers simply more skilled at hiding their insincerity? Are there any ways to distinguish the truly good from the merely clever speakers? Why did the ancient sophists, while popular with some, arouse detestation in others?

5. In what ways are the questions of nature and nurture and of nature and convention still relevant? Has modern biology, with its discoveries of the role of genetics, refined the problem? Can you think of any experiments that might help illuminate the various issues involved?

6. Are the sophists more to be admired than scorned? In what ways did they further understanding? In what ways were their methods at least potentially corruptive? Is it true that any good thing can be used for ill (one might, for example, clobber another person over the head with a medical text or book on ethics)? Are the sophists to blame if their teaching was abused by others?

Notes

1. Herodotus, *History of the Persian Wars* 5.105.

2. Herodotus, *History of the Persian Wars*, trans. David Grene (Chicago: University of Chicago Press, 1987), 7.139.

3. Throughout Thucydides' *History of the Peloponnesian War*, Athens justifies her imperial ambitions and indeed her empire by her glorious leadership during the Persian Wars. By the end of the history (6.82–83), the Athenians themselves seem to realize how hackneyed these claims had become.

4. Modern chaos theory has made us aware of how, if variables are slightly altered, results can be very different. In its practical application this is known as the "butterfly effect"; that is, if a butterfly flaps its wings in China, it may affect weather patterns in the United States. Herodotus anticipates this idea throughout his history. At the very beginning he notes how a chance event, a queen's catching sight of someone hiding in her bedroom, brings about the fall of a dynasty. For a discussion of this principle, see James A. Arieti, *Discourses on the First Book of Herodotus* (Lanham, Md.: Littlefield Adams Books, 1995), 1–5 and passim.

5. In Greek, the word *deinos* means both *terrible* (in the sense of *wicked*) and *clever*. To be "clever at speaking" (*deinos legein*) also means to be "terrible at speaking." One might compare the famous chorus from Sophocles' *Antigone* (334), where the same pun is made about human nature.

6. The same distortion would occur in an account by McGovern of Reagan: one might be able to tell from McGovern that Reagan was concerned with the well-being of people who had *a lot* money. But the story would be told from the point of view that since everything Reagan did sprang from a fundamentally

erroneous view of human nature, the long-term consequences were more disastrous than beneficial. The only change is the substitution of "a lot" for "a little."

7. See note 5 above.

8. Aristotle, *Rhetoric* 1414b18 ff.

9. The same sentiment is found later in the *Réflexions ou sentences et Maximes Morales* of Duc de la Rouchefoucauld: *C'est une grande habileté que de savoir cacher son habileté* (It is a height of cleverness to conceal one's cleverness).

10. In antiquity, different styles had their enthusiastic supporters who looked on style with an almost religious zeal—indeed, for many there was no "almost." For example, in the Roman period, the two styles that came to be known as Asianism and Atticism were in sharp conflict. Cicero used the term *Asianism* to refer to two distinct styles of speaking: 1) one marked by epigrammatic, sharp, neat, and charming expression and 2) the other marked by torrid and florid excess of language and delivery (*Brutus* 325). Opposed to Asianism was Atticism, a style deliberately spare, economical, and matter-of-fact. Each had its enthusiastic proponents and opponents. Petronius, writing in the middle of the first century C.E., had the narrator of his *Satyricon* attack Asianism as stained and turgid and windy beyond the norm (*Satyricon* 1). Quintilian, writing at the end of the first century C.E., spoke of Atticism as a cult, some of whose members were still around, "dry, juiceless, and bloodless" (Quintilian, *Institutes* 12.10.14).

11. *Medea* 522. See p. 145, where Jason's statement is quoted. Aristotle surely had Euripides in mind when, in the *Poetics* (1450 b7), he distinguished between the older tragedians, who made their characters speak "politically," and the newer ones, who made their characters speak "rhetorically."

12. Larue Van Hook, *Greek Life and Thought: A Portrayal of Greek Civilization* (New York: Columbia University Press, 1948). The passage quoted is from pp. 165–66, but the whole speech (pp. 164–67) is quite remarkably rendered into English.

13. Modern taste differs with the Greeks in many matters. One very prominent difference is in the painting of marble sculpture. We tend to find the marble itself plainly beautiful, but the Greeks painted their sculpture to make it more lifelike.

14. See, for example, the parody of Agathon in the *Symposium* (197d–e) and of Polus in the *Gorgias* (448c).

15. Quoted in Diogenes Laertius 9.51.

16. *Laws* 716c.

17. Antiphon, frag. 44B. This translation is found in Werner Jaeger, *Paideia: The Ideals of Greek Culture*, vol. 1, trans. Gilbert Highet (New York: Oxford University Press, 1945), 327. He sounds rather like Shylock in his famous speech in *The Merchant of Venice* 3.1.57–66.

18. The question of the origin of civilization seems to have been a favorite of Protagoras, at least as portrayed in the *Protagoras* of Plato, who, even if he cannot be trusted to present Protagoras's views fairly, perhaps reflects Protagoras's interest in the question (Plato, *Protagoras* 322 b–c). The origin of the state is the focus of Herodotus's story of Deioces (Herodotus, *History of the Persian Wars* 1.96–101). The question of the best regime figures in the discussion of the Persian conspirators (Herodotus, *History of the Persian Wars* 3.80–88) and prominently in Aristotle (*Politics*, books 3 and 4). The question of the state as an organism is the model for Plato in the *Republic* and of Menenius Agrippa's speech in Livy (*History of Rome* 2.32). The question of disease as a metaphor for what ails the state is pervasive in Thucydides. See Charles Norris Cochrane, *Thucydides and the Science of History* (New York: Russell & Russell, 1965).

19. Whether poetical skill is a gift of the gods is the subject of Plato's *Ion*. For a balanced discussion of the question of the place of nature and technique in writing, see chapter 2 of Longinus's *On the Sublime*.

20. Aristotle, *Rhetoric* 254 a1. "Counterpart" is the usual translation of the Greek word *antistrophos*. For other possibilities, see George A. Kennedy, *Aristotle: On Rhetoric: A Theory of Civic Discourse* (New York: Oxford University Press, 1991), 28–29 n.

21. Aristotle, *Rhetoric* 1356 a37–b26.

22. This is reported by Sextus Empiricus, *Against the Professors* 2.7, and by Cicero in both *de finibus* 2.17 and *Orator* 113.

23. Diogenes Laertius, *Life of Protagoras* 9.52, 54.

24. Prodicus's influence may be felt in Thucydides, where, for example, the Corinthians draw a careful distinction between a complaint (*aitia*) and an accusation (*kategoria*) (1.69) or give special attention to the meaning of *arbitration* (1.39).

25. Diogenes Laertius, *Life of Protagoras* 9.51, trans. R. D. Hicks (Cambridge, Mass., 1931). Subsequent quotations from Diogenes Laertius are from this edition.

Select Bibliography

THE PERSIAN WARS

Cook, J. M. *The Persian Empire*. London: J. M. Dent, 1983.
Green, Peter. *The Greco-Persian Wars*. Berkeley: University of California Press, 1996.

SOPHISTRY AND RHETORIC

Guthrie, W. K. C. *The Sophists*. Cambridge: Cambridge University Press, 1971.
Schiappa, E. "History and Neo-Sophistic Criticism: A Reply to Poulakos." *Philosophy and Rhetoric* 23 (1990): 307–15.
———. *Protagoras and Logos: A Study in Greek Philosophy and Rhetoric*. Columbia: University of South Carolina Press, 1991.
Segal, C. "Gorgias and the Psychology of Logos." *Harvard Studies in Classical Philology* 66 (1972): 99–135.

CHAPTER 6

Medicine, Tragedy, History

I. Medicine

One of the great accomplishments of the ancient Greek world, and of all antiquity, was the development in the late fifth century of the *scientific* practice of medicine. Doctoring, of course, is as old as civilization itself, perhaps even older, but only when the Greeks developed a purely rational way of looking at the world did medicine become a science.

In early Greek belief, as in the beliefs of other peoples, illness, like all other facets of human life, came at the discretion of the gods. Homer's *Iliad* and Sophocles's *Oedipus Rex* both begin with plagues sent by an angered Apollo. The idea that a deity is responsible for causing or curing illness is also found in biblical writings, especially in the New Testament, where casting out demons and healing the sick are among Jesus' principal activities. Curative powers were attributed to the pagan gods, and votive offerings (many the models of the diseased body parts needing cure) and amulets are common archaeological finds. Greeks believed also in the healing power of dreams, which played a part in the cures at the sanctuaries of Asclepius in Epidaurus and Corinth.[1] An ill person would go to sleep in a special area in these sanctuaries, and there the god Asclepius would converse with the patient in a dream and offer a cure. These nonscientific medical views were never abandoned by the ancient world (nor, indeed, have they been abandoned by the modern world either, as the continued use of amulets, candle lighting, and faith healing all attest) but existed along with scientific medicine.

As we have seen, the philosophers of Ionia sought an explanation of nature that did not rely on supernatural causation. Instead, they sought to show that all nature operated by the same set of physical laws. Perhaps because of the tremendous success of Greek mathematics—and of geometry in particular, with its system of deductive reasoning based on very few axioms—there was a tendency among natural philosophers to develop explanations of the physical universe that were deductive from various assumptions. Deductive reasoning produces the highest degree of certainty, and Aristotle is typical of the Greeks in affording the prize for precise knowledge to sciences like geometry and logic, sciences whose conclusions

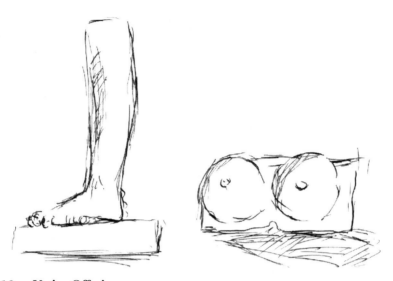

Figure 12.   Votive Offerings
These models of offerings, on display at the Museum of the Asclepeium at Corinth, represent
bodily parts for which cures were being sought. The various sanctuaries to Asclepius enjoyed
excellent reputations, and tablets from grateful patients graced the walls.

99

are reached through deductive reasoning from axioms and definitions.[2]
The early thinkers offered various solutions to the questions of what the
world was made out of and how it functioned, but, as we observed, their
theories were developed from speculative assumptions.[3] Thales made water the basic principle; Anaximander, a substance of indeterminate nature;
Anaximenes, air; Heraclitus, fire. In the fifth century, as we shall see,
Empedocles declared the elements to be four: air, earth, fire, and water.[4]

The results of the natural philosophers, however, were not satisfying.
The material world simply does not yield to purely deductive reasoning.
Medical writers of the fifth century and later very much wanted to separate themselves from the speculative axioms of the natural philosophers.
Celsus (fl. 14–37 C.E.) claims that Hippocrates (about 460–360 B.C.E.)
was the first actually to do so. In *On the Nature of Man*, Hippocrates criti-
cizes those physicians who claim that because humans are a unity, they are
composed of only one of the four elements. He says that their proofs
amount to nothing and that victory in their debates goes to the one with
the glibbest tongue.[5]

A key feature of Greek medical science is its rejection of gods and magic in the interpretation of disease. In popular Greek language, epilepsy was called the "sacred disease." The Hippocratic author who wrote the treatise *On the Sacred Disease* claims that this disease is no more sacred than any other:

> I am about to discuss the disease called "sacred." It is not, in my opinion, any more divine or more sacred than other diseases, but has a natural cause, and its supposed divine origin is due to men's inexperience, and to their wonder at its peculiar character. Now while men continue to believe in its divine origin because they are at a loss to understand it, they really disprove its divinity by the facile method of healing which they adopt, consisting as it does of purifications and incantations. But if it is to be considered divine just because it is wonderful, there will be not one sacred disease but many, for I will show that other diseases are no less wonderful and portentous, and yet nobody considers them sacred.[6]

He continues by attacking as charlatans and quacks those who try to cure the disease by means of charms. He himself explains epilepsy as resulting from a discharge in the brain, and he supports this theory with the dissection of a goat that suffered from the same disease. In addition to the physiological explanation, what is remarkable is that the author sees the same laws of nature operative in both humans and goats.

The man most identified with the development of Greek medicine is Hippocrates of Cos, who is said to have established a medical school on his native island. Virtually nothing is known of Hippocrates himself, though he is treated respectfully by writers of his era. Plato refers to him as a typical doctor, and Aristotle calls him the perfect example of a physician. Plato attributes to Hippocrates the revolutionary idea that in order to understand the body it is necessary to look at it as an organic whole, that is, as a unity whose parts function together. This organic view, however, is not explicitly stated in any of the extant Hippocratic books. And the consensus of scholarly opinion is that there was no single author "Hippocrates." As in the case of Pythagoras, all works were attributed to the head of the school. None of the fifty to seventy surviving books of the so-called Hippocratic corpus agree with all the views attributed in antiquity to Hippocrates, and, in fact, the contents of these books are often at odds with one another. Nevertheless, even if his actual works are not known, Hippocrates appears to have been a real person and to have had— if Plato may be credited—a scientific outlook.

One of the important features of Greek medicine is the inquiry into the causes of disease. As in the case of natural philosophy, where a variety of views explained the universe, so in medicine there were various theoretical formulations, ranging from a single unitary cause for all disease to specific causes for each. The author of the Hippocratic work *On Breaths*, for example, thought that because some breathing irregularity accompanies illness, breath is at the root of every disease.[7] On the other hand, the author of *On Ancient Medicine* criticized physicians who did not distinguish between symptoms and causes.[8] He also criticized those who thought that if a disease follows a certain action, the action was the cause of disease—a mistake known in philosophy as the *post hoc propter hoc* fallacy.[9] An example would be eating a certain food and, when illness followed shortly after, assuming, without any further evidence than the coincidence, that the food caused the illness.

Another feature of Hippocratic medicine, as detailed in the work *Prognostics*, was the careful study of the progress of diseases. Once a physician had diagnosed a particular illness, he could tell the patient what to expect in the future as the disease ran its course. The ability to predict was essential in establishing medicine's credibility as a science.

Diagnosis and prognostication both incorporate the fundamental Hippocratic principle that disease is a part of nature and acts in accordance with natural laws. Because humans share a common bodily nature and diseases share a regular (and hence predictable) nature, a science of medicine is possible. For a disease to be treatable by the art of medicine, what works for one patient must work for another. Thus medicine must carefully analyze nature, catalogue the types of diseases, and define the appropriate treatment for each. The underlying assumption of ancient medicine, as of our own, is that the body functions best when its nature is maintained. Hence the job of a physician is twofold: first, he should not interfere with the body's nature but should maintain it by means of *preventive* medicine, the principal forms of which are diet and exercise; second, if the patient is already ill, the physician, using *therapeutic* medicine, should restore the body to its nature.

From its birth in fifth-century Greece, the scientific practice of medicine has been continually alive in the West. The centuries following Hippocrates saw major advances in anatomy, as postmortem dissections became common. Specialized work in gynecology, orthopedics, and other branches of medicine continued and flourished. Later, in the Roman period, there were major advances in public health, and the Romans bequeathed to posterity insights about hygiene, sanitation, and water supplies.

Medicine provided philosophy a model of a subject that, grounded in scientific naturalism, yields practical benefits in this life. It showed that philosophy is good for bodies as well as for souls.

II. Tragedy

Marcus Aurelius, writing of the origin and use of tragedy, says,[10]

> At first tragedies were produced to be reminders of [life's] accidents, and to remind us that this is the way things happen by nature and that, just as you are not vexed at what happens on the stage, so you should not be vexed at what happens on the greater stage. You see, you observe that these things must be gone through and even those who cried out "Ah, Cithaeron" bear them. Some things are said usefully by those who compose drama, especially, for example: "If I am uncared for by the gods, and my sons / also are uncared for, even this has *logos*."[11] And again, "You see, there's no use in getting your / emotions [*thymos* in Greek] up over things."[12] And "To mow off life as if it were ripe grain."[13] And many similar such things.

Quite to the contrary, in *Paradise Regained*, John Milton has his character Christ reject Greek tragedy as useless:

> Remove their swelling epithets, thick laid
> As varnish on a harlot's cheek, the rest,
> Thin sown with aught of profit or delight,
> Will far be found unworthy to compare
> With Sion's songs, to all true tastes excelling,
> Where God is praised aright, and godlike men,
> The Holiest of Holies, and his saints;
> Such are from God inspired, not such from thee...[14]

Thus Christ lambastes Greek poetry for its lack of true spiritual value. Remove the various poetical figures ("thick laid / As varnish on a harlot's cheek"), he says, and what remains is not much in comparison to the splendors found in Scriptures.

Whose verdict is right? What is the intellectual remnant when tragedy is stripped of art? Do its lessons go beyond the proverbial injunctions to listen to oracles, to behave rationally, to revere the gods, to honor guests, to bury the dead, to refrain from killing one's husband's new beloved? Do remarks concerning tragedy belong in a book about ancient philosophy? And though some ancient philosophers themselves discussed tragedy as a philosophical *subject*, did tragedy have anything to contribute to the intellectual framework?

Perhaps we can affirm that tragedy contributes, though not in a systematic way, to some questions that recur in philosophical discourse. Those discussed here will be the questions of evil, law, personal responsibility, and fate. It is clear, however, that tragedy, especially in the work of Euripides, dramatized many other issues as well.[15]

The oldest of the surviving playwrights, Aeschylus, takes up in the *Oresteia* the problem of evil. This trilogy treats the particular pendulum-like movement of evil from generation to generation that began when, after Atreus married Aërope, Atreus's own brother Thyestes seduced Aërope, his sister-in-law. The next swing of the pendulum occurred when Atreus, in revenge, pretended to be reconciled with Thyestes and invited him to a banquet of reconciliation, where he fed Thyestes his own children. In the next swing, Thyestes and his surviving son Aegisthus killed Atreus and exiled Atreus's two sons, Agamemnon and Menelaus. Later, Agamemnon came back from Sparta, where he had married Clytemnestra, and banished Thyestes and Aegisthus. He then went on to lead the Greeks in the Trojan War, but to secure a favorable wind for the fleet he sacrificed his and his wife's daughter Iphigeneia. Then, when Troy was taken, he allowed the city to be sacked, the people wantonly slain, and the temples of the gods violated. He returned home to his wife, bringing his prize-concubine, Cassandra, herself a priestess, whose virginity had been dedicated to Apollo. In the next movement of the pendulum, dramatized in the *Agamemnon*, the first play in Aeschylus's trilogy, Aegisthus, having seduced Clytemnestra, joined with her to kill Agamemnon and Cassandra.

In the next swing, dramatized in *The Libation Bearers*, the second play of the trilogy, Agamemnon's son Orestes killed the murderers, his own mother Clytemnestra and her lover Aegisthus. In the final swing, dramatized in the *Eumenides*, the third and final play of the trilogy, the Furies, gods whose job is to avenge murder of kin, pursued Orestes.

Aeschylus was not interested in the *origin* of evil. It was enough for him to recognize first that evil exists and has existed from as far back as the beginning of mankind and second that it is the nature of evil to breed more evil. Evil, once let loose into the world, produces consequences that cannot be controlled by the originator of the evil act. Thus, when Thyestes seduced Atreus's wife, he could not have foreseen that this action would

Figure 13.   Orestes Kills Aegisthus

While Agamemnon is at Troy fighting to take back Helen, his wife Clytemnestra (Helen's sister) is seduced by Aegisthus. When Agamemnon returns, in the first play of Aeschylus's trilogy *Oresteia*, the adulterous couple slay him. In the second play, *The Libation Bearers*, Agamemnon's son Orestes slays the murderers. Here he is shown slaying Aegisthus. In the final play, *The Eumenides*, the Furies pursue Orestes.

result initially in his eating his own children and ultimately in the extermination of his branch of the family. But he might have known that some terrible consequences would follow. Or again, when Agamemnon slew Iphigeneia, he did not know that this sacrifice would first result in stirring his wife Clytemnestra to betray and murder him and then stir his son Orestes to murder his mother Clytemnestra. The question raised by the myths is, of course, what would have been a suitable punishment or compensation for each crime. What should Thyestes have done to compensate Atreus for seducing his wife? What should Agamemnon have suffered to pay for having slain his daughter for the Greek passage over the Aegean? When a person wrongs another, should the person who suffered the wrong commit an equal wrong in return, thus obtaining justice, or should he add a little bit more wrong as punishment and retribution? Would an absolutely equal retaliation satisfy the demands of justice? At what point should action and reaction end?

Aeschylus's solution is perfectly harmonious with what we have discussed as characteristic of the Greek mind, that is, the imposition of order on nature. In the last play of the trilogy, Orestes is tried for parricide, the crime of killing a parent. Athena testifies on his behalf that he is not really guilty of the slaying of a *parent*, for—and here she becomes what nowadays we call "an expert witness"—only the father is a parent, the mother being the soil in which the paternal seed grows. Now, in this particular case and generally when it comes to trials and justice, we may come to the conclusion that a law was wrong; and when we do, this conclusion causes in us a peculiar ambivalence with respect to the law and law courts. We tend to admire law in the abstract but to despise it in the particular. Though we approve of law courts, we often hate lawyers. Reason will show us, however, that we cannot have law in the abstract; we cannot have law courts without lawyers. And we ought not to let our disgust at mankind's application of laws blind us to the supreme realization that the Greeks made for us, that law is the foundation both of the operation of the cosmos and of the operation of civilization. We might say of law what Edmund Burke said of order: "A particular order of things may be altered; order itself cannot lose its value."[16] Aeschylus knew that law and order of one kind or another would always exist. Anarchy is impossible, for anarchy is a vacuum that nature abhors; and if anarchy fills the vacuum with no other kind of law, then might makes right. Anarchy is impossible except in a chaos, but the universe to the Greeks was no longer a chaos; it had evolved into a cosmos, an ordered place operating according to law. The triumph of Zeus over his chaos-born ancestors symbolized this evolving cosmos for Aeschylus; and since to him heaven and earth were not divided and distinguished worlds, what occurred in heaven had its correspondence on earth: the evolving cosmos on earth was the order achieved by Greece, and especially by Athens, over the chaos of Greek prehistory and Asiatic barbarism.

Concerning the question of personal responsibility, perhaps it is best to glance at Aristotle's definition of the finest tragic plot. It involves

> the man who, not differing from us in virtue and justice, and hence being one of those who have a great reputation and good fortune, changes to misfortune not because of vice or wickedness but because of some error, as in the case of Oedipus and Thyestes and other famous men from families of this sort.[17]

The key word here is *mistake* (*hamartia* in Greek)—error in judgment.[18] The word has several implications. First, it implies that there is an agent. Mistakes do not simply happen; *someone* makes a mistake. Second, the existence of a mistake guarantees that there is a right answer. Third, if someone makes a mistake, he must either know the right answer or have reasonable access to the right answer. Fourth, if someone has made a mistake, he is responsible: the chain of causes must stop with him, the error in judgment has no external cause. The etymology of the Greek word helps to understand the meaning. Literally it means *missing the mark*, an image drawn from marksmanship. Throughout the *Iliad*, warriors are described as throwing spears at the enemy and either hitting them or missing them. When someone shoots at a target, he may hit it six times in a row and then on the seventh time miss. If he is asked why he missed, he may find a valid excuse. He might say that the wind blew, that the sun shone in his eyes, or that someone yelled and distracted him. While these may be phony excuses, quite often they are real explanations—the wind did blow, the sun did shine, or someone did yell—and all of them are outside, external causes that forced him to miss. But sometimes the wind does not blow and the sun does not shine in his eyes—and he still misses. What is the explanation then? There really is none. He can only say, "I missed." The blame for missing rests solely with him—for there are no outside sources to blame. Thus the word *mistake* refers to an action for which the agent is responsible.

Aristotle distinguishes between a misfortune, an injustice, and a mistake.[19] A *misfortune* is an accident; that is, it is irrational, and it does not arise from any internal wickedness on the part of the sufferer. An *injustice* is no accident but is the result of thinking, and it does arise from internal wickedness. A *mistake* is not an accident; that is, it does result from thinking, but it does not result from internal wickedness. The soul of tragedy, then, is that human beings, through a mistake for which they are responsible, bring about their own change of fortune.

Finally, we may take up the question of fate, the word *moira* in Greek. *Moira* originally seems to have meant *share* or *allotment*. Even Zeus, whose will is paramount, is subject to certain limitations and conditions that *moira* has set down for all things, humans and gods.[20] The notion behind *moira* is that when the primordial chaos settled down into order, things developed a nature, a set of properties—in short, a *moira*. The reason for the particular allotment of properties and potentialities was of no special interest to the Greeks; for them it was simply the way things are. When everything had been given its *moira*, it was expected to stay within these boundaries. If it did not stay within its boundaries, it would, necessarily, step over into something else's *moira* and would thus cause pain, injustice, and a return to chaos. The Greeks were quite aware of this principle. As Heraclitus says, "The sun will not transgress its boundaries; otherwise, the guardians of Justice, the Furies, will find it out."[21]

Let us examine the operation of *moira* more carefully. Perhaps we may start with a rose seed. It is the *moira* of a rose seed to become a rose bush, and to be a rose bush with blooming roses is its end or purpose (*telos* in Greek, from which comes the English word *teleological*). In general, Greek culture assumed that everything has a purpose. Aristotle, for example, rejected the idea of a thing's not having a purpose as manifestly absurd.[22] Now if nothing interferes with its assigned potentialities, the rose seed will become a rose bush. But, of course, things may interfere: a rabbit, a drought, an incompetent gardener confusing it for a weed. But only external forces can affect the seed. It has no will of its own; it cannot choose to violate its *moira*. It cannot even make a mistake. Humans, to move to a

107

more complex example, are beings who can have their *moira* violated by external forces, including other humans, but who can also violate their own *moira*, either by mistake or intention. The *moira* of humans is not fixed like that of a stone; it is dynamic and active. The job of each person, as the Delphic Oracle attests, is to fulfill his allotted potentialities, to fulfill his *moira*. The first of the Delphic maxims is usually translated as "everything in moderation," but it is more accurately translated as "nothing in excess," that is, "don't *overstep* the boundaries of your *moira*." The second Delphic maxim is "know thyself," that is, "know your limitations." If "nothing in excess" advises us not to *exceed* our limitations, "know thyself" advises us to *reach* them, not to fall short. The great Aristotelian doctrine of the golden mean, of excess and deficiency, was writ large in Greek culture long before Aristotle.

The Greeks realized that if the universe was *teleological*, that is, if it moved to purposes or ends, then one could trace the course of the movement that led to the end (the *telos*). They then saw that somewhere in the course of the movement came a critical moment when a decision was made that either brought the end inevitably about or frustrated it. This moment they named the *kairos*, "the critical moment." Aristotle gives as an example merchants caught in a storm at sea who save their lives by throwing their cargo overboard to lighten the ship. The decision to throw the cargo overboard is the critical moment that produces the end of safety. Perhaps another example will illustrate the matter more clearly. When the space shuttle *Challenger* was on the launching pad, there were many moments when the process could be stopped and the disaster of its destruction averted. But there came a point when the process could not be stopped. Once the shuttle was launched and the defective O-ring leaked, the end was inevitable. Any interval between the moment of launching, when the O-ring failed—the critical moment or *kairos*—and the explosion, the end or *telos*, was irrelevant. The interval was only a few seconds in the case of the *Challenger*. In the story of Oedipus, it was protracted to many years. That interval was waste and suffering; and the longer it was, the greater the waste and suffering. If the critical moment brings about the end inevitably, then the interval of time between them serves no purpose. Yet it must be gone through. It is here, perhaps, that the nature of tragedy lies. And here, too, perhaps, we find that sense of inevitability that many see as lying at the heart of tragedy. There are doom and inevitability in tragedy, but they come about because of the voluntary actions of human beings. This is the irony of tragedy, that men bind themselves to their fates by their actions. As Heraclitus said, "Character is fate."

This sense of the tragic nature of human life helped foster the conditions of the enterprise of philosophy. Aware of the tension between *moira* and freedom, aware of the heavy responsibility that attaches to all human actions, reflective individuals sought to understand just how things worked.

III. History

The development of history as a separate activity represents yet another example of the extent to which philosophical thinking penetrated the Ionian mind. Herodotus, known to the world as "the father of history," a native of the Ionian city of Halicarnassus, announces his project in the opening sentence of his *History of the Persian Wars*. He promises to discuss the great and wonderful deeds of both Greeks and barbarians and, in particular, "why the Greeks and Persians fought against one another." The first task had perhaps already been performed since time immemorial by record-keeping scribes. The second task appears to be new with Herodotus.

The word translated above as *why* is the Greek word *aitia*, which, though often translated *cause*, means chiefly *the thing that is responsible*. Now it is no easy matter to find a war's "cause" in this sense. For example, imagine a college course on the American Civil War. If a professor wished to begin the course with "the thing that was responsible," where would he begin? With the first shots fired on Fort Sumter? With the second Missouri Compromise? With the First Missouri Compromise? With the Constitutional Convention? With the importation of the first enslaved human beings into North America? It is obvious that every professor must choose *some* moment at which to begin. Yet any chosen moment will involve some assessment of the appropriate starting place, some interpretation of the event.

When Herodotus says, "I know the man who was the *aitia* of the Persian Wars,"[23] he means that he can locate the beginning of the war and place the responsibility. In doing so he is at one with the great Ionian thinkers—philosophers and scientists—who were his countrymen, such men as Thales, who predicted the first eclipse and who argued that all things were made out of water. Democritus, the inventor of the atomic theory, once said, "I would rather show one *aitia* than rule over the Persian Empire."[24] That attitude is the essence of Greek culture, and it is a part of the essence of our own culture.

Now even in Aristotle, who distinguished four kinds of *aitia* and who makes the simple notion of responsibility found in Herodotus subtle and abstract and complex, the notion of responsibility is fundamental, for his famous "four causes" are arranged in a hierarchy; and the most important element of that hierarchy is the "final cause," that is, the purpose for which something was done.[25] The concept of purpose *implies* someone or something capable of having a purpose; and such a person or thing can be held responsible.

In Herodotus one is responsible if no outside force compels one to do what one does. A mistake or an act of madness, originating within an individual, would not free one from responsibility, for there is no outside source. In this respect Herodotus is in the tradition we found in the Milesian thinkers of seeing the soul as a kind of unmoved mover or originator of its own actions.[26] Indeed, this is how the Greeks accounted for free will. They did not concern themselves with what stirred a soul to have an irrational thought; for them it was simply a given. Thus, for example, Herodotus writes that "this Candaules was erotically fixated on his wife,"[27] and the ensuing story proceeds from Candaules' erotic obsession. The obsession arises entirely in Candaules; Herodotus does not find it necessary to psychoanalyze Candaules, to look into his relationship with his mother, to probe the depths of his unconsciousness, or even to find a physiological aberration. The erotic fixation is the *aitia* of his actions. Since no external cause is present, the responsibility and origination of the action can be attributed to the performer of the action. No further hunt for an *aitia* is necessary.

A second important feature of history, also a manifestation of the influence of philosophy, is Heraclitus's principle of change. It is perhaps self-evident that the subject matter of history is change. The greater the change produced by an event, the greater its historical importance. Since wars are the greatest single concentrated cause of change in human affairs, wars are the preeminent subject of history.

When people hear that things change and that life is uncertain, though they nod their heads in agreement, their actions show that they do not really believe the rule applies to themselves. The general tendency of human nature is to assume a continuance of present conditions into perpetuity and to make plans for the future on the basis of this assumption, seldom imagining a change, especially for the worse. As long as human nature remains the same, people will probably nod at the truth that life is uncertain while refusing to believe that it pertains to themselves. Herodotus, no doubt, was warning his fellow Greeks that the reversals of fortune that had affected other human beings could affect them—the demises of long-lasting dynasties, the defeats of giant empires, the peripeties of fabulously rich kings who became slaves. At the beginning of his history, Herodotus announces his program and this great truth:

> I shall go forward in my account, covering alike the small and great cities of mankind. For of those that were great in earlier times most have now become small, and those that were great in my time were small in the time before. Since, then, I know that man's good fortune never abides in the same place, I will make mention of both alike.[28]

Here is Herodotus's statement of the principle of vicissitude, that history is ever changing and that human fortunes are in a constant state of alteration. In history, truly "everything flows" (*panta rei* in Greek).

A careful reading of Herodotus's history pays rich rewards. Herodotus is, first of all, a marvelous storyteller. He does not tell his stories such that they are interesting only in themselves; his telling evokes deep insights into the human condition. And, of course, for those interested in ancient philosophy, he wonderfully reflects the various debates occurring in the Greek world of his century and anticipates many of the philosophical issues that will come.[29] His work offers many lessons to his contemporaries, lessons that, if they had been taken to heart, might perhaps have prevented the Peloponnesian Wars and their devastating consequences. Perhaps, however, the tragic sense that pervades Greek thought was proved true here, too, and it was not the *moira* of the Greeks to live in peace with one another.

———

Discussion Questions

1. At least two revolutionary ideas are attributed to Hippocrates of Cos, the "father of medicine." For Celsus, one was the rejection of the speculative assumptions of the natural philosophers; for Plato, the other was the idea of the body as an organic unity, where each part functioned together with other parts. In what way was each idea "revolutionary"? Are both ideas accepted today? Is one more accepted than the other?

2. In what ways is the science of medicine dependent on the same principle as ancient philosophy, namely, that there are general laws that describe reality?

3. Marcus Aurelius, a philosopher, attributes an educational function to tragedy. The ancients often credit art with providing either a combination of education and pleasure, or education alone, but the possibility that art could provide pleasure exclusively is not discussed. Yet, unless human nature has changed quite remarkably, many people surely enjoyed art for pleasure alone. Is art better if it teaches as well as pleases? If it teaches, is it possible that its teaching can be corruptive? If it simply pleases, is it possible that the pleasure it provides can be corruptive? Would a philosophic mind, seeking the good for human beings, want to control the effects of art? Why or why not?

4. The *Oresteia* of Aeschylus ends in a trial in which Athena testifies that only a father is an actual parent. Now for Aeschylus's theatergoers, the so-called trial had taken place at a fictive date of nearly a thousand years earlier. What would they have thought of this "expert testimony"? Would they have been prompted by the play to consider the nature of scientific claims or of science in general? Would the play have prompted them to reflect on the nature of jury trials? If so, would they have concluded, as the text suggests, that trials were a good thing, promoting the rule of law?

5. To what degree do philosophical concepts of responsibility and nature underlie Greek tragedy? Does the frequent intervention of deities in human action clarify, muddy, or have no effect on the nature of the philosophic influence?

6. Is there a fundamental distinction between the search for historical causes and the search for natural causes? If so, what is it? If not, why doesn't the presence of human free will (unless it does not exist) constitute a fundamental difference between the two types of causes?

7. For Aristotle, *change* is a genus with three species: coming into being (that is, *generation*), going out of being (that is, *destruction*), and motion. Motion, also according to Aristotle, comes in four kinds: alteration, locomotion, increase, and decrease. In what ways does history exhibit all these kinds of change?

Notes

1. An ancient work describing such cures is the *Oneirocritica* of Artemidorus (second century C.E.).
2. On Aristotle's philosophy of science, see pp. 207–12.
3. See chapter 2.
4. See pp. 116–18.
5. Hippocrates, *On the Nature of Man* 1. The same author, though attacking others for their lack of evidence, accepts as axiomatic that humans are made of four humors—blood, yellow bile, black bile, and phlegm, each derived from one of the four elements. This is an indication perhaps of how the principle of the four elements seemed virtually self-evident to early scientists. It ought to serve as a caution to us all.
6. Hippocrates, *On the Sacred Disease* 1, trans. W. H. S. Jones (Cambridge, Mass.: Harvard University Press, 1943).
7. Hippocrates, *On Breaths* 5.
8. Hippocrates, *On Ancient Medicine* 21.
9. Hippocrates, *On Ancient Medicine* 21.
10. Marcus Aurelius, *Meditations* 11.6.
11. Euripides, *Antiope*, frag. 207.
12. Euripides, *Bellerophon*, frag. 289.
13. Euripides, *Hypsipyle*, frag. 757.
14. *Paradise Regained* (4.343–50).
15. In Euripides, the issues raised by the sophists come up over and over again: the place of women, the power of language to be abused, the value of war.
16. Edmund Burke, "A Letter to a Noble Lord," in *The Harvard Classics*, ed. Charles W. Eliot (New York: P. F. Collier & Son, 1909–1914), vol. 24, part 4, paragraph 32.
17. Aristotle, *Poetics*, trans. Hippocrates G. Apostle, Elizabeth A. Dobbs, and Morris A. Parslow (Grinnell, Iowa: Peripatetic Press, 1990), 1453 a8–12.
18. My understanding of *hamartia* and of tragedy and of much else, such as it is, I owe to my teacher and later colleague John M. Crossett. For a discussion of *hamartia*, see my article "History, *Hamartia*, Herodotus," in *Hamartia: The Concept of Error in the Western Tradition: Essays in Honor of John M. Crossett*, eds. D. V. Stump, James A. Arieti, Lloyd Gerson, and Eleonore Stump (New York: Edwin Mellen Press, 1983).
19. *Rhetoric* 1374b6–10.
20. Zeus might have the power to transgress these limitations, but he does not. The point is beautifully illustrated in *Iliad* 16, where Zeus knows that *moira* has determined that his son Sarpedon is to die in battle. Zeus asks himself whether he should save his son, and his wife Hera hears him anguishing. She tells him that if he saves Sarpedon, all the gods will save their favorites. Zeus refrains from exercising the power that he has and watches his son die.
21. Heraclitus, frag. 94.
22. Aristotle discusses the impossibility that something may arise in nature by chance and without purpose in *Physics* 198 b10–199b33. In *On the Heavens* 271 a34, he explicitly says that God and nature create nothing that is pointless. He expresses the same view repeatedly (for example, *On the Soul* 415 b16, 432 b21, 434 a30, and many other places).

23. Herodotus, *History of the Persian Wars* 1.5.
24. Democritus, frag. 118.
25. See pp. 201–2.
26. See the discussion of Thales on pp. 45–46.
27. Herodotus, *History of the Persian Wars* 1.8.
28. Herodotus, *History of the Persian Wars* 1.5, trans. David Grene (Chicago: University of Chicago Press, 1987).

29. For example, when Gyges tries to dissuade King Candaules from making him look at the queen naked, he explicitly embodies both sides of the nomos/physis controversy to show that looking on the queen is wrong by both standards. See the discussion in James A. Arieti, *Discourses on the First Book of Herodotus* (Lanham, Md.: Littlefield Adams Books, 1995), 18–19.

Select Bibliography

MEDICINE

Web resource: http://medweb.bham.ac.uk/histmed/biblio.html.
Langholf, V. *Medical Theories in Hippocrates: Early Texts and Epidemic*. Berlin: De Gruyter, 1990.
Longrigg, James. *Greek Medicine from the Heroic to the Hellenistic Age: A Source Book*. London: Duck-worth, 1998.
Pinault, Jody R. *Hippocratic Lives and Legends*. Studies in Ancient Medicine, vol. 6. Leiden: E. J. Brill, 1992.

TRAGEDY

Web resource: www2.warwick.ac.uk/fac/arts/classics/modules/gktrag/bibliography.
Knox, B. *The Heroic Temper*. Berkeley: University of California Press, 1966.
Meier, C. *The Political Art of Greek Tragedy*. Translated by Andrew Webber. Baltimore: Johns Hopkins University Press, 1993.
Nussbaum, M. C. *The Fragility of Goodness: Luck and Ethics in Greek Tragedy and Philosophy*. Cambridge: Cambridge University Press, 1986.
Padel, R. *In and Out of the Mind: Greek Images of the Tragic Self*. Princeton, N.J.: Princeton University Press, 1992.
———. *Whom Gods Destroy: Elements of Greek and Tragic Madness*. Princeton, N.J.: Princeton University Press, 1995.

HISTORY

Arieti, James A. *Discourses on the First Book of Herodotus*. Lanham, Md.: Littlefield Adams Books, 1995.
Boedeker, Deborah, ed. *Herodotus and the Invention of History*. *Arethusa* Special Volume 20 (1987).
Evans, J. A. S. *Herodotus*. Boston: G. K. Hall, 1982.
Flory, Stewart. *The Archaic Smile of Herodotus*. Detroit: Wayne State University Press, 1987.
Gould, John, *Herodotus*. London: Duckworth, 1989.
Lateiner, Donald. *The Historical Method of Herodotus*. Toronto: University of Toronto Press, 1989.
Romm, James. *Herodotus*. New Haven, Conn.: Yale University Press, 1998.

CHAPTER 7

Empedocles, Anaxagoras, and Democritus

I. Empedocles

In terms of longevity of influence, it would be difficult to find a philosopher whose views lasted longer or were more broadly accepted as true than those of Empedocles of Acragas (modern Agrigento), in Sicily. Where earlier philosophers had picked one substance and had based their physics on it, Empedocles cut to the quick and asserted that there were four such substances or *roots*, as he called them, that made up the universe—earth, air, fire, and water. With this system it was no longer necessary to devise an explanation of how water transformed itself into fire, for water and everything else keeps its basic nature, and our familiar world of things is made by a chemistry that combines the four roots in differing proportions. In Empedocles' system, for example, bone is an eight-unit compound formed from two parts of earth, two of water, and four of fire. In addition to these four substances, Empedocles posits two forces, *love* and *strife*, that either bind unlike things together (this is the work of love) or bind like things together (this is the work of strife). Empedocles wrote in verse, considered quite good in antiquity (it is praised by Aristotle), and he used poetic names for both substances and forces. Sometimes he refers to the four substances by the names of the gods, so that fire is either Zeus or Hephaestus, air is Hera, earth is Aidoneus, and water is Nestis. Love is sometimes Aphrodite, sometimes Harmonia; strife is sometimes Neikos, sometimes Ares. The things of the world all contain a mixture of parts, and when the balance is right, health and excellence occur.

The challenge for Empedocles, as for all the ancient thinkers, was to account for change. Parmenides and Zeno explained change by denying that it existed. The Milesians tried to show that a single substance might undergo various changes. One problem was how a substance could transform itself into another substance with contradictory qualities. How, for example, could water, which is destroyed by fire (for fire boils it away), actually *become* fire? In Empedocles' scheme, such radical transformations were not necessary, for the basic roots remain true to their bounded natures. In a sense, they preserve a kind of Parmenidean unity and oneness. It was only "kind of Parmenidean," for, according to Parmenides, there was in fact *no change* or plurality whatsoever.

Thales, Anaximenes, and Heraclitus had suggested water or air or fire as the basic substance, perhaps because they all exhibit a movement that seems to exist internally, that is, a self-motion, and so each could stand as the single principle of the world, one that contained both matter and a principle of motion—what today we call "force." Empedocles, as we have said, constructed a system with four principles of matter and two *external* principles of motion: strife and love. By these antithetical principles, the world comes into being and goes out of being. Four cyclic periods constitute the life of the universe. The first occurs when all the roots—air, fire, water, and earth—are perfectly and homogeneously mixed together by love. Thus things that are unlike (the four different roots) are brought together. During the second period, love passes out of the universe, and strife enters. While the universe is in the second period, the elements are partially combined and partially separated. After strife has entered sufficiently, in the third period, love is banished altogether, and the elements are separated completely. Thus, strife binds together things that are like (that is, by putting together the same elements), a process that results in separate accumulations of the elements. In the fourth period, love enters, and strife begins to move out, and, with the influx of love, the elements are again combined. It is not clear whether Empedocles thinks our present world in the second or fourth period, but it is certain that the first and third are impossible, for in those periods there is either too much combination or too much separation. The dynamic periods are those in which there is mixing. We might imagine a pantry with four Empedoclean ingredients. If they are totally separated, eggs in egg crates, flour in flour bags, and so on, then we have nothing particularly splendid. If, on the other hand, they are perfectly and homogeneously mixed, without the correct proportions found in cakes and breads and muffins, again we have nothing splendid. The ingredients need to be in one of the intermediate stages, where they are mixed together in the right proportions, to make splendid cakes, breads, and muffins.

Love works by taking the elements that are unlike and blending them harmoniously. In the case of bones mentioned before, harmonia mixes the two units of earth and two of water with four of fire, that is, roots that are unlike, to produce bone. Strife works by taking the units that are alike and separating them out of the mixture. For example, if we had a perfectly blended bowl of granola, with nuts, raisins, and flakes of grain all mixed

117

together, strife would remove all the nuts and put them in a separate pile and then do the same for the raisins and the flakes. In Empedocles' model the separation is of the roots themselves, so that all air, water, earth, and fire are in separate piles.

Empedocles came up with many other fascinating notions. He claimed that living things came about by chance combinations of the roots and that where the combinations did not prove conducive to life, the animals died, but where they were conducive, the animals survived.[1] He theorized that sensation involves particles flowing out from senses and landing on the openings of our senses. He followed up this theory of how we perceive light with the startling counterintuitive idea that light itself travels.[2] His mind was so resourceful that it is not perhaps entirely shocking to learn that he thought himself a deity.

Empedocles does not confront Parmenides' logic straight on, and we may observe also in his system the usual difficulties of the ancient physicists of explaining exactly how their systems worked. Despite these shortcomings, Empedocles' ideas proved fertile in the West. Their influence was nowhere stronger than in medicine, where, through Hippocrates and Aristotle, the four roots developed into the theory of the humors—that the bodily parts and their actions result from varying combinations of the four elements and that health is a harmonious balance and blending of the four humors.[3] The psychology based on humoral theory, that of the four basic temperaments—choleric (or bilious), sanguine, phlegmatic, and melancholic—can also be traced to Empedocles. Inasmuch as this was the basic theory of human psychology until the nineteenth century, the influence of Empedocles on Western culture was extensive, long, and deep.[4]

II. Anaxagoras

Anaxagoras, born in Clazomenae, a city on the eastern shore of the Aegean north of Ephesus, emigrated to Athens. His precise dates are confused in the tradition, but by the mid-450s, he was probably already mature and in Athens.[5] His writings continued to circulate for over a thousand years, as Simplicius, in the sixth century C.E., quotes him extensively, presumably from a text that he possessed.[6] No doubt Simplicius was trying to discover in the writings of Anaxagoras what caused Aristotle to refer so often to him.

Like his contemporary Empedocles, Anaxagoras speculated on a wide variety of matters, though he was interested primarily in the nature of the physical world and in astronomy. When someone asked why he had been born, he replied, "In order to study the sun, moon, and starry sky."[7]

Also like Empedocles, he tried to account for the world mindful of Parmenides' powerful arguments about being and nonbeing. Taking from Parmenides the premise that nothing can come from nothing, he accepted that there was no void, no emptiness, and that the universe was filled with matter. Concerning matter he speculated, quite contrary to the views of the monists (those who believed that there was only one principle of matter) or of Empedocles, that there are infinitely many fundamental forms, not one principle or four roots, and that these infinitely fundamental forms do not transform themselves one into another. His view may be clarified by a contrast with the contemporary understanding of stem cells: stem cells have the *potential* to develop into different bodily parts. But in Anaxagoras's scheme, all bits of matter *actually* contain everything else in them. Thus, for example, the grass that a cow grazes on *already* contains milk and hamburger as part of its structure. It also contains hair and teeth and blood as well as marble and smoke and water and all the other parts of everything in the universe. Parmenides might be partly satisfied because nothing comes into existence, for the infinite kinds of stuff, hamburger, marble, milk shakes, and papyrus already exist. Of course, since Parmenides denied the possibility of plurality, he would not have been wholly satisfied.

According to Anaxagoras, the world began with everything already present in a mixture, but, because of the infinitesimal size of all the fundamental forms, this truth was not evident.[8] Unlike the other early physicists, who could not account for how the world came to look the way it does now, Anaxagoras had an explanation. For this explanation, Anaxagoras, together with an otherwise unknown fellow citizen of Clazomenae, received high praise from Aristotle:

> When someone said that Intelligence exists in nature, as in animals, and that He is the cause of the arrangement and of every kind of order in

nature, he appeared like a sober man in contrast to his predecessors who talked erratically. We know that Anaxagoras openly made these statements, but Hermotimus of Clazomenae is credited with having made them earlier. Those who had such beliefs, then, posited as principles of things both the cause of what is noble and the moving cause.[9]

The word that Aristotle is using for *Intelligence*, *nous*, is often translated as *Mind*. For Aristotle what is "sober" about this view, in contrast to the views of the other thinkers, is that it accounts for the order and beauty of the world. The world did not arise from random mixing and separation but from a rational principle. The primordial mixture, which had been stable for an infinite time, was put into motion by Mind, and the movement caused the various things to separate.[10]

It is not clear exactly what this Mind is. It seems somehow physical, though of a very pure substance,[11] and while it is distinct from the universal mixture, it nevertheless affects it.[12] As we have noted,[13] the ancients tried to explain self-motion. It appeared to them that self-motion originates in a will and that will exists only in things that are alive. It was perhaps for this reason that the monists (those who sought a universal principle in one thing) had established things like water and air and fire as the principle of the world, for these things seem to move on their own. But, of course, the motion of fire and water and air is neither rational nor ordered, nor does it appear aimed at any purpose. It was perhaps because of the purposelessness of the prior explanations that Aristotle called these thinkers erratic. The Mind that the sober Anaxagoras claimed to be the principle of motion is unmoved by anything else and unaffected by it.[14]

The view that Mind is responsible for the order of the universe, whether original to Anaxagoras or Hermotimus, has been profoundly influential in the history of philosophy. If Plato can be believed, Socrates himself found the idea inspirational, even if he was ultimately disappointed in Anaxagoras's failure to explain just *how* Mind functioned to create the world.[15] Later, Aristotle's universe, in which everything aims at a purpose, depends on mind[16] as a moving cause, for only mind is capable of acting for a purpose. In the last days of ancient philosophy, when Boethius awaited execution in a prison cell and the allegorical figure of

Lady Philosophy consoled him, what provided the spark to restore Boethius to philosophical equanimity was his belief that the world is ruled by Mind. And it is the idea that Mind brought about the universe that lies at the heart of the argument from design, perhaps the most ubiquitous argument for the existence of God.

Some of Anaxagoras's other views are worthy of note. Plato credits Anaxagoras with believing that the moon receives its light from the sun, though he adds that Anaxagoras derived this view from earlier sources.[17] Anaxagoras thought that the moon was made of the same substance as the earth and that it possessed hills and valleys.[18] He thought that the sun was many times larger than the Peloponnese[19] and, notoriously, that the sun was a rock.[20] Aristotle attributes to Anaxagoras the view that it is because of hands that humans are the most intelligent animal. Aristotle disagrees, arguing instead that it is because of their intelligence that humans have hands. Aristotle's discussion is quite splendid in itself and, in addition, gives insight into how both Anaxagoras and Aristotle saw Mind work:

> Now it is the opinion of Anaxagoras that the possession of these hands is the cause of man being of all animals the most intelligent. But it is more rational to suppose that man has hands because of his superior intelligence. For the hands are instruments, and the invariable plan of nature in distributing the organs is to give each to such animal as can make use of it, nature acting in this matter as any prudent man would do. For it is a better plan to take a person who is already a flute-player and give him a flute, than to take one who possesses a flute and teach him the art of flute-playing. For nature adds that which is less to that which is greater and more important, and not that which is more valuable and greater to that which is less. Seeing then that such is the better course, and seeing also that of what is possible, nature invariably brings about the best, we must conclude that man does not owe his superior intelligence to his hands, but his hands to his superior intelligence. For the most intelligent of animals is the one who would put the most organs to good use; and the hand is not to be looked on as one organ but as many; for it is, as it were, an instrument for further instruments. This instrument, therefore—the hand—of all instruments the most variously serviceable, has been given by nature to man, the animal of all animals the most capable of acquiring the most varied arts.[21]

121

Anaxagoras is said to have been the friend and teacher of Pericles, the Athenian leader during the zenith of the Athenian Empire. Diogenes Laertius, in the first half of the third century C.E., reports that Cleon, Pericles' rival, brought a charge of impiety against Anaxagoras for having described the sun as a red-hot rock and though Pericles himself defended him at trial, he was nevertheless fined and banished. Diogenes reports several accounts of the trial, and, alas, it is impossible to know which, if any, is true. That a variety of stories was circulating more than six hundred years after the death of Anaxagoras attests, however, to his fame and the abiding interest in his fortunes.

III. Democritus

The glory of originating the idea that there are indivisible atoms of matter has traditionally been given to both Leucippus (fl. 425 B.C.E.) and Democritus (born c. 460–457 B.C.E.). Although the original insight might well belong to Leucippus, our ancient sources do not clearly distinguish what was properly Leucippus's and what Democritus's. Because Democritus is generally recognized to have developed the insight into a complete theory with implications for physics, ethics, biology, epistemology, and politics, here the name Democritus will refer to the entangled Leucippus–Democritus composite.

Democritus offered yet a different solution to Parmenides' denial of plurality and motion. One of the logical consequences of Parmenides' idea that nonbeing cannot exist is that there cannot be any empty space. Empty space or emptiness, of course, would be nothing, and, as Parmenides observed, nothing cannot be. If, however, the universe is completely full—if it is what is called a *plenum* (from the Latin word *plenus* for *full*)—then there can be no motion. The world would be like a 1950s telephone booth crowded with playful teenagers, so packed that no one could move in any direction. As a solution to this conundrum, Democritus proposed that in addition to matter there exists what he called *void*, sometimes alternatively translated as *vacuity* or *empty space*. The void allows for plurality by separating the bits of matter and allows for motion by giving matter space in which to move. In declaring the void one of the fundamental principles of nature, any possible Parmenidean objections are simply ignored.

In Democritus's universe the bits of matter separated by void are called *atoms*, tiny, indivisible units, themselves unchanging and eternal—miniature Parmenidean spheres, as it were. The Greek word *atom* means *un-split*. Atoms, constantly in motion through the void, make up all the different visible objects by their different combinations, just as different structures may be made out of different combinations of identical Lego blocks. Also like Lego blocks, the atoms differ in shape and size. *Everything* is constructed out of these atoms—mountains, rivers, bodies, souls, even gods. Visual and auditory images are made of atoms too. Finally, according to Democritus, atoms are infinite in number.

How, we might wonder, did Democritus come up with the theory of atoms? Because he could not see atoms directly, they were an intellectual model, devised by genius alone, that resulted from various thought experiments and from attempts to make sense of such observed phenomena as plurality and motion. Because matter is divisible into smaller and smaller pieces, one might think that the process of division could in principle go on forever. Perhaps because as far as we can see every bit of matter is capable of being divided, the indivisible units of matter must be invisibly small. In any case, Democritus assumed that there must be an end to smallness, an absolute smallness that defines the units of matter. As with the existence of a void, he established this absolute smallness as a premise. The existence of all sorts of invisible things, such as wind, smells, and sounds, lent credibility to the idea that there are also invisibly small, indivisible units of matter.

Aristotle objected to the Democritean scheme on two grounds. First, he said that any single piece of matter, no matter how small, *is* able to be divided, at least potentially. Second, he said that there cannot be an infinite number of atoms, for such an actual infinity is impossible. Thus, Aristotle's distinction between potential infinity and actual infinity was employed to criticize atomism.[22]

Democritus introduced atoms to avoid the repugnant notion of infinite divisibility. He introduced the notion of the void to elude Parmenides' equally repugnant argument against motion. Whereas Parmenides argued that, because nonbeing cannot be, motion is impossible, Democritus argued the reverse: because motion is observed all the time and is therefore possible, there *must* be a sort of nonbeing—void—that makes motion possible. He cut the Gordian knot of Parmenides' problem not by denying that motion requires nonbeing but by refusing to deny the existence of motion and by therefore accepting the "being" of the void. One might perhaps compare Democritus to Samuel Johnson discussing Bishop Berkeley's proof of the nonexistence of matter. Describing the moment, James Boswell writes, "I observed, that though we are satisfied that his doctrine is not true, it is impossible to refute it. I shall never forget the alacrity with which Johnson answered, striking his foot with mighty force against a large stone, till he rebounded from it, 'I refute it thus.'"[23]

Democritus also had to account for how atoms actually combine into things rather than collect in a pile at the bottom of the universe. His proposal was that the constant motion of atoms enables them to fulfill their function. Both their absolute motion in the universe and their motion relative to one another account for the coming into being and going out of being of everything. Nothing is created or destroyed; atoms are simply rearranged. Furthermore, the rearrangement is, ultimately, random. This universe, with its particular arrangements of atoms, did not have to come to be as it is; all its atomic configurations originate by chance. For all we know, there may be many other worlds, with many other configurations of atoms.[24]

As to the question of where the motion of atoms originates, Democritus again avoided the issue entirely by taking eternal motion as a given. With regard to the question of why atoms collide rather than fall straight down, a later atomist, Epicurus, asserted that occasionally atoms swerve on their own and so, instead of falling in parallel descents, collide and thereby combine. The swerve also accounts for the appearance of what seems to be free will.[25] This solution, of course, begs the question, for it does not explain how the swerve itself comes to be. Hence, the sober Cicero rightly rejected the notion of the swerve as an arbitrary contrivance.[26]

Although the physical system of Democritus constitutes an ingenious proposal that embraces a nonteleological explanation of causes, it does not explain the source of motion or of atoms (other than by stipulating that they have no source), does not satisfactorily account for how atoms collide, and does not provide a philosophically satisfying explanation of how nonbeing in the guise of the void can exist. In short, it addresses specific problems in Parmenides in a groundbreaking but explanatorily incomplete manner.

The Democritean view seems to reduce the universe to purposelessness and meaninglessness, despite the existence of gods, which are, like everything else, made of atoms. After all, if atoms can combine to create men, then atoms can combine to create gods.[27] The gods of the atomists are bright, beautiful, radiant creatures who inhabit the interstellar spaces, lead lives of transcendent happiness, and never give the slightest thought to men. Given the gods' lack of concern for human beings, no atomist would ever dream of praying to the gods. He might, of course, try to imitate them, for they embody the Democritean ethical ideal of cheerfulness. If the universe is meaningless and purposeless, one might as well try to be cheerful.

What is cheerfulness for an atomist? The atomist must first understand how the physical system works. Once he understands the theory of atoms and the void, he can see that the universe is meaningless and that certain ethical consequences follow. For one thing, attempting to do anything that has meaning is meaningless. There is no sense, as Epicurus later argued, in engaging in what we today call "meaningful activity," in aiming for a career, for fame, for wealth, for power, for success. "Stay out of community activities," the atomists advise. For an atomist, citizens who fight for their country or who participate in political affairs are foolish. The moment they become involved, the moment they care about an issue—any issue—they have sacrificed their happiness. In the face of these seemingly grim considerations, cheerfulness is achieved in the liberating realization that meaning need not be actively pursued and that death need not be feared because it is simply the re-forming of atoms into other objects with no afterlife full of horrible punishments.

125

IV. Summing Up the Early Philosophers

Although these few chapters have not by any means given a complete account of the early philosophers and their various theories, it is possible, perhaps, to draw some general conclusions about their approach to philosophy. Working with only their minds and the evidence of their unaided senses, the early philosophers from Miletus and elsewhere in the Greek world tried to comprehend the material and dynamic forces of the cosmos.

In doing so they anticipated many of the questions that continue to puzzle scientists: Are the underlying principles one or few or many? Does change take place by an alteration of accidental qualities such as color and shape, or do the fundamental principles themselves undergo essential metamorphoses? Is there in physical reality a particle so small and unitary that it cannot be divided? How is motion possible, and what are its limits? These thinkers shared with one another, and with modern physicists, the view that because the universe is intelligible and orderly, its wonders might yield to human intelligence. For the atomists, to be sure, all structures are the result of chance collisions, but this very fact about chance is able to be known—and in this sense even chance succumbs to human reason.

Despite its genius, this early philosophy was fundamentally flawed. The major theories were largely independent guesses at the principles of nature. If a part of one theory turned out to be clearly unsatisfactory, a later thinker would come along with a new theory that would substitute for the unsatisfactory element a new principle designed to resolve the difficulty. But there was no experimentation whatsoever, no steady refinement or progress in the course of knowledge. The theories stand with the names of their authors like works of sculpture in a museum, with no sense of approaching closer and closer to the truth. Perhaps because the thinkers did not have much of a scientific vocabulary at their disposal, they relied too heavily on easily misleading metaphor to stretch their meaning.

For the most part, the writings did not survive long as works worth copying. What we possess remains because it was included in summaries by later thinkers, such as Aristotle or his commentators, who present only a partial précis of what the early philosophers said. These summaries are often neither accurate nor fair but are shaped so as to render more acceptable the summarizers' own views. Thus, in most cases, the full original meaning has been lost. Still, to ask questions, to frame inquiries, to wonder about nature as the early philosophers did is one of the great achievements of the human race. When Thales speculated that the fundamental principle of nature is water, he initiated a process of mental activity that would change human life on our planet. His insight that a human mind can explore the secrets of nature because those secrets are at bottom intelligible was a fruitful seed that multiplied, first in Miletus and then in the rest of the Hellenic world, wherever it found fertile minds.

Discussion Questions

1. Empedocles' theory seemed so intuitively right that for two millennia it was accepted as true, and it allowed for corollary theories that explained health and psychology. It what ways was Empedocles' theory of matter clearly superior to the theories of his predecessors? Imagine that you were a parent in antiquity trying to explain the physics of nature to one of your inquisitive children. How would you present this theory?

2. Look at Aristotle's discussion and rejection of Empedocles' theory that light travels (The sources are cited in footnote 2 of this chapter). How fairly do you think Aristotle presents the theory? (You will have to make this determination solely on the basis of internal evidence, for Aristotle is our only source for Empedocles on this point.) How well does Aristotle refute Empedocles' theory? Why does Aristotle take the idea seriously enough to mention it so often?

3. While much of what Anaxagoras thought passed quickly from the scene, his idea that Mind is somehow responsible for order in nature was central to Western science until the Darwinian revolution took hold. What are the shortcomings of Anaxagoras's theory? How would you have challenged Anaxagoras if you had heard him?

4. How do the ideas that the moon is made of the same substance as the earth and that it possesses hills and valleys or that the sun is a rock square with Anaxagoras's idea of Mind?

5. Perhaps we who live in the twenty-first century favor the thought of Democritus over that of other ancients, for it most seems to resemble contemporary theories of physics. But Democritus's theory had less influence on Western civilization than many of the competing theories. What are the features of ancient atomism that rendered it implausible, even when it was introduced? Was there any way that Democritus could have repaired the deficiencies of atomism, or were both its strengths and its weaknesses inherent parts of his system?

6. Does the fact that Democritus devised his theory of atoms solely by the application of his logic render it less credible? Is there a similar problem with the theories of modern physics? To what degree is there *direct* evidence for quarks, electron spin, and the Big Bang? To what degree is secondary (or tertiary) evidence reliable? Exactly what is the difference between direct and indirect evidence?

7. Are Aristotle's criticisms of atomic theory persuasive? How would those criticisms apply to the contemporary model of the atom?

8. Should the science of how to live well, the branch of philosophy we call *ethics*, be based on physics? Does a theory of how to live ethically depend on what the world is made of? Can you think of any kind of physics that would lead as a logical consequence to what most people would reckon as unethical behavior (for example, blatant selfishness, injustice, or lying)?

9. As you look over the range of early philosophical thought, would you want contemporary scientists to have included some investigation of it in their education? Would there have been some gain in such study, either for general intellectual growth or for their scientific careers, or would it have been simply a waste of time?

Notes

1. This remarkable claim seems to have anticipated Darwin's theory of natural selection.

2. Aristotle, who is the source of our knowledge of Empedocles on this point, disagrees quite strongly with the notion. See Aristotle, *On Generation and Destruction* 324b26–35; *On the Soul* 418b21–27; *On Sensation and Sense Objects* 437b26–438a5 and 446a27–447a11.

3. An excess of one of the humors results in *dyscrasia*, an unhealthy mixture.

4. The theory underlay the psychological assumptions of most writers, including Shakespeare and Molière, just as the theories of Freud underlay much twentieth-century literature.

5. The source of the confusion is the account in Diogenes Laertius, who puts his birth in the Seventieth Olympiad (500–497), but says that he began to study in Athens at age twenty, during the archonship of Callias. But since Callias was archon in 456, the dating is impossible as reported. Someone named Calliades, however, was archon in 480, and an assumption of a confusion of names might easily resolve the difficulty.

6. Simplicius (fl. 532 C.E.) was one of the last philosophers of the ancient world. He was teaching in Athens when, in 529, his school of philosophy was closed and the teaching of philosophy prohibited. If it were not for the commentaries that he wrote on various works of Aristotle, in which he quotes the ancient thinkers, much of what we now possess would have been lost.

7. Diogenes Laertius, *Life of Anaxagoras* 2.10.

8. Anaxagoras, frag. 1.

9. Aristotle, *Metaphysics* 984 b15–22.

10. Anaxagoras, fragment 13 and Aristotle, *Physics* 250b24.

11. Anaxagoras, fragment 12.

12. Anaxagoras, fragment 14.

13. See pp. 45–46.

14. Aristotle, *Physics*, 256b24.

15. Plato, *Phaedo* 97c ff. Perhaps Plato's *Timaeus* is an attempt to supply the explanation of how Mind brought about the universe.

16. When *mind* begins with a lowercase *m*, it refers to a rational principle. When it begins with an uppercase *M*, it refers to a divine intelligence. The distinction of when *mind* is a deity and when it is a principle of nature is not always clear among the ancients. Perhaps the confusion in this text reflects the fuzziness of the ancients themselves.

17. Plato, *Cratylus* 409a.

18. Hippolytus, *Refutatio* 1.6.

19. Hippolytus, *Refutatio* 1.8.

20. Plato, *Apology* 26d.

21. Aristotle, *Parts of Animals* 687 a7–23, trans. W. Ogle, in *The Complete Works of Aristotle: The Revised Oxford Translation*, ed. J. Barnes (Princeton, N.J.: Princeton University Press, 1984).

22. For more on what Aristotle means by his important doctrine of the impossibility of an actual infinity and for its place in Aristotle's philosophy, see chapter 11, pp. 199, 204, and 209.

23. Boswell, *Life of Johnson* 1.545.

24. This particular view is attributed by Diogenes Laertius to Leucippus, *Life of Leucippus* 9.31.

25. See p. 250.

26. Cicero, *de Finibus* 6.19, *de Fato* 22.46–48.

27. Democritus, frag. 166.

Select Bibliography

For a general bibliography on the Presocratics, see the bibliography in chapter 2.

EMPEDOCLES

Inwood, B. *The Poem of Empedocles: A Text and Translation with an Introduction*. 2nd ed. Toronto: University of Toronto Press, 2001.

Kahn, Charles. "Religion and Natural Philosophy in Empedocles—Doctrine of the Soul." In *The Pre-Socratics: Critical Essays*, ed. Alexander P. D. Mourelatos. Garden City, N.Y.: Anchor Press, 1974.

ANAXAGORAS

Kerferd, G. B. "Anaxagoras and the Concept of Matter before Aristotle." In *The Pre-Socratics: Critical Essays*, ed. Alexander P. D. Mourelatos. Garden City, N.Y.: Anchor Press, 1974.

DEMOCRITUS

Taylor, C. C. W. *The Atomists: Leucippus and Democritus. Fragments: A Text and Translation with Commentary*. Toronto: University of Toronto Press, 1999.

Vlastos, Gregory. "Ethics and Physics in Democritus." *Philosophical Review* 54 (1945): 578–92; 55 (1946): 53–64.

The Peloponnesian War:
Socrates, Thucydides, Euripides

I. Socrates

Very little—alas—is known about some of the most inspirational figures who have ever lived. What seems most certain about Socrates is that he lived to age seventy, that he was executed by the Athenians in 399, and that he was disdained by some and virtually worshipped by others. He is said to have been a stonecutter, and six and a half centuries after his death, Pausanias (fl. 150 C.E.) reports having actually seen a statue of Hermes that Socrates sculpted.[1] Socrates is said to have been married to a wife who complained that he was too often in the marketplace arguing with his talking companions.[2] A great many stories from many sources have survived, but each of the stories is contaminated—its veracity perhaps fatally distorted—by the particular motive of the storyteller. Even the famous bust that has given us a way to picture Socrates was not chiseled from life but portrays what the sculptor imagined Socrates to have looked like.[3] In the myths of European cities, the founders were named as individuals who had participated in the Trojan War. Thus Rome was founded by Aeneas, Britain by a great grandson of Aeneas, and the area between the Danube and the Rhine by a party of exiled Trojans. In a similar way, it was customary, in establishing a school of philosophy, to trace its spiritual founder to one of Socrates' pupils. Thus the Academy traced its founding to Plato, the school of the Cynics to Antisthenes,[4] and the school of the Cyrenaics to Aristippus.[5]

Because Plato's large corpus survived and because the dialogues are quite beautiful and stimulating and because Plato presents Socrates as the main character in a variety of lovely settings and because—despite the fact that Plato's Socrates sometimes says inconsistent things—the portrait shows a consistent *personality*, Plato's portrayal of Socrates has seared the Western consciousness. For the history of philosophy, it does not matter that Plato's dialogues are almost certainly fictions, that they present chronological impossibilities for the sake of setting scenes where Socrates might converse with prominent people, and that Socrates himself probably would not have recognized his own portrayal. Diogenes Laertius tells this story:

They say that, on hearing Plato read the *Lysis*, Socrates exclaimed, "By Heracles, what a number of lies this young man is telling about me!" For he has included in the dialogue much that Socrates never said.[6]

The anecdote itself may be making an ironic point, for the dialogue *Lysis* deals with friendship, and whoever originated the anecdote might have

Figure 14. Socrates
The longest verbal description of a philosopher occurs in Plato's *Theaetetus* (143e), where Socrates' friend Theodorus compares Theaetetus to Socrates thus:

> If [Theaetetus] were handsome, I would be afraid to use excessive language, lest I seem to be in a frenzy for him. But now, and do not be annoyed with me, he is not handsome, but he resembles you in your snubness and in your protruding eyes. But he has these [features] less than you. Indeed, I speak fearlessly.

This statue of Socrates was sculpted about a half century after Socrates' death and was probably based on the description in Plato. In short, it is essentially impossible to form a verifiable picture of what ancient philosophers looked like on the basis of portrait-sculpture. Classical literature, like biblical literature, does not in general provide verbal descriptions of characters, and depictions in art derive from the imaginations of the artists.

intended to imply that the friendship between Plato and Socrates was not so warm as Plato presented it.

The attempt to find "the historical Socrates," like the attempts to find the historical Jesus or the historical Moses or the historical Pythagoras, is hopeless. And it is unnecessary. The Socrates that has affected the West is the Socrates that Plato bequeathed to us. What Xenophon writes in his *Memorabilia*, *Symposium*, and *Apology* or Aristophanes in the *Clouds* or Aeschines in the fragments of his *Alcibiades* are useful to scholars who gladly wander into the maze of finding the real Socrates.[7] They are working on what is called "the Socratic problem." But, for most people, Plato's picture has won the day.[8]

Plato shows Socrates in pursuit of definitions. In times of turmoil, words tend to change their meanings, and a certain fuzziness, both intentional and accidental, infects normal idiom.[9] During the tumultuous years in which Socrates lived, the concepts of defining words and of drawing fine distinctions were developing. Aristotle credits Socrates with creating inductive arguments and with defining things universally.[10] Plato, and Xenophon,[11] too, portrays Socrates arguing with others about the meaning of such words as *justice*, *love*, *friendship*, *virtue*, *courage*, and *piety*, and these portrayals are among the most accessible and stimulating of the dialogues. Everyone, after all, thinks he knows the meaning of these simple words, and yet only a few questions expose the complex difficulties of finding definitions that at once capture the way the words are used, cover their connotations, and lack self-contradiction.

It must have been amusing for young men to stand around watching Socrates argue with people who, though supremely confident of their knowledge, were quickly deflated by a few simple questions.[12] Indeed, over and over again in the dialogues we see people who affirm a proposition with great heat and certitude but after a few Socratic questions abandon their original position altogether. Socrates' method of arguing, which produced this effect, amusing to spectators but exceedingly painful for its victims, is known as Socratic dialectic. Plato's dialogues suggest that the use of this method was one of the reasons Socrates was executed. The method engendered suspicion, for interlocutors—the persons participating in the dialogue with Socrates—often felt frustrated. They were convinced that some kind of verbal trick or sophistry was being practiced on them, but they could not put their finger on how.

Successful dialectic rests on the following assumptions: 1) that truth exists; 2) that truth is the reasoned agreement of two human beings following the rules of reason; 3) that inconsistency, that is, contradiction, is the surest sign available that the conclusion reached is not true, that is, is false; and 4) that both people must be willing to "stay at their posts" and argue until consistency is reached. Of these points, the one that generated the greatest suspicion in most of Socrates' interlocutors is the importance placed on consistency. Such suspicion takes two forms: 1) consistency can be narrow-minded and rigorous and hence impractical, and 2) too often it degenerates into mere pedantry, into hairsplitting and quibbling about words, a kind of philosophic legalism.[13]

Coupled with this suspicion is one about the very method of inquiry—the technique of question and answer. Most people feel that they are being manipulated by the questioner and driven into saying things that they do not believe or, perhaps even worse, into having some minor inconsistency in their position exposed. Although most people are unwilling to believe that a "minor" inconsistency invalidates their views, for a dialectician truth allows no inconsistency at all.[14]

The source for much of the Western world's portrait of Socrates is Plato's *Apology*, Plato's version of the defense speech that Socrates delivered to the Athenian court that found him guilty and condemned him to death. Plato's is not the only version that survives from antiquity, but its beauty and power have canonized it as the standard.[15] In Plato's canonical portrait,[16] when Socrates learns from a friend that the oracle at Delphi has declared no one wiser than Socrates, he reacts with perplexity, for, on the one hand, he does not feel that he is wise, while, on the other, he does not believe the oracle can tell a lie.[17] His way out of his dilemma is to test the oracle by means of questioning those with a reputation for wisdom in order to determine whether they are wiser than he. What he learns is that while those he questions do not actually know anything beyond their area of narrow expertise, they *think* they do. Socrates, however, *knows* that he does not know anything, and in virtue of this knowledge he is wiser than they. This questioning has irritated his fellow citizens, he adds, as a gadfly might irritate a sleeping horse, but in stirring them to examine their actions to avoid wrongdoing, he is doing the god's work. He has kept out of politics because a voice, his *daimon*, which speaks to him only to warn him against certain actions and which only he can hear, has advised him to avoid politics. When at a critical moment toward the end of the Peloponnesian Wars Socrates was asked by the Council of Thirty Tyrants to bring an admiral to trial, at great risk to his life he refused to carry out the unjust order. Refusing at his trial to influence the jurors by appeals to pity, he was narrowly convicted. Then, during the penalty phase, he flippantly suggested that he be "punished" with free meals for life, and the jurors responded by condemning him to death by a margin larger than that which convicted him.

To readers of Plato's *Apology*, Socrates emerges as a martyr to goodness, preferring death to wrongdoing, and readers shake their heads at the folly of the Athenians who committed the injustice of condemning him. Through Plato, Socrates became the model for subsequent heroes of philosophy, brave thinkers who were wrongly punished by ignorant and tyrannical sovereign powers. In this way the memory of Socrates has provided a noble comforting model to those who risked their lives and fortunes for an intellectual or moral cause.

For all readers, the most inspiring quality of the Socrates represented in the dialogues is the enactment of his courage to pursue truth no matter the cost. What gives meaning to his life is his decision to die rather than to abandon his post as philosopher of Athens. If he had accepted banishment, like Protagoras or Anaxagoras or, later, like Aristotle, who declined to "allow Athens to sin twice against philosophy,"[18] he would not serve as the exemplar of the philosophic man, the man who values truth and justice above everything else. Plato portrays Socrates throughout the dialogues as willing to stand up to bullies like Thrasymachus and Callicles and Meno, who praise the tyrannical life over the virtuous life and threaten Socrates personally. Nor is he intimidated by such famous intellects as Protagoras, Parmenides, Gorgias, and Aristophanes, but he more than holds his own with them.[19]

Socrates' most heroic moments came at the end of his life. On trial on the charges of corrupting the youth of Athens and of not believing in the gods of the city but of making up new gods, he defended his way of life, as we have seen, proclaiming that his life spent in argument with his fellow citizens made them better and stirred them to virtue. He refused to appeal to the jury's emotions in order to gain an acquittal,[20] and, after he was condemned and had the opportunity to propose a suitable penalty, he contemptuously proposed that he receive free meals for life, declaring that justice required he be rewarded for his services. When he was in prison awaiting execution and a friend tried to persuade him to flee, Socrates insisted on working through the arguments, believing that one should determine his actions on the basis of the best argument and the best argument alone. Despite the stress of imminent execution, Socrates did not say, "I'll escape and look for a better argument another time." Instead, he decided on the basis of the best argument he had at the moment when the decision had to be made, and, in the drama of the dialogue, he chose to stay and die. Finally, on his last day he was visited by a number of friends and argued with them about whether the soul survives death. Here too he willingly took on the arguments and did not let any vexing ones slip by. By the end of the dialogue it was clear that none of the arguments was conclusive and that Socrates would die not knowing whether the soul survives death but *knowing that he did not know.* The drama beautifully shows that because he knew that he did not know, he was able to be courageous in facing death. If he had learned conclusively that the soul happily survived death, no courage would have been necessary, for he would have *known,* but courage, it seems, depends on knowing that one does not know an outcome and requires staying at one's post when the risk is worthwhile. The willingness to persist in argument, not knowing whether a conclusion will be found, is Socrates' inspiring example of philosophic courage.

137

Perhaps it is safe to conclude that in life Socrates was a polarizing figure. Athenians must have been sufficiently annoyed with him or with his political allies such as to execute him. At the same time, whether or not Plato's picture of Socrates is true, even in part, the real Socrates was inspirational to many who knew him. And he has continued to be a source of inspiration throughout Western history. Dante placed him among the virtuous pagans; Erasmus invoked him in his prayers, saying, "Holy Socrates, pray for us." And for those who begin their study of philosophy with a Platonic dialogue, he continues to inspire.

II. Thucydides

The Persian Wars ended in 479 B.C.E.; they had lasted for about twenty years. Although twenty years sounds like a long war, the actual fighting took place in just a few years and, in fact, in just a few days. Most of that time was spent in elaborate preparations and expeditions. After the war, for the next fifty years, the history of Greece was, in effect, the history of Athens. A lesser power when the Persian Wars started, Athens displayed such heroism and virtue in the war, especially in the sea-battles, that she came out of the war joining Sparta as what we would call "one of the two great superpowers." Almost from the day that peace with Sparta came, Athens and Sparta were engaged in "a cold war"—again to use a modern expression. That cold war was broken intermittently by confrontations and even by battles; but the actual hot war did not begin until fifty years later, in 430. That war—known as the Peloponnesian War—is the subject of the book written by Thucydides.

The rise of Athens, her growing power, was—according to Thucydides—the cause of the war, for the growing power of Athens produced fear in Sparta and compelled her to go to war. There seems to be a rule of the human psyche that anything that grows up too big too fast produces fear. The bigger the transformation, people feel, the slower the change ought to be. Earthquakes are a simple example: we do not mind a canyon's being created by the slow attrition produced by water, but a violent convulsion of the earth produces fear.

Such is what happened to Athens in relationship to the other Greek city-states after the Persian Wars. Athens became powerful, seemingly overnight. In consequence, she was afforded the leadership of a group. That group was originally formed as a protective league against further invasions by Persia. It was called the Delian League and was located on neutral ground, the island of Delos, sacred to Apollo. It was the job of each member of the league to contribute ships to a common navy; but each member also had the right to contribute money to a common treasury, out of which ships could be purchased. As one might expect, many city-states preferred paying money to working, and so the treasury was built up.

Athens, as the leader, was primarily in charge of expenditures. And, as it is a universal rule that he who pays the piper calls the dances, so Athens, willy-nilly, found her power increasing. As the bureaucratic administration of the treasury became more and more to depend on Athens, Athens found it more and more convenient to have the treasury located at Athens. One day the other members of the league woke up to find that the transfer had been made. And the Athenian Empire was a going concern.

Figure 15.   Acropolis of Athens
With amazing prescience, Thucydides wrote (*History of the Peloponnesian War* 1.10): "If Sparta were to become desolate, and only the temples and foundations of public buildings were left, as time went on, there would be a strong disposition with posterity to refuse to accept her fame as a true exponent of her power. . . . Whereas if Athens were to suffer the same misfortune . . . any inference from the appearance presented to the eye would make her power to have been twice as great as it is." The Acropolis of Athens, reconstructed after the Persian Wars under the leadership of Pericles, shows the political power of Athens as prominently as her aesthetic judgment. The funds for the project were extracted from Athens' onetime allies who had been forcibly converted into subject states.

In this brief sketch—crude and not fair in its details—lie a number of philosophical questions. Did the leadership of Athens grow up out of her will, her choice? Was it thrust upon her? Or was it some combination of both? Perhaps most of us would answer that it was some combination of both. But in giving such a fair and thoughtful answer, we—like Thucydides—let loose into the world an idea that still comes back to haunt us—the notion that there are "forces" or "causes" in the sense of powers either different from human powers or human powers only when taken collectively and not individually.

Thucydides, the author of *The History of the Peloponnesian War*, who is locating the cause—the thing responsible (the *aitia*)—of the war in fear, writes in a genre that he intends to be factual, not fictional. Because historical facts do not of themselves fall into a pretty pattern that can be grasped and remembered, we find it less interesting to read Thucydides than storytellers like Homer or Sophocles. Thucydides is full of facts, and his "theory"—if he has one—is not easy to discern. Also, he stubbornly refuses to give us a theory. He is unlike historians such as Arnold Toynbee or Jonathan Edwards or the Marxists. He is more like a Bacon than a Descartes; he submits himself to his data and tries to record and observe them. To this extent he fully deserves the name given him as the first scientific historian.

Thucydides' Greek is very hard, and some have called it obscure. Cicero describes the style as "stately in the choice of words, rich in thought, from comprehension of matter brief, and for this reason sometimes obscure."[21] This hardness is not just accidental, a trait of Thucydides' personality; it comes about in large part because he was wrestling with new ideas for which his language was not yet prepared. Or, to put it more precisely, he was trying to use a language rich in supernatural and irrational terminology to explain phenomena that he thought could and should be explained in natural and rational terminology.

In the opening chapters of his book, Thucydides observes the distinction between the real and apparent causes of history, a distinction so profound that we now take it for granted. To see the distinction is to be theoretical; and Thucydides is not incapable of theory. But he has no explicit theory of human nature—except to assume that it will not change. Unlike the Marxists, who find economic motives for every action, or behavioral psychologists, who find painful or pleasant stimuli, he has no explicit formula for human motivation. For Thucydides, human beings are not merely symptoms of historical forces. Instead, human beings are themselves "forces." As a result, Thucydides fills his book with characters who make speeches as well as do deeds. They exemplify the Homeric and ancient ideal of human excellence: to be speakers of words and doers of deeds—what Peleus taught his son Achilles.[22] Figures in Thucydides' history—Pericles, Cleon, Brasidas, Nicias, and Alcibiades—loom as real and active agents, with full dramatic vividness. Yet, clearly, Thucydides is no Carlyle, a devotee of the belief that human beings and human beings alone shape history. There is no formula for Thucydides. Perhaps one sign of artistic greatness is its resemblance to life, that the world the artist creates is greater than any theory offered to explain it, just as it is true that the world we live in defies formulaic explanation.

Some have tried to convert Thucydides into art—to explain his history as tragedy. The attempt is often quite successful, and it is not difficult to imagine Athens as a tragic hero of history. Like Oedipus, Athens is of high and prosperous position, is not eminent in goodness though clearly possessing great virtue, and falls into disaster because of some mistake, some error in judgment. Athens has the external appearance of a tragic hero; all we need to do in order to fulfill the criteria is to find out what her *error* is, where her fatal error in judgment (her *hamartia*) lies. Tragedy looks for the laws that govern human nature when it acts individually or typically, for a tragic hero is a type of mankind. Hence Aristotle can say that poetry is more philosophic than history because history deals with what a particular man did, while poetry deals with what a particular type of man did.[23]

Yet there are great similarities between poetry and history. As Quintilian says, history is the closest thing to poetry.[24] In our own day we have seen repeated attempts to combine the two, as in the historical novel and the fictionalized biography. Only when we convert history into tragedy, only when we see Athens not as an abstract entity or a force but as a character, a heroic culture, do we elevate history into the universality of art. It is Thucydides' great art that, without ever using the supernatural or the merely aesthetic, he enables us to see Athens as a tragic hero at the same time that we are always firmly sure that what we are reading is history and not fictionalized fact.

At the end of the section called "Archaeology," Thucydides writes that his book is designed as a possession for all time.[25] His book will be valuable, he avers, as long as human nature remains the same. Underlying this claim is a notion of the static nature of human affairs, a notion very different from our modern idea of "development" or "growth" or "progress," words that generally carry positive connotations. In the history of Thucydides, there is no notion of development in a positive sense. There is, however, one area in modern usage where words like *growth*, *development*, and even *progress* can be used without any positive sense—the field of medicine. Doctors can speak of cancers as *developing* and use tones customarily reserved for objects and utility. A word like *tumor*, which strikes terror into the ears of most of us, can be, to a doctor, benign as well as malignant. If we wish to talk of *development* in Thucydides, we must see it as medical. Such is the burden of Charles Norris Cochrane's very fine book *Thucydides and the Science of History*.[26]

The great plague that strikes Athens occurs early in Thucydides' description of the war. Cooped up in the city because of Pericles' eminently sane policy, the city falls sick. This paradox was clear to Thucydides, who devotes some of his most vivid and dramatic passages to the plague. He describes its symptoms in detail and recounts the responses of the populace in stark and dramatic terms. The plague is both a symptom and a symbol of Thucydides' method of treating history. For what happens to Athens and to Sparta is like a disease, which runs a describable course, with a development consisting of a rise and a fall, and which, in this respect, resembles a tragedy.

The Greeks established the pattern of future historians; that is, they made history deal not with what human beings as human beings do but with what states or nations or tribes do—human beings as groups rather than as individuals. The actions that affect the largest numbers of people or that affect the individuals who in turn affect the largest numbers of people and affect them most severely are the most historical. Thus, as said earlier,[27] wars dominate historical attention.

So Thucydides is interested in the laws that govern human beings when they act collectively. He does not, of course, see human beings as the victims of forces, economic or psychological or social. For him, to repeat, human beings themselves are forces. It has, perhaps, remained for our own day to "dehumanize the history of humanity"—to use Cochrane's vivid phrase[28]—by seeing humanity as a response, not as a stimulus; as a sufferer, not as a doer; as a victim, not as an agent. According to this prevailing contemporary view, humans are a product—something produced, something passive—a result of the two forces that we sum up in the words *heredity* and *environment*. Underlying most of our views on this difficult subject is a picture of what the medievalists called *natura naturata* rather than *natura naturans*, of nature as a *product* rather than nature as a *power*. It is no accident that a favorite analogy of physics is a set of billiard balls, purely passive things. When we think that the word *physics* comes from the Greek word meaning *nature*, whose root means *to grow*, we can see how bald and bare our world has become.[29]

For Thucydides, Cochrane says, *nature*, as applied to man, "included the whole environment which creates him and which he helps to create."[30] Man's will is a subdivision of nature and manifests itself both as a product and as a power. Like nature, human nature is subject to scrutiny, observation, interpretation, and formulation—perhaps not so precise as that of science but still useful and usable. Medicine is not so exact as physics, but it is still good to have. So, too, history, which for Thucydides consisted of using techniques of medical analysis on society. Human nature manifests itself in actions, not in states or conditions; hence it has progress, development, retrogression, and evolution downward and upward. The job of the historian is to trace this movement, this process, in groups of men.

In the story of Athens, its rise and fall, Thucydides perhaps had a perfect symptom and symbol of social growth. Other states have been larger, but in their very largeness lurked a complexity that defies analysis—such as the causes of the downfall of Egyptian civilization. But in Athens Thucydides had a specimen like that which a scientist puts under a microscope. Unlike those scientists who, to see a very small object, must use an electron microscope, which kills the specimen and lets them see it only as dead, Thucydides used an electron microscope that enlarged and vivified. He saw not a dead specimen but one engaged in dying, a whole culture committing suicide.

143

The following passage shows Thucydides analyzing the kind of behavior that will always occur in war. Note the medical language of the description:

> The sufferings which revolution entailed upon the cities were many and terrible, such as have occurred and always will occur as long as the nature of mankind remains the same; though in a severer or milder form, and varying in their symptoms, according to the variety of the particular cases. In peace and prosperity states and individuals have better sentiments, because they do not find themselves suddenly confronted with imperious necessities; but war takes away the easy supply of daily wants and so proves a rough master that brings most men's characters to a level with their fortunes. Revolution thus ran its course from city to city, and the places which it arrived at last, from having heard what had been done before, carried to a still greater excess the refinement of their inventions, as manifested in the cunning of their enterprises and the atrocity of their reprisals. Words had to change their ordinary meaning and to take that which was now given them. Reckless audacity came to be considered the courage of a loyal supporter; prudent hesitation, specious cowardice; moderation was held to be a cloak for unmanliness; ability to see all sides of a question incapacity to act on any.[31]

144

Perhaps Thucydides' view is that human nature obeys its own unvarying laws. The motives that human beings manifest—greed, fear, hope, honor—can no more change than can the physical parts of our nature—tongues, nails, digestive systems. A medical or biological approach to human anatomy, when it looked for the purposes of various organs, led to a teleological viewpoint, to the discovery of purpose and, ultimately, to the idea that mind was responsible for the perfect harmony of form and function. Thucydides' approach is also medical, but with somber clinical acumen he finds not purpose but a process that simply exists in the nature of political organisms. This process is Thucydides' great discovery, and it is for this discovery that his work will remain a possession for always. It is why his history of the great war between Athens and Sparta rings true, why every war reflects its observations, and why, alas, the same human follies and errors continue to recur.

III. Euripides

In Euripides' works we can see the intellectual maelstrom produced by the winds of change that swept over the fifth century. Since Euripides was a playwright and therefore says everything through his characters and nothing in his own person, we must look at what his characters say and how they say it to detect the spirit of his age, whose optimism was shattered by the infinitely varied horrors and suicidal madness of the Peloponnesian War. We can then see how much the culture had changed from a century earlier, when the threat of Persia loomed over Greece but at the same time a hopeful sense of the powers of freedom was emerging. Euripides, the chroniclers tell us, was born at the time of the Battle of Salamis and died in self-imposed exile in Macedonia in 407, just before the end of the war between Athens in Sparta. Though victorious only five times for his plays, he was admired and popular with theatergoers during his lifetime and in the next century.

Like the other tragedians, Euripides based his plays on the myths that constituted the Greek cultural heritage. It was said in ancient times that the difference between Sophocles and Euripides was that Sophocles portrayed men as they ought to be and that Euripides portrayed men as they are. If this distinction was the case, what sort of men and women there were in Athens when the poet was writing! Athens was accused of being a most litigious society,[32] and, in fact, in Euripides' plays we often see the characters talking more like lawyers than, say, like man and wife. In the *Medea*, when Medea and Jason are arguing privately to each other, Jason says,

> It seems necessary for me to be no bad speaker,
> but like a skilled helmsman on a ship
> to set a full sail to escape
> from your endlessly babbling tongue, woman.
> Since you excessively boast [your] goodness,
> I tell you that it was Cypris alone of man and gods
> who was the savior of my voyage.[33]

The characters, an estranged husband and wife, are conversing only with each other, yet they have objectified one another into a jury who will judge on the basis of how well the rules of oratorical debate are followed. To Jason it appears more important to be a master of the rules of persuasion than actually to persuade—as though mastering the rules would be the same as mastering the situation. But the tragedy shows that no one is a master of the situation. Medea, whose genuine passions, as distinct from Jason's hypocritical sophistries, render her a recognizable human being, is enslaved to those passions, and her depravity in killing the very children she loves because of her hellish scorn for Jason proves more deadly than the less sympathetic hypocrisy of her unfaithful spouse.

The ability of language—the expression of reason—to deceive, to lie, to corrupt even while perfectly exhibiting the rules of persuasion is a major theme of Euripides.[34] Thus, after Jason has explained how he will speak with worthy oratorical skill, we hear him claim that he owes thanks not to Medea, who killed her brother and uncle to save him, but to Cypris (that is, Aphrodite), the goddess of sex. It was Medea's sexual desire for

him, of which the goddess was the cause, that drove Medea to do what she did. Still, he adds, Medea got more than she gave: she lived in Greece instead of in her own barbarous land, she lived under law, and she obtained fame.[35] As for his abandonment of Medea and his wedding to Creon's daughter, it was 1) clever, 2) wise, and 3) in Medea's interests. It was *not* because he was tired of Medea's bed that he was marrying the girl but because it was a good move, done for wealth. He concludes that Medea would think it a good plan if she were not jealous.[36]

We have discussed earlier how marriage is a key behavior that distinguishes the sophisticated art and culture of civilization from the raw power of nature.[37] In play after play Euripides brings the nature of marriage to the fore, placing it squarely in the contemporary debate about nature and convention (*physis* and *nomos*). His characters ask whether the force of nature, with her unbridled sexual desires—excited through the goddess Aphrodite—is greater than reason and self-control. Thus, in *Troad*, Helen explains her adultery as an excusable act because she was under the compulsion of sexual desire and hence under the directive of a god;[38] thus, in *Hippolytus*, the nurse endeavors to persuade Phaedra that Phaedra should yield to the natural impulses of her erotic obsession with her stepson. Euripides asks the hard questions that the sophists raised: Is human life a life of nature or of arbitrary convention or of a blend of the two? How do men and women differ, and what is the proper job of each in marriage? These are a few of the questions, embodied in his drama, that his audiences debated as they left the theater and that philosophers still speculated on in the next century. Both Plato and Aristotle, for example, discuss the nature of marriage in their works, a topic that in all likelihood would have been outside the bounds of discussion before Euripides and the sophistic program that he reflects. Before Euripides and the sophists it would have been as superfluous to discuss seriously the role of women in marriage as to discuss the role of a domesticated dog or cat in the household.

Euripides' genius discovered in the ancient myths the theological and ethical questions of his day. If Aphrodite can actually make someone commit adultery, is she a goddess? Is what the gods do right because they do it, or should they too be subject to an absolute standard of goodness?[39] And if a goddess does fill one with a passion, where is the role of human free will? Does Helen's claim that "Aphrodite made her do it" really free her from blame? When in the *Ion* the title character discovers that although Apollo has told him that his father is Xuthus, Apollo is really his father, Ion asks whether a god is capable of telling a lie. The audience may ask the more general question: is a god who lies really a god? This was, of course, the question Xenophanes had asked a century earlier in his lyrics.[40] Now Euripides was asking it on the stage of Dionysus before an audience of twenty thousand.

Euripides portrayed the brutal actions of Greeks in *The Trojan Women*, produced just after Athens's brutal behavior in the destruction of the neutral island of Melos. In the play's implicit condemnation of the Trojan War, Euripides is questioning the glory and worthiness also of the Peloponnesian War and of war generally. In *Helen*, Euripides suggests that Helen was not in Troy at all during the Trojan War but in Egypt, and the implicit proposition is that the Greeks would not have been so stupid as to fight a war over a woman.[41]

Perhaps it is no wonder that Euripides was awarded victory in the tragedy competition so rarely. The judges were obliged to respect the traditions of their ancestors, and even if Euripides adhered to the myths religiously, faithfully recording the details, somehow, in his literalness, he was following up the logical implications of the myths and exposing the ethical and philosophical problems that lay at their core. For example, the myths celebrated Jason as the great "hero" of the *Argo*, the man who obtained the golden fleece. But—Euripides makes us ask—was it Jason's heroism or Medea's sacrifice that brought home the fleece? And how great a feat was bringing it home anyway? The story that had seemed to end "happily ever after" actually had another chapter still, the story of the play *Medea*. The play, produced in 431, just on the eve of the Peloponnesian War, was perhaps Euripides' attempt to warn Athens. Perhaps he was acknowledging that winning the Persian War and preserving Greek freedom had been a great heroic action. But probing further, he was also asking whether, after the glories of Salamis and Plataea, it would have been correct to conclude of the Greeks, as of Jason, that "they lived happily ever after." His play warns that it is not possible to rest on laurels after a heroic action and to expect the future to flow along nicely; perhaps, he warns, there is a need for continued virtue. We may imagine Euripides telling his countrymen, "Let us say that Jason *had* exhibited virtue in the adventure of the golden fleece, just as our Athens *had* exhibited virtue in conquering Persia. Did both then retain the self-control that brought them glory? Or did both become so materialistic as to forget their virtuous pasts?" In the *Medea*, as in the other plays of Euripides, we discover a tragic fear in the power of human passions and in the willingness and ability of human beings to abuse reason and language. In Euripides' drama, we do not experience a calming catharsis, a purging of pity and fear. Before Medea murders Creon's daughter, the chorus pray to Earth and Sun to avert the calamity.[42] There is no mention in the play of what Earth did, but the Sun sent his chariot to rescue the murderess. Perhaps Euripides is suggesting that even one of the powers of the universe, the Sun, is on the side of the murderess Medea. If the sun is Medea's ally, this fact cannot but stir up our anxieties. Perhaps, the play would be saying, the cosmos is not so friendly. This view would be quite different from that in Sophocles' plays, where oracles are proved true and the cosmos is a place of order.

If Euripides reflected the anxieties of his age and if his plays enacted the dangers that the philosophical energy of the fifth century had uncovered, he nevertheless challenged intellectuals to use their powers of mind to put order back into the scheme of things and to turn the world back into a cosmos, a place of ordered beauty and harmony and symmetry. Restoring order became the project of the fourth-century philosophers. While the old political world changed and as the city-state of Pericles, the *polis*, underwent a metamorphosis into the world-state of Alexander, the philosophers with cheery optimism discovered in both the world of ethereal ideas and the world of down-to-earth pragmatism a path to serenity.

Discussion Questions

1. Law professors are said to use the "Socratic technique." Talk to some law students about their classes after you have read a dialogue or two of Plato's. How "Socratic" is the teaching that goes on in law schools? Does law school education enhance its stature by calling itself "Socratic"?

2. Look up in a dictionary one or two of the words whose definitions Socrates used to argue about in the marketplace—*justice, love, friendship, virtue, courage,* and *piety.* How valid or complete is the definition in the dictionary? Where does it hit the mark? Where does it miss the mark? What is the difference between a philosophically satisfactory definition and the kind you find in most dictionaries?

3. In what ways was Socrates a polarizing figure? If he were alive today, would he still be as polarizing as he was in fifth-century Athens? Does the answer to this question depend on the particular place and country where this question is asked? Of the possible reactions to Socrates—admiration, hostility, tolerance, ridicule, and so on—which is most appropriate? What does the answer to this last question tell us about a particular culture?

4. Do people tend to respond to stimuli in the same general ways? Does knowledge of the general way people behave enable people to alter their responses or does it stir them to justify their response by saying, "I'm only human. It's natural and normal for me to respond in this way." What bearing does this issue have on the value of history as a subject of education?

5. Do people have a tendency to see their lives in terms of contemporary artistic genres? For example, do people today describe their lives in terms derived from television situation comedies or cinema or video games? In ancient Athens, would it have been the tendency to see events as consistent with tragedy as a poetic genre? Are some genres more enlightening than others? What is gained and what is lost by understanding our lives as structured in terms of an established genre?

6. Thucydides seems to have been influenced not only by tragedy but also by the science of medicine. To what degree can these two metaphorical motifs for human life as his history describes it—tragedy and medicine—enable a consistent understanding of history? Are there places where the metaphors are inconsistent?

7. Is Euripides concerned with the same topic—the power of language with its ability to enlighten and deceive—as the Socrates of the Platonic dialogues? How do dialectical and dramatic approaches to this topic differ?

8. Like Thucydides, Euripides also inquires into the extent to which human beings have control over themselves. In Euripides' plays, the powers of sexual impulses or of alcohol are presented as powerful gods, Aphrodite or Dionysus, who exert control over our lives. Thucydides suggests that humans, by their nature, are constrained to behave in certain ways. How do we try today to express these same underlying questions about human freedom? Are our metaphors more or less apt than those of the ancients?

9. It rarely happens that the most popular writers are also the most esteemed by critics. Thus Euripides, whose plays were more popular with Athenian audiences (as measured in revivals in the next century), won fewer prizes than Aeschylus or Sophocles. What might account for this phenomenon, that critical and public acclaim so often differ? (In Athens, despite Plato's hint in the *Laws* [659a] that the prizes were awarded on the basis of applause, various measures *were* taken to ensure the independence and honesty of the judges [Isocrates, *Trapeziticus* 34].)

Notes

1. Pausanias, *Geography* 1.22.

2. Shakespeare called Socrates' wife Xanthippe "curst and shrewd" (*The Taming of the Shrew* 1.2.70). The ancient source for Xanthippe's bad reputation seems to be Xenophon, *Symposium*, 15.

3. It was probably sculpted fifty years after Socrates' death.

4. Plato, perhaps not the safest source for information about Socrates, puts Antisthenes at Socrates' death scene (*Phaedo* 59b).

5. Plato says that Aristippus was *not* present at the death of Socrates (*Phaedo* 59c). Are either of these claims true (see preceding note)? Who can tell? Is it possible that by denying Aristippus a place at Socrates' death, Plato is making the point that the founder of a school that put momentary pleasure as the good would *not* have been present at such an unpleasant event? (Diogenes Laertius, *Plato* 36, says that this comment of Plato is meant to disparage Aristippus.) My point is that where the facts are not known, a storyteller can put his story together in any way he wishes, each detail full of meaning or not, according to the teller's wishes.

6. Diogenes Laertius, *Plato* 35.

7. Concerning Socrates, Alfonso Gómez-Lobo, in limiting his discussion to Plato, writes, "I have assumed that we have little to learn from Aristophanes and Xenophon" (*The Foundations of Socratic Ethics* [Indianapolis: Hackett, 1994], 5). I differ from Gómez-Lobo only in thinking that in absolute terms, we have little to learn, qua knowledge, about the actual Socrates from Plato, too. It is, however, Plato's portrait

that has become our portrait. Perhaps we might draw an analogy with the fate of *La Bohème*: Puccini's version is so beautiful that other versions have been virtually forgotten.

8. This is not to say that Aristophanes, Xenophon, and Aeschines are not worth reading. They are fascinating in themselves, raise interesting questions, and shed light on one of the most fertile periods in our history. More important, Plato's victory is not an argument for its historical validity. Much as we would like the actual Socrates to have been the relentlessly steadfast pursuer of truth that Plato portrays, it is not possible, on the basis of the extant evidence, to be certain. Aristotle addresses himself to the question of the historical Socrates (*Metaphysics* 987a32–b10, 1078b17–32, 1086b2–7; *Parts of Animals* 642a28), and perhaps for those who attended Plato's Academy a pastime was separating the teachings that were Socrates' from those that were Plato's.

9. Thucydides observes (*The History of the Peloponnesian Wars* 3.82) that war accelerates the change in language. It is useful to keep in mind that a major part of Socrates' adult life took place during the long war between Athens and Sparta. A contemporary example of how politics changes the connotations of words is evident in the use of the word *moderate*. Once a term of praise, it has come, in such expressions as "Republican moderate," to be an expression of weak allegiance to the fundamental principles of the party. In the same way, the word *adult* has come to mean *pornographic*, as in "adult film."

10. Aristotle, *Metaphysics* 1078a28. In the next sentences Aristotle points out a difference between Plato and Socrates even though in the dialogues Plato's view is put in the mouth of Socrates. Inasmuch as Socrates died two decades before Aristotle was born, Aristotle's knowledge was from the tradition, and once again it is impossible to know with any certainty exactly whose views are truly whose.

11. *Memorabilia* 4.6.

12. A good example of how this occurs is portrayed in the dialogue *Gorgias*, almost certainly a work of fiction. In the dialogue's various conversations, Socrates speedily reduces the famous rhetorician Gorgias, his student Polus, and the (probably fictive) politician Callicles to embarrassing self-contradiction. The dialogue shows how amusingly absorbing people found Socrates: when, at various times, the dialogue is on the verge of breaking up, the people observing the conversation press the participants to continue.

151

13. These are the complaints made by the interlocutors Callicles in the *Gorgias* (482c–e) and Thrasymachus in the *Republic* (338d).

14. For an example of complaints against Socrates' nitpicking over a "trivial" inconsistency, see *Gorgias* 461b.

15. A version by Xenophon also survives. Perhaps fourth-century B.C.E. students of rhetoric were assigned the exercise of writing their own versions of the speeches of both prosecution and defense. A speech of prosecution was written by the sophist Polycrates.

16. I wish to stress, as I shall again in the chapter on Plato, that the description offered here is that bequeathed by Plato and that it may be entirely a fabrication of Plato's imagination or a mixture of imagination and fact.

17. In the context of a legal defense against the charge of not believing in his city's gods, Socrates' remarks would serve to show his piety and would thus affirm his innocence of the charge.

18. Aelian, *Historical Miscellany* 3.36; also Diogenes Laertius, *Life of Aristotle* 5.9.

19. It needs to be repeated that he meets these individuals in the *dialogues*, Plato's plays about Socrates. It is probable that all these encounters were invented by Plato for the sake of a dramatic conversation.

20. Perhaps Plato is deliberately drawing a contrast to Pericles in his defense of Anaxagoras. Diogenes Laertius relates a story from the *Scattered Notes of Hieronymus* (*Anaxagoras* 14) that Pericles made all sorts of appeals to emotion. It is probable either that the anecdote about Anaxagoras was invented somewhere in the tradition for the sake of a sharp contrast with Socrates' noble behavior in court or that Plato invented the remarks of Socrates to draw the contrast.

21. Cicero, *Brutus* 29, trans. G. L. Hendrickson (Cambridge, Mass.: Harvard University Press, 1988). Cicero comments further on Thucydides' difficult Greek in *Orator* 30.

22. See p. 8.

23. Aristotle, *Poetics* 1451 b5–8.

24. Quintilian, *Institutes* 10.1.31.

25. Thucydides, *The History of the Peloponnesian War* 1.22.

26. Charles Norris Cochrane, *Thucydides and the Science of History* (New York: Russell & Russell, 1965).

27. See p. 110.

28. Cochrane, *Thucydides and the Science of History*, 23.

29. Perhaps the biblical notion of the world as *created* is responsible: we see the world as created by a Maker, rather than as the dynamic interplay of various forces—a pagan notion.

30. Cochrane, *Thucydides and the Science of History*, 177.

31. Thucydides, *The History of the Peloponnesian War* 3.82.

32. For an Athenian defense against the charge of litigiousness, see Thucydides, *The History of the Peloponnesian War* 1.77.

33. Euripides, *Medea* 522–28. Translation the author's.

34. See Carol Lindsay, "Aphrodite and the Equivocal Argument: *Hamartia* in the *Hippolytus*," in *Hamartia: The Concept of Error in the Western Tradition: Essays in Honor of John M. Crossett*, ed. Donald Stump et al. (New York: Edwin Mellen Press, 1983), 51–73.

35. Perhaps Pericles has this passage in mind when he says that the best thing for a woman is never to be spoken about (Thucydides, *The History of the Peloponnesian War* 2.45.2).

36. Euripides, *Medea* 549.

37. See the discussion of the art in Greek temples on pp. 24–28.

38. Euripides, *Troad* 948.

39. This is, of course, the question that Plato's Socrates asks in the *Euthyphro*.

40. See pp. 61–62.

41. Euripides seems to be borrowing here this idea from Herodotus (*History of the Persian Wars* 2.120).

42. Euripides, *Medea* 1327.

Select Bibliography

SOCRATES

Guthrie, W. K. C. *Socrates*. Cambridge: Cambridge University Press, 1971.

Ross, George MacDonald. "Socrates versus Plato: The Origins and Development of Socratic Thinking." *Thinking* 12 (1996): 2–8.

THUCYDIDES

Web resource: www.rci.rutgers.edu/~edmunds/thuc.html.

Cochrane, Charles Norris. *Thucydides and the Science of History*. New York: Russell & Russell, 1965.

Connor, W. R. *Thucydides*. Princeton, N.J.: Princeton University Press, 1984.

Finley, J. H. *Thucydides*. Cambridge, Mass.: Harvard University Press, 1942; reprint, Ann Arbor: University of Michigan Press, 1963.

Kagan, Donald. *The Peloponnesian War*. New York: Viking, 2003.

EURIPIDES

Conacher, D. J. *Euripides and the Sophists: Some Dramatic Treatments of Philosophical Ideas*. London: Duckworth, 1998.

Mossman, Judith, ed. *Oxford Readings in Classical Studies*. Oxford: Oxford University Press, 2002.

Powell, A., ed. *Euripides, Women, and Sexuality*. London: Routledge, 1990.

Segal, Erich, ed. *Euripides: A Collection of Critical Essays*. Englewood Cliffs, N.J.: Prentice Hall, 1968.

CHAPTER 9

Rhetoric and the Philosophers

I. Rhetoric

It is difficult for us, who live in an era of a dizzying assortment of entertainment, to imagine a time back in the fourth century B.C.E.—long before the invention of the internet, or television, or radio, or cinema, or the printing press—when the chief form of amusement was spoken discourse. What a diversity of topics speeches could cover! Every area of humanity, nature, or the universe could be elucidated by speech. What opportunities for criticism and dissection or for tribute and applause! What genius, what resourcefulness a clever speechmaker could reveal! The human race appears to give the greatest honors to those who excel in the activities that *all* people participate in. Hence we esteem the greatest runners or writers or singers because we can *all* run or write or sing, while we esteem the greatest surgeons or greatest cellists less, for their skills are very rare. In ancient Greece, the most dazzling speakers achieved a fame we grant only to our greatest rock stars.

In the fifth and fourth centuries, when democratic forms of government showed how effectively oratorical ability could help clever speakers acquire power or prevail in the courtroom, teachers of rhetoric proliferated like yoga gurus or psychics in the 1920s. With the different rhetoric teachers came various specialties. Thus Evenus of Paros specialized in secret allusions and indirect compliments or censures; Tisias, in dressing up trifles as matters of significance and novel matters as matters of antiquity and vice versa and in arguing at length about anything and everything; Polus, in maxims and similes; Thrasymachus, in stirring up and then soothing the passions of the audience.[1] Prodicus practiced the artful drawing of subtle distinctions, Protagoras, the art of drawing deep philosophy from interpretations of poetry—a talent burlesqued in Plato's dialogue *Protagoras*.[2] Teachers of rhetoric wrote innumerable handbooks, many of them sterile and repetitive, multiplying distinctions that vie in subtlety with those of the most refined medieval scholastics. No doubt ancient aficionados of rhetoric were able to identify an author from a brief quotation. They could also recognize dozens and dozens of rhetorical devices, just as we recognize the hackneyed formulae of spy novels or the cinematic clichés of action films or the familiar platitudes of political advertisements. Though critics like Aristotle would later teach that the challenge for an artist is to conceal his art, yet, in the quest for notoriety, a speaker might wish rather to make his art conspicuous than to disguise it.[3]

II. Extemporaneous and Prepared Speeches

It is not surprising, then, that this awareness of the power of speeches should spur the establishment of schools that claimed to provide it.[4] And among the different schools there naturally arose a rivalry for students. Among the various rivalries of the fourth century was a lively one between two students of Gorgias of Leontini, who had been the most famous rhetorician of his day. These students, Isocrates and Alcidamas, debated whether superiority lay in the skill that Alcidamas offered to teach—techniques of delivering speeches extemporaneously—or in the skill Isocrates offered—techniques of preparing splendidly crafted speeches for reading or memorizing. Their contemporary Plato, though he did not see himself as primarily a teacher of discourse for courts or deliberative assemblies, also participated in the debate.[5]

155

Though the rivalry may seem arcane to us, it was actually of great import in its day. In Athenian courts, a defendant had to defend himself,[6] with words from his own lips, and, if he failed to persuade a jury over whom he had no peremptory challenges, he could be fined, exiled, or executed. If he could either speak extemporaneously himself or could memorize a speech provided to him by a master rhetor, he might have a fighting chance. An ability to persuade might make the difference between life and death.

Alcidamas is said to have been so devoted a student of Gorgias that he succeeded Gorgias as head of Gorgias's school.[7] Alcidamas is reported to have boasted of an ability to answer extemporaneously a question on any subject.[8] Not only could he answer any question, but, he claimed, he could answer it eloquently and teach others to do so too.[9]

Alcidamas presented his views in a brief treatise "On the Writers of Written Words."[10] The ability to speak extemporaneously, said Alcidamas, shows a quick vocabulary, a ready supply of enthymemes (rhetorical syllogisms with conclusions deduced from probable premises or signs[11]), and a sharpness in adapting oneself to the exigencies of the moment and to the desires of the audience. In short, it reveals the speaker as quick-witted, intelligent, and sincere. Composing a speech over a long period, polishing it at leisure, adding borrowed felicities from old masters, and revising it after much reflection is a process, says Alcidamas, that even mediocre minds can perform. Moreover, those who think on their feet can, with some effort, write, but those who can write may not be able to think on their feet. The ability to speak on a moment's call will serve one in all the crises of life, but the ability to write a good speech will not help if one needs a speech immediately. It is impossible to keep a memorized speech ready for every one of life's occasions, he continued. A man who is used to preparing beautifully composed written speeches in the comfort of his study will appear ignorant and uneducated when called on to speak spontaneously, for he will have come to rely on the necessity of having everything written out in advance. Written speeches, he concluded, are imitations of real speeches and bear to real speeches the semblance that bronze or marble statues bear to living bodies: they are lifeless and useless when real work is to be done. They are more like labored poems than speeches.

Isocrates, Alcidamas's adversary, was born in 436 B.C.E., just a few years before the Peloponnesian War, and died in 338, just two years before Alexander became king of Macedonia. Possessed of a weak voice himself, he wrote speeches for others and taught speechwriting. Among his students were many of the most celebrated writers and statesmen of the fourth century. Isocrates discussed his views on written speeches in two works written nearly four decades apart, "Against the Sophists" (in about 391) and "On the Antidosis" (in about 353). Isocrates attacked the claim of some teachers of rhetoric of being able to turn anyone whomsoever into a polished speaker. In modern terms, such teachers would be like colleges and universities that practice open admissions and promise to turn any human being, so long as he has a pulse, into an expert scholar and honest citizen. Isocrates was in the philosophical mainstream in believing that art and technique achieve their perfection only when applied by a person of natural ability.[12] A student with promise should study and imitate models provided by earlier speakers and by the teacher. Memorizing and imitating models on noble subjects would habituate a young man to nobility and contemplation of significant issues and would thus improve his soul. A serious student of oratory should be ready to practice his writing constantly, for assiduous practice would yield the fruit of eloquence.

At first glance, Alcidamas and Plato appear to be allies in opposing writing. Plato wrote in the *Phaedrus* that a sage warned King Thamus of Egypt about the dangers of writing—how it encourages forgetfulness because it releases people from reliance on memory and gives a semblance of knowledge without real knowledge.[13] In the same dialogue, Plato's character Socrates added that written words cannot defend themselves or answer questions.[14]

A surprisingly large number of Plato's dialogues investigate the value of extemporaneous speeches. The most conspicuous are the *Phaedrus*, *Symposium*, and *Menexenus*; but others, the *Laches*, *Republic*, and *Timaeus*, may also be considered as comments on the controversy.[15] While we can never be sure exactly what Plato means, for he writes dialogues and does not speak in his own person, he represents the controversy dramatically. It turns out, not surprisingly for so original a thinker, that Plato is not a fan of either extemporaneous or prepared speeches. The *Phaedrus* shows that an extemporaneous speech that has a solid organizational principle, defines its terms, and has a beginning, middle, and end *will* in fact be better than a prepared speech that lacks these qualities.[16] But the *Menexenus* shows us how very easy it is to put together such a speech, especially if one has a bank of prefabricated parts from which to draw. And the *Symposium* shows that even beautiful speeches that carry off the palm for eloquence do not necessarily contain an iota, nay, not even an *i*'s dot, of truth.

The dialogues often show that prepared speeches, even polished ones, are no better. Such dialogues as the *Meno*, *Hippias Minor*, and *Gorgias* show that the mere memorizing of set remarks is not beneficial and in fact results in one's cutting a pretty poor figure.

The *Meno*, for example, opens with a question from the title character:

> Can you tell me, Socrates—is virtue something that can be taught? Or does it come by practice? Or is it neither teaching nor practice that gives it to a man but natural aptitude or something else?[17]

The question is startlingly abrupt—a sophisticated and complicated inquiry into the nature of virtue. The formulation of the question shows a substantial training in philosophy—or sophistry. Meno knows all about the controversy between nature and convention (*physis* and *nomos*) and is open to the possibility that something else may be responsible for a man's acquisition of virtue.[18] The question is designed to make Meno appear to think himself intelligent.[19] To ask so complete a question, one that so well covers all the possibilities, shows Meno's confidence in having worked out the intricacies of the matter. The question—so fulsomely formulated—has as its motive a desire to show off, to initiate a debate that will illustrate the questioner's learning and ability in the art of controversy called *eristic*. In Meno's opening speech, Plato portrays a man who knows all the answers and is certain of his ability to acquit himself in any debate. Meno's question does not seek understanding; it is a challenge to a fight.

When Socrates gives an unexpected response to the question, he trips up Meno completely. What the *Meno* shows, in fact, is the inability to carry on discourse when there is a complete reliance on prefabricated philosophy, memorized set pieces, in short, the kind of "philosophy" taught by Gorgias and Isocrates in which speeches are prepared in advance.

Perhaps Plato's most authentic judgment on the controversy comes in the *Apology*, where we read a philosophical version of Socrates' defense to the Athenian court. We find here three speeches. First is a long, formal defense speech that Socrates will have prepared in advance, even if he did not write it out. That Socrates would have prepared a defense is probable, despite a declaration in his opening that he will speak "not with forethought, in language that just comes."[20] Two "extemporaneous" speeches follow,[21] one delivered after the guilty verdict, when Socrates must propose a penalty, and a second when Socrates addresses a few last words to those who voted for conviction and then to those who voted for acquittal. The two speeches that required action from the jurors were, of course, failures: after the first speech, Socrates was convicted; after the second, he was sentenced to death.

The critical verdict of humankind, however, has been that the speeches *are* persuasive. The biographical passage at the beginning of the *Apology* ought to have persuaded the jurors (as it does readers) that Socrates should not be confused with Anaxagoras; the cross-examination of Meletus ought to have convinced the jurors that the charges of believing in no gods at all and of creating new gods were inconsistent; the rehearsal of Socrates' courageous actions during the oppression of the Thirty Tyrants ought to have given proof of his patriotism and justice. In the penalty phase, Socrates' insistence on not being unjust to himself ought to have convinced the jury that the defendant was at least true to his principles. Each of Socrates' speeches proceeded in an orderly manner, and, as the many famous lines from them attest, each contained a number of purple patches. Instead, perhaps the question should be, Could *any* speeches have persuaded the jurors? Or were they so embittered, so injured, so absorbed in themselves that no good argument, not even one that appealed to their own self-interests, could induce in them a rational choice? Perhaps the *Apology* shows us that a good speech will fail in the absence of an intelligent, philosophically imbued audience. The problem, then, was not that Socrates did not understand the psychological composition of his fellow Athenians; the problem was that philosophy had not taken hold of their souls such that they could let go of the old stories about Socrates they had heard from Aristophanes or of their own irritation at Socratic dialectic. If this speech could not persuade the Athenians, perhaps no speech could. Socrates' arguments and language did not fail; what failed, Plato was saying, was the moral ability of the Athenians to recognize the good man in their midst.

159

III. Isocrates (436–338)

We have only one work from Alcidamas, "On the Writers of Written Words," appropriately, perhaps, since he valued only extemporaneous speeches. From Isocrates, on the other hand, we have a good deal, and because he was quite influential to the Western intellectual tradition, a few words about him and his career are fitting. He was a much greater rival of Plato than of Alcidamas, and it will be best to turn to Plato with an awareness of this rivalry.

Isocrates lived to be a very old man. He was born before Plato and died after him—and Plato himself lived to be about eighty. Isocrates lived to be ninety-eight. Though Isocrates' name is far less familiar than the names of his contemporaries Plato and Aristotle, in some ways he affected the Western world more than they did. What Isocrates taught took form in political reality, not merely in ideas, and in terms of *actually* affecting the political landscape of his era, Isocrates was, perhaps, the most important thinker of the fourth century.

In the *Nicocles*, Isocrates says that we "practice justice and the other virtues not so that we can be less well off than others but so that we can lead lives full of good things."[22] Who would practice virtue, he asks, if it brought no *practical* benefit? For the Socrates of Plato's dialogues, philosophy is concerned essentially with ethics and the state of the individual soul and especially with the state of the soul in the afterlife. For the pragmatic Isocrates, however, philosophy is the kind of culture embodied in what we call "liberal arts education," and it takes aim at this world. Isocrates asks what the world must be like for a liberal education to be of value. His answer is that the world must be like Athens. The attempt to make the Western world like Athens begins in Isocrates. In his first major work, a speech titled the *Panegyricus*, he explains this notion. *Panegyricus* is the word from which we derive our word "panegyric," which signifies in Greek a great cultural festival held at set intervals, like the Olympic Games, at which not only athletic contests but also cultural competitions were held. Athens, Isocrates said, was a year-long cultural festival, and the whole world was invited to attend. Isocrates took the culture of Athens and sought to make it universal. In doing so, he envisioned, perhaps for the first time in the history of the world, a universal state based not on power but on a culture, a state open to all. He writes,[23]

Philosophy, then, which has shared with us equally in discovering all these goods, and shared with us equally in establishing them, has educated us with respect to actions and has civilized us with respect to each other. Out of the accidents and disasters that come to us, philosophy has distinguished those that arise because of our ignorance and those that arise from necessity; and it has taught us to guard against the first, as it has taught us to endure the second, nobly. Our city, Athens, has displayed its love of philosophy and has given honor to the power of speech, that power that all men desire, and for which, if others possess it, we envy them. Athens fully recognizes that we alone, of all the animals, are born having this power as our special quality; and, because of the advantage that it gives us, we are superior to all other animals. Athens has observed that, in most actions of life, chance is so intermingled and confused that often sensible men come to grief, fools to success; in the power of speaking intelligently, however, the foolish have no share, for to be able to do so is the function of a soul endowed with good sense. Nothing so distinguishes fools from wise men as this quality. Furthermore, even if men have been brought up free from both, even if they have courage or wealth or other such good things, they are not judged on the basis of such things but most especially on the basis of whether they speak intelligently. Such power of speech is the surest and most demonstrable token of their culture; and people who possess this power not only have control over themselves but also are honored by others.

Athens has left other cities so far behind in the ability to think sensibly and speak intelligently that those who have studied liberal arts here have gone back home to become the teachers of others. The name "Greek" no longer signifies a race but instead a way of thinking, and those who share in our culture[24] are called Greeks more than those who share in our race.

Isocrates maintained one political end: that Athens should combine the various Greek states into a political unity and conduct a cultural war on Asia. In essay after essay, he set forth this view and preached this cultural union. To further this end, he established his school, to which the sons of the leading princes and kings of Greece came to study. Isocrates lived long enough to see his ideas translated into action. His dream of a pan-Hellenic—an all-Greek—attack on Asia to spread Greek culture became a reality as Plato's *Republic* never did. Of course, the dream did not succeed in the way he hoped: a Macedonian king, Alexander the Great, not Athens, unified Greece and launched Greek culture on its way. Nevertheless, even in this diluted spread of Greek culture there developed the intellectual offspring of Athenian philosophy—the philosophies of Stoicism and Epicureanism, which, as we shall see, turned out to be philosophies more widely appealing than those of Plato and Aristotle.

IV. Rhetoric and Philosophy

As Aristotle observes in the *Rhetoric*, there are many forms of persuasion, among them torture, laws, witnesses, contracts, and oaths.[25] The intellectual spirit most admires the persuasion that comes through *argument*. It is likely that one of the principal reasons that philosophy developed in the *Greek* world was the pervasive esteem given to mental acuity in debate. Since logic could help construct adamantine arguments, logic was a valuable tool. If the logical principles of mathematical proof could persuade in mathematics, then such principles were valuable tools. If manipulating the emotions of an audience could help persuade, then the skills of such manipulation were valuable too.

Toward the end of antiquity, an anonymous rhetorician addressed himself to the question, Why rhetoric? In his answer we see the importance that the discipline had for men who knew from experience that, without the form of *logos* called speech, there could be no culture or civilization:

> Why rhetoric? To order and ornament the life of men and the polity. This is why the rhetorician is called "political" . . . there are three species of rhetoric—legal, advisory, panegyrical, and without these the polity cannot be established.[26]

The author then examines each kind—its operation and its aim: the legal aims at justice, the advisory at counseling us to turn toward the good and away from vice for our own advantage, the panegyric at what is fine. At the end of each, like a refrain from a chorus, come the words "without this, the polity cannot be established." What was true of the polity was certainly true of all the branches of philosophy, for without rhetoric—the art of persuasion by *speech*—there would have been no natural philosophy, no metaphysics, no mathematics, no ethics, no political theory, in short, none of the jewels in the Greek intellectual crown. The competitive spirit, as it expressed itself in the struggle for persuasive supremacy among the rhetoricians and among the philosophers and between the fields of rhetoric and philosophy, proved highly creative for the Western intellectual tradition.

Discussion Questions

1. Surely it was very common for those not intimately involved with the schools of philosophy to confuse the teachers of philosophy with those of rhetoric. In Aristophanes' *Clouds*, for example, they are all "sophists," and in Plato's *Apology* Socrates claims that he is a victim of mistaken identity. Is philosophy open to the charge of "making the worse argument" appear better? Do philosophers ever seem to argue for victory rather than aiming for truth? In other words, are there grounds for confounding rhetoric and philosophy?

2. On the one hand, we admire those who can think on their feet, who are spontaneously articulate, who respond with just the right riposte. On the other hand, we claim also to respect those who "look before they leap," who think before speaking, who speak with studied preparation. Are the two approaches to rhetoric, the spontaneous and the prepared, the extremes of which there is a golden mean? Is there some way to synthesize them into some third form of rhetoric?

3. In those dialogues of Plato where the issue of extemporaneous and prepared speeches arises, is Plato himself able to avoid the charge of writing in a medium that gives the appearance but avoids the reality of spontaneity? After all, in the dialogues, Socrates *seems* to respond with nimble agility to his interlocutors, but Plato may have taken *hours* to think of the appropriate remark. How well does Plato succeed in persuading his readers that the conversations of the dialogues are virtually live recordings?

4. Isocrates claims that virtue brings practical benefits to our lives. He also claims that a "liberal arts education" has value in cities whose culture is like that of Athens. Those who teach at modern liberal arts institutions often claim that the education they provide is not aimed at practical applications (this is left for vocational training) but at fashioning students into good human beings and good citizens. Administrators at these same colleges try to sell their schools because of how well they will help the graduates prepare for the world of work. Are the different goals compatible? Does your education, especially in philosophy, seem to serve a practical purpose? Should an education be focused on making one a productive worker, leaving the liberal arts as something to be picked up on the side? Or should an education be focused on developing a soul, leaving work skills as something to be picked up as an apprenticeship or in vocational training?

Notes

1. So reports Plato in the *Phaedrus* 267a–d.

2. For a discussion of the parody, see James A. Arieti, *Interpreting Plato: The Dialogues as Drama* (Savage, Md.: Rowman & Littlefield, 1991), 117–31, esp. 124–25.

3. On concealment of art, see p. 88.

4. On such schools as the only common form of post-elementary education in the classical world, see G. Kennedy, *A New History of Classical Rhetoric* (Princeton, N.J.: Princeton University Press, 1994), 28.

5. Yet rhetoric seems to have been one of the subjects taught in the Academy, perhaps even introduced into the curriculum by Aristotle. See Diogenes Laertius, *Life of Aristotle* 5.3; see also Werner Jaeger, *Aristotle: Fundamentals of the History of His Development*, 2nd ed. and trans. Richard Robinson (London: Oxford University Press, 1948), 37.

6. For a brief description of Greek legal procedures, see Kennedy, *A New History of Classical Rhetoric*, 15–16.

7. Suda 388. (The Suda is a tenth-century C.E. Byzantine encyclopedia of the ancient world.)

8. In this respect he is just like Gorgias and Hippias, who are portrayed as making the same claim about themselves in the Platonic dialogues (*Gorgias* 447c; *Hippias Minor* 363d).

9. L. Van Hook, "Alcidamas versus Isocrates: The Spoken versus the Written Word," *The Classical Weekly* 12 (1919): 89.

10. The treatise sometimes goes by the name "On the Sophists."

11. Aristotle, in the *Prior Analytics* (70 a10–16), gives these as examples of enthymemes: that a woman is pregnant is concluded from her having milk; that wise men are good is concluded from the fact that Pittacus (who is good) is wise.

12. For a later history of the idea, see *Longinus: On the Sublime*, trans. with commentary J. A. Arieti and J. M. Crossett (New York: Edwin Mellen Press, 1985), 11–15.

13. Plato, *Phaedrus* 274c–275b. In this way it resembles some of my students who triumphantly declare that they have the information in their notes, even if it resides nowhere in their minds.

14. Plato, *Phaedrus* 276c.

15. The *Laches* may be an amoebic dialogue (one in which two parties continuously cap what the other has said in an escalating battle of wits) between Nicias and Laches with Socrates mediating. The *Republic* begins as a competition between Socrates and Thrasymachus and continues as Socrates' young interlocutors challenge him with various problems to solve rhetorically. The *Timaeus* is dramatically presented as a sequel to the *Republic*, where Socrates drew an analogy between the human soul and a state; in the *Timaeus*, the speaker caps Socrates with an analogy of the human body and the entire universe. See the various chapters on these dialogues in Arieti, *Interpreting Plato*.

16. In the *Phaedrus*, Socrates gives two extemporaneous speeches, one on the repugnant theme that a person ought to yield sexually to a nonlover and one on the nature of love. Socrates rejects both speeches as "mad" (265a).

17. Plato, *Meno* 70a, trans. W. K. C. Guthrie, in *The Collected Dialogues of Plato*, ed. Edith Hamilton and Huntington Cairns (Princeton, N.J.: Princeton University Press, 1961).

18. For an overview of the controversy, see W. K. C. Guthrie, *The Sophists* (Cambridge: Cambridge University Press, 1971), 55–134.

19. The question shows Plato's dramatic art. Plato formulates it as part of his characterization of Meno.

20. Plato, *Apology* 17c.

21. *Extemporaneous* is put in quotation marks because the speeches are extemporaneous in the drama as *Plato* is presenting it, and it is, of course, Plato who is composing them.

22. Isocrates, *Nicocles* 2.

23. Isocrates, *Panegyric* 47–48.

24. The word here translated as *culture* is *paideusis* and means something between a system or process of education and the broader characteristics of our word *culture* that include popular tastes and habits. Pericles calls Athens the *paideusis* of Greece in Thucydides' *History of the Peloponnesian War* (2.41).

25. Aristotle, *Rhetoric* 1375 a25.

26. *Rhetores Graeci*, vol. 14, *Prolegomenon Sylloge*, ed. Hugo Rabe (Leipzig: Teubner, 1931), 14–15.

Select Bibliography

ISOCRATES

Benoit, W. L. "Isocrates and Plato on Rhetoric and Rhetorical Education." *Rhetoric Society Quarterly* 21 (1991): 60–71.

Heilbrun, G. "Isocrates on Rhetoric and Power." *Hermes* 103 (1975): 154–78.

Ijsseling, S. "Isocrates and the Power of Logos." In *Rhetoric and Philosophy in Conflict*, edited by S. Isseling. The Hague: Martinus Nijhoff, 1976.

Jaeger, W. *Paideia: The Ideals of Greek Culture.* Translated by Gilbert Highet. Oxford: Oxford University Press, 1971.

Johnson, R. "Isocrates' Method of Teaching." *American Journal of Philology* 80 (1959): 25–36.

PLATO

Ferrari, G. R. F. *Listening to the Cicadas: A Study of Plato's* Phaedrus. Cambridge: Cambridge University Press, 1987.

Gonsalez, F., ed. *The Third Way: New Perspectives in Platonic Studies.* Lanham, Md.: Rowman & Littlefield, 1995.

Kahn, C. *Plato and the Socratic Dialogue.* Cambridge: Cambridge University Press, 1996.

Press, G., ed. *Plato's Dialogues: New Studies and Interpretations.* Lanham, Md.: Rowman & Littlefield, 1993.

ARISTOTLE

Fortenbaugh, W. W. *Aristotle on Emotion: A Contribution to Philosophical Psychology, Rhetoric, Poetics, and Ethics.* New York: Barnes & Noble Books, 1975.

Kennedy, G. A. "The Composition and Influence of Aristotle's Rhetoric." In *Essays on Aristotle's Rhetoric,* edited A. Rorty. Berkeley: University of California Press, 1996.

Nussbaum, M. "Aristotle on Emotions and Rational Persuasion." In *Essays on Aristotle's Rhetoric,* edited A. Rorty. Berkeley: University of California Press, 1996.

Rorty, A., ed. *Essays on Aristotle's Rhetoric.* Berkeley: University of California Press, 1996.

CHAPTER 10

Plato

I. Plato (428–348 B.C.E.)

Born in the first years of the Peloponnesian War, Plato was in his early twenties when Athens was finally defeated by Sparta. Probably some time during his teenage years, he had the pivotal experience of his life, meeting Socrates. Meeting and then admiring Socrates inspired Plato to abandon his ambition of becoming a playwright and instead to devote himself to philosophy.[1] According to an ancient story, the night before he met Plato, Socrates dreamed that a cygnet sat in his lap, immediately developed into a fully grown swan, and flew away into the sky singing a song that delighted all who heard it.[2] In about 387, Plato founded the Academy as an institute for political and scientific research, and he served as its director for the rest of his long life. When he was in his sixties, he tried to influence the politics of the Sicilian city of Syracuse, one of the most important Greek *poleis*, by educating Dionysius II, the successor to the throne. When the plan failed, Plato resumed his directorship of the Academy. His surviving works are dialogues, most of which portray an imaginary Socrates arguing with various personages, historical and invented, on various topics by means of questions and answers—a technique that has come to be called "Socratic dialectic."[3]

These highly provocative dialogues have influenced the intellectual history of the Western world now for well over two millennia. When one first reads them as a young man or woman, the effect is rather like coming up to the Grand Canyon for the first time. As one approaches the edge, the landscape appears simply level desert plain. Then, all of a sudden, the magnificent chasm appears and completely overwhelms by its grandeur. One realizes that the planet earth is capable of wonders far beyond expectation. When, in reading a Platonic dialogue for the first time, one sees Socrates, by the mere force of argument, overthrowing notions that one has accepted, and overthrowing them by means of a few simple questions, one experiences the same sense of new possibilities and of awe, not this time at the power of nature but at the power of human reason.

The ability of philosophy to seize a young mind is beautifully illustrated by the story of Polemon, a profligate and dissipated youth who not only carried money with him so that he might immediately gratify his desires but also left money in hiding places all over Athens so that he would always have funds at hand for the same purpose. One day, Diogenes Laertius reports, on a dare from his fellow rowdies, he burst into the Academy just as Xenocrates, the head of the school, was giving a lecture. Polemon, wearing a festive garland on his head, was completely drunk. As the Roman poet Horace embellishes the story, while Polemon stood in the doorway of the lecture hall intending to mock, the content of Xenocrates' lecture lit a fire in him, and philosophy clutched his soul. As he listened to the lecture, he slowly plucked the leaves from the garland. By the time the garland was bare, his conversion to philosophy was complete.[4] Polemon later succeeded to the headship of the Academy.

Unfortunately for those who wish to know exactly what Plato thought about this or that issue, the dialogues provide merely clues and not certainties. They are works of art, and in them Plato never speaks in his own person but always puts the words in the mouths of his characters. Whether the few surviving writings that are not dialogues, when Plato *does* appear to speak in his own person, are genuine or are exercises by his students or others to produce the kind of thing *they* thought he would say is a matter of continuing controversy.

The next section of this chapter will discuss the difficulties in understanding exactly what Plato said. It will also discuss how one might safely read the dialogues—deriving the lessons of each dialogue when it is considered a unified work of art in which the characters take positions that are not necessarily those of Plato. Readers are advised that here they will find the general interpretation of the ancient thinker the author put forth in *Interpreting Plato: The Dialogues as Drama*, issued by the same publisher as this volume. Part III of this chapter will look at the views generally associated with Platonism, that is, the views traditionally attributed to Plato and his school that have influenced subsequent Western philosophy. Part IV will examine what is known about the Academy, the school Plato founded. And part V will discuss Plato's legacy to the Western tradition.

II. Reading Platonic Dialogues

Most of the problems in understanding Plato arise from studying the dialogues as if they were a part of the tradition in which Plato did not participate. When readers try to find systematic, consistent, straightforward positions in the dialogues, with clear arguments and unambiguous meaning, they are at once frustrated, for the dialogues imitate the rambling and disjointed talk of living conversations. They are neither consistent nor straightforward, and they often portray arguments that contain equivocations, logical errors, and intellectual gamesmanship.

Some scholars have tried to account for discrepancies in the dialogues by assigning them to different periods in Plato's life, and they divide the works into early, middle, and late dialogues—with transitional periods for those that do not fit neatly into any period. While it is almost certainly true that Plato wrote the dialogues sequentially, it is not possible to ascertain with any confidence the actual order in which he wrote them. Determinations based on style or content depend on the whim of the chronologist.[5] In addition, the theory of chronology ignores the crucial question of audience. Since we do not know who Plato's audience was for any particular dialogue, we cannot presume to know why he did or did not include various arguments. Different levels of complexity are suitable for different audiences. A discussion of the Federal Reserve Bank by a university professor of economics with students in a junior high school will be very different from a discussion with colleagues at a professional conference. It would be dubious to date a transcript of the discussions on a basis of style or even content.

In general, it is a mistake to require the understanding of one dialogue to depend on what is said in another. This point is clear when we think about other authors. For example, it would be folly to base an interpretation of Sophocles' *Antigone* on a reading of the *Oedipus Rex*. They were written many years apart, and one play makes no reference to the other. Moreover, it would be absurd to suppose that an earlier text (like the *Antigone*) requires a later one (the *Oedipus Rex*, written two decades afterward) in order to be comprehended: if the author had died before completing the later one, would comprehension be lost forever? Scholars of an author can, perhaps, gain some insight into an author's developing mind by reference to a later work, but full understanding cannot rely on the other work. In fact, such reference is as likely to contaminate understanding as to promote it. And yet we often hear that such and such a point in Plato can be understood *only* by reference to an argument in another dialogue. In short, it is safest to read each dialogue as an independent work.

Much can be gained by rejecting the assumption that Plato wrote the same kind of philosophical works as Aristotle, where positions are deliberately laid out in as straightforward a way as possible. Instead, it is useful to assume that Plato is writing works of drama—the intention of which is principally to inspire—and that the inspiration is engagement in a life of the mind, to doing philosophy with other *people*. It can hardly be denied that Plato has been enormously successful in this enterprise, for very many who have chosen an impoverished life devoted to philosophy have done so because of the inspirational capital he bequeathed.

Long after a reader has forgotten the wandering maze of arguments in the *Phaedo*, he still remembers the heroic figure of Socrates cheerfully drinking hemlock, and he thinks to himself, "I wish I could be like that!" What has moved the reader has been Socrates' courage in pursuing the arguments about the immortality of the soul wherever they led. Again, when one has finished reading the *Crito*, he is similarly inspired. The dramatic situation tells all: the ship sent to Crete for the annual religious rite is about to dock, so executions can again take place in Athens. Crito tries to persuade Socrates to escape from prison. It is difficult to imagine a situation more stressful than that in which Socrates finds himself. Though he has a sure sense of his innocence, he is to be executed, and he now knows the precise hour of his execution. Death is no longer a theoretical far-off possibility but a certainty in three days. How does he respond? Despite all the temptations to live, despite the temptation of Crito's arguments, Socrates inquires into the philosophically correct course of conduct. Even in the midst of the urgent crisis, he engages his mind in order to determine the conduct that would most accord with *logos*. Much of the scholarship on this dialogue debates whether the arguments of the imaginary Laws, which persuade Socrates to stay and face execution, are valid. But the arguments of the Laws are not the heart of the dialogue's teaching.

171

Their truth or validity is not the main point. What matters in the play is that the *character* Socrates cannot refute them, that the character Socrates believes them to be the best arguments available. At the end of the dialogue, Socrates challenges Crito to produce a better argument if he has one. He does not, and Socrates decides to follow the best argument he has. He does not say, "I'll escape now; maybe I'll come up with a better argument tomorrow." The drama shows him acting on the basis of the best argument he has at the critical moment when he has to make his decision. And here lies the inspirational and dramatic message of the dialogue: a person of the mind, no matter how stressful and unnerving his situation, decides—even in matters of his own life and death—on the basis of the best rational argument that he has at the moment when he must decide. This is the dramatic purpose of the dialogue, and it does not matter whether scholars find defects in the arguments of the Laws for this point to be true.[6]

It might appear from these remarks that Plato did not have a philosophy or any philosophical positions. Such is not the case. Surely Plato held positions. The question is whether we can discern those views with any certainty in the dialogues.[7] Perhaps we can see hints of some positions through the mist of the dialogues, just as we can see hints in the works of Shakespeare, Sophocles, and Euripides of what they thought. But it is not easy. We can, however, identify many of the issues to which they directed their attention; we can then turn our minds to deducing what each play *as a whole* tells us, if anything.

Perhaps it would help to give a few examples of the teaching to be derived from the dialogues when we look at them as unified plays. Let us remember, however, that the kind of teaching we receive from art is very different from that we receive from philosophical treatises; art aims primarily at stirring our emotions, and the dialogues—insofar as they are products of art—work in this way, too. When we read or see a tragedy, the lessons perhaps seem rather obvious: honor the gods, do not commit hubristic actions, believe oracles, bury the dead. As these lessons unfold through the situation enacted in a play, we in the audience feel that human life and the order of the cosmos depend on their being true. If the lessons do not dazzle with breathtaking novelty, they nevertheless convey matters of significance. The teaching in the dialogues is more like this teaching in drama than the teaching we find in technical philosophical texts on metaphysics and logic.

A few of the dialogues seem to have as their lesson the inspiration of Socrates' memory. Thus the *Phaedo* shows how courageously Socrates met his death; the *Crito* shows him sticking to his post and choosing to stand by the best argument he has, even when such a choice means death. The *Euthyphro* shows how little Socrates corrupted youth. Even if his conversations with the various characters in the dialogues are inconclusive and leave the youths bewildered, how has bewilderment harmed them? In the case of Euthyphro, the conversation seems to have had no effect at all, and if there has been no effect, there has obviously been no corruption.

Some of the dialogues attack presumption. No doubt Plato was continuing the Socratic mission of testing those who proudly trumpeted their wisdom to the world. Thus the *Symposium* mocks those who presume a knowledge about the gods; it teaches us to beware of those who make up stories about the gods and expect them to be believed: people tend to create gods in their own images or to promote their own interests. This surely is a teaching usefully learned in all generations. The *Phaedrus* is an attack on an uncritical enthusiasm for listening to speeches. Cleverness like Lysias's is no guarantee of truth or sense. Almost the same teaching is found in the *Menexenus*, where Socrates shows how easily speeches on set themes may be made up. The *Meno* shows the emptiness of memorizing set-piece arguments, which do not require the speaker to understand the subject in his soul.

In other dialogues, like the *Cratylus* and (perhaps) the *Symposium*, we learn to follow the mean. In these dialogues various extreme positions are taken, by Socrates or the interlocutors, and the absurdity of each extreme is depicted. The audience or reader goes away realizing the folly of the extremes and thinking that perhaps wisdom lies in the mean. Thus, in the *Cratylus*, we learn that the positions of excess naturalism and excess conventionalism are equally unable to explain language; in the *Symposium*, we see perhaps the sorrows that come from both the excessively sexed life of Alcibiades and the deficiently sexed life of Socrates.

These are some of the teachings that emerge from a dramatic reading of Plato.[8] Perhaps they lack the metaphysical, epistemological, ontological, logical, political, ethical profundity that many scholars have found in the dialogues. Yet they are positive teachings of the kind that art provides.

They are teachings that would improve our souls. The history of the world—the dismal record of theological charlatans, of demagogic propagandists, of bleary-eyed philosophers and mindless politicians, of scientific hucksters, and of people who abandoned argument whenever it threatened some practical advantage—shows how important to the world were the lessons Plato had to teach in his dialogues.

In Plato we observe the elements that we found in earlier writing. We find myth and mythology, as there are myth and mythology in Homer. We find historical setting and criticism, as they are in Herodotus and Thucydides. We find drama and dialogue, as they are in Aeschylus and Euripides. And we find, in the Platonic Socrates, a phenomenon that literary critics say cannot be done: a successful dramatization of a wise and good man. Critics often say that novelists and poets cannot portray a good man in any way that interests us. But Plato gives them the lie, for he, and he almost alone in the annals of literature, shows a good and wise man being wise and good. We are not simply told that Socrates is wise and good; we actually see him being so. Plato shows us a wise and good man being good and wise in a way that arouses our attention, commands our belief, and makes us care what happens, both to Socrates and to his ideas.

III. A Compendium of Views Associated with Plato

It cannot be repeated too often that Plato does not "do" philosophy in his own person. Indeed, views that may appear near and dear in some dialogues come in for what seems annihilating criticism in others.[9] Plato perhaps had an inkling of the difficulty readers would have in determining just what he did think. In the "Seventh Letter," if it is genuine, he suggests that he never committed his truly held ideas to writing.[10] The very late Neoplatonist Olympiodorus tells the story that just before dying Plato saw himself become a swan, and, leaping from tree to tree, he defied the attempts of hunters to catch him—a dream Olympiodorus interpreted as a prediction that later interpreters of Plato's doctrines would not be able to hunt down the ideas and catch them.[11]

To distill the thought of a great literary artist into a bald listing of ideas is a daunting task. It is like trying to extract and list the views of a painter from the way in which he portrays his subjects: it might perhaps provide a glimpse at some of the artist's underlying notions, but at what a price! The translation of a canvas—with its resemblance to life, its rich and evocative ambiguity, its fertile meaning that extends rooting tentacles in all directions—into a formal system, a meticulously exacting graph-paper chart, is an offense against the memory of the artist. Still, in the interest more of elucidating the *history of philosophy* than the works of Plato himself and with the hope that Plato's ghost will forgive this effort as it smiles condescendingly from its perch in the Elysian Fields, we proceed.

A. METAPHYSICS

Perhaps it will be useful to consider how mathematics, a field to which Plato was devoted (he merged his school with that of the mathematician Eudoxus), may have contributed to his understanding of metaphysics and its corollary issues, such as the problems of change and the place of the soul.

In geometry, when we speak of points, lines, circles, triangles, and the rest, we are able to distinguish the geometric figures that we draw from the perfect ones that exist only as concepts in our minds. This distinction is critical, for it enables us to recognize at once that the mental points and other figures are indestructible, unchanging, eternal, and universal. They are apprehended only by the mind. The approximate physical embodiments of geometric shapes, on the other hand, whether portrayed by chalk or paint or shapes in wax, are destructible, changing, temporary, and particular. In other words, the mental figures are akin to things spiritual; the drawn shapes, to things physical. It follows also that our senses are unable to perceive what is nonphysical. The tongue cannot taste a mental image of a triangle, the ears cannot hear it, the eyes cannot see it, the nose cannot smell it, and the hands cannot touch it. It can be apprehended only by the mind, which itself is not perceived by the senses.

The intelligibility of perfect, unchanging things, to which Plato gives the name *ideas* or *forms*—like geometric shapes—suggests that alongside the physical realm there exists an abstract realm that is perfect and unchanging. *Ideas* or *forms* are not limited to mathematics. Everything for which there is a name has a perfect *form* in an eternally changeless, immaterial reality of Being. What is true of things is true also of qualities, and perhaps for this reason many of the dialogues are concerned with trying to define the form of such intangibles as courage or justice or virtue. With the insight that reality consists of two different realms, Plato found his solution for the problem of change. For the physical world, the realm of Becoming, everything is change—all things flow, just as Heraclitus proclaimed. For the realm of intelligible forms, the realm of Being, however, all is constant, unchanging, and universal.

This solution, known as Platonic dualism, is one of the most powerful and abiding conceptions in the intellectual history of the West. Its advantages are considerable. It accepts the apparently true fluid condition of the materiality with which we are familiar. At the same time, it accepts as true the apparent constancy that enables us to recognize things and to communicate with one another by referring with fixed names to things that are in some sense fixed. Plato succeeds in reconciling the opposite views of Parmenides and Heraclitus by means of the insight that each view is partly right but refers to a different part of reality, one to the realm of Being, the other to the realm of Becoming.

What is fixed seems to be the immaterial part of reality. A physical house may change, but the *idea* or mentally conceived *form* of a house remains the same. Indeed, one's idea of a house may remain the same in one's memory even while the house grows old and things in it fall apart.[12] Living things, or things that appear to be alive, seem to change more than inanimate materials. Animals change more than rocks. Nevertheless, we also say that living things have an identity that remains the same even in the midst of a changing corporeal part. Now if we say that an unchanging fixed identity is akin to the immaterial ideas, perhaps we can call this part the living thing's soul. Hence we can define *soul* as the part of a living entity that remains the same or has the greatest claim to remaining the same. It is not too difficult a stretch of the imagination, then, to see why for Plato the abode of souls is the realm of Being, and the aim of each person is to prepare his soul for habitation there. His body will decay and remain in the realm of Becoming. And so a person should worry over his soul, not his body.

Platonic dualism includes a dualism of body and soul—of that which changes and that which remains the same. The two are not equivalent, for the one is entirely subject to corruption, while the other may be improved to the point that it can dwell in everlasting peace and stability. The job of some-one during this life is to cultivate the soul, the noncorporeal part, so that it will enjoy a happy permanence. In the Platonic scheme, rewards and pun-ishments are meted out to souls in accordance with their owners' behavior in the realm of Becoming. In some dialogues, perhaps humorously, Plato dis-cusses the reincarnation of souls into bodies suited to their earlier behavior. Souls with no philosophy in them are reincarnated as wild animals whose heads face the ground (instead of the heavens); foolish souls are reincarnated as oysters and fish; flighty, light-minded souls as birds; and so forth.[13]

Because the material world is constantly changing, in a sense it is not so real as the unchanging world of the forms. The job of a philosopher is to try to apprehend the forms. In this way he is always "preparing for death" since in death his soul will always somehow be present with the forms, freed from bodily contamination in the realm of Becoming.

One problem for Plato and for those who subscribe to the reality of forms is whether they actually exist in some separate realm of Being—that is, whether ideas have a separate existence apart from things. Can there ever be any evidence for such existence? A second problem, common to all du-alistic systems, concerns the point of contact. How do immateriality and materiality meet and impinge on one another? The idea of a house, as something without weight or other physical qualities, is clearly nonphysical. The idea exists only as a concept. Yet the abstract idea governs our behavior with regard to the various houses we encounter in the physical world. Cor-poreal human creatures, despite being made of matter, seem always to be discovering or inventing new ideas. Another aspect of this general problem with dualistic schemes is the "mind–body problem," how apparently incor-poreal thoughts can affect our bodies. For example, the beauty of a word or an image may cause a physical sensation. But the beauty itself, even if it is *of* a physical thing, is not itself physical. The question, of course, is how the physical affects the nonphysical, or, to use traditional Platonic language, how the physical *participates* in the forms, and this question remains an ob-ject of study in both philosophy and neuroscience.

B. ETHICS

The various arguments concerning the good for human beings recur very often throughout the dialogues, and some general views seem to emerge. Even here, however, the views, though somewhat compatible, are not entirely congruent. For example, in some of the dialogues virtue is identified with knowledge, and the disparate virtues of courage and justice and temperance all devolve into knowledge; in other dialogues, when happiness is defined as a life of virtuous activity, the identification of knowledge and happiness is not made.

It is advantageous for a human being to discover what is truly good for himself as distinct from what is only apparently good. The good for a human being differs from the good for an animal or plant, for it will be intimately bound with his nature as a human being. What is distinctive of human beings as human beings is the faculty of reason; hence the good for a human being is found in reason. The true good is beautiful, just, and free from anxiety. It is a good of the soul, for it is the rational soul and not the body or possessions or power or glory that is the *human* part. Thus what is good for a person is to be just, for this is to have a good and beautiful soul. If someone performs an unjust act, it is best for him to be restored to a condition of justice by being punished, and a just person will seek punishment for himself and his friends. Indeed, the worst thing for a wrongdoer is to escape being brought to justice, for escaping justice means that his soul avoids becoming better.

Because what makes a human being worse is developing a less perfect soul, and because physical harm, even death, cannot diminish the virtue or goodness of a soul, the evildoing of men does not do harm in a meaningful sense. For evildoers can harm one's body, but they cannot make one less morally good. Thus Athens might kill but cannot harm Socrates. One will probably be rewarded for goodness in the afterlife, where philosophers, the individuals who have cultivated goodness in their earthly lives, go to the best places in the underworld.

Virtue is teachable if one is clear by what is meant by "teachable." As the sophists used the word, that is, to mean "pouring" knowledge into an empty vessel of a mind or dictating arguments that must be memorized, virtue would not be teachable, for such "teaching" would not render a person actually virtuous. The evidence is that many men renowned for their virtues had sons who were not virtuous, who were not receptive to the wisdom "poured in" by their fathers—and, clearly, if there were no students in the sense of those who actually succeeded in learning, then there were no "teachers" in the sense of those who actually succeeded in teaching. But if we understand "teach" to mean employing a process of the dialectical method of question and answer—an intellectual midwifery, as it is called in one dialogue[14]—then it is teachable, for it draws a real understanding of the truly good out of those engaging in the Socratic conversation.

If virtue were not able to be taught, it would mean that virtue was not knowledge (for an object of knowledge can be taught). And if it were not knowledge but merely "right opinion," it would not be a lasting thing, for it would not be fixed in the eternal forms but would be subject to the flux of changing events. If virtue were not knowledge—and knowledge is the unchanging, universal, and eternal truth of things—there would be no objective standards of ethical behavior, and with no objective standards, there would be no truly civilized life, for law and business require objective standards of truth and falsehood to function well.

C. POLITICAL PHILOSOPHY

Plato's two longest works, the *Republic* and *The Laws*, which together constitute just a little less than 40 percent of the corpus, directly or indirectly treat politics. The *Republic* is a brilliant work that takes up a large number of philosophical issues with humor and even satire. Nevertheless, a few serious views emerge that have become part of the legacy attributed to Plato. The *Laws* is a compendium of the legislation necessary to manage a good state; the laws are established by a good legislator working together with a good tyrant.

In the *Republic*, the state is made up of three parts, each corresponding to a part of the tripartite human soul. Workers in the state correspond to the appetitive part of the soul, guardians to the spirited part of the soul, and rulers—"philosopher-kings"—to the rational part of the soul. Only when all the parts of the state perform their proper function and do so in obedience to the properly ruling part is there a good and just state. In the famous formulation of the *Republic*, there will be no good states until philosophers rule:

> Unless either philosophers become kings in our states or those whom we
> now call kings and rulers take to the pursuit of philosophy seriously and

adequately, and there is a conjunction of these two things, political power and philosophical intelligence, while the motley horde of the natures who at present pursue either apart from the other are compulsorily excluded, there can be no cessation of troubles, dear Glaucon, for our states, nor, I fancy, for the human race either. Not, until this happens, will this constitution which we have been expounding in theory ever be put into practice within the limits of possibility and see the light of the sun. But this is the thing that has made me so long shrink from speaking out, because I saw that it would be a very paradoxical saying. For it is not easy to see that there is no other way of happiness either for private or public life.[15]

One of the principal aims of the state is to educate citizens to perform their jobs. For this purpose strict censorship must be practiced so that literature capable of corrupting, like the stories of Homer and the tragedians that show the gods in behavior we would condemn in human beings, will not have the opportunity to undermine the state.

Plato has been seen as an opponent of democracy, for in democracies rule is by the uneducated, the unwise. That all opinions—wise and foolish— should have the same political authority is counter to reason since reason demands that the opinion of the wise prevail. As we would not allow our bodies to be treated by the average man in the street but would insist on a physician expert in the art of medicine, so we should not wish our state to be managed by the average man but should insist on those expert in the art of managing a state.

The history of the fourth century, when Plato wrote the *Republic*, must give us pause in interpreting the dialogue. In the *Republic*, we find that many features of Sparta's constitution serve as models for Plato's imaginary state—a totalitarian control over private lives, with the eugenic considerations governing sexual relations; the elimination of marriage; the education of children left to the state; the elimination of private property among the guardians; and the education of women, including their physical education. Yet we must wonder how serious Plato was here, for in the fourth century, Sparta was very much a failed state: her population was vastly reduced from earlier times (Aristotle says that by 330 there were only one thousand Spartans, while a century and a half earlier, in 479, there had been eight thousand); Sparta's traditional laws about the reversion of property to the state at a man's death had been repealed by a concession to a general desire to choose one's own heirs; and the famed military supremacy had been humiliated at the Battle of Leuctra (in 379), after which Sparta's allies had rebelled. One can wonder whether in having his Republic echo the failed Sparta, Plato wasn't hinting to his readers, as perhaps Socrates was to *his* interlocutors, that the philosophic state, called by Socrates' interlocutor Glaucon a "city of pigs,"[16] was really preferable to the imaginary city of speech.

D. EROS

Though the word *eros* generally means *sexual desire* in Greek, Plato infuses it with a special philosophical significance, a significance developed by many of his successors into a highly influential mystical power. In this way, *eros* becomes a desire not for sex but for the spiritually good.

Since *eros* is a desire, it is not in itself good, for a desire is a wish for some good that is lacked, and since *eros* is a desire for this particular good, it must itself lack the good. *Eros* is a spirit (*daimon* in Greek) that directs us toward the good. It begins with an awareness of beauty in an individual body, then moves us to the beauty of bodies in general, then to the beauty in laws, and continues moving us upward, as though scaling a heavenly ladder, until we come to the idea of beauty in general (that is, the *form* of beauty), of which all beautiful things partake. Knowing the form of beauty is the culmination of a long process of an education that is perfected by dialectic.

Eros is also a yearning for immortality. In its lower manifestations, in animals and in most people, it shows itself in a wish to propagate. But higher than bodily immortality is spiritual immortality, which comes from a creative process in which one who knows anything wishes to teach it to another, "propagating," so to speak, the ideas in another person. Thus a desire to educate is a function of this philosophical *eros*. The desire for immortality is a type of self-love, but self-love is not derogatory in this sense, for it is a desire to immortalize one's soul by having it contemplate the forms and, most especially, the form of forms, the form of the good. In this way it is a striving to complete one's nature, to develop the man in man, by fully subordinating the appetitive and spirited parts of the soul to the reasoning part. Because this concord of the soul can come about only through a mixture of the right kinds of education, "musical," which looks

181

to the wisdom of the spirit, and "gymnastic," which looks to the strength of the body, it is clear that the completeness of the soul cannot come about without a proper education. Once again, we are led to the idea that *eros* is a force for education.

E. TELEOLOGY

Plato's dialogue *Timaeus* is an account of how the universe's rational and intelligible order comes about. The main speaker, Timaeus (whom the tradition dangerously takes as Plato's mouthpiece),[17] says that the visible world in which we live, that is, this physical world, was made by a Craftsman (in Greek, *Demiurge*) as a likeness of an eternal pattern. In the case of Plato's divine Craftsman, the "likeness" is the mental image of ideas that exist in the realm of Being—a repository in the realm of Being of the perfect and eternal and unchanging ideas.

Like any artisan, the divine Craftsman had a purpose and designed each element of his product with a specific purpose in mind. Just as a carpenter might make the various parts of a table to serve subsidiary purposes—for instance, making the top flat to keep objects from slipping off, making the legs equal so that the top will not wobble, allowing the table to be fitted with a removable leaf so that a large group might enjoy a meal together, or using wooden pegs instead of iron nails so that there will be nothing to rust—so too the Craftsman of the universe made every part to serve some subsidiary or ultimate purpose. The basic quality of the universe that Timaeus describes is that it is *teleological*, that is, that everything in it serves a purpose.

According to Timaeus, the world is made by intelligence operating on the necessity in materials. The Craftsman, gazing at the divine pattern in the World of Being, imitates the pattern as intelligently as he can—given the materials at his disposal. He arranges earth, air, and water in due proportions. The universe is made round because, Timaeus says rather arbitrarily, roundness is the perfect shape, the perfect idea; and soul is attuned according to various mathematical ratios that exist as ideas in the World of Being.

Matter had existed in a state of disorderly motion before the creation of the universe. The Craftsman's purpose in making the universe was to put this matter into an order as much like that of its maker as possible, that is, an order that is good and rational.

Teleology is revealed in the construction of human beings. The gods, helping the Craftsman design humans, in addition to giving humans an immortal soul, also gave them a mortal kind of soul, which contains all the passions. From this premise comes an array of anatomical conclusions. To avoid polluting the divine soul, the gods put the mortal soul in the chest and separated it by an isthmus (this is the neck). The gods made the heart to be a bodyguard to tell all the organs (by beating more strenuously than normal) when an unjust deed has been done. To relieve the leaping of the heart, the gods made lungs, the coolness of which enables the heart to be subservient to reason in times of passion. All these anatomical features, and many more, were created for the sake of mind, that is, for the sake of philosophy. Thus the construction of the universe—along with human physiology—fits in harmoniously with the general Platonic scheme, where philosophy is the purpose of human life.

F. OTHER VIEWS

Plato takes up many, many other matters in his dialogues with a mixture of wit and seriousness that both delights and leaves readers scratching their heads about the real purpose of the works. One subject associated with Plato is known as "the doctrine of recollection,"[18] which comes up in the *Meno*. According to this notion, since the soul is immortal, it already knows everything before it is born in a human body; nothing is really *taught*, and what we call learning is really recollection.[19] Whether Plato is serious or joking is a matter of long and heated debate among scholars.[20] In the *Cratylus*, he takes up the origin of language and whether language arises by convention or by nature. Here, too, Plato's own views are a matter of controversy. In the *Phaedrus*, he takes up the question of whether writing has been a boon or a misfortune, and his character Socrates argues that writing has been a misfortune, for it has corrupted the faculty of memory in people.

Like great literature in general, the dialogues benefit from frequent rereading. One can return to them again and again and develop new insights, both about the dialogues and about the subjects that the various characters converse about. If Plato's purpose was to inspire a zeal for philosophy, he must, by anyone's standard, be reckoned a stunning success.

IV. Plato's Academy

The name "Plato's Academy" is misleading, for the Academy was never Plato's. It was, in fact, an area of about 490 by 330 yards situated northwest of Athens about a mile and a quarter from the *agora*, the center of town. Here was located the cult of one Hecademus. Pausanias, writing two centuries or so after Cicero, provides a full description.[21] The comic playwright Aristophanes presents an idyllic picture in contrast to the jaded *agora*.[22] Perhaps in memory of Socratic associations, so charmingly presented in the *Lysis*, Plato chose to commence his academic career there; later, according to Diogenes Laertius, he moved to a spot outside the Academy proper, near the famous hill of Colonus, where he seems to have had a house and garden.[23] The name "Academy" was used loosely in antiquity to designate both the gymnasium or park itself as well as the surrounding area. As the name of the philosopher grew, however, the name of the cult hero shrank, and "Plato's Academy" it has been ever since.

The philosopher engaged in his educational work for about forty years, from about 387 to his death in 347. In practical terms, the Academy was enormously successful. To Plato's school came councilors and lawgivers for republics and sovereigns—reigning and future. As H. I. Marrou writes,

> Plutarch gives a list of statesmen Plato helped to produce, and they were to be found in every part of the Hellenic world: Dion of Syracuse, Python and Heraclides (the liberators of Thrace), Chabrias and Phocion (the great Athenian generals), Aristonymos the law-giver of Megalopolis in Arcadia, Phormion of Elis, Menedemus of Pyrrha, Eudoxus of Cnidus, Aristotle of Stagira, and lastly, Xenocrates, adviser to Alexander the Great. But even this long list is incomplete, for we must add Callipus the murderer of Dion of Syracuse, Clearchus the Tyrant of Heraclea in Pontus and his opponent Chion; Euphraios, who was adviser to Perdiccas III of Macedonia before he became the champion of democracy and independence in his native city of Oreos in Euboea; Erastus and Coriscus, who governed Assos and were the allies of Hermeias of Atarneus.[24]

From later evidence we can deduce some of the activities that took place at the Academy after Plato's death: 1) mathematical research; 2) the harmonizing of mathematics and philosophy, especially Platonic philosophy—and, by implication, the continuous development of that philosophy; and 3) initiation of the young into the methods of philosophy, especially definition and division. The relationship of mathematics and philosophy became very close, so close that Aristotle—sounding like a modern humanistic philosopher speaking of symbolic logicians—remarks that philosophy there had become mathematics.[25]

Though to go into what went on in the Academy would be highly speculative, perhaps it would be appropriate to mention the problem posed by the claim in the "Seventh Letter" (if it is genuine) that Plato never committed his true ideas and theories to writing—what some claim to be the unwritten teachings (*agrapha dogmata* in Greek) mentioned by Aristotle.[26] Closely connected with the problem is the famous "lecture" or "lectures" on the Good. Aristoxenus, a pupil of Aristotle's, reports an anecdote about this lecture that he says was told by Aristotle himself.[27] The anecdote shows that even the divine Plato had the power to be dull. We hear that Plato once gave a lecture titled "On the Good." It was a very abstruse lecture, and he opened it up to the public. According to Aristoxenus, the audience was absolutely bored, as the lecturer droned on and on, until at last people began to leave, one by one. As Plato finished the lecture, he looked up, only to discover an empty hall, devoid of listeners—except for one man. That man, of course, was Aristotle. From the anecdote we may guess that each member of Plato's audience came expecting, from the title "On the Good," to hear something about the traditional human values such as health, strength, in short, about human happiness. It is unclear whether the lecture was intended for a public audience, for members of the Academy, or for both. If it was only for members of the Academy, then it is clear that many members did not know of the abstruse work that was Plato's special occupation. Finally, the anecdote is suggestive of the relationship that Aristotle may have had with Plato. We tend to think of this relationship of teacher and student as rather a familiar one, but the anecdote suggests that perhaps the older man was remote and that Aristotle did not wish to lose a rare opportunity to learn Plato's sincerely held views. Like Aristotle, we too might have this wish!

V. After Plato

After the death of Plato in 347, the Academy was taken over by his nephew Speusippus. The other leading contenders for the headship were Aristotle and Xenocrates,[28] both of whom left Athens, perhaps in disappointment or from a lack of sympathy for the focus on mathematics that was then occurring. Indeed, Aristotle says that Speusippus was falling under the influence of the Pythagorean school and was rejecting Plato's Idea of the Good for an idea of a "One beyond being."[29] When Speusippus died in 339, Xenocrates returned to Athens and became head of the Academy until his death in 315. He was so devoted to philosophy that he hardly ever left the grounds of the Academy. His resistance to female charm was celebrated in the stories of his valiant and successful resistance to the notoriously attractive courtesans Phryne and Laïs.[30] The Academy underwent changes as the decades passed. For a while it was identified with skepticism, the doctrine by which it was doubted that anything at all could be known. Later, the Academy became somewhat eclectic, mixing Stoic elements with those more traditionally ascribed to Plato. It was finally closed in 529 C.E. by the Christian emperor Justinian, who objected to it as a pagan institution.

Discussion Questions

1. Throughout antiquity we find individuals whose lives were somehow turned to philosophy through an encounter with a philosopher. What qualities, in addition to mental acuity, do you think a philosopher has to possess in order to convert someone to preferring intellectual over material rewards?

2. If you put three or four geometers in a room, it is difficult to imagine fervent debates over the truth of this or that theorem. But put in a room three or four Plato scholars, or Shakespeare scholars, or James Joyce scholars, and it is impossible to imagine there *not* being fervent debates. What is it about literary works that invites debate about their meaning? In the case of Plato's dialogues, the debates are perhaps more complicated since people will argue over both the literary purposes and the philosophical issues that Plato

has his characters discuss. Do you think that this complexity has increased Plato's appeal?

3. The author of this book has argued that one can be reasonably sure that some positive lessons do emerge from Plato's dialogues, for example, to follow the mean and to be wary of those who claim to know the minds of the gods. Has the author overstated *his* case, and is Plato in fact *not* attempting to teach these lessons?

4. What in Plato's system of Forms might be appealing to religions with a concept of a transcendent deity? What challenges to such religions does the theory of Forms present?

5. To what extent are school systems, as well as handbooks on parenting, based on the notion that virtue can be taught? Should our penal systems also be based on this notion? Are there limits on the extent to which virtue can be taught? Are there limits that depend on age, or intelligence, or religion, or class, or ancestry, or race, or body type, or high school record? Have there been individuals who wished to deny to certain kinds of people the ability to be taught virtue?

6. Would *you* want to live in a state governed by philosopher-kings? What would be the actual advantages or disadvantages of such a regime? Can you think of any states that have actually been governed by such individuals? One sometimes thinks of the rule of the Antonines during the Roman Empire and of Antoninus Pius and his adopted son Marcus Aurelius. Were these men truly philosopher-kings? Can any general or philosophical lessons be drawn from their experiences?

7. When Plato uses the word *eros* to signify a desire to move us toward the realm of Forms, how far is he stretching the metaphor inherent in this term? To what degree do such metaphors clarify or obscure an author's meaning?

8. Plato's teleological approach to understanding the physical world has been profoundly influential in the history of science, and for most of Western history it seemed compatible with a religious understanding of the universe and God's role in it. In the nineteenth and twentieth centuries, teleology has been rejected by most, though not all, physicists and biologists. While the specific scientific views of Plato today would probably find no supporters at all, does he nevertheless help define the broad philosophical questions that apply to understanding nature? What elucidation does he provide in articulating the questions?

9. The Academy stayed in business for nearly a millennium after Plato's death. One of its challenges must have been whether to preserve and transmit

the founder's teaching or to examine, refine, and reject it and then expand the frontiers of knowledge. If you had been present, what arguments would you have made for Academic (understood literally and narrowly as "belonging to the *Academy of Plato*") orthodoxy? What arguments would you have used to reject such orthodoxy?

Notes

1. Diogenes Laertius, *Life of Plato* 3.5. Like all ancient anecdotes, this one too must be taken with a grain of salt. The purpose of the story may have been to illustrate the inspirational effect of philosophy, that it could make a man give up a talent and its promise of fame for a higher calling. It is equally possible that the purpose of the story is to explain why Plato wrote dialogues, for they would have been a way to keep his childhood ambition and yet write works of philosophical value.

2. Alice Swift Riginos, *Platonica: The Anecdotes concerning the Life and Writings of Plato* (Leiden: E. J. Brill, 1976), 21.

3. On dialectic, see pp. 134–35.

4. Diogenes Laertius, *Life of Polemon* 2.16; Horace, *Satires* 2.3.254 ff.

5. For example, one scholar would place the *Phaedrus* as Plato's first dialogue "because Plato could not have written so passionately about love unless he were a young man himself," while another would put it among the late dialogues because it mentions the world of ideas. For a discussion of the dating of the *Phaedrus*, see W. K. C. Guthrie, *A History of Greek Philosophy*, vol. 4 (Cambridge: Cambridge University Press., 1978), 396 n. 1.

6. In fact, the more loopholes they find, the more likely it is that Plato wants us to see the dramatic point. When we see a drama, we understand that the characters say what is appropriate for them to say as *characters* in the drama; the "truth-value" of what they say is of interest as it enhances their characterization. Only when it comes to Plato's philosophical drama do readers simply assume that Socrates is to be understood as speaking in perfect arguments.

7. In the "Seventh Letter," if the letter be genuine, Plato denies ever committing to writing his serious doctrines. The letter's authenticity is with remarkable cyclical regularity either affirmed or rejected. I do not know whether the letter be spurious or not; its sentiments seem to me valid. For a discussion of the letter, with references to the relevant secondary material, see James A. Arieti, *Interpreting Plato: The Dialogues as Drama* (Savage, Md.: Rowman & Littlefield, 1991), 14–15.

8. For more, see Arieti, *Interpreting Plato*, 247–50.

9. For example, the concept of the "form"—usually a bedrock notion of "a Platonic system"—is dealt a blow in the *Parmenides*.

10. Plato, "Seventh Letter" 344c. On Plato's true ideas see pp. 172–74; see also Socrates' anecdote about Plato on p. 133.

11. Riginos, *Platonica*, 24–25.

12. The problem is more vexed, as Plato himself knew (and as he revealed in his dialogue *Parmenides*). If a person redecorates his house, he has produced a new idea of his house. So now he has a fixed idea of his house at time A (before the redecoration) and at time B (after the redecoration). And what about every other moment? Does each moment of each thing reflect a different fixed idea? Does each number? These are very difficult questions for a Platonist.

13. Plato, *Timaeus* 91d–92c.

14. Plato, *Theaetetus* 149a–151d.

15. Plato, *Republic* 473c–e, trans. Paul Shorey (Cambridge, Mass.: Harvard University Press, 1953).

16. Plato, *Republic* 372d.

17. Diogenes Laertius says that Timaeus is one of four characters who expounds Plato's own views (*Life of Plato* 52). The other three are Socrates, the Athenian Stranger (in the *Laws*), and the Eleatic Stranger (in the *Sophist*).

18. Even though Socrates—presumably Plato's mouthpiece in the dialogue—himself admits that he doesn't subscribe to the theory (86B), it has been taken as a serious part of the Platonic system.

19. *Meno* 81A–D.

20. For a brief review of the debate concerning Plato's theory of recollection, see Arieti, *Interpreting Plato*, 226–27 n. 7.

21. Pausanias, *Geography of Greece* 29.2 ff.

22. Aristophanes, *Clouds* 1005 ff.

23. Diogenes Laertius, *Plato* 3.5.

24. H. I. Marrou, *Education on Antiquity*, trans. George Lamb (Madison: University of Wisconsin Press, 1982), 64–65.

25. Aristotle, *Metaphysics* 992 b32.

26. Aristotle, *Physics* 209 b13–16.

27. *Elements of Harmony* 2.1.

28. Xenocrates, about whom little is known, was from Chalcedon (a city on the Asiatic side of the Bosphorus opposite Byzantium), and Aristotle was from Stagira (a city in Chalcidice in northern Greece).

29. Aristotle, *Metaphysics* 1080 b11–18.

30. His heroic steadfastness is recorded by Diogenes Laertius, *Xenocrates* 7.

Select Bibliography

Web resource: www.platon.org/eng/eng-web.htm.

Arieti, James A. *Interpreting Plato: The Dialogues as Drama*. Savage, Md.: Rowman & Littlefield, 1991.

Friedländer, Paul. *Plato*. 3 vols. Translated by H. Meyerhoff. Princeton, N.J.: Princeton University Press, 1969.

Grube, G. M. A. *Plato's Thought*. London: Methuen, 1935.

Jaeger, W. *Paideia: The Ideals of Greek Culture*. Vol. 2. Translated by Gilbert Highet. New York: Oxford University Press, 1943.

Shorey, Paul. *What Plato Said*. Chicago: University of Chicago Press, 1933.

Taylor, Alfred Edward. *Plato, the Man and His Works*. New York: Meridian Books, 1960.

CHAPTER 11

Aristotle

I. Introduction

A young person discovering Plato feels the exuberant exhilaration of falling in love for the first time. When he puts down his book, he exclaims, "This is better, much better, than I dreamt it would be." A young person coming upon Aristotle feels like a child coming face to face with the *Encyclopaedia Britannica* who, filled with dread, withdraws a ponderous volume from the set, notes that it is almost completely devoid of colorful illustrations, yet has the reassuring sense that though he does not wish to contend with it just now, should a pressing need come in the future, it will serve him well. If the chief good of Plato is that he excites one to engage in philosophy, the chief good of Aristotle is that he makes one confident that philosophy is worthwhile and actually has truths to promote our understanding.

Aristotle, born to a physician in Stagira, in northern Greece, came down to study at Plato's Academy when he was about seventeen years old, in or about 367 B.C.E. By now the Persian Wars had been over one hundred years; the Peloponnesian War more than thirty-five years. Athens was prosperous, active, civilized: the external scars of defeat had passed. Tragedy, philosophy, and rhetoric were flourishing. The rival schools of Plato and Isocrates were flourishing; Demosthenes, perhaps the greatest orator the world has seen, was commencing his career; trade and manufacturing, depressed during the Peloponnesian War, were in vigorous revival. And the world came to Athens to be educated. In the crowd of those who came was the seventeen-year-old Aristotle. He entered Plato's Academy. He stayed there for twenty years.

When Plato died in 347, Aristotle went to Assus, on the Asiatic side of the Aegean, to the court of Hermeias, who had been a fellow student at the Academy. He married Hermeias's daughter Pythias and fled with her to Lesbos when Hermeias was betrayed and killed. From there Aristotle was summoned to the court of Philip of Macedon, where he became the tutor of Prince Alexander. In 334, as Alexander commenced his conquests, Aristotle, perhaps funded by Alexander, moved to Athens and established his school, known as the Lyceum, a lovely gymnasium surrounded by gardens and covered walkways. He taught there until after the death of his patron Alexander, when he fled Athens, which had brought a charge of impiety against him.[1]

It would appear that while studying at Plato's Academy, Aristotle began to work out the rules of analytical thinking. The forging of his *Organon*—the tool we call logic—led him to break away from Plato's genre of expression, the dialogue, and into a different way of looking at things. He created a new style for philosophy, one that can easily be detected in translation: lean, spare, expository, analytical, full of technical terms and precise distinctions.

We have only a fraction of what Aristotle wrote, though we know from Diogenes Laertius many of the titles of the lost works.[2] In addition to writing on logic, he wrote on ethics, politics, metaphysics, poetry, physics, animals, dreams, and on many, many other subjects. He applied his methods of research to everything he did. When he wished to write about starfish, he and his students collected starfish and studied them. When he wished to write about constitutions, he and his students collected one hundred and fifty constitutions. He was the first man to organize research and to departmentalize knowledge. He often writes, "On this point, see my work on such and such."

In organizing the various sciences and disciplines, Aristotle noticed that they fell into three kinds. These he called the productive, the practical, and the theoretical. Shoemaking, for example, Aristotle would classify, like poetry, as a productive art—that is, the art aims at producing something actual. In the case of a shoemaker, the aim is to produce a pair of sandals or shoes; in the case of a poet, a lyric or an epic. The next kind of discipline is the practical. A man who teaches the art of surgery is not aiming to produce a thing; he is aiming at a certain activity, removing or repairing parts of the body. So too those who concern themselves with etiquette and ethics; they aim at a certain kind of activity—polite conduct or ethical behavior. The last kind of art is the theoretical. Here the art or science aims neither at the production of a thing nor at an activity but at knowledge for its own sake. The study of the origin of the universe and of black holes, knowledge of which has no productive or practical value, is pursued wholly for its own sake. Aristotle considered the theoretical sciences to be superior to the productive and practical ones.[3]

In this chapter it will be impossible to do more than discuss a few topics to serve as an introduction to Aristotle. These will commence with an overview of his works on logic and especially the *Categories*. We shall then take a look at what has come to be known as "Aristotle's four causes" before moving on to his response to the challenge of Parmenides, his notion of the Prime Mover, his philosophy of science, and, finally, his ethics and psychology. There will not be an attempt here to do even an injustice to his work in biology, zoology, meteorology, politics, rhetoric, and poetics, or, indeed, many other subjects.

II. Logic

Aristotle did not use the word "logic," nor was it he who organized what are known as his works on logic into the collection called the *Organon* (Greek for *tool*). He most likely thought of these works as lessons in persuasiveness, and while some aimed at the means for establishing truth, others explicitly aimed at the means for demolishing an opponent in debate and achieving victory for oneself. The various "schools" of philosophy were competing for students, and the most practically efficacious part of the curriculum was that devoted to the art of persuasion. Though Aristotle drew hundreds of distinctions, he does not seem to have drawn the particular line separating technical logic from rhetoric.

Given the number of these writings on persuasiveness, perhaps, for the purposes of this book, a brief overview of the individual works would be most useful. These will be taken up in the traditional order.

The first book of the *Organon*, *Categories*, covers the kinds of things that can be affirmed or denied about things or subjects. What is affirmed or denied is called a *predicate*. Examples of the kinds of things that may be a predicate are quantity (three yards), relation (half), acting (he is painting), and being acted on (the wall is being painted). This fundamental work will be taken up in more detail in the next section.

On Interpretation, sometimes called, more accurately, *On Propositions*, deals with propositions and their parts (nouns and verbs), the kinds of propositions (denials, affirmations, assertions that are contrary, and assertions that are contradictory), and the relation of propositions to truth. For example, Aristotle investigates both specific statements like "it will rain tomorrow" and universal future statements like "the sun will always come up."

Prior Analytics, perhaps the most technical work, deals with the nature of the syllogism—the deductive argument having two premises and a conclusion. It discusses the premises (also called *terms*) and the relation of the premises to each other and to the conclusion. *Posterior Analytics* is the work that most fully presents Aristotle's philosophy of science, for it deals with demonstrative knowledge. It investigates premises, definitions, and the types of questions that can be asked and classifies the kinds of demonstrations that can be made.

Topics and *Sophistical Refutations*, which together make up about half of the *Organon*, are the least technical of the works on logic. They deal with defeating an opponent in argument and constitute a comprehensive cookbook of argumentation. Since most arguments that one is likely to encounter are inductive, that is, drawn from life's examples, these books deal extensively with how to handle inductive claims. Much of the advice is practical. For example, Aristotle points out that it is much easier to poke holes in a definition that someone else offers than to establish a definition oneself. He observes also that one will be much more persuasive if one gives the *appearance* of impartiality, an appearance one can establish by an occasional objection to one's own position.[4] The rules for demolishing another's argument are laid out with impeccable common sense, and a reader will immediately recognize their effectiveness.[5]

A reader who is fond of classifications and distinctions will find a mother lode in *Sophistical Refutations*. Here, among a myriad of other classifications, Aristotle describes the four classes of arguments (didactic, dialectical, examinational, and contentious), the five aims of those who argue as competitors (refutation, falsity, paradox, solecism, and reducing the opponent to simply repeating himself), the seven kinds of fallacies, the two styles of refutation, the six ways of creating an illusion dependent on language, and so on. The student who learned these and could employ them at will at the proper occasion would clearly become a champion arguer.

III. Aristotle's Ten Categories

One way to avoid equivocation and the resulting confusion is to know precisely just what can be said about a thing and all the ways in which it can be classified. Aristotle's *Categories* teaches how to avoid equivocations by telling us how to classify things. After studying the book, Augustine was convinced, for a while, that he knew just about everything.[6] Armed with the ten categories, Aristotle or one of his students could examine some thing—in Aristotle's words—some *this*. The notion of a *this* is very important for Aristotle: if things did not exist, there could be no system. Things must be detectable by human beings; each thing must be—to use his word—a *this* (*to on* in Greek). What does Aristotle mean by a *this*? Well, he does not mean any particular thing, that is, any one thing. By a *this*, Aristotle means a kind of thing, of which at least two specimens must exist. For if two things of the same kind exist, we have a universal; we have a genus, and so we can generalize about them. If there were only two elephants in the whole world, even though there were only two, since they would be the only ones of their kind, we would be justified in treating them as a genus, as a universal, and we could say, "All the elephants in the world are gray" or "All the elephants in the world have thick skin." So long as there are at least two, we can make a generalization. But if there is only one, we cannot. For Aristotle, a *this* is a technical term for a thing that is different from other things, that belongs to a set of two or more things of the same kind, and about which generalizations can be made. In Aristotle's language, a *this* is a thing that has being (in Greek, an *ousia*) and can thus be a subject of discourse. The Greek term *ousia* was translated into Latin as *substantia* and is traditionally rendered as *substance* in English. Substance is the first of Aristotle's ten categories.

When a *this* has been identified, we may look to see whether it is the kind of a *this* that has quantity. If the *this* is a dog, it may have a variety of quantities that are meaningful—weight, width, height, and so forth. There are, of course, some things that we can identify that would not have quantity in a meaningful way. For example, pity or irritation are identifiable things for which the category of *quantity*, the second of Aristotle's categories, has no significance.

We may then look to see what kind of *this* the thing is; that is, we may look to see its qualities. The dog, for example, may be a retriever, male, and black. *Quality* is the third of the categories.

We can also categorize a *this* by its *relationship*—the fourth of Aristotle's categories—with people and other things. The retriever is a pet, for it has a master; it is a littermate since it has male and female siblings. It is a companion of the other dogs in the neighborhood.

Next we can categorize a *this* by its *location*—the fifth category—that is, where it is. The retriever may be on my street or on the lawn in front of my house. Later it may be in the garage or down the road chasing a tennis ball.

We may also look at the *position* of a *this*. For example, the retriever may be lying down now; later it may be standing. Position is different from location, for the dog could be sitting or lying down in a particular location on the lawn or in the garage. Position is the seventh category.

A *this* may be characterized by its state or *condition*—the eighth category. For example, the dog may just have been washed and may now be clean. A few hours ago, it had tangled with a skunk and was odiferous and dirty.

A *this* may be categorized by what it is doing, by its actions. The dog is now eating. Later it will be retrieving a tennis ball. *Actions* are the ninth category.

Finally, a *this* may be categorized by what is being done to it, that is, *how it is being affected*. A while ago the dog was being washed; later it will be brushed. We distinguish between a subject doing and having something done to it by the active and passive voices.

About a *this* we may also make generalizations concerning its matter, its form, its essence, its universality, its potentiality, and its actuality. Perhaps it would be useful to discuss here what these terms mean.

B. MATTER AND FORM

For Aristotle, *prime matter* is what is left when all form is removed. Because we experience matter only when it is joined with a form, in a thing that is a composite of matter and form, it is impossible to give an example of pure matter.[7] Perhaps it will be helpful, though, to explain the meaning by analogy. A gold statue is made up of a matter or material called gold. But it is not a statue until it receives a form. When it receives a form, it is a composite of matter and form. Before the gold is formed into a statue, it has some *other* form, for example, as a cube, bar, or hunk of ore. Pure matter by itself does not actually exist since all actual objects have a form.

Trying to think of gold itself without any form is like thinking of water or gas apart from the particular shape they take from the receptacle that contains them. Each of the things we make out of gold—statues, cups, dishes, guns, and so forth—is distinguishable *by its form* from other things made out of gold. We make a statue out of gold by getting the gold to have a certain form. We do not start with some gold on the one hand and some form on the other and then put the two together. No form is ever separable from its matter, any more than matter is capable of existing without some form. We cannot take the form out of the gold statue and leave just the gold over here and the form over there: all we can do is destroy the form, as when we melt the gold statue and thereby impart a new form to the gold. Even if the newly formed gold lacks the aesthetic excellence of a statue, it has a form nonetheless.

By considering the relationship between form and matter, we can further clarify the meaning of the term *matter*. Suppose we take a wooden chair as our example. The matter is wood; the form in which the matter appears to us is the form of a chair. Suppose that we chop the chair up into small pieces with an ax. We can see at once that we have deprived the wood of the form of the chair—that is, the remnants of wood no longer look like, or can be used as, a chair. But the remnants of the chair are still wood—that is, the matter has not changed; instead, it has a new form, in this case, the form of a pile of wood chips. Now suppose that we take another wooden chair, but, instead of chopping it up with an ax, we burn it. Once again, we can see that the form of the chair has been destroyed. In addition, however, the matter of the chair—the wood—has been changed: in destroying the form, we do not end up with wood but with ashes (and some gases, as well, although they dissipate and are not easily detectable). Now ashes are not wood—that is, we cannot take the ashes and, using the techniques of carpentry, make a chair out of them. But the ashes are matter (in the form, perhaps, of a loose pile on the floor), and we can take the matter that is ashes and do something with it.

If we reflect on this imaginary experiment, we can see that both the wood and the ashes are what Aristotle calls "proximate" or "intermediate" matter, not "prime" matter. Wood and ashes are proximate matter because they have different characteristics, different forms, that distinguish them—for example, smell, color, and solidity. Reduce a chair to wood chips or ashes, and you have reduced it to its proximate matter, not to entirely formless, prime matter. Underlying both the ashes and the wood is what Aristotle calls *primary matter* or what today we might call *matter/energy*.

C. ACTUALITY AND POTENTIALITY

Let us return to our chair for a moment to consider two other Aristotelian concepts, those of actuality and potentiality. When the wood is in the form of a chair, we have an actual chair. Since the chair's wood could be used to make something else, say, wooden dice, the wood can be said to be *potential* dice. When a thing undergoes the process of becoming actually that which it was potentially (for example, when the chair undergoes transformation into dice), the transformation is called *change*. When the chair becomes dice, the composite of matter and form-of-chair no longer exists. To be sure, the matter continues to exist, but it now exists with the form-of-dice. Prime matter is thus incapable of either destruction or generation. We speak of generation and destruction only of composites, when there is the addition or privation of a form.

Even though ultimate matter has no form in and of itself, there must be such a thing as ultimate matter lying behind all the matter/form composites in the world. If we do not posit ultimate matter, we end up with what Aristotle absolutely and unequivocally set himself and his powerful intellect against: an infinite regress. If the wood can be changed into ashes—which are matter plus form—and if the ashes can be changed into something else that is matter plus form, and if this process can go on indefinitely, we end with an infinite regress of potential changes, with no starting point.

D. ESSENCE

We come now to the third item—*essence*.[8] An essence is what a thing is in itself, in virtue of itself, without accidents or properties. It answers the question, What is the thing? For example, of a reader one might ask,

"What is a reader?" And the answer is, "An individual who reads." Or, to use a more Aristotelian example, one might ask, "What is a human being?" The answer: "An animal that reasons." Now any given human being will have many attributes or qualities or properties that have little or nothing to do with being an animal that reasons. For example, a particular human may be bearded, male, and suffer nearsightedness. But none of these has anything to do with being a human being. To arrive at the essence of a thing, we must strip away everything that might be accidental to an individual instance of the thing to arrive at what is left, that is, at pure form plus pure matter, and then we have the essence of a thing, whether a reader, a human being, a bird, or anything else. And that essence is—to use a synonymous term—the individual's *nature* as a reader or human being. In order for accidental properties and qualities to exist in this individual, the individual must first have a special kind of essence—that special kind that we call a "reader" or "human being." So after we determine what the matter is, and the form, we have to see the combination of matter and form in its purest state, and when we see that, we see the essence.

A universal is any two or more *thises* of the same species or kind. Thus the only two elephants on the planet would be a universal. So, too, all women constitute a universal. As long as there are at least two *thises*, we have a universal; and if we have a universal, we can make universal or general statements. For example, we can say of the universal *woman*, "All women are mortal."

Each *this*, however, is an individual—by which Aristotle means that it is of a nature such that, if it is divided or cut in two, we don't end up with two *thises*, but—instead—the *this* ceases to be. And of an individual, or a particular, no general or universal statements can be made. Thus, for example, we cannot say, "All John Jacob Jingleheimer Smiths are shoemakers." As there is only one John Jacob Jingleheimer Smith, to say "all" is silly.

E. ADDITIONAL THOUGHTS ON ACTUALITY AND POTENTIALITY

To examine further the meaning of potentiality, let us think once again of rose seeds. A rose seed is a *this*; there is more than one rose seed, and so we have a universal; and every rose seed has potentiality—that is, every rose seed is a potential rose bush. Contained within that small seed is a complicated genetic makeup that enables the rose seed—if nothing interferes—to grow and develop into a rose bush. Of any *this* we need to understand what its potentialities are if we are going to understand its nature, its essence. The rose has many potentialities. It can become a gift for a beloved, or it can have its odor-bearing properties extracted and made into the fragrance of a perfume. Some of the potentialities of the rose seed exist, as we say, by nature. Other potentialities develop only because humans work on them by means of art and sciences. By itself, a rose seed has only natural potentialities.

Finally, we may turn once more to actuality. If a rose seed is not interfered with, it will actualize its potentialities. And once it has actualized its potentialities, it becomes an actuality. We might also say it "ends up" as a rose bush. In the phrase "ends up" lies the Greek conception of *telos*, from which we get our word "teleological." A *telos* is the condition that any *this* is in when its potentialities have been most fully actualized. For a rose seed, the *telos* is to be a rose bush; for a baby, the *telos* is to be a man or a woman.

We do not have much trouble in recognizing that a rose bush is the fulfillment of the potentialities of a rose seed. It is, however, much more difficult to know what the fulfillment of a baby's potentialities are. What constitutes the *telos* of a human being is one of the topics Aristotle takes up in his work on ethics.

201

IV. Aristotle's "Four Causes"

Part of Aristotle's genius lay in enunciating the various patterns that constitute knowledge and in showing how, if any of these are incomplete, knowledge will be incomplete. When we talk about a thing, Aristotle said we want to know 1) what it is made of—the material cause, 2) who or what made it—the efficient cause, 3) what it looks like and how it is put together—the formal cause, and 4) what its end is—the final cause. These are known as "Aristotle's four causes." If we are speaking of a house, for example, we want to know that it is made of bricks and pipes and glass and so on; that it was constructed by Sam and Ruth and Uli and Patrick, the carpenters, electricians, and plumbers; that it is a colonial house; and that it was made for the end of housing the Kidd family. We want to know, in other words, how to categorize the house: as "brick house," "colonial house," and so forth. Aristotle's four causes provide four fundamentally different ways of categorizing things, four fundamentally different aspects of knowing things. If we knew only that the house was made of bricks, our knowledge would be incomplete, as it would be if we knew everything about the house *except* what it was made of.

Aristotle's formulation works best for things made by human beings for express preconceived ends and less well for things in the natural world. For example, we might ask about a certain mouse that nibbled some chocolates we left on our kitchen counter last night. We might be able to say what the mouse was made of; we might be able to explain "who made it"—its mouse parents; we might even understand its anatomy and shape. But what is its purpose? Those who grant purposes to nature might say that the mouse's purpose is to supply food to snakes and so to participate in the chain of being; others might say that the mouse is fulfilling a purpose assigned it by God. Aristotle would perhaps say that the mouse is achieving the end of doing what a mouse does for the most part and therefore not by chance, that is, nibble at whatever food it finds. Aristotle would probably agree with the vast majority of evolutionary biologists, who claim that the mouse has no ultimate purpose. In denying a pre-planned purpose to things in the world, Aristotle perhaps exposes a tension in rational human psyches, which do not normally find closure unless all four causes are apprehended in terms applicable to things in the human world. Cosmic objects, such as asteroids orbiting the sun, pose similar difficulties to the understanding. The search for ends—whether those that consist of things acting according to their nature or, in the case of human intentionality, the rationally conceived goals we call *purposes*—is called *teleology*. Ancient thought is dominated by teleological thinking because the ancients, with some notable exceptions, could not easily conceive of a universe or anything in the universe that lacked ends. Aristotle, though admitting that it is very difficult to articulate even the *questions* involved in attributing a *telos* to plants, himself dismisses the notion of things and events existing in nature without ends as absurd.[9]

V. Aristotle's Response to Parmenides

Let us recall, for a moment, that Parmenides denied all motion and all coming into being. He based this denial on the idea that if something comes into being, either it has to come from something that is—in which case it would already be—or it has to come from something that is not—an impossibility since nothing can come from nothing.[10] Aristotle attacks Parmenides' dilemma by distinguishing between actuality and potentiality. Every object has the potentiality to become something else. For example, a rose seed has the potentiality to become a rose bush, and it becomes one by actualizing its potentiality to be one. In a sense, the potentiality to become a rose bush actually *is* in the rose seed, as is the rose's potentiality to be made into a bouquet or a perfume. In the sense that the potentiality has being, Parmenides is correct. Aristotle thus suggests that Parmenides is right insofar as nothing comes into being *absolutely* out of nothing. Things do come into being out of what they are not, but, for Aristotle, the things they are not exist potentially, even if not actually. Thus the rose bush comes into being out of a thing that is potentially but not actually a rose bush (but is actually a rose seed).

What sort of being is capable of turning potentiality into actuality? It must be something that, in a broad sense, moves the thing and is different from the thing itself. In order to understand this idea, let us recall that according to Aristotle's conception of matter, *matter* is what is left when all form is removed.

The connection between Aristotle's doctrine of matter and form and the issue of how potentialities become actualities lies in Aristotle's insight that matter is to potentiality what form is to actuality. Gold in the *form* of a statue is an *actual* statue, although in virtue of its matter it has the potentiality of being formed into any number of other things. But gold does not spontaneously form into statues, nor do rose seeds into rose bushes. States of potentiality must be actualized by someone or something. And the actualizer must itself be in a state of actuality with respect to the form being actualized. The sculptor does not, of course, have to *be* a golden statue in order to make a statue, but the form of the statue must be present in his mind before he can render that form in gold. In the sense that the idea *is* in the mind of the sculptor, it already has being, and in this sense Parmenides is correct that being does not come into being.

VI. *The Prime Mover as Aristotle's Deity*

Natural processes, such as the maturation of rose bushes and even the motions of the stars and planets (although these latter motions do not involve matter taking on new forms), are, for Aristotle, made actual by a being that is actual in the highest sense and that uses a special mode of actualization. The key to understanding the most fully actual sort of being and how it works is to appreciate Aristotle's aversion to infinite regress. If *all* motion and actualization were accomplished by transitions from potentiality to actuality, there would be an infinite regress of such transitions, and there could never be any *first* motion or actualization.[11] When we speak of motion, says Aristotle, we are not speaking about the causes of motion itself, for motion itself has no cause: it is uncaused and eternal. The rustling of leaves, to be sure, is caused by the wind, which itself is caused by other winds. But nothing moves motion itself. This means that there never was a time when motion began. In the same way, time must always have existed, and the terms *before* and *after* are meaningless with respect to an (imaginary) period in which there was no time.[12] By this argument, there is no reason for the motion ever to have had a beginning or ever to have an end. Hence, there must exist a being of pure actuality, one that actualizes and moves *itself*, without the help of anything else and without a hint of potentiality. This self-moved being, moving eternally, is the ultimate source of all motion and actualization in nature.

How does a self-moved being move other beings? In a dazzling insight, Aristotle defines the unmoved mover—*unmoved* in the sense of self-moved or not moved by anything else, not unmoved in the sense of "not moving"—as the object of *desire*. Aristotle is capitalizing on the fact that a thing may move other things by being the object of their desire. For example, a river may move a woodchuck or a human being to it by offering to fulfill its desire to drink water. An astronomer may be moved to study the distant stars by a desire for understanding. Neither the river nor the knowledge the astronomer seeks is itself affected or moved in any way by those who are doing the desiring. Neither is even aware that it is desired. As objects of desire, they move others—hence the term *unmoved movers*.

We can easily see the implications of this concept in the human world. As Aristotle observes in the opening of the *Nicomachean Ethics*, every action and every intention aim at some perceived good. Even our actions that are in an absolute sense bad are aiming at *some* good, such as pleasure or wealth or fame. For example, the person who smokes is aiming at the good of pleasure or acceptance by his peers; the person who robs a bank is aiming at the good of wealth. But, of course, Aristotle would say that real goods—health or virtue—are rational, whereas goods that are *perceived* to be good but are not actually good are irrational. In the claim that we always aim at some perceived good and that this good is the object of our desire, Aristotle is saying that the good moves us. If the highest good subsumes all lower goods, and if the highest good is identified with God, we can see that the unmoved mover, God, in an important respect does move every action and every intention.

The problem, as Aristotle's student Theophrastus observed, is how "desire" can move lifeless things. This is a real problem, for how can we speak of stars or trees as having desires? The problem is aggravated because the distinction between living and lifeless is not always clear in Aristotle. In *On the Soul*, Aristotle suggests that "living" things are what have self-nourishment, growth, and decay, but in the *Physics* he suggests, with Plato and perhaps Thales, that self-motion is what distinguishes the living.[13]

Perhaps Aristotle's insight can be made intelligible by taking his reference to desire as metaphorical. Aristotle talks about the natural impulses and natural motions that inhere in a thing's essence—the tendency of rocks to fall and fire to rise, for example—in much the same way that modern scientists speak of the gravitational "attraction" between bodies or the "attraction" between differently charged particles. Similarly, in modern parlance, systems "seek" equilibrium, and various cells "seek out" their counterparts. Aristotle's metaphor of desire should not be unintelligible to those familiar with similar metaphors in modern science.

One of the advantages of this notion of "desire" is that it eliminates the need for physical contact between mover and moved. A necessity for such contact would be a significant obstacle to any plausible concept of the unmoved mover, for in most cases we do not experience any physical contact between the object moved and the mover. In the most obvious physical sense, we do not see any physical contact between, say, a rock let go out a window and the ground to which it is drawn or any physical contact between a celestial object and its orbiting satellite. Today we say that there is gravity, an invisible "unmoved mover," and we believe that gravity is a physical force, even though the mechanism of it is not yet understood. For an ancient like Aristotle, a psychological force, like desire or its metaphorical extension in lifeless things to powers like "attraction," was an intelligible way of expressing the notion. In the case of gravity, would it be so very different to say that objects "have a desire" for one another in proportion to their masses?

One of the problems with Aristotle's conception of the Prime Mover concerns what the Prime Mover does with itself. Here is Aristotle's description of the Prime Mover's eternal contemplation:

Such, then, is the principle upon which depends the heaven and nature. And its activity is like the best which we can have but for a little while. For it exists in this manner eternally (which is impossible for us), since its actuality is also a pleasure. And it is because of this [activity] that being awake, sensing, and thinking are most pleasant, and hopes and memories are pleasant because of these. Now thinking according to itself is of the best according to itself, and thinking in the highest degree is of that which is best in the highest degree. Thus, in partaking of the intelligible, it is of Himself that the Intellect is thinking; for by apprehending and thinking it is He Himself who becomes intelligible, and so the Intellect and its intelligible object are the same. For that which is capable of receiving the intelligible object and the substance is the intellect, and the latter is in actuality by possessing the intelligible object; so that the possession of the intelligible is more divine than the potency of receiving it, and the contemplation of it is the most pleasant and the best. If, then, the manner of God's existence is as good as ours sometimes is, but eternally, then this is marvelous, and if it is better, this is still more marvelous; and it is the latter. And life belongs to God, for the actuality of the intellect is life, and he is actuality; and his actuality is in virtue of itself a life which is the best and is eternal. We say that God is a living being which is eternal and the best; so life and continuous duration and eternity belong to God, for this is God.[14]

Though this God, whose activity is thinking of himself thinking, is an entity that we would be hard pressed to love in an emotional way, the reasoning that led to this conception of the deity force nevertheless exerted a powerful influence for the next two thousand years in the most serious theological reflection.

VII. Aristotle's Philosophy of Science

A. THE STRONG MEANING OF KNOWLEDGE

When we speak of Aristotle's quest for *scientific knowledge*, we are speaking redundantly. For Aristotle, *science* and *knowledge* are the same word, the Greek word *episteme* (from which we derive the branch of philosophy called *epistemology*, which deals with the nature of knowledge). The philosopher puts such strong requirements on knowledge (that is, *science*) that very little can actually meet his requirements of being known in the strict sense.

Briefly stated, for Aristotle scientific knowledge is universal knowledge of necessary truths through their causes. Because the goal of attaining this sort of knowledge is difficult, if not impossible, to reach, Aristotle distinguishes between the exact and the inexact sciences. For example, in chemistry one might learn that if chemical X is mixed with chemical Y, the resulting compound is chemical Z. While the facts may be true and it may indeed be true that every time chemicals X and Y are mixed they produce chemical Z, the science is inexact, for there is no knowledge of the cause: it is not known *why* these two chemicals result in the third. For example, all cooks know that if they apply heat to a raw egg in a frying pan, the egg hardens, but few can explain why. In such cases, there is knowledge of *what* happens, but not *scientific* knowledge. In the same way, we might turn on our televisions and change the channels by pushing a button. If we do not understand the full causality of *why* the channels change, we do not have scientific knowledge. And, of course, a full knowledge of the causes would involve an explanation of all four causes.

Moreover, scientific knowledge explains causes and effects in such a way as to be universally applicable. To know scientifically would be to know the *why* for *all* eggs or to know the *why* about changing the channels on *all* televisions. Scientific knowledge discards accidental, contingent, and irrelevant factors such as the color and size of an egg or the brand of a television.

This is Aristotle's philosophy of science as he lays it out in his *Posterior Analytics*. We should note, however, that the conclusions presented in most of Aristotle's philosophical, biological, and other writings are not so strictly scientific as he himself deems desirable. Indeed, few, if any, scientific results have ever met Aristotle's full requirements. Yet the views in the *Posterior Analytics* are significant in that they set a very rigorous standard for knowledge.

B. WHERE KNOWLEDGE COMES FROM

Aristotle says that all teaching and learning that comes through discourse, either spoken or written, proceeds from previous knowledge. The first level of knowledge in discourse is, of course, knowing the meanings of the words we use in order to learn from others. But knowledge of the meanings of most words falls short of knowledge in the strong Aristotelian sense, for it is not universal knowledge of necessary truths through causes. For example, when we hear the statement, "The monkey is sitting in a cage," we understand the meaning of the remark because we understand the meaning of the separate words, but we do not know the word *monkey* in a scientific sense because we do not know the causes that have resulted in the universal concept of "monkey."

Understanding a word means knowing the general category into which the word fits and also the various qualities that make the thing denoted by the word different from everything else. A monkey will fit into the general category of animals and also has certain simian characteristics that distinguish it from all other animals. But scientific knowledge, which includes a knowledge of definitions, requires more: it requires knowing the cause through which something exists and knowing that the thing cannot be other than what it is.[15] When it comes to monkeys and most everything else, neither we nor anyone else has this full knowledge, for such knowledge would include more than what can be comprehended by human minds:

why a particular sperm fertilized the particular egg that led to the monkey, why monkeys have just these and not other characteristics, and so forth.

One of the biggest problems in knowing in the strict sense we have been discussing comes from the apparent truth that all learning and teaching comes from previous knowledge, and the previous knowledge has several requirements of its own. First, the starting principles of the original knowledge must be true; that is, they must accord with the universe as it actually is. Second, the principles must be primary; that is, they cannot themselves be demonstrable. If they were, they would proceed from other principles that had to be demonstrated as well and so on in an infinite regress. Clearly, if there were to be such an infinite regress, we could never know anything, for our lives would be spent in an endless search for more and more basic principles. Third, the principles from which new knowledge is acquired must be more known to us than the new knowledge. For example, if one is studying cell division, one must first understand cells. Or if one is studying triangles, one must first understand lines and angles. The starting principles, Aristotle holds, are the causes of the conclusions because we reason from them to the conclusions.[16]

C. MISTAKES PEOPLE MAKE ABOUT KNOWLEDGE

Aristotle points out that there are two opposite types of mistakes about knowledge. One involves believing that there is no knowledge whatsoever because it is impossible to come up with premises that do not depend on demonstration. Those who hold this view argue that one cannot know unless one knows what is prior, that is, what a claim is based on. But since one is led into an infinite regress in constantly seeking prior premises and since an infinite regress, by its very nature, is impossible to traverse, one can never have knowledge in the strict sense. Because they accept Aristotle's requirement of demonstration through causes, they are unwilling to accept any principles whatsoever. Hence they claim that knowledge in the strong sense is logically impossible. Those children who never tire of asking *why* no matter how far the series of explanations goes seem to share this view.

The second sort of error involves thinking that there can be a demonstration of *everything*. Persons who hold this view are mistaken, according to Aristotle, because they think that premises *can* be demonstrated. When a conclusion is reached, they say, we have a demonstration of the premises. If, for example, a certain club that allows only teenagers to be members actually has only teenagers in it at a certain time, this fact would purportedly be a demonstration of the premise that only teenagers are allowed to be members. But it should be clear that this demonstration would not constitute scientific knowledge of the premise.

Aristotle rejects both positions. In the first instance, he accepts the idea that there can be indemonstrable truths, truths that are understood by intuition or intellect. The axiom that a thing cannot both be and not be is such an indemonstrable truth. Although knowledge of such truths, for Aristotle, is not *scientific* (that is, demonstrated) knowledge, it is knowledge nonetheless. There are very few truths of this sort, however. Concerning the second sort of mistake, Aristotle rejects the kind of circular demonstration illustrated in the argument about the club that admits only teenagers. The problem with these faulty demonstrations is that each of the terms is taken as a prior truth in one context but a posterior one in another. If we allowed such demonstrations, then any statement X could be proved by a circular argument of the form "Given that X is true, it follows that X is true." In the argument about the teenage club, for example, after accepting the premise that only teenagers are allowed to be members—a "prior" claim—we conclude that only teenagers are present—a "posterior" one. When we claim that the conclusion proves the premise, however, the fact that only teenagers are present becomes the prior claim, and the fact that only teenagers are members becomes the posterior claim. Taking one and the same statement to be both prior and posterior obviously prevents the proof from being a satisfactory one. The proof that Bush is president would be that Bush is president.

D. UNQUALIFIED KNOWLEDGE

Now for Aristotle, unqualified knowledge is known in an absolute way and cannot be other than it is. Not only does scientific knowledge (that is, demonstrated knowledge) proceed from necessary premises for Aristotle, but demonstrations are of things that are themselves necessary. Aristotelian demonstrations require necessary, not merely true, premises. As an example of a demonstration that fails to meet Aristotle's criteria because it has a true, but not *necessarily* true, premise, consider the following. From the fact that Einstein knew that Rio de Janeiro was the capital of Brazil it follows necessarily that Rio is the capital of Brazil. But the premise is not necessary: although it is true that Einstein knew about the capital, he merely happened to know about it, and thus the premise stating his knowledge is not *necessarily* true. Hence, the conclusion, although it follows from the premise, has not been demonstrated in the Aristotelian sense of following from a necessary premise. To take an example in which a premise involves a contingent property rather than a contingent truth and in which the conclusion similarly fails to measure up to Aristotelian rigor, consider trying to derive a conclusion from the fact that a carpenter is tall. Tallness may indeed be a property of the carpenter, but it is only a contingent, not a necessary, property of being a carpenter. Therefore, any conclusion derived from the tallness of the carpenter will fall short of being demonstrative, regardless of whether the conclusion—say, that the carpenter is not short—really does follow from the premise. The reason for the nondemonstrativeness of all such arguments is that their premises do not embody necessary truths or do not involve essential attributes.

We have seen that Aristotelian knowledge involves demonstration that is universal, through causes, and from premises that are prior, more convincing, and necessary. Aristotle also argues that if in an investigation the premises are universal, then the conclusion of a demonstration correctly made from these premises will be unchanging. In other words, premises about changeable, destructible things cannot figure into unqualified demonstrations, and hence there can be no unqualified knowledge about destructible things. To be sure, we can make claims about destructible things, but these claims will never be universal. Here again we see the close attention by ancient philosophers to the constant flux of physical things.

The import of the foregoing discussion is that Aristotle effectively limits the kinds of things we can know in the full sense of the term to sciences such as geometry and logic—deductive sciences that have indestructible, immaterial things as their subject matter. All the other branches of learning that we call science—geology, biology, physics, chemistry, botany, physiology, astronomy, and so on—are lesser forms of science for Aristotle because they cannot achieve knowledge in the full sense. In physics, for example, we may know about various constants or about the rate of decay of certain isotopes, and we may draw all sorts of conclusions from this knowledge. But we do not have knowledge in the Aristotelian sense because, perhaps among other shortcomings, our premises are never necessarily true. We know what occurs, but we don't know the causes. A geometric or mathematical proof, on the other hand, is conclusive to those who understand it because the axioms possess an intuitive necessity and the conclusions follow necessarily from what is prior. But a posteriori arguments, that is, arguments from effects, are never known fully known in the Aristotelian sense since they are developed from effects and not from causes.

VIII. Aristotle's Ethics

Aristotle's work on ethics covers a multitude of topics, including the nature of human happiness, the virtues and vices, and friendship. The theory of happiness forms a superstructure that supports the rest of his theory of ethics and paves the way for the theories of his successors.

A. HAPPINESS

Every action and every intention, says Aristotle, aims at a good, and some goods are greater than others. For example, when one bathes, the bather aims at cleanliness—in other words, one bathes *for the sake of* cleanliness. One wishes cleanliness, in turn, for the sake of health or beauty or social acceptability. One wishes beauty perhaps for the sake of attracting others. But goals cannot proceed into infinity, for there can be no actual infinity.[17] Therefore, there must be one goal that includes the rest—that is, one goal for the sake of which we do all that we do. For example, we wish cleanliness for the sake of health, but we wish health for the sake of happiness. It does not make sense to ask why we seek happiness, for happiness is an end in itself. Happiness, then, as our ultimate goal, is the highest good.

If happiness is the highest good, all that remains is to determine the precise nature of the highest good for human beings. Some people think the highest good to be money, but they must be mistaken. For the purpose of money is to buy things, and when one buys things, one wants the things bought more than one wants to keep the money. Hence money is only an intermediary or instrumental good. Some think the highest good to be sensual pleasure, but they too must be mistaken. For many other animals enjoy the pleasures of the senses as much as humans, and we are looking for the highest good for a human being. Some think the highest good to be honor, but they are mistaken as well. For honor depends more on those who bestow it than on those who receive it, and the highest good should not be dependent on others or capable of being falsely awarded. Moreover, since men pursue honor to assure themselves of their goodness, it is clear that they value goodness more than honor.

Determining the good for a thing requires examining its function. Since the function of human beings is to reason and since what comprises the various virtues is correct reasoning, the good for a human turns out to be an activity of the soul in accordance with virtue. Hence the end, or *telos*, of a human being is to be as virtuous as possible.

Aristotle's ethics proceeds from the premise that human beings are animals whose function is to act intelligently—that is, in accord with reason. Ethical conduct will involve the application of reason to the various activities of human beings.[18] Aristotle offers no justification of behavior based on pronouncements of religious authorities, declarations from the gods, or even conduct modeled by the gods (except, perhaps, for contemplation, though this is an activity attributed to the gods only in philosophy and not in the Greek religion that was practiced).[19]

B. THE DOCTRINE OF THE MEAN AND THE VIRTUES

The famous doctrine of the mean defines correct behavior—the virtues—as acting moderately—that is, neither deficiently nor excessively.[20] Incorrect behavior—the vices—consists of opposed contraries. Aristotle's own example of the concept is the set of vices consisting, on the one hand, of rashness—a deficiency of fear—and, on the other, of cowardice—an excess of fear.[21] Rashness and cowardice are thus opposed to one another. The person who is virtuous—the person who acts with courage—lies as a mean between these contrary extremes. It is difficult to achieve the absolute mean, just as it is difficult to hit a bull's-eye in archery. As in archery if one has a tendency to shoot to the left, he compensates by aiming to the right, so in behavior, should one have a tendency to err to one side of the mean, Aristotle advises aiming at the other side.[22]

For an action to be virtuous, it must be voluntary, and so Aristotle takes up the complicated problem of just what makes an action voluntary. In contrast to later philosophers, like the Stoics, who drew very rigid distinctions, Aristotle, using examples drawn from life, draws distinctions qualified with subtle nuances: in one, he discusses the man ordered by a tyrant to commit a crime or have his own parents murdered; in another, he ponders a merchant at sea who hurls his cargo overboard; in yet another, a man who kills another man, intending to kill him, but the dead man turns out to be the killer's own son. To what extent are these actions voluntary or involuntary? For the Stoics, an action was either voluntary or involuntary, with no degrees in between. But for Aristotle, to be fully voluntary, an action must be done with knowledge, without compulsion, and for a desired good.[23] These requirements have their own difficulties, as Aristotle is himself aware. For example, he distinguishes between a man who acts *through* ignorance and the man who acts *in* ignorance. The person who kills his own son thinking him an enemy acts *through* ignorance; the man who robs a bank to gain money acts *in* ignorance, for he is ignorant of what he should do and of what he should avoid doing.

Aristotle individually defines the various ethical virtues. *Generosity* is the virtue that lies as the mean of giving and taking property: its excess is wastefulness; its deficiency, stinginess. *High-mindedness*, the virtue wherein a person, understanding his own excellence and considering himself worthy of high honors, acts appropriately, lies as the mean in handling high honor. Its excess is vanity, its deficiency, low-mindedness. When life calls for moments of relaxation and playful conversation, the virtue that lies as the mean in the handling of humor with propriety is *wittiness*: at its one extreme lies buffoonery; at the other, boorishness. Sometimes the vices lying at the extremes have names, but the virtue at the mean is itself nameless. In the matter of *high* honors, the virtue is high-mindedness. But concerning small or moderate honor, only the vices have names (at least in Greek)—ambitiousness and, for want of a better word in English, "unambitiousness." A category for which there is no name is known as an "anonymous category."[24]

The practice of justice for human beings, is, in a sense, synonymous with human excellence (*areté*). As one might look at the number 144 and consider it as a single unit, or as $72 + 72$, or as 12^2, or in many other ways, and as each way gives us a different sense of the number (as a unity of one gross, or as a duality of two equal unities of 72, or as the square of 12), so one might think of acting justly as abiding by the terms of contracts, or as punishing or rewarding properly, or in many other ways.[25] A general definition of justice, perhaps, would be a disposition, acquired by habit, to do what is fair and lawful where other human beings are concerned. Its two categories are *distributive justice*, which concerns the proper apportionment of good things to members of the same community, and *corrective justice*, which concerns correcting situations in which just relations have been disturbed. These two forms of justice correspond to the two kinds of medicine, *preventive*, which aims at preserving the body's proper nature, and *therapeutic*, which aims at restoring the body's proper nature. The very existence of a good political community, where people can achieve happiness, depends on the carrying out of justice.

Since ethical virtues depend on actions in accordance with proper reasoning, Aristotle considers the intellectual virtues, on which proper reasoning depends, to be an essential part of ethics.[26] One intellectual virtue is *prudence*, which Aristotle defines as the ability to deliberate about the means that lead to true happiness as a whole. Since happiness is virtuous activity, a prudent man will be able to deliberate about the means for achieving a good end. For example, he will be able to calculate the best means to lead a drug addict to recover from his addiction. Other intellectual virtues include *intuition*, the ability to grasp principles; *wisdom*, a combination of both intuition and knowledge about the most honorable things, like good and evil and the nature of the universe and its stars; and *intelligence*, which Aristotle defines as the ability to make good judgments about the matters on which a person deliberates with prudence.

A perfectly virtuous human being will desire only the good, and his faculties of reasoning will be excellent. Unfortunately, most human beings, not being perfectly virtuous, *do* desire things that are not good. Aristotle observes that what distinguishes the continent person from the incontinent is not the absence of wrongful desires but the ability to control them. When a continent person has a desire for something that is wrong, since his intellectual virtue is strong, he rejects the desire. The incontinent person may have the same wrongful desire, but since his intellectual virtue is not strong, he yields to the wrongful desire. Aristotle also takes up why people pursue bodily pleasures when the pleasures are bad. He offers two explanations. The first is that since people experience excessive pains, they seek excessive pleasures to cancel out the pains.[27] For example, when one feels the pain of hunger, the pleasure of eating cancels out the pain. His second explanation says that people who cannot enjoy other pleasures pursue bodily pleasures because they are intensely pleasant.

C. FRIENDSHIP

Friendship receives a major treatment in Aristotle's ethical theory. Indeed, of the three extant ancient philosophical works on friendship (the others are Plato's *Lysis* and Cicero's *On Friendship*), Aristotle's is by far the most exhaustive. To be a friend to another person, Aristotle says, one must wish the person to be well for the person's own sake. This is most easily shown by considering a lifeless object. For example, we wish wine to be well so that it may keep and satisfy our appetite for it. We wish wine well not for its own sake but as a means for our own good.[28] Friendship is the greatest of all external goods. In the *Lysis*, Socrates declares that he would rather have a friend than the best rooster or quail in the world, a sentiment with which Aristotle agrees, for he declares that no man who lacked friends would be called happy.[29]

The philosopher distinguishes three types of friendship. In two, friendships of utility and friendships of pleasure, a friend is liked not for his own good qualities but only insofar as he provides a use or a pleasure. These are the sorts of friendships one might have with one's barber, where the utility is a haircut on the one side and payment on the other, or with one's opponent in racquetball, where mutual pleasure is derived from athletic competition. These are the least stable friendships, for they are easily dissolved when the parties no longer provide either a use or a pleasure to one another. The third and best friendship is that which exists between persons who are equal in as many ways as possible—age, status, interests—and who, being virtuous, share the same virtues and wish good for their friend for the sake of the friend himself. Because virtue tends to be a stable disposition of the soul, these friendships are the longest lasting and the most satisfying of all.

Aristotle reflects on practical questions as well: whether a person ought to come to the aid of a friend or a virtuous person, whether children should always obey their fathers, whether one should sooner repay a debt or help a friend, whether one should love himself and to what degree, how many friends a virtuous person should have, and whether one needs friends in both good and bad times.[30]

D. PLEASURE

In the concluding sections of his work on ethics, Aristotle turns to the vexing problem of pleasure, the nature of which he elucidates, even without providing a precise definition.[31] There is, he says, a pleasure for each faculty, such as sight or hearing, and these activities are most pleasant when the faculty is operating at its best level and is directed toward the best objects. Thus the most beautiful sights or sounds cause the greatest pleasures with respect to these faculties. Since the preeminent faculty of human beings is a capacity for thinking and since this faculty goes to the core of human happiness, it follows that the greatest pleasure for a human being is that in contemplation. Contemplation is the most divine of all activities, and the more one contemplates, the closer one is to the divine.[32] By this analysis, the ethical virtues rank lower than the intellectual. Here Aristotle joins with Plato and the Western philosophical tradition generally in giving the first prize of happiness to philosophers and in establishing the superiority of the contemplative to the practical life.[33]

In the centuries after Aristotle, these conclusions were debated and refined in the various schools of philosophy. The Stoics, for example, argued that Aristotle was mistaken in assigning any role at all, no matter how subordinate, to external goods in human happiness. They denied Aristotle's commonsense claim that someone who was hideously deformed or miserably impoverished could not be happy in the full sense.[34] Stoics maintained that the only thing that counted for happiness is virtue and that a good man might be happy even while being excruciatingly tortured on the rack. Later, in Christian thought, the highest good was identified with God, and happiness—still defined as the highest good—was identified with divinity or union with God. In short, Aristotle's work was not the final answer in ethics but was, as no doubt Aristotle himself would have wished, a spur to further investigations.

IX. Aristotle's Psychology

For Plato, the human soul (*psyche* in Greek, from which we derive *psychology*—the *logos*, that is, "account," of the soul) is imprisoned in its body. A philosopher devotes his life to preparing for death, separating himself as much as possible from his body and living in as pure a world of mind as he possibly can. Since, as Plato's Socrates says,[35] a person is most removed from awareness of his body when he is thinking about ideas—and the more abstract the ideas, like mathematical ideas, the better—he prepares himself best for the permanent separation of death when engaged in this type of thought. For Plato, one's goal is to reach the afterlife as pure soul. Of Plato's tripartite division of the soul, two parts are very closely linked to the body, the appetitive part of the soul, which governs the desires for things like food, drink, and sex, and the spirited part, which controls the emotions. The third part of the soul, intelligence (*nous* in Greek)—the reasoning, thinking part—is not connected to the body. At death, when the soul departs from the body altogether, there is no need for the parts of the soul that regulate the body, and so it is clear that the part of the soul with the greatest likelihood of surviving without a body, that is, of surviving into an afterlife, is the rational part of the soul, the intelligence.

Aristotle's views on the soul are quite different from those of his teacher. For Aristotle, all living things are a composite of body and soul. Their body is the matter, their soul, the form. While it is easy to distinguish body and soul, as it is the convex and concave sides of a lens, they are no more separable than the sides of a lens. Thus, for Aristotle, the destruction of the body is the destruction of the soul, just as the destruction of the convex side of a lens is the destruction of the concave. In a few passages, however, Aristotle, perhaps worried about his own death or perhaps in a particularly Platonic mood, suggests that if any part of the soul *were* to survive death, it could be only the reasoning part.[36]

Aristotle maintains that the soul takes on three forms and that these are arranged in a hierarchy: nutrition, sensation, and intellect. What they have in common is that they are self-moving and aim at a goal. Nutrition aims at the maintenance and reproduction of the living thing; sensation, which includes locomotion and desire, stands above nutrition and helps nutrition achieve its goal of maintenance and reproduction. Intellect, which includes reason, the highest form of soul, exists in human beings and is the power that acquires true principles. The lower forms of soul are a precondition for the higher, and the higher forms change the behavior and nature of the lower. For example, animals, which share with plants the lowest form of soul (nutrition) but also possess sensation, by virtue of this higher form obtain food and reproduce in ways quite different from plants. Human beings, because they have the additional form of reason, engage in the same activities of obtaining food and reproducing in ways different from animals.

In terms of Aristotle's four causes, the soul is the cause of the body as all but the material cause. It is the efficient cause of the body because it brings about movement, for soul provides desire, and desire is what aims the body toward a goal.[37] For example, desire prompts a person to move toward an ice cream sundae. Since behavior is a tendency or capacity to act in a certain way, the soul is the formal cause of an action: a person who is driving a car to the ice cream parlor to purchase his sundae is exercising his knowledge of the rules and procedures that form the action of driving. The soul is the final cause of an action by the body because it alone understands the "why" of the action, that is, for what sake an action is undertaken. For example, only the soul understands that the action of seeking a sundae is undertaken for the sake of pleasure.

For Aristotle, physiology is related to the various levels of the soul. At the lowest level, the function of the nutritive part is to acquire nourishment, and its goal is for the body to reproduce, and both of these operations require their physiological instruments, that is, the organs that feed and those that reproduce. Sensation requires organs that can receive sensible forms, and these are the organs related to the five senses, the organs of seeing, hearing, and so forth. Each sensory organ accepts only a certain moderate level of sensation, for too little would not register, as when something is too tiny to be perceived; and too much might be destructive of the organism, as when too bright a light would cause blindness.

The rational form of the soul, in addition to thinking, includes imagination, recollection, and memory. Imagination occurs when forms that are provided by sensation are manipulated by the mind in the absence of any sensation of physical objects. For example, by means of imagination we might take wings that we have seen on a bumblebee and attach them to a cow: we then picture in our minds a winged cow that our eyes have never observed. Memory combines imagination with an understanding of the past. For example, we might picture in our minds an old friend who is now distant. Recollection, for Aristotle, differs from memory, for it includes both an image from the memory and the energizing of other images that are related. For example, we may recollect an old currently distant friend as he rode a horse twenty years earlier. Imagination is crucial for action, for it enables us to picture in our minds the end that we desire. We are able to picture the chocolate sundae before we leave the house for the ice cream parlor.

Aristotle's work on psychology involves distinctions and analyses of desire, belief, thinking, judgment, error, and many other topics. Because it makes good intuitive sense and because it actually explains a good deal of animal and human behavior, it was the major work on the subject until the Enlightenment in the eighteenth century. Whether the psychological notions that succeeded it, including the work of Freud, were an improvement is perhaps a matter of debate. Modern neuroscience has already validated many of Aristotle's views as against those of the modern Descartes. Where Descartes reiterated the Platonic mind–body dualism as against the composite unity of Aristotle, modern neuroscience is once again investigating the relation between human chemistry and biology and human behaviors. Research into how the brain functions and the link between behavior and physiology is wholly in the spirit of Aristotle's ancient work.

X. Aristotle's Legacy

If Plato is a rock star, Aristotle is a player of baroque chamber music. It is no wonder that in antiquity it was the dazzling Plato, who promised immortality, whose winged prose soared to the ethereal World of Being, whose influence was deeply felt among intellectuals, while the more sober Aristotle, whose major writings survived as cragged, difficult-prose torture dungeons, was relegated to scholars.

At the end of antiquity, Boethius, who loved Aristotle and Plato equally and who planned to translate the works of both into Latin and then reconcile them, made the fateful decision to begin his work with Aristotle's logical works. Thus these were preserved for the West as other Greek works were not, and they became the basis of the study of dialectic during the Middle Ages. As part of the famous educational *trivium*, along with grammar and rhetoric, dialectic was a major part of the curriculum of the relatively few who undertook an education. When, beginning in the twelfth century, dialectic was applied to theology, a revival of Aristotle occurred, and when the University of Paris was chartered in 1200, a major project of reconciling Scripture with Aristotle was initiated, culminating in 1273 with the *Summa Theologica* of Thomas Aquinas.

Aristotle remained in ascendance until the fifteenth century, when, during the Renaissance, the West rediscovered Plato and (largely) forgot Aristotle. Among the characteristics of the Renaissance was an enthusiastic faith that humans, by imitating the divine, could achieve divinity for themselves. This faith was famously celebrated in art and architecture. Plato, with his mystic streak and breathtaking prose, seemed to have discovered the secret way to heaven. In the sixteenth century, the Protestant Reformation brought a heated rejection of scholasticism, the subtle analytical attempt to apply logic to theology. Since Aristotle and his works on logic were closely associated with scholasticism, they were rejected by the guilt of association. A century later, the zeal of Francis Bacon (1561–1626) for a brand-new approach to science stirred a renewed rejection of Aristotle and everything connected to what was considered outdated or erroneous science.[38] Nevertheless, the work of Aristotle has continued to generate insights, and philosophers, literary theorists, and psychologists continue to learn from his pioneering works, to develop his discussions, and to debate his conclusions. One would indeed be a rash thinker to ignore Aristotle's deliberations.

Discussion Questions

1. Does Aristotle's preference for "knowledge for its own sake" rather than for a practical purpose reflect the snobbism of the intellectual elite? On

what basis can one make the argument that knowledge is valuable in itself? How, given the very high tuition at modern colleges and universities, not to mention what economists call "opportunity cost," can a modern student justify to his parents a major in philosophy or classics? What Aristotelian arguments might the student use?

2. Aristotle devised his formulation of logic to establish the principles of persuading other people. Now, while one always wishes his own arguments to be strictly logical, one often suspects that the logic of others might be somehow deceptively defective. How hard is it to come up with arguments whose logic is flawless? Are there any logical fallacies so subtle that they are really difficult to detect? Any that logicians themselves might disagree about? Have you ever been aware of any lapses in your own logic that you hoped would not be detected by others?

3. After Augustine had studied Aristotle's *Categories*, he felt he knew just about everything. In a similar way, after the work of Newton and Maxwell, some physicists were confident that most everything in physics had been explained. How might comprehensive explanatory systems generate such arrogant delusion, and how might it be prevented?

4. While Aristotle's categories and his four causes may not explain all there is to know, how do they help us think about things systematically and in helpful ways?

5. Parmenides, as we have seen, presented a great challenge to ancient thinkers. How well has Aristotle responded to the conundrums posed by the earlier thinker? Are Aristotle's distinctions valid in clarifying the logical problems posed by Parmenides?

6. For Plato *eros* was instrumental in leading philosophers to the reality of the Forms. For Aristotle *desire* (in Greek, *epithumia*) draws philosophers to the Unmoved Mover. Are there any connections between Plato's *eros* and Aristotle's *desire*? Is Aristotle borrowing or translating into his own terminology these or any other notions from Plato?

7. Aristotle's strict definition of knowledge as a demonstration that is universal, through causes, and from premises that are prior, more convincing, and necessary severely limits the number of things known. Is it nevertheless useful to have so rigorous a standard? Will such a standard inspire—or demoralize—those in fields like biology, chemistry, geology, and astronomy, where the material nature of the subject matter prevents these strict criteria of knowledge from ever being met?

8. Aristotle's theory of ethics depends on the underlying rationality of human nature. But one who surveys the history of humanity will find that rea-

son has rarely worked well enough to provide peace and justice. Is there any alternative to an ethics based on rationality? Could there be an ethics without an underlying theory? Could there be any theory of ethics that didn't depend on a basic human rationality?

9. Compare Aristotle on why people sometimes seek to fulfill a desire that is bad with Plato, who says a man never chooses what he knows is bad. Does either of these philosophers seem closer than the other to the truth? Is there a way of explaining human wrongdoing that is perfectly compatible with the rationality of humans? Or, if human wrongdoing reveals an irrational side to human nature, is there any ethics that can eliminate it?

10. How well has Aristotle defined the various virtues? Does knowing the definition of a virtue increase one's likelihood of practicing it? Can you think of any virtues that don't fit his definition of virtue?

11. Do you agree with Aristotle in judging the intellectual virtues as the highest aspiration of human beings? Are the moral and intellectual virtues, by Aristotle's own standards, strictly separable? Is it likely that a person who spends his life in contemplation would ever act unjustly or selfishly?

12. How consistently with the rest of his philosophy does Aristotle's understanding of the human soul fit? Do his views about human happiness, about ethics, and about the way logic works form a system in which one part helps elucidate the others?

Notes

1. Athens had earlier banished Protagoras (see p. 93) and Anaxagoras (see p. 122) and had executed Socrates.

2. For the enormous list, see Diogenes Laertius, *Aristotle* 22–27. Diogenes totals the corpus at 445,270 lines. By way of comparison, the *Iliad* and *Odyssey* together total only about 27,800 lines, or about 6 percent that attributed to Aristotle. Only a small portion of this work survives.

3. Of course, Aristotle was shortsighted here. It would be difficult to defend trivial knowledge for its own sake (like the cost of an actor's shoes) as more worthwhile than lifesaving practical knowledge (like how to perform the Heimlich maneuver).

4. Aristotle, *Topics* 156b16.

5. Examples of such advice are in the hundreds. Typical is Aristotle's advice on pointing out an opponent's equivocations, that is, the use by the opponent of words with more than one meaning, or his making claims of permanence for things that are in fact temporary.

6. Augustine, *Confessions* 4.16.

7. See chapter 2, note 11, on *hyle*, Aristotle's word for matter.

8. There is a simple linguistic formula for understanding an essence: *any verb in the infinitive* is the essence of the verb root + *-er*. For example, *to read* is the essence of a *reader*; *to swim* is the essence of a *swimmer*; *to teach* is the essence of a *teacher*.

9. Aristotle discusses the difficulty of articulating this subject in *Physics* 199b11 and the impossibility that something may arise in nature by chance and without ends in *Physics* 198b10–199b33. In *On the*

Heavens 271a34, he explicitly says that God and nature create nothing that is without ends. He expresses the same view repeatedly (for example, *On the Soul* 415b16, 432b21, 434a30, and many other places).

10. Aristotle summarizes this dilemma in *Physics* 191a27–31.

11. Aristotle is not speaking of temporal but of *logical* priority, a distinction used later by Christian philosophers in discussing the Trinity (see pp. 346–47). Perhaps the meaning may be clarified by thinking of efficient causes. A paperweight that lies on a desk is supported by the desk beneath it, the desk by the floor, the floor by the foundation, the foundation by bedrock, and so on until we find something that supports without itself being supported. All these efficient causes are occurring simultaneously with respect to time; but those on which something else is supported are prior logically to those that are in turn supporting other things. Thus, the bedrock is logically prior to the foundation, the foundation logically prior to the floor, and so on.

12. See Aristotle, *Metaphysics* 1071b5–15.

13. Aristotle, *On the Soul* 412a13, *Physics* 255a5–7. For the discussion of self-motion and Thales, see pp. 45–46.

14. Aristotle, *Metaphysics* 1072b14–31.

15. On the distinction between definitions through genus and differentia and definitions that involve knowledge of causes and on Aristotle's occasional use of one or the other, see A. Gómez-Lobo, "Definitions in Aristotle's Posterior Analytics," in *Studies in Aristotle*, ed. D. J. O'Meara (Washington, D.C.: Catholic University Press, 1981), 25–46.

16. Aristotle, *Posterior Analytics* 71b27–72a5. For Aristotle the causes of a thing are its starting principles, and these may be explained in terms of the four causes. The material principle (or cause) of a house is what it is made of; the efficient principle is who brought it about and so on.

17. Here we can perhaps see clearly how Aristotle's philosophy forms a *system*, where notions about infinity and final cause, which were discussed earlier in connection with works of Aristotle on logic and metaphysics, are critical to his theories of ethics.

18. In the *Politics*, Aristotle will show also how the good *polis* is one constructed on the premise that man is a rational animal. Indeed, for Aristotle, politics is simply ethics on a larger scale. In the last paragraph of the *Nicomachean Ethics*, we can see the transition to his treatment of politics.

19. "Imitation of God," which for medieval Christians became the very soul of virtue, is not found in Aristotle, who goes so far as to say (*Nicomachean Ethics* 1145a26–28) that neither virtue nor vice exists in the gods, for their state is more exalted than anything at the human level, and just as the behavior of a brute animal cannot be called vice, for it is generically different from vice, so the behavior of gods is generically different from virtue. Later, in the conclusion of the *Nicomachean Ethics*, he says that all forms of behavior that humans find virtuous are small and unworthy of the gods (1178b8–20). If some human beings resemble (and *to resemble* is not *to imitate*) the gods in any way, it is in the practice of contemplation (1178b20 ff.).

20. *Nicomachean Ethics* 1103b26–1105a16. This teaching is sometimes called the "Doctrine of the Golden Mean," where *golden* figuratively denotes the value of achieving it.

21. *Nicomachean Ethics* 1108b11 ff.

22. *Nicomachean Ethics* 1109a20–b26.

23. *Nicomachean Ethics* 1110b19–1111b4.

24. The discussion of the various virtues, of which a sample only is given here, takes place in Book 4 of the *Nicomachean Ethics*. The ambitious man is called (1125b14–16) in Greek *philotimos* ("one who loves honor"), the unambitious man *aphilotimos* ("one who does not love honor").

25. Speaking in the language of philosophy, one might say that $72 + 72$ or 12^2 are predicated of the same thing (that is, 144) but that the definitions of the two expressions differ.

26. The intellectual virtues are taken up in Book 6 of the *Nicomachean Ethics*.

27. *Nicomachean Ethics* 1154a30 ff.

28. In Aristotle's philosophy, the song that proclaims that "a diamond is a girl's best friend" cannot be true, for the diamond is only a means to make the girl more beautiful or more wealthy and is not loved as an end in itself. The example of wine is found in *Nicomachean Ethics* 1155b27–34.

29. Plato, *Lysis* 211d–e; *Nicomachean Ethics* 169 b9–10.

30. These questions and others are the subjects of Book 9 of the *Nicomachean Ethics*.

31. In *The Rhetoric for Alexander* 1422a17, he defines *pleasure* as "that which causes joy."

32. *Nicomachean Ethics* 1177a12–1178 a8.

33. The debate over the relative merits of the contemplative and practical lives begins, of course, in Homer. See the discussion on pp. 8–9.

34. Aristotle, *Nicomachean Ethics* 1099a32–b8.

35. *Phaedo* 65a–e.

36. Aristotle, *On the Soul* 429a10–11; 429a 17–19. Aristotle's views are the subject of much debate. The hint that Aristotle believed in the ability of the soul to exist apart from the body is perhaps suggested by his view that reasoning, unlike seeing or hearing, is not located in an organ (*On the Soul* 408a).

37. In this way God, as the object of desire, is an efficient cause: it moves a human being to seek divinity. For a discussion of this notion, see above, pp. 204–6.

38. Bacon pointedly titled one his works *The New Organon* to distinguish it from the "Old" *Organon*, the name used for the collection of Aristotle's works on logic.

Select Bibliography

Web resource: www.epistemelinks.com/Main/TextName.asp?PhilCode=Aris.

Barnes, Jonathan, ed. *The Cambridge Companion to Aristotle*. Cambridge: Cambridge University Press, 1995.

——. *A Very Short Introduction to Aristotle*. Oxford: Oxford University Press, 2000.

Gill, Mary Louise. *Aristotle on Substance: The Paradox of Unity*. Princeton, N.J.: Princeton University Press, 1989.

Kenny, Anthony. *Aristotle's Theory of the Will*. New Haven, Conn.: Yale University Press, 1979.

Lear, Jonathan. *Aristotle: The Desire to Understand*. Cambridge: Cambridge University Press, 1988.

Lloyd, G. E. R. *Aristotle: The Growth and Structure of His Thought*. Cambridge: Cambridge University Press, 1968.

CHAPTER 12

The World of the Third Century

I. Alexander and His Aftermath

Isocrates' dream had been a cultural war of Greece against the barbaric East. In the murky fashion of dreams, the dream became reality in the latter part of the fourth century, as Alexander of Macedon defeated the might of Persia. Perhaps at the outset of Alexander's career the hopes of the philosophic elite were high. Alexander seemed at first much more receptive to his tutor Aristotle than Dionysius of Syracuse had been to his tutor Plato. Moreover, the young Macedonian king took Aristotle's great-nephew Callisthenes on his marches to collect scientific data. By the late fourth century, few if any sober individuals held to any faith in the efficacy of democracy, for its defects were obvious both from the experience of a century and a half of failure and from the theorizing of the best philosophers. The Athenian Isocrates, in the *Nicocles*, had written a very fine praise of monarchy. Though political theorizing would continue, and such writers as Polybius would have useful things to say regarding the mixed Roman constitution, people came to accept that one-man rule was as much the way of the human world as it was of the world of the gods, where Zeus presided over an orderly cosmos.

Whatever hopes there may have been that Alexander would be a philosopher-king were dashed by the brutal reality of his psychopathic, megalomaniacal behavior. Whether this behavior was brought on by alcoholism or disease or wounds or simply (or complexly) as a result of his preternatural military success is impossible to determine, and the ancients themselves were unsure. After his early death his empire showed its fragility. Insurrections within the conquered lands loosened Macedonian control, and quarrels among his successors resulted in a division of the empire. The dream of a single world-state that would reflect the oneness of the universe would have to wait a few centuries longer, for Rome.

The period from the death of Alexander until Rome's conquest of Egypt, the last of kingdoms ruled by Alexander's successors, is known as the Hellenistic period. This era witnessed momentous changes, and these would profoundly affect the development of philosophy. Perhaps the most important was the disintegration of the *polis* as the fundamental political unit and its replacement with a centralized imperial government. A part of Alexander's megalomania was perhaps manifested in a desire to found cities. Some of these, like the Alexandria in Egypt (as distinct from a number of other cities that he established named Alexandria[1]), in the course of a relatively brief time grew to enormous populations. The successors of Alexander continued the practice of founding cities, and the new cities provided opportunities for city planning, a field invented by Hippodamus a century earlier.

What made founding new cities possible, along with the various extensive public works that accompanied their construction, was the fabulous wealth that entered the Hellenic world as a result of the Asian and Egyptian conquests. The chief effect of this wealth, at least for the first six or seven decades following Alexander's death, was to provide material prosperity as a compensation for and distraction from the political freedom that the Greeks had previously enjoyed. But as the initial effects of the new wealth subsided and as inflows diminished and, as inevitably happens, when the inequalities between the rural poor and the urban rich reappeared conspicuously, discontent and rebelliousness increased. In these poorer times, people now felt less loyalty to a monarch whose capital was far away than they had felt to the regime of their *polis*, to which, so to speak, they had been married "for richer or for poorer." This ominous weakening of the political structure would make the Hellenistic kingdoms easy prey for Rome in the second and first centuries.

II. Intellectual Developments

Perhaps by the beginning of the third century there was a sense that the greatest philosophical contributions in ethics, metaphysics, and politics had already been made. Or perhaps the great monarchs were unwilling to fund or even allow broad free-thinking independent speculations that might prove dangerous to their hold on power. Whatever the cause, intellectual pursuits ventured in new directions in the third century B.C.E.,[2] when the principal developments were in mathematics and astronomy, biology, city planning, and literary and textual studies.

A. MATHEMATICS AND ASTRONOMY

No one would begrudge immortality to the names associated with the mathematics of the Hellenistic period. Among the mathematical stars were Euclid (fl. 300), whose name became synonymous with geometry, and Apollonius of Perga (fl. 275), whose work on astronomy established a model of the planetary system that would last until Galileo and Kepler. Euclid and Apollonius both seem to have lacked the triumphant pride of many of the early thinkers, who spared no laudatory effusions in speaking of their own work. In his renowned *Elements*, Euclid modestly claims to do no more than summarize and organize the work of his predecessors. Similarly, Apollonius, author of the dazzling *Conic Sections*, acknowledges that half his work is borrowed from the *Conics* of Euclid, a work no longer extant. Also during the Hellenistic period, Hipparchus (fl. 165) began the development of spherical trigonometry, which analyzes the properties of triangles drawn on spheres. And, of course, Archimedes (287–212), often considered the greatest mathematician of antiquity, not only founded the science of hydrostatics, which examines the properties of bodies floating in water, but also made many contributions in the understanding of spheres, cones, cylinders, levers, and the calculation of pi.

In Euclid, who probably studied at Plato's Academy, we find the influence of a philosophical education. Following Aristotle, he distinguished between *axioms*, as common notions true for all sciences, and *postulates*, truths that apply only to geometry.[3] The correctness of Euclid's choice of which propositions to call postulates, while not devoid of controversy, has stood the test of time. Perhaps the most controversy concerns the fifth postulate, which, because of its complexity, seems amenable to proof yet defies attempts to prove it.

Apollonius left Perga in Asia Minor to study mathematics and astronomy in Alexandria with Euclid's successors. As a mathematician, his major work was the *Conic Sections*, where, in four hundred and eighty-seven propositions, he established the terminology and methodology for conics, among other things, and introduced the terms *ellipse, parabola*, and *hyperbola* to describe the curves formed by cutting a cone with a plane. In astronomy he was the first to suggest epicycles, an ingenious solution to make observed astronomical data conform with revered philosophical assumptions. According to Aristotle, the motion of all the celestial spheres is circu-

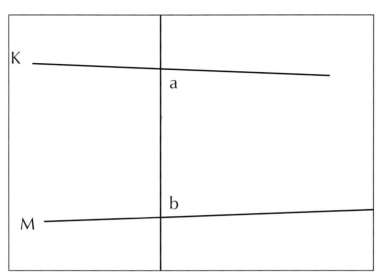

Figure 16. Euclid's Fifth Postulate

Postulates one through four are very simple: (1) it is possible to draw a straight line from any point to any point; (2) it is possible to extend a finite straight line continuously in a straight line; (3) it is possible to describe a circle with any center and distance; (4) all right angles are equal to each other. The fifth postulate is quite different: if a straight line falling on two straight lines makes the interior angles on the same side less than two right angles, the two straight lines, if produced indefinitely, meet on that side on which the angles are less than the two right angles. In the figure, angles *a* and *b* are less than right angles, and so lines K and M will eventually meet on the right side. From Euclid's time on, it seemed as though the fifth postulate *ought* to be provable from other postulates and axioms, and through the centuries, such mathematical luminaries as Ptolemy (100–178), Proclus (410–485), Nasiraddin at-Tusi (1201–1274), John Wallis (1616–1703), Johann Heinrich Lambert (1728–1777), and Adrien-Marie Legendre (1752–1833) all tried and failed to prove it. It is thus a testimony of Euclid's insight to have seen that the proposition had to be offered as a postulate.

lar because circular motion is the only form of eternal, uniform, perfect motion. But since planets seem to move backward in their nocturnal course (in what is called *retrograde motion*), the notion that the planets move in simple circles around the earth had to be modified. Apollonius proposed that each planet moved uniformly around a small circle—an epicycle—whose center moved uniformly around the earth on a second larger circle. Since the motion of the planet was composed of two different circular orbits, the planet's observed motion in the sky appeared retrograde to a viewer on earth. Though modern astronomy does not, of course, agree with Apollonius's scheme, it was a brilliant success and lasted, with improvements by later astronomers like Hipparchus and Ptolemy (fl. 140 C.E.), for nearly two

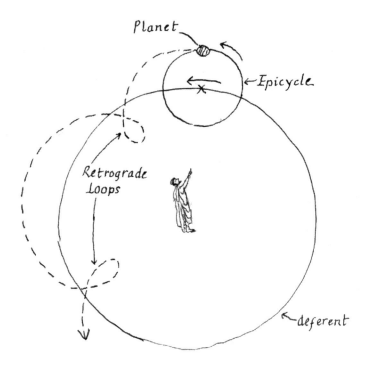

E P I C Y C L E S

Figure 17.   Epicycles

Because the ancients believed that the only motion appropriate to a heavenly body is motion at a constant speed in a perfectly circular orbit, ancient astronomers combined simple circular motions to explain the wanderings of the planets. The backwards motion of planets (retrograde motion) could be explained by assuming that each planet moves in a circle called an epicycle. The center of the epicycle is carried around the earth in a circular orbit called a *deferent*.

thousand years.[4] By the power of mere intellect, Apollonius had produced a model that preserved both the most fundamental (if erroneous) assumption of perfect circular motion for celestial bodies and the observed data. In addition, it also allowed for accurate predictions.

Hipparchus, the mathematician and astronomer who developed spherical trigonometry to provide a means for telling time at night by observation of the stars, is most celebrated for his discovery of the precession of the equinoxes (the slow westward movement of the location of the equinox), a discovery he was able to make by comparing his own careful observations with old records—work that had also probably been undertaken so that time records could be maintained by reference to the predictably regular paths of heavenly bodies. Hipparchus is credited with being the first to use parallax (the apparent motion of a close object with respect to a more distant background as the observer changes location) to determine the sizes and distances of the sun and moon. And he also devised a system for ranking stars according to their brightness.

The fame of Archimedes, a mathematician of Syracuse in Sicily, was so great that numerous anecdotes were told about him and many quotations attributed to him. As in the case of many notable individuals, the stories took on a life of their own and, whether or not they actually occurred, became a part of the intellectual tradition of the West. In military history, he achieved lasting fame for his skill in practical engineering in the defense of Syracuse from Rome. Though credited with a number of ingenious devices, he followed the Platonic and Aristotelian schools in disdaining machinery in favor of theoretical studies.[5] Perhaps the most famous story about Archimedes is how he was ordered by the tyrant of Syracuse to determine whether an ornate crown was alloyed with base metals without damaging it. While sitting in his bathtub, the story goes, he had the insight that a body in water is buoyed up by a force equal to the weight of the displaced water. He was so thrilled by this insight that he ran naked from his tub through the streets shouting "Eureka" (I have found it!). Another anecdote tells how, when discussing the lever and the fulcrum, he said, "Give me a place to stand, and I shall move the world." In another, he is said to have rigged up a system of cogs and pulleys such that he could draw a fully equipped ship up onto land all by himself.

In his nine extant treatises, there are many genuine discoveries laid out with extremely rigorous proofs. He calculated the surface area of a sphere (four times the greatest circle enclosed, that is, $S = 4\pi r^2$) and its volume (two-thirds of the cylinder it inscribes, that is, $V = \frac{2}{3}\pi r^3$). He determined π to lie between $3\frac{1}{7}$ and $3\frac{10}{71}$. He worked out various problems of integration (for example, the area of any segment of a parabola, the volumes of the segments formed by the revolution of conic sections, and so forth). In his book the *Sand-Reckoner*, he shows how to express a big number—the number of grains of sand that would be required to fill the universe, and to do so he imaginatively establishes a place-value system with a base of 100,000,000. While this work may not startle modern readers, who are used to physicists telling us how many atoms make up the universe or how many light years away shines a faint star, the work is unique in antiquity.

233

B. BIOLOGICAL SCIENCES

Theophrastus, who became head of the Lyceum after Aristotle, was, to judge from Diogenes Laertius's list of his works, amazingly prolific.[6] Among those that survive are the *Characters*, a compendium of different personality types, and several treatises on plants. It is for his work on plants that Theophrastus is now most known. He describes the kinds of plants, their parts, their geographical distribution, their uses, and their medicinal qualities. The work was standard until the Renaissance.

Of the researchers into human anatomy and physiology, the branch of medicine that most carried on the philosophical interest in teleology, the most important were Herophilus of Chalcedon (fl. 270) and Erasistratus of Ceos (fl. 260). These men are said to have been helped by the ruling Ptolemies, who allegedly gave them living prisoners whom they could dissect alive.[7] These accusations of horrific cruelty run counter to the Greek abhorrence of human sacrifice and are probably the propaganda first of anti-Greek Romans and then of anti-pagan Christians. Among the achievements of Herophilus, whose works have not survived, were a diagnostic technique that distinguished types of pulse, the distinction of veins and arteries, a description of the form and function of the duodenum (which he also named), and, from his dissection of the eyeball, descriptions of the retina, iris, and optic nerve. Perhaps his most outstanding contributions concerned the nervous system, where he added to the knowledge of the meninges and drew the distinction between motor and sensory nerves.

Erasistratus, sometimes called the father of physiology, gave a more detailed description of the brain and traced the course of the cranial nerves going to the parts of the head. He seems also to have described the form and function of the valves of the heart and to have thought that both veins and arteries originate in the heart, though, of course, he did not understand the function of the heart itself. He is also credited with having discovered the proper function of the epiglottis.

After these scholars, research on anatomy and physiology diminished. Perhaps the reverence of the Romans for the bodies of the dead made dissection illegal, or perhaps the influence of the Hellenistic religions and philosophies, which emphasized knowledge of the soul over that of the body, discouraged studies of human physical structures.

C. CITY PLANNING

According to Aristotle, Hippodamus of Miletus (fl. 460) invented the art of city planning.[8] The idea that reason be used in laying out streets and locating important civic buildings is perhaps one more genuine contribution of the sophistic movement. It may also reflect a sense of the safety that was felt after the Persian War. One of the advantages of a confusing maze of streets in unplanned cities was the disorder into which it threw invaders, especially in night encounters. Aristotle explicitly describes how an invading enemy might be wholly flummoxed by the complex of narrow winding streets, while natives might easily find their way in the familiar complexity.[9] Hippodamus is credited with having laid out the grid plans of the Athenian harbor of Peiraeus and of Thurii, a pan-Hellenic colony that Pericles established in 443.

Alexandria, in Egypt, according to ancient accounts, appears to have been laid out on the Hippodamian model.[10] There was a central avenue thirty-one meters wide running east to west and a wide avenue cutting it from north to south.[11] Porticoes kept the streets shady, so that people did not have to fight for a position near the wall for the shade. The population was divided into the fourths of the city created by these cross streets: Egyptians into the western two fourths, the Jewish population into the northeast fourth, and the royal palace, Museum, Library, temples, and parks into the southeast fourth. Though Hippodamus had established the optimal population at ten thousand citizens, Alexandria, like other Hellenistic cities, had a population in the hundreds of thousands. That cities of such immensity could be made habitable is perhaps evidence of the success of the application of mind (*nous*) to urban planning.

D. LITERARY STUDIES

Perhaps it was Macedonia's political domination, with the consequent reduction of the *polis* as the keeper of culture, that was responsible for the diminution of literary genius in the Hellenistic period. During this period, the Greek mind found an outlet for its energies in the preservation and study of the writings that had been handed down from a freer age. The great texts of Homer, Hesiod, and the tragedians were a quarry that could be mined for a variety of precious ores—grammar, prosody, archaic words, mythological allusions. Among the greatest of these literary miners were the critics Zenodotus (fl. 285), Aristophanes (fl. 217), and Aristarchus (fl. 180). If these names are unfamiliar to modern readers, it is because they toiled in the unglamorous field of textual scholarship. Yet their work preserved for us many of the classics, and their genius was in itself quite remarkable.

Zenodotus of Ephesus, the first head of the Library at Alexandria, is credited with having established textual studies. He collated various manuscripts of Homer in an attempt to establish the original text. He noted passages that he felt were not genuine. He established the principle that a text should make sense. Hence he deleted or inserted lines into the text or moved them around. And he is the one who arranged the *Iliad* and the *Odyssey* into twenty-four books each—an arrangement that has lasted for over two millennia. His *Homeric Glossary*, a study of obscure words in the epic writer, is perhaps the world's first work of lexicography.

Aristophanes of Byzantium became chief librarian at Alexandria when he was sixty. In addition to taking up Zenodotus's work on the text of Homer, he produced editions of Hesiod, Pindar, Euripides, and his namesake Aristophanes. His work in lexicography consisted of compilations of foreign and unusual words. With his colleagues he established philology as a serious branch of learning.

Aristarchus of Samothrace is the scholar whose claim to fame remains his critical edition of Homer, which in most respects is our modern text. His scholarship was varied and included grammar, orthography, etymology, and textual criticism. In antiquity he was celebrated as the consummate polymath,[12] and his work was carried on by such famous students as Dionysius Thrax (170–90), who compiled a work on grammar that served as a manual until the Renaissance and beyond,[13] and Apollodorus of Athens (fl. 140), who, also a polymath, wrote on chronology, mythology, geography, and theology.

236

Discussion Questions

1. One would imagine that if any teacher could have educated a true philosopher-king, it would have been Aristotle. Yet Aristotle's student

Alexander the Great established his genius as a soldier and conqueror, not as a thinker. Both Aristotle and Alexander affected the future of the world for millennia. Which of the two would you judge the greater? Be sure, in working out your answer to this question, to establish in as Aristotelian a fashion as possible the criteria of greatness.

2. What does the controversy about Euclid's fifth postulate reveal about the interest in pure logic? In what philosophical ways does it matter whether the fifth postulate is an actual postulate or is itself capable of proof?

3. The belief that underlies the theory of epicycles, that perfect motion is perfectly circular, endured for over two millennia, until it was superseded by Kepler's work. To what extent is the notion of perfect circularity an aesthetic notion peculiar to the individuals who thought of it? To what extent is it a feature of human psyches generally? Would a Greek have had any way of determining whether the belief about circularity was natural or conventional?

4. How are mathematical formulae persuasive in ways that rhetoric cannot be? What is the difference in the persuasive force of the subject matter of rhetoric versus that of mathematics?

5. The work of the Hellenistic physiologists ground to a slow halt. What are the limitations of scientific research in general, and of biological research in particular, in the absence of instruments such as microscopes that extend the human senses?

6. Aristotle said that the location of a city had to be suitable for health, defense, and political activity (perhaps commerce, housing, and assemblies) and had to possess beauty. Pausanias (fl. 150 C.E.) forbears to classify a place called Panopeus as a city because it had no gymnasium, no theater, no marketplace, and no public fountains. Taking our contemporary suburban areas into consideration, do Aristotle's requirements for being a city need to be modified? What is lost and what is gained by the facts of today's culture?

7. Is it possible that cultures, having exhausted their creative energies, simply wear out, in much the same way that television series, having exploited all the potentialities of their basic premises, come to an end (sometimes—alas—after having been protracted beyond their natural end by artificial life support)? Can there be a revival of creativity in *scholarship* on the achievements of the past, or is such scholarship likely to be a dry and barren business? Do courses in the history of philosophy allow for the same free range of human thought as courses in the latest new thought?

Notes

1. Among the various franchise Alexandrias are Alexandria in Areia, Alexandria on the Gulf of Issus, Kapisa-Alexandria, Alexandria on the Tigris, and Alexandria Troas.

2. To be sure, two major comprehensive systems, Epicureanism and Stoicism, do arise early in the third century and grow and compete and thrive into the Roman period. A discussion of these will occur in the next two chapters, when, in the Roman period, their greatest extant proponents (Lucretius for Epicureanism and Epictetus and Marcus Aurelius for Stoicism) flourished.

3. Information about Euclid's life is derived from one paragraph in Proclus's *Commentary*. For the distinction between axioms and postulates, see Morris Kline, *Mathematical Thought from Ancient to Modern Times*, vol. 1 (New York: Oxford University Press, 1972), 56.

4. What appears to moderns as a simpler solution than epicycles to explain the apparent retrograde motion of the planets is the idea that the stars and the sun are motionless and that the earth goes around the sun. Archimedes (*The Sand-Reckoner*, introduction) reports that the idea actually was suggested by Aristarchus of Samos (fl. 275 B.C.E.) and that the suggestion would yield a universe much greater than what was believed. Unfortunately, Archimedes dismissed the notion as impossible.

5. According to Plutarch, this disdain accounts for his lack of writing on his inventions.

6. The works are listed in Diogenes Laertius, *Theophrastus* 42–50. Diogenes computes his output at 232,808 lines (as compared to 444,270 for Aristotle).

7. This charge is asserted by Celsus, *De Medicina*, Proemium 23–24, trans. W. G. Spencer (New York: Loeb, 1935), I:12–15. It is repeated by Tertullian, *Treatise on the Soul* 10.

8. Aristotle, *Politics* 1267 b26. For Hippodamus, city planning seems to have included the constitution, the number of citizens, and other attributes of a city. Aristotle describes and then rejects these in great detail in 1267 b22–1269 a28.

9. Aristotle, *Politics* 1330 b22–27. Thucydides graphically shows how citizens familiar with the layout of a town might overwhelm a confused invader (*History of the Peloponnesian War* 2.3.4).

10. Strabo, *Geography* 17.1.10.

11. Ioanna Phoca and Panos Valavanis, *Architecture and City Planning* (Athens: Kedros Books, 1999), 24.

12. Cicero, *Atticus* 1.14.3; Horace *Ars Poetica* 450.

13. Gilbert Murray reports ("The Value of Greece to the Future of the World," in *The Legacy of Greece* [Oxford: Oxford University Press, 1921], 3) that he knew a gentleman from a good English school in the nineteenth century who had been taught the principles of grammar entirely out of Dionysius of Thrax.

Select Bibliography

ALEXANDER

Green, Peter. *Alexander of Macedon, 356–323 B.C.: A Historical Biography*. Berkeley: University of California Press, 1991.

Hamilton, J. R. *Alexander the Great*. Pittsburgh: University of Pittsburgh Press, 1974.

Hammond, N. G. L. *Alexander the Great: King, Commander, and Statesman*. Park Ridge, N.J.: Noyes Press, 1980.

Tarn, William W. *Alexander the Great*. Chicago: Ares Publishers, 1981.

MATHEMATICS AND ASTRONOMY

Gow, James. *A Short History of Greek Mathematics*. Mineola, N.Y.: Dover Publications, 2004.

Kline, Morris. *Mathematical Thought from Ancient to Modern Times*. Vol. 1. Oxford: Oxford University Press, 1972.

Sonneborn, Henry. *Archimedes and the Sands of Space and Time*. Larchmont, N.Y.: Eagle Press, 1994.

CITY PLANNING

Lawrence, A. W. *Greek Architecture*. New York: Penguin Books, 1983.

Murray, Oswyn, and Simon Price, eds. *The Greek City: From Homer to Alexander*. Oxford: Oxford University Press, 1990.

Ward-Perkins, J. B. *Cities of Ancient Greece and Italy: Planning in Classical Antiquity*. New York: G. Braziller, 1974.

Wycherley, R. E. *How the Greeks Built Cities*. New York: Norton, 1976.

BIOLOGY

Lennox, James G. "The Disappearance of Aristotle's Biology: A Hellenistic Mystery." *Apeiron* 17 (1994): 7–24.

Pellegrin, Pierre. *Aristotle's Classification of Animals: Biology and the Conceptual Unity of the Aristotelian Corpus*. Translated by Anthony Preus. Berkeley: University of California Press, 1986.

LITERARY STUDIES

Cole, T. *The Origins of Rhetoric in Ancient Greece*. Baltimore: Johns Hopkins University Press, 1991.

O'Sullivan, Neil. *Alcidamas, Aristophanes, and the Beginnings of Greek Stylistic Theory*. Stuttgart: F. Steiner, 1992.

Russell, D. A. *Classical Literary Criticism*. Rev. ed. Oxford: Oxford University Press, 1989.

CHAPTER 13

Epicureanism

I. Introduction

Epicureanism and Stoicism, the major rival philosophical systems during the six centuries of the Hellenistic Age and early Roman Empire—the period from about 300 B.C.E. to about 300 C.E.—were starkly opposed to each other on many fundamental issues: Epicureanism maintained that the world was dominated by chance, Stoicism, that everything was predetermined; Epicureanism, that the gods were remote and disinterested in human affairs, Stoicism, that the gods carefully oversaw what happened in the human world; Epicureanism, that death was the total end of life, as the constituent atoms of all things dissembled and became other things, Stoicism, that the soul continued to live; Epicureanism, that the highest good was *ataraxia*, freedom from pain, Stoicism, that the highest good was *apatheia*, freedom from emotional involvement in both the trials and the triumphs of daily life. Each philosophy had prominent adherents, and, despite their common goal of unflappable, cool, detached calm, they were frequently moved by fervent passionate zeal for their systems.

II. Epicurus's Antecedents

A. ARISTIPPUS OF CYRENE (435–360)

Aristippus, like Plato, who was about a half decade his junior, is reported to have been a close disciple and companion of Socrates. Perhaps because Plato did not approve of the direction in which Aristippus developed Socrates' ideas, he pointedly informs us that Aristippus was not present at Socrates' death but was on the island of Aegina.[1] While only a few fragments of his work remain, Diogenes Laertius reports many stories about him, and the outline of his philosophical positions seems clear. Aristippus was famous for his philosophy of hedonism, which emphasized the value of immediate pleasures.

There is perhaps no more basic motive in all animals than the pursuit of pleasure and the avoidance of pain. In the case of the other animals, since they do not seem capable of abstracting future goods, it seems plain that the goal of immediate pleasure drives them to engage in action. Eating, mating, and scratching all bring instant gratification. In the case of human animals, philosophers from Democritus to Plato to Aristotle had emphasized that pleasure has a different force. Democritus maintained that rather than immediate pleasure, one should seek the pleasure of a whole life. Plato developed this idea into a rational calculation of the most accurate pleasure. When something is near, said Plato, it appears large, and just as a hand appears larger than the sun when the hand is held before one's eyes, so immediate gratification, because it is near, appears greater than a pleasure far off in the future. But just as one understands by his intellect that the sun is actually larger than his hand, so an accurate calculation by the intellect reveals whether the far-off pleasure is in fact the larger one.[2] Plato also developed the idea that for human beings the truest pleasures are those of the mind.[3] For Aristotle, too, the happiest human beings lead a life of contemplation.[4]

Aristippus maintained that people do everything they do to seek pleasure or to avoid pain. Even actions that involve hard work, like helping a friend carry a heavy load or fighting in a battle, are ultimately done for these motives. We choose all our actions according to the pleasure they bring, for pleasure is something that we can feel with a clarity that eludes other experiences. We *know* when we like something, even if we know nothing else about the thing. Physically pleasurable sensations, he avers, are more intensely felt than intellectual pleasures; eating an ice cream is a sharper pleasure than solving a problem in arithmetic. Because the past is gone and the future exists in the imagination, only the present is real, and so pleasures of the moment are as good as pleasures get. The job of philosophy is to guide us to the greatest pleasures.

One corollary of this philosophy was that we should not become slaves to pleasure, for this would bring dependence and pain. We should be the masters of pleasure; it should not be our master. As Aristippus said of his courtesan Laïs, "I have Laïs; she does not have me."[5]

Aristippus is said to have been a thoroughly delightful person, refined, witty, and good natured. He was well paid for his teaching and enjoyed a conspicuously luxurious life. His daughter Arete kept up his school after his death and instructed her son, named Aristippus for her father, in the doctrines of hedonism. The younger Aristippus continued this "work" and was known by the epithet "mother-taught" (*metrodidaktos*). The influence of Aristippus will exert itself in Epicureanism, both by the pattern of his life and by his views concerning pain and pleasure.

B. PYRRHO OF ELIS (C. 360–275)

Xenophanes lamented the treatment philosophers received from their cities. Unlike athletes, who were celebrated as heroes and given free meals, philosophers were ignored or even scorned. The life of Pyrrho presents the opposing case: he was so esteemed as a philosopher that he was appointed high priest in his native city Elis, in the Peloponnesus, and, in what was perhaps the most generous fallacy of hasty generalization in history, *all* philosophers were exempted from taxation.[6] This very circumstance, that the reception of Pyrrho contrasts so sharply with that of Xenophanes, reflects one of Pyrrho's major views, that to all philosophical questions one can bring equally strong opposing arguments such that they cancel each other out. As a result, one is left not knowing and should suspend judgment concerning the truth. The philosopher, acknowledging his lack of knowledge, should in fact be sensible enough to keep silent about matters.[7] If a person lived in conformity with this modest surrender to self-limitation, accepting the customs and laws of his community (which might differ very greatly from those of another community, but since equally strong arguments could be made against each set of laws and customs, one might as well accept the local ones), he would enjoy great tranquillity of mind. For this happy tranquillity of mind, Pyrrho used the word *ataraxia*.

This philosophy of doubt, known as skepticism, sometimes called "Pyrrhonism," after Pyrrho,[8] is one of the possible reactions to the frustration from seeing conflicting persuasive arguments. The ancients were aware of the paralysis that could arise from equally strong opposing claims. When Herodotus describes the deliberations of Xerxes concerning his planned invasion of Europe, Xerxes' uncle Artabanus prudently lays out the challenges and pitfalls that await him. Xerxes responds, "If all opposing arguments must be considered, nothing will be accomplished!"[9] In the comedy *Phormio*, the Roman playwright Terence presents a very funny scene in which a father is at a loss of what to do about his son who had married a girl without his father's knowledge. The father asks three friends for advice. One gives him an argument for rejecting the marriage, a second gives him an equally strong argument for accepting it, a third tells him that the matter requires further deliberation. At the end of the scene, the father is left wholly perplexed, a state Plato called *aporia* (literally, "no exit"—in Greek, from *a-*, a prefix that negates, and *poria*, "way out" as in English *pore*).[10] In the *Phaedo*, Plato portrays Socrates discussing what is coined *misologia*, or "hatred of arguments," a condition that arises from listening to opposing arguments and coming to the conclusion that there is no truth, that all argument is wordy persiflage, tales told by idiotic prattlers, signifying nothing. In the dialogue, Socrates is portrayed as having a reaction different from the acknowledged ignorance (*akatalepsia*) and silence (*aphasia*) recommended by Pyrrho. Though one argument after another about the immortality of the soul is found wanting, Socrates boldly keeps on wrestling with the question, heroically undeterred by each roadblocking perplexity (*aporia*) that he and his interlocutors encounter. In the end, the *Phaedo* proves to be what is called an *aporetic* dialogue, that is, one that does not yield a solid conclusion about the matter at hand.[11]

Pyrrho's skepticism seems to have been prompted by the basic question about what constitutes the stuff of what we see around us. Things have qualities that produce different sensations. For example, in the very same room one person may feel warm, another chilled. Moreover, we do not penetrate with our understanding to the inner nature of things. What, really, he asks, does it mean to understand the nature of wood or water or fire?

Pyrrho's contemporary Aristotle claimed in the opening sentence of the *Metaphysics* that all human beings by nature desire understanding. One implication of this claim is that if understanding is not achieved, a desire goes unfulfilled, and the result is the perturbed pain of longing, of unfulfilled desire. Pyrrho takes the other side and finds in ignorance not painful longing but *ataraxia*, imperturbability, and he makes this imperturbability the goal of life. The admiration of calmness is revealed in many anecdotes that Diogenes Laertius tells about Pyrrho. In one, after being frightened by a dog that rushes on him, he confesses to his friends that his fear was a human weakness that he should strive against.[12] In another, he applies excruciatingly painful remedies to a wound without so much as a frown.[13] In another, he is on a ship during a storm, and all the other passengers are panicked while he himself stays calm; he points to a pig that is eating serenely on the deck and tells his companions that they ought to be as unperturbed as the pig.[14]

Diogenes Laertius suggests that Pyrrho first developed his views when he accompanied Alexander on his conquests and met the group of Indian wise men known as "Gymnosophists" (Greek for "naked wise men," because they wore no clothing), whose basic views were to revere the gods, to abstain from wrongdoing, to be courageous, and to despise death.[15] As discussed earlier in this book,[16] showing calm in moments of great stress was a fundamental ideal of the Greek mentality, portrayed in the temple friezes, in athletic sculpture, and, philosophically, in the calm and cheerful disposition of Socrates as he drank the poisonous hemlock. Perhaps, when Pyrrho found this same ideal among the naked wise men of India, he concluded that if such diverse cultures could share the same goal of imperturbability, it was one notion that could be established as beyond doubt.[17]

Pyrrhonism, or radical doubt, has a long history in the West. It was refined in the second century C.E. by Sextus Empiricus, in *Outline of Pyrrhonism* and other works. It was revived during the Renaissance by Michel de Montaigne (1533–1592) and later became the bedrock of the philosophies of René Descartes (1596–1650) and David Hume (1711–1776). Pyrrho's ideal of *ataraxia* is the chief goal too of Epicureanism.

III. Epicureanism

A. EPICURUS

Unlike Stoicism, which is named after a place—a covered portico of shops in Athens called the Stoa—Epicureanism is named after a man, Epicurus. This fact, interesting enough as a mere historical curiosity, is not without significance. When a movement or a group is named after a man, we can guess that the character of the man was of extreme importance, that the imprint of the man, both his character and personality,[18] marks the group or movement. Just as the character and personality of the one known as Jesus Christ dominate the movement called Christianity, so the character and personality of Epicurus dominate Epicureanism.

Although we have only two small volumes of the three hundred books that Epicurus wrote, and although the surviving writings are rather dull, perhaps intentionally so,[19] we can tell that the man Epicurus must have had an extraordinary impact on those who knew him and that—as in the case of the Christians who associated with Jesus—those who knew him were successful in transferring a sense of that impact to later generations. A contemporary named Colotes, on first hearing Epicurus speak, embraced his knees and worshipped him like a god.[20] Some three hundred years after his death, the Roman poet Lucretius wrote *On the Nature of Things*. The poem is still our principal source for Epicureanism. Lucretius mentions Epicurus many times, each time with a reverence ordinarily reserved for a god. Here is what Lucretius writes when he mentions Epicurus for the first time:

> When man's life lay, for all to see, oppressed
> Foully on earth by heavy superstition
> Showing its head from regions of the sky
> To threaten mankind with its dreadful aspect,
> Then first a man, a Greek, a mortal, dared
> To raise his eyes against it and resist.
> Neither the reputation of the gods,
> Nor lightning bolts nor thundering menace checked him;
> Nay, such threats only spurred his mind more keenly
> To be the first to break the bonds
> Of nature's gates. And so the living force
> Of intellect triumphed, and marched beyond
> The flaming limits of the universe,
> Traversed the infinite all by means of thought,
> And from that infinite like a victor came
> Bringing us knowledge of created things—what can be born,
> What can't, each power's limit,
> Together with its rationale that lies
> Deep at the basis. Then did superstition
> Take its turn at subjection. His victory
> Made mankind equal with the very heavens.[21]

This reverential attitude of Lucretius toward Epicurus is not an isolated phenomenon. Five centuries after his death, a man named Diogenes of Oenoanda erected, at his own expense, a kind of shrine to Epicurus— a wall on which he engraved long quotations from Epicurus's writings.

247

Dying of heart disease, Diogenes wished to share with his fellow human beings the true source of *ataraxia*, or imperturbability. Remnants of the wall still survive.[22] Among the remnants are several columns on which are inscribed the more famous sayings of Epicurus.

Perhaps an examination of the life of Epicurus will reveal the several reasons for the peculiar devotion that he aroused. He was born in 341 on the island of Samos. Athens had lost control of this island in the Peloponnesian War but had regained it in 363 and sent settlers, among whom was Epicurus's father Neocles. When Epicurus was a teenager, Neocles sent him to study in Teos, on the coast of Asia just north of Samos, at the school of Nausiphanes, who had been a disciple of Democritus, the inventor of atomic theory. In 324 Alexander issued a decree that all political exiles be returned to their native soil, and among these were the residents of Samos expelled in 363, whose lands had been assigned to Athenian settlers like Neocles. As a result, Epicurus, now without a home, was plunged into poverty.

After a two-year residence in Athens for military service, Epicurus lived variously in the eastern part of the Aegean, in Colophon, on the island of Lesbos, and on the Hellespont. There he seems to have worked out his philosophical system and to have met some wealthy young men with whom he formed friendships that would continue throughout his life. In 306 he moved to Athens, where, with the financial help of his friends, he purchased the estate that would be his Garden, the school he founded. He lived and taught there until his death in 270.

Epicurus had an electrifying effect on many who knew him. Perhaps his most inspiring activity was what was celebrated in Lucretius's eulogy— the suppression of superstition. As he looked around, he saw people engaging in fearful rituals from the moment they awakened in the morning until the moment they fell asleep at night. Fear of the gods and fear of death pervaded their every moment. One of Aristotle's students, Theophrastus, wrote a book, *Characters*, in which he described the various personality types, one of which is the superstitious man (in Greek, the *deisidaimon*, "the one who fears the divine"). On certain days of the month, the superstitious man decorates the statues in his house with garlands and drinks warm wine; he avoids the pollution that comes from coming close to a corpse, a tombstone, a menstruating woman, a madman, or an epileptic. (Pliny warns in detail what results from contact with a menstruating woman: new wine turns sour, crops become barren, grafts die, seeds in gardens are dried up, bright mirrors are dimmed, the edge of steel and the gleam of ivory are dulled, hives of bees die, and bronze and iron are seized by rust.[23]) The superstitious man believes in the power of dreams, of the purifying olive, of garlic, of leek, and of seawater.[24] Superstitious fear governs all the rituals of his daily life. Lucretius, perhaps putting into Latin Epicurus's own examples, describes the fatally erroneous power of superstition (which for him is identical to religion) in his account of the sacrifice of Iphigeneia, whom King Agamemnon slew in order to obtain favorable winds for the expedition to Troy.[25] Men fear death, Lucretius says with great wit, because they imaginatively attribute their present sufferings to the afterlife. Here is an example:

> As for all those torments that are said to take place in the depths of Acheron, they are actually present here and now, in our own lives. There is no Tantalus, as the myth relates, transfixed with groundless terror at the huge boulder poised above him in the air. But in this life there really are mortals oppressed by unfounded fear of the gods and trembling at the impending doom that may fall upon them at any moment by the whim of chance. . . .[26]
>
> Sisyphus too is alive for all to see, bent on winning the insignia of office, its rods and ruthless axes, by the people's vote, and is embittered by perpetual defeat. To strive for this profitless and never-granted prize, and in striving toil and moil incessantly, this truly is to push a boulder laboriously up a steep hill, only to see it, once the top is reached, rolling and bounding down again to the flat levels of the plain.[27]

249

But, says Lucretius, death is not to be feared, for there is no afterlife and hence no need to fear punishments there. Nor is there any consciousness after death, nor is there pain, for death is nothing other than the falling apart of the atoms that constitute our being.

B. EPICURUS'S SYSTEM

Epicurus's philosophical system was based on the physics of atomism, the fundamental principle of which is that all existence consists of two and only two things: a void and atoms. The word *atom*, in Greek, signifies something that cannot be divided or cut or split. When in the nineteenth century chemists discovered an elemental form of matter that they believed could not be split, they revived the ancient Greek term as its name. In the twentieth century, physicists managed to split what the nineteenth century called the atom. But they did not split the etymologically correct atom—for the atom is not capable of being split; they split only what the nineteenth century thought was the atom. Now there may not be any such thing as the atom; or it may be what physicists today call a quark or some as yet to be discovered part of a quark, but if there is an atom, it will—if we ever discover it—be unsplittable.

Epicurus accepted from Democritus that there are such things as atoms and that these are the "ultimate building blocks of the universe." Like Democritus, he thought of these atoms as moving around in empty space, in the void. Out of their accidental collision came everything that exists—rocks, sky, mind. Democritus had suggested no particular mechanism for the atoms to collide. Epicurus introduced the notion of a "swerve," a completely indeterminate minute aberration from a downward fall. As modern physicists had to introduce various constants to make their systems work, so Epicurus introduced the swerve (in Greek *parenclesis*, "a leaning sideways"). Without the swerve, the atoms would simply continue to fall through the void at the same speed (for the void would offer no resistance to slow them down) in parallel paths, never colliding with another and never combining to make the world.

According to Epicurus, the swerve was the cause of free will. Strict atomism would preclude free will, as everything would be determined by the laws that controlled the behavior of atoms. The inherently indeterminate nature of the swerve, applied to the atoms of the mind, accounts for the unpredictability in human life. Epicurus took what appeared to him as the brute fact of free will and tried to account for it by means of a physical cause. If his solution seems to beg the question, that is, to take as an assumption (the existence of the swerve) what ought to be its conclusion (the existence of the swerve and the swerve as free will), at least he is aware of the labyrinthine nature of the problem.[28] Modern theories of human psychology that begin with the premise that all behavior can be explained by chemical and physical means are still straining either to explain free will or to dismiss it altogether as an illusion.

Epicurus stressed the connection between his physics and his ethics, and his fervent follower Diogenes of Oenoanda included on his pillars Epicurus's criticism of those who neglect physics:

> Some philosophers, and especially those of the Socratic school, say that the study of nature and worrying about things up above is superfluous, and they do not condescend to spend time on such things.
>
> [Others do not dare to say outright that we should not study nature], being ashamed to make this statement, but they employ another method of getting rid of it. For when they allege that things are incomprehensible, what else are they saying but that we should not study nature? For who would choose to search for something he will never find? Aristotle, therefore, and those who follow the same line as Aristotle, say that nothing can be scientifically known; things are always in flux and because of the swiftness of the flow they escape our apprehension.[29]

In our best, and very entertaining, source for the details of Epicurus's scientific system, the majestic verse of Lucretius's six books of *On the Nature of Things*, we read the arguments for the existence of atoms, the reasons for their invisibility, the nature of their movement, the variety of their shapes, and details of their swerve. In addition, the poet describes the soul's atomic composition; the soul's mortal nature; the nature and operation of sensations, dreams, and illusions; the imperfection of the world, which shows that the world cannot have been made by gods; the origin of human beings and of civilization; and the causes of earthquakes, thunderbolts, and other phenomena usually attributed to the gods. Nevertheless, despite their call to study nature, it is for their manner of life that Epicureans were chiefly known and for which their philosophy was popular. Epicurus's life in the Garden served as an *agoge* (Greek for *a manner* or *model of life*) for others to follow. Unlike the schools of Plato and Isocrates, the aim of Epicurus's school was not to prepare pupils for a political career. The aim was a life of imperturbability, *ataraxia*. In the Garden one spent time with one's friends, enjoying sweet conversation and mental exercises. Unlike the other schools, the Garden admitted women, even courtesans, and they could enjoy an intellectual life on an equal basis with the men. As the Garden was separated from the community, so the Epicurean lived as uninvolved as possible apart from the political whirl that surrounded him (or her).

251

At the beginning of the second book of *On the Nature of Things*, Lucretius provides an extended metaphor of *ataraxia*:

> What joy it is, when out at sea the stormwinds are lashing the waters, to gaze from the shore at the heavy stress some other man is enduring! Not that anyone's afflictions are in themselves a source of delight; but to realize from what troubles you yourself are free is joy indeed. What joy, again, to watch the opposing hosts marshaled on the field of battle when you have yourself no part in their peril! But this is the greatest joy of all: to possess a quiet sanctuary, stoutly fortified by the teaching of the wise, and to gaze down from that elevation on others wandering aimlessly in search of a way of life, pitting their wits against one another, disputing for precedence, struggling night and day with unstinted effort to scale the pinnacles of wealth and power. O joyless hearts of men! O minds without vision! How dark and dangerous the life in which this tiny span is lived away! Do you not see that nature is barking for two things only, a body free from pain, a mind released from worry and fear for the enjoyment of pleasurable sensations?[30]

Epicurus, whose health had always been poor, died at the age of sixty-nine from a very painful kidney disease. As he lay dying, he wrote to his friends, "This is the happiest day of my life. It is the last. The pains in my bladder and stomach, always extreme, continue their course, and lose none of their violence. But against all that I place the joy in my soul when I recall the conversations we have had together."[31] Perhaps here we may see, with its profoundest implications, the doctrine described metaphorically by Lucretius in the passage just quoted. Epicurus, on his last day alive, was not, of course, delighted to be in the excruciating pain of his disease. But, like the person sitting on the cliff and watching the ships tossed by a storm, he was able to appreciate that it was only his "detached" body and not his true self—his mind—that was buffeted by pain. In other words, he was able to withdraw into a garden of his mind and look with imperturbable detachment on his body as on a stranger.[32]

So Epicurus had a small house, a garden, some very close friends, and—for his amusement—did problems in philosophy. That life is, of course, at variance with the conventional view of Epicureanism, which imagines a life surrendered to materialistic pleasures—eating, drinking, sex, and so on. A person who gives himself to those pleasures is really a *hedonist*, that is, one who pursues *pleasure for the moment*. An Epicurean was as interested in pleasure as a hedonist, but he thought more about it. For Epicurus, as for the hedonist, the ultimate standards of happiness are pleasure and pain. Epicurus's aim is lasting pleasure, pleasure that will not ultimately lead to pain. The problem with sensual pleasures is that they are short lived and invariably lead to pain: drinking leads to hangovers; sexual liaisons, to physical and emotional suffering. The truest pleasures are those of philosophy, and for Epicureans consist fundamentally of friendship, though friendship without the kind of intense feeling that can lead to pain. The friendship of the Epicureans is famous, and justly so. In the face of a meaningless and purposeless universe, what pleasure is there greater and more lasting than that of friendship?

In his analysis of pleasure, Epicurus introduced the distinction between "settled" pleasure and pleasure "in movement," a distinction that applied to both bodily and mental pleasures. A settled pleasure occurs when the body experiences an absence of pain, when, for example, the body is not hungry, not thirsty, not aching. "Pleasure in movement" occurs when the body is in the process of eliminating a pain, when, for example, a body scratches itself, eliminating the pain of an itch, or when a body eats, eliminating the pain of hunger. Both these types of pleasure have their mental counterpart. A mind free from fear or exuberance or from any kind of perturbation enjoys *ataraxia*, imperturbability, that is, settled pleasure. A mind ridding itself of a mental pain experiences pleasure in movement, as when the mind solves a mystery, where there had been the pain of ignorance.

Where, one might wonder, are the gods, and where is their attentiveness to the world and to human life? The *ataraxia* sought by men, says Epicurus, is the permanent state of the gods. The gods cannot possibly be as Homer portrays them, prone to anger or grief or erotic titillation or jealousy; they cannot care who wins or loses a war or who suffers or who rejoices, for any such care would destroy their imperturbability. Like the heavenly bodies, which immortally rise and set, the gods go about their business serenely.[33] That the gods exist is certain, for human beings have a clear vision of them,[34] but nothing that humans do riles or pleases them.

Consciousness of a meaningless universe became pervasive among intellectuals in the classical world at the same time that the *polis*, the kind of

city-state that Athens represented, ceased to be the dominant social structure. When Alexander the Great created a world-state out of the numerous independent *poleis*, he destroyed that community. People no longer
felt themselves significant members of a group that was finite, whose limits
they knew, and to whose well-being they were fully committed. The Hellenistic Age—the period from the rise of Alexander to the rise of Rome—
was only a foreshadowing of the greatest superstate, Rome. There was no
polis anymore; there was only the *cosmo-polis*, the world-city. The philosophy of Epicurus provided intellectual Romans with a way to cope with the
politically remote Roman Empire, where the will of the emperor ruled
supreme. Like Epicurus, Romans could withdraw into a garden of their
minds, gazing with detachment at the worldly terror around them.

The members of the immediate circle of Epicurus and his successors,
filled with the enthusiasm of those convinced that they have found the
true way, wrote treatises attacking other philosophical systems. Colotes of
Lampsacus wrote a book colorfully titled *That the Doctrines of the Other
Philosophers Actually Make Life Impossible*. Among the works attacked by
Colotes and by Epicurus's good friend Metrodorus were various dialogues of Plato. Of course, Epicurus was not himself immune to criticism.
Among Hellenistic rhetoricians, "Epicurean" was perverted into "hedo-
nistic," and in rabbinical literature and that of the Church fathers, "Epi-
curean" became a synonym for "atheist."[35]

Discussion Questions

1. What is the attraction of defining the good in terms of *pleasure* and *pain*?
Is it possible to manipulate the meanings of these terms in such a way as to
expand their scope over a broad range of human life?

2. Pyrrho, believing that equally strong pairs of opposing arguments regarding all philosophical questions could be constructed such that they cancel
each other out, maintained that the true philosopher, acknowledging his
lack of knowledge, should keep silent. Do you think that *equally* strong opposing arguments can always be constructed or, with John Milton, that truth
will always win in a fair fight? What are the implications for philosophy,
law, history, and any other subject where debate plays a key role of the
claim that equally strong arguments can be made for opposing sides?

3. In your experience, has the ability to see the opposing arguments on a matter resulted in philosophic humility à la Pyrrho, or has it resulted in paralysis from an inability to choose, or in an assertive arrogance for one side, or in some other nonhumble outcome?

4. Is the kind of personal devotion that Epicurus stirred in his disciples somehow unseemly in philosophy, where we expect—or do we?—that people will respond to solid arguments and not to personal charisma? In your own academic choices, to what extent has the charm of the instructor, as distinct from the subject matter itself, influenced your decisions? How would you defend or attack such decisions?

5. How well are Epicurean physics and ethics integrated into a coherent system? Can modern physics, which is (somewhat) similarly based in material particles, be integrated into a consistent ethics? Should ethics and physics be related to each other in the first place?

6. Is Epicurus's acknowledgment of the gods sincere, or does it seem a transparent attempt to avoid a charge of impiety? If you could be a pagan god, would you choose to be the kind of god described by Epicurus or the kind of god we find in Homer's epics?

7. Does Epicureanism as a philosophy provide a way of either finding meaning in life or coping with the vast impersonality of the Hellenistic Age, when the *polis* had ceased to be the fulfilling focus of people's lives? How similar is devout Epicureanism to a religion?

Notes

1. *Phaedo* 59c. Plato also points out that he was the lover of Meno (*Meno* 70b). That Meno was a notorious scoundrel we know from Xenophon's *Anabasis* 2.6.21.

2. *Protagoras* 353d–357d, esp. 356c–357a.

3. For example, *Republic* 585 d–e, *Philebus* 52–c.

4. *Nicomachean Ethics* 1177 a20–1178 a8.

5. So reports Cicero in *Ad Familiares* (9.26.2): *habeo, non habeor, a Laide.* Cicero adds that the line is better in Greek.

6. Diogenes Laertius, *Life of Pyrrho* 9.64.

7. For the suspension of judgment Pyrrho used the term *epoche*; for the acknowledgment of ignorance, Pyrrho used the term *akatalepsia*; and for the laudable silence, Pyrrho used the word *aphasia*.

8. Diogenes wittily reports that a certain Theodosius denied that skepticism should be called after Pyrrho, for, said Theodosius, if the most one aspires to is doubt, then one can never be certain of what Pyrrho actually meant, and without such knowledge, doubters should not be called Pyrrhonians (*Life of Pyrrho* 9.70).

9. Herodotus, *History of the Persian Wars* 7.50.

10. Terence, *Phormio* 445–464.

11. The conversation in the *Phaedo* deals with the immortality of the soul. By the end of the dialogue, no convincing proof has been offered. Instead, Socrates knows that no proof has been found and that he lacks knowledge about the soul's immortality, and he thus exhibits *akatalepsia*, acknowledged ignorance. Only in this way, however, is he able to face death courageously, for had he *proved* the immortality of the soul and his own future journey to a happy place, he would have had no need for courage. For a full discussion of this dialogue as a dramatic call to philosophic courage, see *Interpreting Plato: The Dialogues as Drama* 215–229.

In reading the Platonic dialogues, one would generally be prudent to withhold judgment about Plato's own views, and the scholarship on Plato, in which strong opposing views are advocated, makes an attitude of Pyrrhonism attractive.

12. Diogenes Laertius, *Life of Pyrrho* 9.66.

13. Diogenes Laertius, *Life of Pyrrho* 9.67.

14. Diogenes Laertius, *Life of Pyrrho* 9.68.

15. Diogenes Laertius summarizes these views of the Gymnosophists in the "Prologue" to his *Lives of the Philosophers* 1.6. Their influence on Pyrrho is suggested in *Life of Pyrrho* 9.61.

16. For the discussion of calm in temple friezes, see chapter 1, pp. 28–29.

17. Moses Hadas is reputed to have observed wittily that if one wishes to know what a culture really was like, it is necessary to look at the culture's ideals and to assume that it behaved in a way opposite to those ideals. After all, one does not have to aspire to qualities that one already possesses. Perhaps Hadas's insight can reveal a great deal about ancient and modern cultures.

18. Perhaps it would be useful to draw a distinction between the words *character* and *personality*. A *character* is, literally (in the Greek), an engraving, a gouging out, a mark; then, by extension, it is the mark of a person, his characteristic sign or way of doing something. Such a way is formed by repeated similar actions or habits: when these habits possess moral rectitude and are socially useful, we call the character good; when the habits are immoral and so antisocial, we call the character bad. There is a nice distinction to be made between those characteristics that are socially uniform and those that are personal and unique. Good character is non-individualistic and universal, just as is bad character, for good and evil actions fall into universal classes. Between them lies the area in which the uniquely personal may operate, traits that do not affect the basic morality of actions but that give them an individual charm or repulsion, called *personality*. The word *personality* is derived from the Latin word meaning *mask*; it refers to that part of ourselves that we present to the outer world; for example, we are cheerful or morose or sparkling or dull. But such traits are not directly functional to the operations of our character; hence a man may be charming but evil, dull but good.

19. It appears that strict Epicureans deliberately avoided literary artistry as dishonest persuasion. Later, this view seems to have had a rival, as some Epicureans argued that rhetoric was an art.

20. Epicurus, frag. 31, "To Colotes," in Cyril Bailey, *Epicurus: The Extant Remains* (Oxford: Clarendon Press, 1926), 129.

21. Lucretius, *On the Nature of Things* 1.62–79.

22. For a translation of what remains, see C. W. Chilton, *Diogenes of Oenoanda: The Fragments* (London: Oxford University Press, 1971).

23. Pliny, *Natural History* 7.64.

24. Theophrastus, *Characters* 16.

25. Lucretius, *On the Nature of Things* 1.80–101.

26. Lucretius, *On the Nature of Things* 3.978–983, trans. R. E. Latham (New York: Penguin Books, 1994). Subsequent quotations of Lucretius are from this translation.

27. Lucretius, *On the Nature of Things* 3.995–1002.

28. John Milton wittily has the fallen angels amusing their idle hours debating free will as an activity in Hell (*Paradise Lost* 2.557–561):

> Others apart sat on a hill retired
> In thoughts more elevate, and reasoned high

> Of providence, foreknowledge, will, and fate,
> Fixed fate, free will, foreknowledge absolute,
> And found no end, in wand'ring mazes lost.

29. Diogenes of Oenoanda, in Chilton, *Diogenes of Oenoanda*, frags. 3 and 4.

30. Lucretius, *On the Nature of Things* 2.1–22.

31. Diogenes Laertius, *Life of Epicurus* 22.

32. This interpretation of Epicurus's last day is suggested in the poem of John M. Crossett, "Epicurus," *Columbia University Forum* 9 (1966): 43.

33. Epicurus, *Epistle* 1.76–77.

34. Epicurus, *Epistle* 3.123.

35. In the Mishnah, for example, the word "Apikoros" (from the name Epicurus) is used for someone who forfeits his share in the world to come (Sanhedrin 10:1).

Select Bibliography

Festugière, A. J. *Epicurus and His Gods*. Translated by C. W. Chilton. Cambridge, Mass.: Harvard University Press, 1955.

Jones, Howard. *The Epicurean Tradition*. London: Routledge, 1992.

Long, A. A. *Hellenistic Philosophy: Stoics, Epicureans, Sceptics*. Berkeley: University of California Press, 1986.

Warren, James. *Epicurus and Democritean Ethics: An Archaeology of Ataraxia*. Cambridge: Cambridge University Press, 2002.

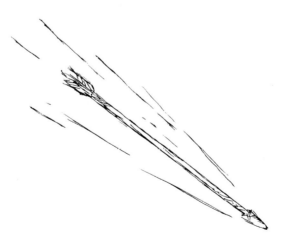

CHAPTER 14

Stoicism

I. Introduction

Diogenes Laertius devotes the longest chapter in *Lives of the Philosophers* to Zeno of Citium, the founder of the school of Stoicism, an indication, perhaps, of the importance of this school during Diogenes' time. Unlike Epicureanism, its major rival, Stoicism seems to have been open to internal debates, and, as a result, we find more freely expansive thought among Stoics than among Epicureans. Epicurus himself was largely responsible for Epicurean orthodoxy, for he claimed that since the views he laid down were perfect and complete, they were not subject to modification or correction—an intellectually tyrannical view that can produce atrophy rather than dynamic growth, as it did in Pythagoreanism. Among other subjects, Stoics debated the relative importance of the various branches of philosophy, the place of external goods in human happiness, and the relationships among God, nature, and fate.

Both Epicureanism and Stoicism provided a means of coping with the major social change of the Hellenistic and Roman periods—the replacement of the *polis* with the *cosmopolis*, the world-state, with its attendant evils of social fragmentation, loneliness, and despair. Epicureans thought it best to withdraw, to lie on the high cliff of philosophy and look down on those who were toiling and suffering in civic life. In practical terms, this philosophy was clearly not for everyone, for it required an independent income. In fact, Epicureanism seems to have been a philosophy for the rich.

Stoicism, however, was for all men in all seasons. Zeno, who made and lost a fortune of worldly gold, invented a philosophy that would allow equal happiness to paupers and millionaires, and of the three most famous Stoics of Rome, Epictetus was a slave, Seneca a fabulously wealthy aristocrat, and Marcus Aurelius an emperor. One chapter in a book on ancient philosophy cannot do justice to a comprehensive system that developed over six centuries. It won't try. Instead, after a look at its antecedents, this discussion will note a few highlights of its development and of its basic concepts. It will conclude with a look at Stoicism's three most prominent Roman adherents.

II. Cynics

Because the Cynics ignored physics and logic and devoted all their attention to ethics, some people considered Cynicism to be a way of life rather than a philosophy.[1] Cynics believed that the entire purpose of life was to live virtuously and that nothing else mattered. To lead a virtuous life was to live "according to nature." From this principle Zeno first developed Stoicism. For the Stoic, as for the ancients more generally, a philosopher's manner of life (in Greek, his *agoge*) was a vital part of his teaching, perhaps even more influential than his books. Indeed, philosophers seem sometimes to have lived with the express purpose of serving as models for imitation. Surrounded by pupils who would record their masters' virtue and wit, philosophers lived as though they were acting on a stage, themselves the playwrights. Devoted their pupils were, and their reminiscences produced the hundreds of sources Diogenes Laertius cites in *Lives of the Philosophers*.

Antisthenes of Athens (446–366) is credited with having founded the "school" (one flinches in using the word *school* of this particular assemblage of individuals) of Cynics. He was about midway between the age of Socrates, who was twenty-three years older, and the age of Plato, who was seventeen or eighteen years younger.[2] Having been a student of Gorgias, Antisthenes wrote dialogues in Gorgias's flamboyant style, giving them names like *Truth* and *Exhortations*.[3] When he heard Socrates' discussions in the marketplace, he became a "Socratic" and brought his followers with him. When Socrates died, he resumed his own teaching.[4] He chose as the site for his teaching a gymnasium named Cynosarges (in Greek, "white [*argos*] dog [*cynos*]"), and it is probably from the name of this gymnasium, as well as from their serendipitous resemblance to dogs, who, like these particular thinkers, snap at the heels of the mighty, that the Cynics took their name.

Antisthenes borrowed from Socrates the idea that the soul should be as free of the body as possible.[5] Where Socrates went barefooted, Antisthenes went in a ragged cloak. He admitted no rich men into his presence, took no money at all for teaching, and, when asked what good he derived from his study of philosophy, replied, "The ability to converse with myself."[6]

His most celebrated pupil was Diogenes of Sinope (404–323), who groused that Plato's talks were a waste of time, that the tragedies in the Theatre of Dionysus were peep shows for morons, and that politicians were the lapdogs of the mob.[7] And yet Alexander the Great said, "If I were not Alexander, I would be Diogenes."

According to the account in *Lives of the Philosophers*, the young Diogenes adulterated some currency his banker-father had entrusted to him, and, as a result, his father was imprisoned and died.[8] Banished, Diogenes went to Athens, where he asked to become Antisthenes' pupil. Accustomed to discourage pupils, Antisthenes rejected Diogenes until finally one day, when Antisthenes was about to strike the young Diogenes with his staff, Diogenes said, "Strike, for your staff is not hard enough to keep me away from you so long as I find what you are saying worthwhile."[9] From then on he was Antisthenes' pupil and an imitator of the Cynic life.

Diogenes, by all accounts, surpassed his master in strict Cynicism. Diogenes had three possessions: a tub (which served as his home), a bowl, and a cup. One day, when he saw a boy cup his hands to drink, he realized the superfluity of the cup and threw it away. Another time, when he saw a child break a plate and eat his lentils with the hollow part of a piece of bread, he threw away his bowl.[10] Though he injured no one physically, he was full of biting comments. Once, when he saw officials of a temple taking to prison someone who had stolen a bowl from the temple treasures, he said, "The big thieves are leading away the little thief."[11] And when he was short of money and asked his friends for some, he said it was not alms he was asking for but repayment of what was due.[12] In perhaps the most famous story of the Cynic, Alexander came to visit Diogenes while he was sunning himself and told the philosopher, "Ask me any favor you like." Diogenes replied, "Stand out of the light."[13]

Diogenes had an enthusiastic follower, Crates (fl. 326), who gave up an inheritance to lead the impoverished life of a Cynic. He extolled what he called the "natural life," which meant for him a life devoid of luxury and pride. Crates himself had two notable students, his wife Hipparchia and Zeno. Hipparchia cared little for her good-looking rich suitors but fell in love with both Crates' teaching and the pattern of his life. Her parents begged Crates to dissuade her, and, in conformity with the Cynic disposition to reject pupils, he stripped naked before her and said,[14] "This is your bridegroom, and here are all of his possessions. Make your choice, for unless you adopt this type of life, you will be no companion." She chose to adopt his dress and way of life, and the two of them extended the "life of nature" to having sexual relations in public.[15]

The ideas that one ought to live "according to nature" and that nothing done "according to nature" can be bad anywhere (activities that included sexual relations and excreting) were Cynic principles. The idea that a life "according to nature" was self-sufficient would be developed in Stoicism. As the anecdote of Diogenes and Alexander shows, the self-sufficient man, no matter how impoverished, is, in Cynic belief, every bit the equal of the master-ruler. Whatever we may think of Cynic brazenness today, Cynics seem to have won the esteem of their contemporaries. When a boy broke Diogenes' tub, the Athenians gave him a new one, and when he died, the Corinthians put both a pillar and a statue of a dog in Parian marble over his grave.[16] Perhaps these eccentric philosophers were not so threatening as Socrates, who was executed, or Aristotle, who had to flee Athens.

III. The Early Stoa

A. THE FOUNDING OF STOICISM: ZENO (336-265)

The Athenians thought so highly of Zeno, who had come from Citium (a town on the island of Cyprus), that they entrusted him with the keys to the city walls, gave him a gold crown, and erected a statue in his honor.[17] His was a riches-to-rags-to-spiritual-riches story. According to the tale, when he was thirty years old, he was shipwrecked while transporting a rich cargo of purple dye from Phoenicia to the Piraeus, the port of Athens. He survived the wreck and wandered the five miles to Athens, where he decided to pass some time in a bookshop. He was browsing in Xenophon's *Memorabilia* about the life of Socrates and was already well into the second book when he looked up and sighed, "Where are men like Socrates today?" The bookseller, at that precise moment just happening to see Crates down the street, told Zeno, "Follow that man!" Whether the bookseller was trying to rid himself of an idler who was reading books for free or whether, as the Stoics might perhaps aver, he was the instrument of

Providence is, of course, impossible to say. But from that moment, Zeno became the Cynic's pupil.[18]

Zeno was more personally modest than his Cynic friends, who flouted convention for its own sake. In conformity with this modesty, he developed a philosophy that did not so conspicuously set itself against the prevailing social conventions. In his earliest work, called, like Plato's masterpiece, *Politeia*[19] (Greek for *Republic*), he expressed the Cynic belief that all human beings are equal, all brothers with souls made of the same fire that infuses the universe. Since class and rank are social conventions and since, stripped naked of such accoutrements, all people are the same, Zeno argued that there should be one world-state for all humanity in which all people would be equal citizens. Unlike Plato's imaginary state, where the philosopher would rule as king, in Zeno's republic the wise man—the man who lived according to nature, human nature, that is, in accordance with reason—would be a citizen like everyone else. Laws would be unnecessary, for people would live with rational self-control.

He was active at the same time that Epicurus was attracting followers. Against Epicurus's standard of rational pleasure as happiness, Zeno opposed the standard of virtue, or behavior in strict accordance with reason. When Zeno was challenged on the precise superstructure of his views on politics and virtue, he responded by expanding his insights into a broad philosophical system that included epistemology, logic, and physics.[20]

Zeno taught at the *Stoa Poikile*, the "Painted Stoa," in the marketplace of Athens, and for this reason he and his students were soon called not "Zenonians" after the founder but "Stoics"—a name reflecting significant contributions to the system by others besides Zeno.

B. ZENO'S SUCCESSORS

When Zeno died in 265, he was succeeded by his student Cleanthes of Assus (301–232), who arrived in Athens with only four drachmas in his pocket, or about what an ordinary workman would earn in four days.[21] His only surviving work is the *Hymn to Zeus*, a poem of fifty-one lines that expresses the strong religious feeling we find in Stoicism—a feeling perhaps introduced into the Stoic School by Cleanthes himself. He was a poor ascetic and earned a living carrying water by day so that he could argue philosophy by night.[22] He taught that the universe is a living being whose soul somehow penetrates its entire extent—an idea called *pantheism*.[23] Since the universe's soul is identical to the human soul, the essence of the universe and of human beings is the same.

Cleanthes was succeeded as head of the school by Chrysippus of Soli (280–207), an incredibly prolific writer of seven hundred books. These books, most of which dealt with logic, language, physics, and the other parts of philosophy aside from ethics, are credited for having made Stoicism a comprehensive system. Unfortunately, none of Chrysippus's works have survived, but his views, as reported by other writers, seem to have established the basis of orthodox Stoicism. These included the explication of the phrase "life according to nature," the formulation of logic, and the division of the universe into two principles, the active and passive, whereby matter (defined à la Aristotle as substance without quality[24]) is the passive principle and God, or the reason that inheres in the matter, the active principle. He held to the idea that the human soul is a unity, not the tripartite composite that Plato had suggested, and that therefore there was no conflict between emotions and reason. Emotions, he claimed, were simply false judgments, and when a person is conflicted about a choice, it is not a contest of emotion versus reason but a conflict of reasoned judgments.[25]

265

C. THE MIDDLE STOA

The poet and Latinist A. E. Housman wittily remarked, "It has been a well known fact for a long time that the Romans read nothing that came before Posidonius."[26] Housman was referring to the impression one has from texts of Posidonius's student Cicero and from scholarly commentaries on Cicero's works that Cicero and every other Roman learned everything they knew from Posidonius of Rhodes (135–51), the most famous Stoic of the Middle Period.[27] His fame was transient, for he seems to have been largely ignored after the second century C.E., and his works survive only in fragments.[28] These works show that he was not bound to the views of his predecessors by a sense of orthodoxy but was, in fact, an independent thinker.[29]

A polymath, he wrote books on geography, tides, seismology, geology, mineralogy, botany, military tactics, the ethnology of the Jews, and historiography[30] as well as on the traditional branches of Stoic philosophy—logic, physics, and ethics. For Posidonius, physics was prior to logic and ethics.

Soul was subject to analysis in physical terms, and logic was the order of the physical world as reflected in the rational mind. The relationship of the branches of philosophy was shown by an analogy: physics was the flesh and blood, logic the bones and nerves, ethics the soul. How—and whether—Posidonius's works all fit together to form an integrated, coherent philosophical system is, perhaps, not ascertainable from the surviving texts.

We may speculate that Posidonius was particularly influential in his own times because of his view that the world-state envisioned by Zeno was to be actualized in the Roman Empire. The Stoic mission to the world, he maintained, was the same as the mission of Rome: to spread the rule of law, which, in its earthly manifestations, is a reflection of the cosmic law of the universe. Posidonius, perhaps because of the esteem for his varied works, perhaps because of his celebrated congeniality, seems to have wielded a great deal of intellectual authority, and this authority gave credence to the political applications of his thought. In this respect he would bear the credit for having made Stoicism the most dominant philosophy in Rome.

266

IV. Tenets of Stoicism

A. INTRODUCTION

While Epicureans, in compliance with the will of their founder, were absolutely united on the matter of teaching physics first and then ethics, Stoics were divided. Posidonius, as noted previously, compared the parts of philosophy to the parts of a human being, with ethics as the soul. Other Stoics, also dividing their subject hierarchically, compared logic to a wall, physics to a tree protected by the wall, and ethics to the fruit of the tree. In this analogy, logic was prior because it established the rules by which the truth of propositions could be judged; using these rules and protected by them as by a wall, physics investigated the nature of the universe; finally, ethics taught people how to lead a good life given the universe in which they dwell. Since Stoic thought is quite varied, what is described here will not be congruent with what every Stoic believed, though it will lay out views mostly agreed on (as far as we can determine given the fragmentary remains of Stoic writings on most subjects).

B. LOGIC

Aristotle, who invented the science of logic, did not actually name this branch of philosophy. His treatises on logic were divided into separate works collectively called the *Organon* (Greek for *tool* or *instrument*).[31] It was left to the Stoics to organize these studies under the name *logic*. And though, as for Epicureans, the aim of the philosophical system was a manner of life, Stoics expended much effort in working out a logic and the definitions of terms.[32]

The logic of the Stoics dealt with a method of connecting meaningful utterances, which they named *lekta* (from the Greek for *things said*)—propositions, questions, or commands. Stoics were interested principally in classifying the way these utterances are connected by the conditional, or hypothetical, word *if* and in determining where the utterances stand on a scale from true to false.[33] For example, the argument "If Dion walks, then Dion is in motion; but Dion is walking, therefore Dion is in motion" they called "a syllogistic" argument and deemed "conclusive." The argument "If it is day, it is light; but it is day, therefore Dion walks" was deemed "inconclusive" because a contradictory conclusion, that "Dion is not walking," is also possible. The numerous commutations depend on the hypothetical quality or on the truth of the various parts of statements.

Stoics also enjoyed pondering what they deemed "insoluble" arguments. An example is what they called the "Nobody" argument. As Diogenes Laertius describes this argument, it is one "where a major premise consists of an indefinite and a definite clause, followed by a major premise and a conclusion: if anyone is here, he is not in Rhodes; but there is someone here; therefore there is not anyone in Rhodes."[34] They also believed that a certain number of undemonstrated claims were the foundation for all syllogisms, though they disagreed about the exact number of the indemonstrable claims.[35]

Because Stoics believed that the universe was an organic whole in which all the parts were related to each other—a relation shown in the analogies for the interconnectedness and dependence of the branches of philosophy—they wanted to show how assertions (*lekta*) were connected, and this project was the focus of their logic. Hence they endeavored to establish the criteria by which claims could be adjudged true, and here, as frequently occurred in other philosophical systems, they opened themselves up to assault. The history of philosophy shows over and over again that it is easier to challenge truth claims than to establish them.[36] For the Stoics, beginning with Zeno, knowledge is based on sense impressions. These sense impressions forcibly affect our minds and establish the conviction that they are true. A sequence leading to knowledge begins when the sense impressions create a picture (*phantasia*) in the mind. The mind assents mildly to this picture (the assent is called a *synkatathesis*). This assent is followed by a comprehension of what has occurred (the comprehension is called a *katalepsis*), that is, a "taking into the memory" of the mental picture. Finally, there comes knowledge (*episteme*). Zeno described the sequence by an analogy: sense impression is like the fingers of a hand extended, assent of the mind is a closed hand, comprehension is a tight fist, and knowledge is the left hand enclosing the tight fist of the right hand.[37] But, as perhaps is plain, no theory of knowledge, that is, of absolute, total apprehension of truth, can be based on sense impressions, which, regardless of how intensely they assert themselves, may not be reliable. Even when everyone on the planet has the same sense impression, and the truth is acclaimed by what the Stoics called "universal assent," the inference from the impression, as well as the impression itself, might be wrong. (For example, everyone has the same impression that the earth stands still, and yet the earth is moving through the cosmos.) Skeptics attacked the Stoics on just these very grounds.

268

Whatever the defects of their logic, Stoics were convinced that the wise man must be fully versed in the subject, for all the truths of physics and ethics could be discerned only with the tool of reason. In this they were at one with the other schools of ancient philosophy.

C. STOIC PHYSICS AND ITS RELATION TO ETHICS

Stoics maintained that there were two principles: the active principle and the passive principle, that is, a principle that did something and a principle that suffered or underwent what the active principle did.[38] The passive principle was what might be called *matter*, or *being*, a kind of cosmic stuff lacking in any quality whatsoever; the active principle was what might be called *god* or *logos* and existed *in* the cosmic stuff. Stoic physics was akin to what is called *pantheism*, that is, the doctrine that God (sometimes called by the names *Zeus*, or *fate*, or *reason*) and the universe are identical.[39] The active principle, they said, is invisible and, operating throughout the cosmic stuff, creates each individual thing.

Although both Epicureanism and Stoicism start with two principles, the two sets of principles are not at all analogous. We might be able to draw some kind of crude comparison between Stoic matter and Epicurean atoms, but there is no conceivable way in which the Stoic *logos* corresponds with Epicurean void. And just as Stoics and Epicureans have radically different principles, so, too, they have radically different notions of space: for the Epicureans, it is infinite, actually infinite; for the Stoics, it is finite.[40]

The lonely atoms colliding accidentally in the void led the Epicureans to extol friendship as the highest pleasure.[41] For Stoics, the universe is a synthesized penetration of cosmic stuff by *logos*; the *logos* is divine. Hence any part of matter, of cosmic stuff, is divine because it is informed by the divine *logos*. The implication therefore is that each man is divine—not his body, which will eventually be destroyed, but his divine *logos*. An Epicurean could look forward to a state of complete annihilation at death: both his body and soul would be reduced to accidental atoms, and the soul would be troubled no more, for all consciousness would disappear— after all, consciousness is only the result of certain combinations of atoms. A Stoic, however, was much less clear about all this. He believed that his body would be reabsorbed into the cosmic stuff, out of which new things would be created. But what about his *logos*? Note the use of the word *logos* instead of *soul*. *Logos* cannot exist apart from the cosmic stuff. Or, if it does, it does not exist for long; eventually it, too, is reabsorbed into the cosmic *logos*. An Epicurean had to worry about himself only so long as the entity that he was existed; but when his atoms fell apart, what happened to them was up to chance. But a Stoic had an obligation not to violate the cosmic order, the cosmic *logos*. As he carried in him a divine spark, it was his job to make that spark correspond to the cosmic divine spark: the individual Stoic's *logos* had to be like the cosmic *logos* because if it were not, the cosmos—the universe—would be disordered. And if it were disordered, the individual Stoic would be disordered, too. The Epicurean had no obligations except to himself; the Stoic had obligations to everyone and everything. Thus obligation, a sense of duty, is the mark of true Stoicism.

269

The Stoic had first to understand what the universe, what Nature, was like; then he had to act in accordance with it. Since Nature was this amalgam of cosmic stuff and *logos*, everything was the way it ought to be. As Alexander Pope put it in his *Essay on Man*, "Whatever is, is right."

D. ETHICS

Just as Epicureans are falsely accused of being hedonists, of being devoted to a life of sensual and immediate pleasure, so Stoics are accused of—as Pope puts it—"lazy apathy." The Epicurean ethical idea was to live a life of *ataraxia*, imperturbability. The Stoic ideal was a life of *apatheia*. The root of this word is *pathos*, which, in Herodotus, means "suffering," and, as Herodotus and Aeschylus say, "in suffering is wisdom" (*en pathei mathos*). In Aristotle, the word *pathos* has various senses: in the *Poetics* the tragic hero falls into *pathos* as a result of a mistake; yet, in Aristotle's more colorless works, like the *Physics*, the word signifies simply *attribute*. In Longinus, the great literary critic, the word signifies *feeling* or *emotion*—things like hate, pity, fear, love, and so forth. In Stoicism, the word signifies one of the two principles of the universe, the passive principle—that which submits or undergoes or suffers. The *a-* in front of the word *apatheia* signifies a privation, a lack of suffering or of feeling emotion, that is, a lack of undergoing changes in attributes. The Epicureans did not wish to be upset—that is, they wished to avoid pain—but they did not wish to avoid pleasure. To achieve happiness, the Stoics wished to avoid *both* pain and pleasure.

One avoided feeling pain and pleasure by understanding how nature operated and then by imitating it—by "following nature," as the Stoics put it. Make yourself like the universe. They were like Christians in this sense: as Jesus told his disciples to "be perfect, even as your father in heaven is perfect,"[42] so, too, the Stoic sages told their disciples to "be perfect, even as the universe is perfect." Once a person saw that something was in accordance with nature, then it was his job to adapt his psyche to accept it. Stoic ethics, then, developed the following principles: 1) some things lie within one's power, 2) some things lie outside one's control, and 3) some things do not matter. If something lies in one's power, he should control it in such a way as to be like nature; if something lies outside one's power, he should put up with it; if something does not matter, he should disregard it. The formula was simple: "hold up and hold off" (*aechou kai arechou*). If we expand this crisp saying, we have something like this: "bear and forbear"; or, "endurance and restraint."

Where Epicureanism appealed to an elite, Stoicism appealed to everybody. Whether a person was at the top or bottom of society, or even in the middle, he could be a Stoic. Three famous Stoics of Roman antiquity illustrate the extraordinary range of appeal: Seneca the Younger, Epictetus, and Marcus Aurelius. Seneca, an aristocrat, served as Nero's tutor, was later exiled and was eventually forced to commit suicide; Epictetus was a slave; and Marcus Aurelius was a Roman emperor. After a glance at some other Stoic views, we shall visit these three thinkers.

E. ASSORTED STOIC VIEWS

Stoics, in general, shared a number of other views. These included the ideas of the "World *Logos*" and its related conception of Providence, the figure of the sage, the periodic destruction of the universe by fire (what they called *ecpyrosis*), and the paradoxical notion that all wickedness is equal.

Perhaps Epicureans and Stoics were most opposed on the idea of Providence (Latin for "seeing in advance"; in Greek, the term is *pronoia*, "planning in advance"). For Epicureans, the universe was the result of chance collisions of atoms. For Stoics, the universe is the way it is because of the controlling power of God, who is equated with a universal reason, the World *Logos*, that pervades the universe and everything that happens in it.[43] This complete control, coming as it does from the divine mind, is Providence. A favorite Stoic metaphor is that life is a stage and we are actors on it. Our job is to perform as well as we can the script that the playwright Providence has written out for us. To the objections the Skeptics made of these views, that the world is too imperfect to have been made by a divine mind, Stoics replied that the world's evil, even if it appears to our limited vision as bad, would in fact appear good if we understood the entire scheme of things.

The sage, or wise man, is a figure of profound respect in Stoicism. He is the person who has achieved a life of supreme happiness. It is not clear exactly what constitutes the extent of his knowledge. At times he appears omniscient, but the idea of *human* omniscience seems impossible since it would require knowing everything about the past, present, and future. At times his knowledge seems to be a kind of prudential wisdom, that is, knowing about good and evil and possessing the ability to choose the good regardless of how complex the particular problem that presents itself. Whether there actually were or had been any actual sages or whether it was simply a goal to aspire to is also unclear, but the goal and the image of the sage remained fixtures in Stoic thought.

Early Stoics seem to have believed that the world is destroyed when the mix of elements becomes such that the amount of fire overwhelmingly exceeds the amounts of other elements. After this destructive cosmic fire has taken place, the other elements come into existence again and the universe is renewed in a cycle of generation and destruction, in a fashion somewhat akin to the cycles Empedocles proposed.[44] This Stoic theory implied questions for human life: would a human soul, also made of fire, last until the cosmic conflagration, or would only the soul of the sage?[45] By the period of Middle Stoicism, some Stoics were revising this view of periodic conflagration and maintaining instead that the world was eternal and indestructible.

Perhaps one of the Stoic views strangest to those outside the school was the notion that all wickedness is equal.[46] Cicero discusses this paradox with a reaction somewhere between bemusement and contempt.[47] The underlying Stoic view is that life should be lived "according to nature." Thus an action that strays from the straight path of nature even by only one degree, insofar as it is not on the straight path of nature, is equally *not* on the path as one that strays by thirty degrees or one hundred and eighty degrees. Either a person follows the straight path or he does not. If, to use the Stoic example, one wrongly kills a cockerel or one's own father,[48] one has equally killed wrongly. Since for human beings the way of nature is the way of reason, any wicked conduct whatsoever is a departure from reason. The correct way is absolute. If the sum of several numbers is one hundred, calculations of ninety or twenty-five are equally not one hundred. This idea is related to the idea of the sage, for the sage *never* strays from the right path by any degree; those who are not the sage are foolish, and they have *every* vice (even if all the vices do not manifest themselves at all times).

By the time that many prominent Romans in public life had adopted a mild Stoic philosophy, many of these peculiar views had been set side, relegated to the status of curiosities, in much the same way that later Protestants largely set aside the inflexible belief in absolute predetermination that Luther and Calvin had preached from their pulpits.

V. Roman Stoicism

A. SENECA (4 B.C.E.–65 C.E.)

Seneca was an enormously wealthy Roman aristocrat, the tutor of Nero, and for five years (54–59) virtual ruler of Rome. Then, when Nero began to feel his power, Seneca was banished; a few years later, Nero gave his former teacher the choice of being executed or committing suicide.

In sharp contrast to his Cynic forebearers, Seneca was fabulously wealthy: he had 500 tables of cedar wood and inlaid ivory,[49] at which he used to sit writing essays in praise of poverty. Some perhaps might think such an activity hypocritical. But Seneca was a Stoic and as such believed that the universe had placed him in life as a wealthy aristocrat. Whether he liked it or not, he had to put up with it. As a matter of fact, he did not seem to like it much: he preferred a life of thought. Personal preferences do not matter to a Stoic: his job is to do whatever job nature assigns him and to do it well. The essays extolling poverty were Seneca's way of reminding himself not to take his position seriously, not to value his wealth. They were, in effect, his "meditations."

Seneca's philosophical works cover a vast array of ethical topics, as is attested by their titles, *On Anger*, *On Clemency*, *On the Shortness of Life*, and *On the Constancy of the Sage*. In them he consistently and eloquently advocates a life of practical wisdom, and his works are full of lessons on how to cope with life's sorrows. He seems to have achieved a level of Stoic detachment toward his own life such that when he was executed by Nero he was thinking of how it would "play" to posterity, and he followed the script of a philosopher like Socrates, dying with equanimity. Seneca died, saying to his companions, "As I am prevented from showing my gratitude for your services, I leave you my sole but most beautiful possession—the image of my life. If you bear this in mind, you will reap the reward of loyal friendship in the credit accorded to virtuous

273

accomplishments."[50] With these words he joined the immortal ranks of those who "died for Athens."

B. EPICTETUS (55-135)

Epictetus was the son of a slave and was himself a slave for many years. One of his owners, Epaphroditus, was an ex-slave who became an important figure in Nero's administration. Epictetus came from Phrygia, in Asia Minor, and exhibited both Oriental joie de vivre and Roman seriousness. At some time in his life, one of his masters seems to have beaten him so severely as to leave him crippled. While a slave in Rome, he was allowed by Epaphroditus to study philosophy—Stoicism. Eventually he earned his freedom and began to teach philosophy at Rome. Under Emperor Domitian, in 92 C.E., all philosophers were banished from Rome; Epictetus went to Asia Minor, where he continued to teach.

His life was even more frugal than that of an Epicurean: he never locked his house in Rome, for his only possessions were a straw mattress and a rush mat. In Asia Minor, his standard of living was much better: he had an iron lamp, but when it was stolen, he got along with one made out of clay. The only difference between his life as a slave and his life as a philosopher was freedom. Like Socrates, he did not write books: Arrian, one of his disciples, wrote down his sayings, and two volumes of these have survived. In addition, we have his *Encheiridion*, one of the most famous books of philosophy in the world though it is only about fifty pages long. *Encheiridion* means, literally, "something small that fits in the hand." In Herodotus, it signified a dagger. By extension, it came to mean any small useful item that could be carried in the hand; then it came to mean a handbook. The *Encheiridion* of Epictetus was a kind of weapon to be used throughout life, to protect oneself from the attacks of pain and pleasure, the two great enemies of *logos*, reason.

Here are some sample passages from the *Encheiridion*. In the first passage, the manual's opening two sentences, Epictetus concisely sums up the essence of Stoic ethics:

> Of things some are in our power, and others are not. In our power are opinion, movement toward a thing, desire, aversion (turning from a thing), and in a word, whatever are our own acts; not in our power are

the body, property, reputation, offices (magisterial power), and, in a word, whatever are not our own acts. And the things in our power are by nature free, not subject to restraint or hindrance; but the things not in our power are weak, slavish, subject to restraint, in the power of others.[51]

The next shows how this attitude would be expressed in response to loss:

If you have a favorite cup or mug, say that it is not your favorite; then, when it breaks, you won't be disturbed. If you kiss your wife or child, say to yourself that you are kissing something mortal [that is, something that will break]; in that way, when your wife or child dies, you won't be disturbed.[52]

Epictetus elaborates this seemingly callous attitude:

We can learn what the will of nature is by considering how we are like others. For example, if another man's slave breaks the master's favorite glass, you are ready to say, "that's the way things go." You ought to feel the same way when your own favorite glass is broken, for rest assured, it will break. In the same way you would, if another's man's wife or child dies, say, "It's the human condition." Well, if your own wife or child dies, don't moan or groan; remember how you felt when the other man's wife died.[53]

Perhaps a reader might say that Epictetus was a slave and that such a philosophy perhaps befits a slave, who cannot help suffering. But Epictetus held the same views after he was free.

C. MARCUS AURELIUS (121–180)

Our last example of Roman Stoicism is Marcus Aurelius, emperor of Rome for nineteen years. He was a thoughtful, sorrowful, meditative man—one who would have preferred a life far different from that which he led. Most of his reign was spent on the frontier, defending Rome from attacks; he seems to have written his book, *Meditations to Himself*, in his tent, in the evening, at the end of the day's battles. It is a kind of Stoic pep talk, a rehearsal—for such is what the word *meditation* means—of the right attitudes to take. But his preference did not matter: the universe had made him emperor, as it had made Seneca an aristocrat and Epictetus a slave—and he had to put up with it. He is generally regarded as one of the

275

finest of the Roman emperors: he tried to reduce the brutality of the gladiatorial games, he was merciful to political prisoners, and he persecuted Christians—all actions consistent with his Stoicism.[54]

VI. Concluding Remarks on Stoicism

All three men—Seneca, Epictetus, and Marcus Aurelius—lived during the first two centuries of the Common Era, that is, until about 180. The first century saw the worst of the Roman emperors; the second century saw the best. In that first century were such depraved emperors as Caligula, who had his horse elected to the Senate, and Nero, who killed his mother, his wife, and his teacher. In the second century were such emperors as Trajan—one of only two pagans who find their way to heaven in Dante's *Divine Comedy*—and Marcus Aurelius. It was of this period that Edward Gibbon wrote,

> If a man were called to fix the period in the history of the world during which the condition of the human race was most happy and prosperous, he would, without hesitation, name that which elapsed from the death of Domitian to the accession of Commodus [the period from about 90 to 180].[55]

Similarly, it is difficult to think of many worse times than, say, the rule of Nero. For both times, the worst and the best, Stoicism was an appropriate philosophy. There are two ways of coping with the world. The first way is to be resourceful, resilient, adaptable, versatile, an Odysseus or a Thomas More—men for all seasons. The second way is to be consistent, unyielding, inflexible, tougher than the circumstances that press in on you, to be like Seneca, Epictetus, Marcus Aurelius. In the ancient world, Stoicism was the closest the world had to a philosophy for all seasons.

———

Discussion Questions

1. In the Gershwin opera *Porgy and Bess*, Porgy sings, "I've got plenty of nothing, and nothing's plenty for me"—in an aria that expresses the philosophy of the Cynics Antisthenes and Crates perfectly. Is there a pride in the

claim of being satisfied with nothing? If there is, is it consistent with being a shoeless and penniless Cynic?

2. Zeno put forth the view that there should be a world-state, with all people as equal citizens. Surely he was inspired by Alexander's failed attempt at creating such a state. Can you think of any arguments *against* a world-state? Are there advantages in having separate countries? What are the advantages of a world-state? On which side does the balance come down?

3. Is there anything in the *personalities* of the founders of Stoicism that allowed a growth and development of the system independent of their personalities (as distinct from the personality of Epicurus, which did not allow such independence and instead demanded orthodoxy)? Are there essential *doctrinal* positions in Stoicism that would have allowed for its independence from both personality and orthodoxy?

4. How well integrated is Stoic logic with the other parts of the philosophy? Does a philosophy's well roundedness, its comprehensiveness, enhance its appeal? If one branch (for example, logic, or ethics, or epistemology) is especially persuasive, are individuals likely to accept the less persuasive branches as well? Is there a value in a philosophy's being a *system* as distinct from a collection of disparate insights?

277

5. Neither Stoic nor Epicurean physics offered a completely convincing proof of its imaginatively conceived claims, and perhaps for this reason both schools concentrated on ethics, where the arguments could be more directly related to observable human life. In which system do the ethics and physics more closely depend on each other?

6. Would someone like the Stoic sage, who led a perfectly Stoic life, be fulfilling his human potential for a good life? Or would he, qua human, be missing out on something?

7. Examine the Stoics' use of metaphors that describe their philosophy and the nature of the world. In what ways do the metaphors illuminate our understanding? Are there any ways in which the metaphors hinder it? If so, how?

8. What do you think of the Stoic view that all wrongdoing is equal? What is attractive about the view? What is unattractive? Given human behavior as it actually exists, could a practical judicial system be established on the Stoic view?

9. Romans seem to have found in Stoicism a philosophy friendly to their empire. In what ways is Stoicism more suited for life in an imperial regime than are the philosophies of Plato, Aristotle, or Epicurus?

10. Which of the Roman Stoics discussed in the chapter most seems to have lived consistently with his philosophy?

Notes

1. Diogenes Laertius, *Life of Menedemus* 6.103.

2. Plato, perhaps showing his respect for Antisthenes, places him at the scene of Socrates' death (*Phaedo* 59b).

3. Diogenes Laertius, *Life of Antisthenes* 6.2. For an example of Gorgias's style, see pp. 88–89.

4. Perhaps there was a motif in ancient literature of the instantaneous or near-instantaneous adoption of a new course of life. The stories of Polemon, Plato, Antisthenes, Zeno, and many others tell of people whose souls are ignited by an inspirational moment. The phenomenon of the sudden conversion is adopted or shared by Christianity. In the Gospels we read of Peter and Andrew, who, upon seeing Jesus pass by, instantly drop their nets to become "fishers of men" (Matthew 4:19). In Acts we read of Paul's sudden conversion on the road to Damascus. And several centuries later, in the *Confessions* of Augustine, we read of Antony and Victorinus, who serve as models for Augustine's own conversion in a Milan garden. In Roman literature, such as the *Metamorphoses* of Ovid or the *Golden Ass* of Apuleius, we may observe the interplay of the internal, psychic conversions with the external, bodily transformations.

5. For the discussion of Socrates' description of philosophy as a preparation for death, that is, the freedom of the soul from the body, see p. 336.

6. Diogenes Laertius, *Life of Antisthenes* 6.6.

7. Diogenes Laertius, *Life of Diogenes* 6.24.

8. Diogenes Laertius, *Life of Diogenes* 6.21.

9. Diogenes Laertius, *Life of Diogenes* 6.21.

10. Diogenes Laertius, *Life of Diogenes* 6.37.

11. Diogenes Laertius, *Life of Diogenes* 6.45.

12. Diogenes Laertius, *Life of Diogenes* 6.46.

13. Diogenes Laertius, *Life of Diogenes* 6. 38. Plutarch tells the story, too, in *Life of Alexander* 14.

14. In *Utopia* Thomas More describes the law of his imaginary islanders that men and women should see one naked before marrying. Perhaps the bold action of Crates was his inspiration.

15. Diogenes Laertius, *Life of Hipparchia* 6.97.

16. Diogenes Laertius, *Life of Diogenes* 6.43 and 6.78.

17. Diogenes Laertius, *Life of Zeno* 7.6.

18. Diogenes Laertius, *Life of Zeno* 7.2–3.

19. In Greek, the word *politeia* signifies something between *constitution* and *the things relating to the polis*. If one thinks of Plato's famous dialogue and calls it, instead of *Republic*, *Things Relating to a Polis*, one conceives of the work in a way perhaps more in keeping with Plato's intention. In a similar way, if one calls Paul's book *Actions of the Apostles* instead of *Acts of the Apostles*—again perhaps a more accurate rendering in modern English—one thinks of the work somewhat differently from normally.

20. These will be discussed later in this chapter under the general discussion of Stoic views.

21. This wage would have provided for a very meager style of life. For a discussion of ancient monetary values and the difficulties of comparing them to modern ones, see C. E. Robinson, *Everyday Life in Ancient Greece* (Oxford: Clarendon Press, 1933), 92–95, and Frank J. Frost, *Greek Society* (Lexington, Mass.: D.C. Heath and Company, 1971), 55–59.

22. Diogenes Laertius, *Life of Cleanthes* 7.168.

23. This is one form of pantheism. For a variant form, see pp. 264–65.

24. See the discussion of Aristotle's conception of matter on pp. 197–99.

25. It is possible that this view influenced Virgil. When Aeneas experiences his crisis with Queen Dido of Carthage and seems required to choose between his duty to sail to Italy as the gods wish or to follow his emotion and stay with Dido, the conflict seems one between emotion and reason. But if one realizes that Aeneas has an obligation to the queen, who has rescued him and his crew and has also given him her love, then one sees that for a man of piety like Aeneas there are really two duties, one to the gods and one to Dido, and the conflict may take place wholly within the rational faculty.

26. Commentary on Marcus Manilius, *Astronomicon* 2.5.93 (Hildesheim: G. Olms, 1972).

27. He was known as Posidonius of Rhodes though he was born in Apameia, Syria.

28. These fragments have been gathered and published in the edition of L. Edelstein and I. G. Kidd, *Posidonius: Volume I, the Fragments* (Cambridge: Cambridge University Press, 1972).

29. For example, against his teacher Chrysippus and more consistently with Plato and Aristotle, he taught that emotions were not simply false judgments but separate irrational forces that must be subordinated to reason.

30. So says Sextus Empiricus, frag. 88 in Edelstein and Kidd, *Posidonius*.

31. See, on Aristotle's logic, pp. 194–95.

32. For example, Chrysippus wrote a book called *Dialectical Definitions*; the Stoic Antipater wrote one called *On Terms*.

33. Diogenes Laertius, *Life of Zeno* 7.76.

34. Diogenes Laertius, *Life of Zeno* 7.82.

35. Diogenes Laertius, *Life of Zeno* 7.79. Perhaps in this respect they were attempting to be like the geometers, who reduced the number of axioms to as small a number as possible. See, on Euclid, p. 230.

36. This fact, that it is easier to challenge than to establish positions, is also put forth by Aristotle (see p. 195).

37. Cicero, *Prior Academics* 2.144.

38. Diogenes Laertius 7.134; Edelstein and Kidd, *Posidonius*.

39. For Cleanthes' version of pantheism, see pp. 264–65.

40. For the Stoic view of a finite universe, see Diogenes Laertius, *Life of Zeno* 7.140. For the Epicurean argument for an infinite universe, see Lucretius's clever example of a man standing on the edge of the universe and throwing a spear (*On the Nature of the Universe* 1.968–983).

41. See p. 253.

42. Gospel of Matthew 5:48.

43. Diogenes Laertius, *Life of Zeno* 7.138.

44. See p. 117.

45. Diogenes Laertius reviews the different opinions of Cleanthes and Chrysippus on this subject. It is never clear whether the soul maintains an individual identity as it survives or whether it is somehow reabsorbed into an undifferentiated cosmic fire. The notion that the sage's soul survives longer is suggestive of the former view but is not conclusive. One particularly independent Stoic, Posidonius's teacher Panaetius (185–109), seems to have denied the doctrines of periodic conflagration and of the soul's surviving death (Cicero, *Tusculum Disputations* 1.79).

46. I am using the word *wickedness* to translate the Greek word *hamartemata* and the Latin word *peccata*. The usual translation used in discussing this matter is *sin*, but this word carries too much of a Judaeo-Christian connotation for a pagan philosophy. *Wickedness*, like *sin*, nicely includes both actions and what are known as affective states, that is, both wicked actions like murder and wicked emotions like envy or haughtiness.

47. Cicero, *Stoic Paradoxes* 3.

48. Cicero, *Stoic Paradoxes* 3.24.

49. Tacitus, *Annals* 13.42.

50. Tacitus, *Annals* 15.62. I have altered the quotation only to the extent of changing it from the third to the first person. Tacitus himself suggests (15.63) that Seneca may have been aiming these remarks to a wider audience than the friends who were there.

51. Epictetus, *Enchiridion* 1, trans. George Long (Amherst, N.Y.: Prometheus Books, 1991). Subsequent quotations are from this translation.

52. Epictetus, *Enchiridion* 3.

53. Epictetus, *Enchiridion* 26.

54. Marcus refers to Christians only once in the *Meditations*, in 11.3, where he rebukes them for their obstinacy (a crime to Roman authorities) and for the theatrical manner of their deaths (perhaps, as a Stoic, he finds their joy at martyrdom repugnantly emotional). Marcus's predecessors Trajan, Hadrian, and Antoninus Pius seem to have adopted a policy of "benign neglect" toward Christians, not rigidly enforcing the

laws against them. But, as G. M. A. Grube points out in the introduction to his translation of the *Medita-tions* (Indianapolis: Bobbs-Merrill, 1963, xxi), by Marcus's time Christians were refusing military and civil duties, and a better-organized Church was claiming more authority over its members—a provocative chal-lenge to imperial rule. And so, perhaps actuated by a sense of duty to uphold the law, Marcus renewed the vigorous persecution.

55. Edward Gibbon, *Decline and Fall of the Roman Empire*, chap. 3.

Select Bibliography

CYNICISM

Dudley, Donald R. *A History of Cynicism: From Diogenes to the 6th Century AD*. London: Bristol Classical Press, 1998.

STOICISM

Campbell, Keith. *A Stoic Philosophy of Life*. Lanham, Md.: University Press of America, 1986.
Colish, Marcia L. *The Stoic Tradition from Antiquity to the Early Middle Ages*. 2 vols. Leiden: Brill, 1990.
Edelstein, Ludwig. *The Meaning of Stoicism*. Cambridge, Mass.: Harvard University Press, 1966.
Rist, J. M. *Stoic Philosophy*. Cambridge: Cambridge University Press, 1969.
——, ed. *The Stoics*. Berkeley: University of California Press, 1978.

CHAPTER 15

Rome and Cicero

281

I. Rome

The rise of Rome from an insignificant village to master of the Western world must have seemed as improbable to the ancients as it would for us if Farmville, Virginia—a town distant from the great centers of civilization—conquered its neighbors and then became a colossus ruling the entire Western Hemisphere. Yet just a century and a half after the death of Alexander, Rome had conquered all Italy, Greece, and her great enemy Carthage.

Like other cities, Rome traced her origins to Troy, for her mythology told that Aeneas, the son of Venus (*Aphrodite* in Greek) and perhaps the second greatest fighter on the Trojan side, escaped burning Troy for Italy. The myth presented Rome with a dilemma: was her allegiance to the East, where her origins lay, or to Greece, where she wished to locate her spiritual and intellectual affinity. On the one hand, the East meant a monarchical regime where the monarch was believed to be a god or close to it, where the individual existed to serve the ruler, and where size and wealth were equated with goodness. On the other hand, the Greek intellectual heritage meant an adherence to Greek logic; a high and even supreme value placed on the worth of the individual, either as a human being or as a soul; a concern for a form of government that would allow the greatest possible freedom consonant with political stability so that the individual could develop his potentialities; a consequent belief in the efficacy of some form of democracy; and a commitment to education, to the individual psyche in the methods of logic and reason, so that it might make wise choices for its own development. In general, the Greek credo might be summed up in the paradoxical notion that the individual must be subservient to the majority so that the majority itself can find happiness as individuals. Throughout her history Rome oscillated between these two allegiances, often with devastating consequences.

The founding of Rome dates to the eighth century B.C.E. But Rome was not noticed by Greece for at least three hundred years—and even then the story about a tie with Greece is probably Roman propaganda intended to lend stature to Rome. Livy, one of the great historians of Rome, writes that in the fifth century Rome sent a delegation to study Athenian politics and the Athenian constitution. The story survives nowhere in Greek literature. But as Greece lost her independence to Alexander, and as Alexander's empire shattered, Rome slowly, patiently grew, expanding onto the surrounding parts of Italy, and, unlike the Greeks, kept whatever she conquered. Suddenly, in the third century B.C.E., Greece experienced Rome's conquering armies. Polybius, a Greek diplomat, who spent seventeen years as a hostage in Rome, predicted that Rome would be greater than any empire the world had ever seen and wrote a history of Rome to persuade his fellow Greeks of the truth of this prediction.

As Polybius looked at the rise of Rome, he speculated on the causes for her greatness. He found many, but he gave special attention to one, Rome's "reverence toward the supernatural" (*deisidaimonia* in Greek).[1] On this point, Cicero, perhaps the single greatest mind that classical Rome produced, saw the cause in the same way. He wrote,[2]

> It was not by our numbers that we overcame the Spaniards, nor by our strength the Gauls, nor by our cunning the Carthaginians, nor by our arts the Greeks . . . but by piety and religion and this one wisdom . . . our recognition that all things are ruled and directed by the will of the gods. This is how we overcame all races and all peoples.

283

These views do not reflect a naive faith. Instead, for the Romans piety meant a reverence for the order in both the law that governs nature and the law that governs human life. In other words, for Rome, piety was practical.[3]

By the time of Cicero's birth (106 B.C.E.), Rome had enjoyed several centuries of steady growth. Carthage, Rome's greatest enemy, had been decisively beaten in 202 and brutally annihilated in 146. Conquest offered opportunities for fabulous wealth, and the Romans became fabulously wealthy. They knew what to do with their wealth externally; they never did master what to do with it internally. Rome simultaneously experienced "progress" in her wealth and in her corruption. Materially the Romans made good progress; morally their progress was like what Thucydides and the physicians might have referred to as the progress of a disease.

Cicero's life (106–43) spanned a period of extraordinary turmoil for Rome—the brutal Social Wars against her Italian allies, the civil war between Marius and Sulla, the dictatorship of Sulla with its fearsome proscriptions, the chaos wrought by the megalomaniacs Pompey and Caesar, the attempted coup d'état of Catiline, and the dictatorship of Caesar, his assassination, and its chaotic aftermath.

II. Cicero the Man

Cicero was born into a middle-class family in Arpinum, a small town between Rome and Naples. His father realized the value of an education and spent his money to educate his son in literature and law. Cicero practiced law and won plaudits for his speeches. Having successfully prosecuted a friend of the tyrant Sulla and, in consequence, perhaps fearing for his life,[4] he left Rome and went to Athens, where he studied at the Academy, and then traveled to Rhodes, where he attended lectures on oratory as well as lectures by the leading philosopher of the age, Posidonius. Plutarch reports that on the way back to Rome he consulted the oracle at Delphi and was told "that he would attain the greatest glory by making his own genius and not the opinion of the people the guide of his life."[5] Back in Rome, in 76, he married the wealthy Terentia and entered politics. In 70, he undertook what turned out to be a glorious prosecution of Caius Verres, who, as governor of Sicily, had accepted bribes, stolen treasures, and in general fleeced the whole wealth of the island for his personal pleasure. The victory in the courtroom catapulted Cicero to the top of the legal profession. In 63, he defeated Catiline for the consulship and then suppressed Catiline's attempt to seize power. To do so, Cicero needed to assume a temporary dictatorship, and, in the heat of the moment, unfortunately he did not follow due process. Later, hoping somehow to preserve the Republic, he turned down an offer to join Caesar and Pompey as triumvirs. In his last years he was somewhat withdrawn from the daily practice of politics. But after the assassination of Julius Caesar in 44, still hoping to restore the Republic, he tried to manage Octavian in order to ward off the threatening dictatorship of Marc Antony. When Antony and Octavian became allies, Antony ordered Cicero murdered.

In his education and in his life, Cicero embraced the ideals of antiquity first summed up in Homer, "to be a speaker of words and a doer of deeds" and "always to excel and to hold one's head above others." After Homer, the Greeks sought to make distinctions, even differences, in these goals, into what we call the active and contemplative lives. Plato and Aristotle perhaps represent for us the archetypes of the contemplative life. Cicero represents the archetype of the man who tried to unite the two lives. As a youth, he had studied ancient culture and had learned it thoroughly. That education informed his every act, whether legal, political, or philosophical. As a lawyer, he brought to the study of law that sense of sympathy and understanding that we call *humanistic*. As a politician, he stood for integrity and openness, values and ideals that we still hold. As a philosopher, he transmitted, almost single-handedly nearly the whole range of Greek culture to the Western world.

He became what he trained himself to be—a great orator. In this, he was like Isocrates, for whom he had great admiration. But where Isocrates was only a teacher of rhetoric, Cicero was a practicing orator. He achieved the highest office in Rome, for he became a consul. His failure to follow due process in assuming a temporary dictatorship to cope with the crisis of Catiline cost him his career. Though he usurped dictatorial power for a very short period of time and with every intention of relinquishing it, he was censured for his action. It is perhaps therefore ironic that his great opponent was Julius Caesar, whose dictatorship was intended to be perpetual. And when Cicero courageously opposed the dangerous Marc Antony, Antony had Cicero's head chopped off.

III. Cicero the Thinker

Cicero was interested in philosophy from his youth. When he was studying in Athens, he nearly decided to give up his political ambitions and take up philosophy as a career. A decade afterward, while he was preparing his prosecution of Verres, his letters show a desire to retire to a life of contemplation, and he expresses the same desire again at the time of his consulship.[6] Philosophy was a source of consolation for Cicero, and his two most productive periods occurred when he turned to philosophy in the period just after the death of his daughter Tullia in 45 and when he reengaged in politics after the assassination of Caesar in 44. Except for *On the Republic* and *On the Laws*,[7] all his philosophical works were written during his last two or three years: *Paradoxes, On Consolation, Hortensius, Academics, Tusculan Disputations, On the Nature of the Gods, On Divination, On Fate, On Old Age, On Friendship*, and *On Moral Duties*. These philosophical works, which are mostly based on Greek originals, transferred Greek learning into Latin. In transferring them into Latin, Cicero made it possible for the Western world to have some access to Greek philosophy during the thousand-year period when the West lost the Greek originals. Some of the originals were lost forever, and Cicero is our only source for them.

Cicero did not merely translate the Greek originals; he adapted them, and in adapting them he found Roman parallels for Greek words and examples. In doing so he taught Rome that she could compete with the Greeks. Even by his writing, which embodies the beauty of rhetoric with a deeply ethical purpose, he sought to reunite the active and contemplative lives. Indeed, so promising was Cicero in his younger years that his teacher of rhetoric in Rhodes, Apollonius, is reported to have said that with Cicero's departure, Rome was robbing Greece of her eloquence just as she had robbed Greece of all else.[8] To be sure, the philosophy of Cicero lacks the expertise of one who devoted all his time to technical subjects; he possessed, however, a very fine mind that was grappling with philosophy as a way of life rather than as a school exercise. In this way he was perhaps like Socrates, though where Socrates dealt with individuals, arguing with them privately, Cicero chose to communicate his philosophy to large groups by his writing.

Cicero identified himself with the Old Academy and the thought of Plato. As a member of the Academy, Cicero believed that truth exists and can be known. But neither the Academy nor Cicero himself accepted *much* as true, for they held to the rigorous Aristotelian standard of knowledge. It was one of the central tenets of the Academy to accept no proposition that had not been proved true (in the strong sense of proof).[9] But in fact Cicero himself was eclectic in his philosophy. Though he had what was to him the patriotic purpose of introducing the philosophy of Plato to his fellow Romans,[10] at times he seems closer to the Stoics than to Plato, and at times he adopts some notions of the Pythagoreans, at times those of the Peripatetics, Aristotle's school. He generally rejects the philosophy of the Epicureans, a philosophy that, while not officially atheistic, was atheistic in spirit. He is an independent thinker who never simply accepts a point of view because it comes from an authority. His basic philosophical assumptions are these: that nature is orderly rather than disorderly and friendly rather than unfriendly; that human beings are a part of nature; that nature operates by law; that humans have free will; that humans are happiest when living in accordance with nature, that is, when they obey the law; that the idea of law is implicit in nature and inherent in humankind—a principle called "right reason" (*recta ratio* in Latin); and that the state should reflect the natural order, an ideal that he terms a "harmony of the classes" (*concordia ordinum* in Latin).

Cicero's earliest ventures in writing philosophy are his Romanizing adaptations of Plato's *Republic* and *Laws*. In these works he reaches the conclusion that the best government has a mixed constitution, that is, the one that combines the pure regimes of rule by one (monarchy), rule by the few best (the type of oligarchy called *aristocracy*), and rule by the many (democracy). He finds the constitution of Rome to be potentially best, where the consuls, who rule with term limits of one year, represent a monarchical authority not polluted by perpetuity; where the Senate represents the aristocracy; and where the popular assemblies represent the many. Perhaps with himself in mind, Cicero saw nothing ridiculous about the notion of a "philosopher-politician," though he was aware of the possibility that if a politician were excessively abstract, he might not effectively deal with the practical issues of statecraft. The most famous part of *On the Republic* is the last section, known as "Scipio's Dream," where we read that the best part of heaven is reserved not, à la Plato, for philosophers but for the good ruler, the idealized Roman statesman like Scipio.

On the Laws defines law in a Stoic fashion as the supreme reason that pervades and works through nature.[11] In the ideal form of justice, which is evidence of the intimate connection of man and gods,[12] a man loves his neighbor as much as he loves himself.[13] Because justice is a law of nature, it does not consist in mere obedience to the rules laid down in the law codes of nations.[14] Thus Cicero would squarely reject the notion of Stephen Decatur's famous toast, "Our country! In her intercourse with other nations, may she always be in the right; but our country, right or wrong," and would approve the correction of Senator Carl Schurz, "Our country, right or wrong! When right, to be kept right; when wrong, to be put right!" This was an idea that Cicero kept close to his heart, and, even if he did not keep it perfectly, for the most part it guided his actions.[15] Finally, he believed that justice was to be sought for its own sake, as the highest good for human beings (the *summum bonum* in Latin).

The bulk of Cicero's philosophical writings came after the death in 45 B.C.E. of his beloved daughter Tullia. The two tumultuous years before Cicero was assassinated by Marc Antony in 43 were Cicero's most philosophically productive. Unfortunately, the earliest of these works have not survived, but they were immensely influential. His *Consolation*, which he wrote to help himself cope with his daughter's death, was perhaps inspired by a work *On Grief* by Crantor, one of Plato's successors. But it was Cicero's work that served as a model for a whole subgenre of philosophical consolations, beginning with those of Seneca and Boethius and continuing down to the present with John Gunther's *Death Be Not Proud*, Harold Kushner's *When Bad Things Happen to Good People*, and Leon Wieseltier's *Kaddish*. Cicero's *Hortensius* is the work that Augustine says turned him to philosophy. It apparently taught that philosophy could free men from the fear of death and from superstition and could direct them to true happiness, which is found in a life of the spirit. While these are familiar Platonic and Aristotelian themes, Augustine leaves the impression that Cicero's treatment was highly inspirational, perhaps in the manner of the Platonic dialogues themselves. This type of inspirational work was known as "protreptic" (*protreptikos*, Greek for *urge forward*) and was aimed at "urging one forward" toward philosophy. Of the *Academica* too much is lost to obtain a sense of its purpose. The work does contain a discussion of happiness, in which one of Cicero's old teachers at Athens defines happiness as the attainment of the natural goods, which are divided into the mental (of which virtue is the most important), the bodily, and the external.

The *summum bonum* (the highest good) is the subject of *De Finibus Bonorum et Malorum* (*Concerning the Definitions of the Good and the Bad*). The work begins with a review of the Epicurean view that pleasure—defined as freedom from pain—is the highest good and with the idea that mental pleasures, since they extend to both the past and the future, are better than physical pleasures, which take place only in the here and now. Cicero rejects the Epicurean view because he believes that humans have been born for some end nobler than mere pleasure. Then he describes and rejects Stoicism, the other leading philosophy of the day. One Stoic view that comes in for lengthy discussion is the famous paradox that all wicked actions are equal and all good deeds are equal. What the Stoics meant is that either an action is in conformity with nature or it is not.[16] An analogy with a right angle will help explain the notion. Either an angle is right or it is not. If it is not, whether it be 89 degrees or 1 degree or 359 degrees, it is equally *not* a right angle. The Stoics and Cicero use the example of a man drowning: he can drown as easily in a meter of water as in the ocean.[17] At the end of the work, Cicero accepts the views of the Academics and the Peripatetics that the core of the *summum bonum* is a life of virtuous activity, but he adds that the Stoics are wrong in making virtue the sole entirety of the *summum bonum*, for other faculties (like bodily health) and externals goods (like having children who live) also count. Here too we see that Cicero's philosophy lacks the extremism that results from fervently following up the logical implications of an inflexibly binary position. As a consequence, Cicero's ethical views are more appealing for practical life, for they are actually achievable by mere mortals.

289

Cicero undertook a series of works that treated matters of theology—*On the Nature of the Gods*, *On Divination*, and *On Fate*. *On the Nature of the Gods* does not address the question of whether gods exist, an existence that Cicero took for granted. Instead, Cicero concentrates on the nature of the gods, an issue about which people differ considerably. The work begins with some general questions: Why did the gods who created the universe suddenly wake up to create it? Why did they create it at all? Did they create it for all humankind or for a special group?[18] If the universe is for the sake of mankind, why did it need to be so big? He then examines the theologies of myriad philosophers from Thales on.[19] He rejects all of these on the basis of their inconsistency, arbitrariness, or plain silliness. He carefully evaluates the argument that the world was made by a designer and looks at the claim that every designed object has a purpose. He asks whether it necessarily follows, even if the universe had a designer, that the designer is an eternal, universal God with all the other divine attributes.

On Divination takes up the question of whether the practice of divination, ubiquitous in the ancient world and common enough in our own, has any validity. If it is valid, says Cicero, it would confirm the existence of the gods, of fate, and of nature. Cicero gives full scope to the argument that divination is false, that chance enters into our lives, and that divination is injurious to life because it promotes superstition.[20] In his last theological work, *On Fate*, part of which has been lost, Cicero, arguing that human beings do have free will, disagrees with his own beloved teacher, Posidonius, who believed that everything was predetermined and that humans did not have free will.

Cicero continued his frenetic output with *On Old Age*, a lovely book that discusses the possibilities of a vigorous old age and asserts the value of believing in the soul's immortality. Cicero writes,

> If I err in believing men's souls to be immortal, I err willingly, and as long as I live I do not wish an error which gives me such satisfaction to be wrested from me. If I shall have no sensation in death as some paltry philosophers think, I have no fear that the dead philosophers will ridicule my error. But if we are not going to be immortal, it is desirable for a man to be erased in proper season; nature imposes a limit upon life as upon all else. Old age is the closing act of life, as of a drama, and we ought to leave when the play grows wearisome, especially if we have had our fill.[21]

One text that is rather extraordinary for Cicero is his *Topics*, a work that deals with Aristotle's various methods of finding arguments and with the nature of the syllogism. Cicero seems to be summarizing in Latin, and from memory,[22] Aristotle's work of the same name, a work that has unfortunately not been preserved. That Cicero would know the book so well shows, in addition to how a splendid memory he possessed, how important he judged the book. Boethius later translated Aristotle's work into Latin and wrote a commentary on Cicero's version, in which he pointed out the differences between the two.

Cicero's last work of philosophy is *On Moral Duties*, composed not long before his death and perhaps not completely polished. The work took a Greek original and made it Roman by using examples from Roman life and literature. The four classical virtues—wisdom, justice, courage, and temperance—are discussed as merging into the single Platonic conception of the "morally good" (*honestum* in Latin). But the main question the book asks is whether there is a conflict between what is expedient and what is good, that is, between an apparent practical good for a person and what is the true absolute good. Consider this example:

> Suppose, for example, a time of dearth and famine at Rhodes, with provisions at fabulous prices; and suppose that an honest man has imported a large cargo of grain from Alexandria and that to his certain knowledge also several other importers have set sail from Alexandria, and that on the voyage he has sighted their vessels laden with grain and bound for Rhodes; is he to report the fact to the Rhodians or is he to keep his own counsel and sell his own stock at the highest price? I am assuming the case of a virtuous, upright man, and I am raising the question how a man would think and reason who would not conceal the facts from the Rhodians if he thought that it was immoral to do so, but who might be in doubt whether such silence would really be immoral.[23]

In good Platonic fashion, Cicero debates the question, giving the views of Diogenes of Babylon and the contrary view of his pupil Antipater. The question is debated entirely on the matter of morality and not of expedience.[24]

IV. Cicero's Legacy

Montesquieu said that in politics Cicero was not destined to be one of the main actors but to play a subordinate role.[25] In the philosophy of the Roman world, however, Cicero was a major player. If he was not original, his lack of originality was characteristic of the Romans generally, who adopted and modified and assimilated what they borrowed, stole, or conquered. With Cicero, Greek philosophy is filtered through the mind of a sensible and discerning critic.

Cicero's influence on the prose style of Europe, in both vocabulary and syntax, can hardly be overestimated. The pagans Quintilian and Pliny the Younger imitated his style, as did the Christians Minucius Felix, Lactantius (who was called the Christian Cicero), Jerome, Ambrose, and

Augustine. In the Renaissance, Erasmus finds it necessary to chastise the exaggerated imitation of the style known as "Ciceronianism."[26]

Moreover, Cicero deeply influenced religious thought, especially the theology of Christianity. Though the Church fathers loved Plato, they loved Cicero more, and, especially in the fourth century C.E., Cicero was the model for both their style and their content. In the sixth century Boethius so reflected the eclecticism and the urbane humanity of Cicero that Gibbon referred to him as "the last of the Romans that Cato or Tully [Cicero] could have acknowledged for their countryman."[27] Boethius's great project of translating into Latin all the works of Aristotle and Plato and then reconciling them is Ciceronian in spirit.

Finally, Cicero demonstrated to the world that philosophy need not be written in crabbed, somniferous, unintelligible prose. The history of philosophy shows, alas, that this lesson has not been learned. But, as in education generally, it is not always fair to blame the teacher when the students haven't learned their lessons.

Discussion Questions

1. In a brilliant passage in *The Decline and Fall of the Roman Empire*, Edward Gibbon writes (end of chapter 3) that "the minds of Romans were not prepared for the slavery" imposed by the emperors. He continues,

> Oppressed beneath the weight of their own corruption and of military violence, they for a long while preserved the sentiments, or at least the ideas, of their free-born ancestors. The education of Helvidius and Thrasea, of Tacitus and Pliny, was the same as that of Cato and Cicero. From Grecian philosophy they had imbibed the justest and most liberal notions of the dignity of human nature, and the origin of civil society. The history of their own country had taught them to revere a free, a virtuous, and a victorious commonwealth; to abhor the successful crimes of Caesar and Augustus; and inwardly to despise those tyrants whom they adored with the most abject flattery.

In the life of Cicero we see a man struggling but failing to keep alive this liberal philosophy in the soul of his state. Yet after his death he continued to serve as a model of Roman probity, and such educators as Quintilian always refer to him in reverential tones. What in ancient pagan philosophy could have helped thoughtful individuals endure patiently (for five centuries!) this bifurcation of loyalty to the regime and freedom of the intellect?

2. To what extent are the underlying philosophical assumptions of Cicero still held, that is, that nature is orderly rather than disorderly and friendly rather than unfriendly, that human beings are a part of nature, that nature operates by law, that humans have free will, that humans are happiest when living in accordance with nature, that the idea of law is implicit in nature and inherent in humankind, and that the state should reflect the natural order, the "harmony of the classes"?

3. In what ways is Cicero's moderation reflected in his philosophic eclecticism?

4. Though Cicero laughed at most theological views, he still seems to have been a religious man. How can the paradox be resolved?

5. Though many contemporary people find Cicero arrogant, even bombastic and dull, the ancients admired him; the humanists of the Renaissance imitated him; and through the middle part of the twentieth century he continued to be thoroughly studied in schools. In short, he would seem to have passed the test of time with high marks. What might we infer about an age like our own, which no longer is enchanted by him?

Notes

1. Polybius, 6.56. *Deisidaimonia* is also the word for *superstition* (see p. 248).
2. *de Haruspicum Responso* 9.19.
3. Livy tells how Numa, the second king of Rome, in order to settle his rambunctious population into civilized life, pretended to meet the goddess Egiria, who dictated the religious observances that Romans needed to follow. Despite the pretense, the religion was genuinely felt by Numa and by the citizens. Perhaps they all decided to accept this "noble lie" for the sake of communal life.
4. Fear is offered as a motive by Plutarch (*Life of Cicero* 14). Cicero himself says that he left for health and to improve his oratorical style (*Brutus* 314–316).
5. Plutarch, *Life of Cicero* 5.
6. *Pro Murena* 21.
7. They were written seven or eight years earlier.
8. Plutarch, *Life of Cicero* 4.5.
9. For this strong sense of proof, which is stated clearly by Aristotle, see pp. 210–12.
10. *de finibus bonorum et malorum* 1.20.
11. Cicero, *On the Laws* 1.18–20.
12. Cicero, *On the Laws* 1.21–27.
13. Cicero, *On the Laws* 1.28–34. Views like this make it plain perhaps why Cicero was so esteemed by the Roman Church fathers.
14. Cicero, *On the Laws* 1.47.
15. Perhaps more than any other ancient writer, we are able to possess a good sense of what Cicero was actually like. This sense emerges through his letters, which, since they were not written for posterity, show him as his candid true self, or at least as much as he was willing to share with family and friends. It has become common for those who write about Cicero to point out his vanity and other personal defects and to show the discrepancies between his ideals and his actual practice. But the sense one gets from reading

extensively in Cicero is that a love of virtue really was the ruling passion of his soul and that in the attempt to be true to his ideas, Cicero achieved all that a force of conscious effort could achieve. For the most part he succeeded, and he showed real personal courage at all stages of his life, from his youthful opposition to the tyrant Sulla, to his defense in middle age of the Republic against the assault of Catiline, and, in old age, to his forceful, and fatal to himself, opposition to Antony. We might only wonder how the world might have been improved if all our politicians had had the integrity of Cicero.

16. See the discussion of this paradox on p. 272.

17. Cicero, *De finibus* 3.46.

18. Cicero, *On the Nature of the Gods* 1.21–23.

19. Cicero, *On the Nature of the Gods* 1.25–43.

20. Cicero, *On Divination* 2.148–150.

21. Cicero, *On Old Age* 85, trans. Moses Hadas (New York: Modern Library, 1951). Subsequent quotations to *On Old Age* are from this translation.

22. There are differences between Aristotle's system and Cicero's, and Cicero's probably also includes "alterations and adaptations of Aristotle by generations of both rhetoricians and philosophical commentators" (Eleonore Stump, *Boethius's In Ciceronis Topica* [Ithaca, N.Y.: Cornell University Press, 1988], 8).

23. Cicero, *On Moral Duties* 3.50, trans. Walter Miller (Cambridge, Mass.: Harvard University Press, 1913).

24. The debate is reported in Cicero, *On Moral Duties* 3.51–54, and is well worth studying.

25. Montesquieu, *The Greatness of the Romans and Their Decline*, trans. David Lowenthal (Ithaca, N.Y.: Cornell University Press, 1968), 116.

26. In his comical dialogue *Ciceronianus*, published in 1528, Erasmus mocks the pedantic slavish imitation of Ciceronian vocabulary and style.

27. Gibbon, *Decline and Fall*, vol. 2, chap. 39.

Select Bibliography

Clarke, M. L. *The Roman Mind: Studies in the History of Thought from Cicero to Marcus Aurelius*. New York: Norton, 1968.

Everitt, Anthony. *Cicero: The Life and Times of Rome's Greatest Politician*. New York: Random House, 2001.

MacKendrick, Paul. *The Philosophical Books of Cicero*. London: Duckworth, 1989.

Powell, J. G. F. *Cicero the Philosopher: Twelve Papers*. Oxford: Clarendon Press, 1995.

CHAPTER 16

Greek Philosophy Finds the Bible and the Bible Finds Greek Philosophy

295

I. The World at the Turn of the Millennium

What startles us about the centuries from the death of Alexander to the victory of Caesar Octavianus at Actium—the period we unify by naming it the Hellenistic Age—is its dynamism. It was a time in the Mediterranean region when thought began to extend from local interests to broader matters, when men began to think of themselves as citizens not of Athens or Sparta or Jerusalem but of the whole world, nay, of the whole cosmos. Alexander's ambition had been perhaps to homogenize the panoply of peoples, to blend them into one, to improve their diet by transplanting the most delicious fruits and vegetables throughout the world, to foster understanding by a common tongue, and to encourage all to accept the Greek philosophers' discovery that under superficial variations in religions, physiognomies, and customs lay a common rational nature.[1] During the Hellenistic period people began to look at one another's cultures and to examine the implications of the differences in manners and religion.

To intellectuals, the light of Greek philosophy had uncovered many of the mysteries of nature and had given hope that reason could uncover still more. With the division of all reality into the Worlds of Being and Becoming, an incorporeal realm of ideas and a corporeal realm of matter, Plato had reconciled the polar thinkers Parmenides and Heraclitus and had largely solved the problem of change. The Pythagoreans and their mathematical successors had shown, as Galileo also would say later, that a good part of nature is written in numbers—that there exists a measurable, rational order governing space and time. Aristotle had tamed and organized logic and had used it to describe the manner of God's existence and how the worlds of nature, supernature, and humankind all yield to investigation informed by logic. A Hellenistic intellectual might reasonably have assumed that these discoveries would transcend all cultures and that regardless of how alien any culture encountering these discoveries, once it understood these truths, it would readily accept them.

For the Western philosophical tradition, one such encounter, that of Greek and Jewish cultures, was to have lasting consequences. Our Hellenistic intellectual would, however, have had his optimism frustrated, for it was not an occasion of love at first sight. The delights of Greek culture, figurative art, athletic competitions, and theater did, naturally enough, appeal to some Jews.[2] But these delights were in sharp contrast to the traditional practice of Judaism, which in the Ten Commandments forbade images of anything above or below the earth or in the heavens, which saw Greek athletic competitions with their accompanying nudity and hero worship of athletic stars as an affront to God and his laws, and which disdained productions of drama as celebrations of idol worship.[3] Victory over the Greeks in the Maccabean Wars of the second century B.C.E. had guaranteed religious autonomy to the Jews, but this autonomy could not insulate them from what was happening culturally, especially the Jews who lived outside Judaea.

In Egypt, where a million Jews lived in Philo's day,[4] the Bible had been translated into Greek during the reign of Ptolemy Philadelphius (285–246). This Greek version, known as the Septuagint, was used by some Jews in religious services.[5] Alexandria, the great center of education, was itself home to a very large population of Jews. It was not always a calm home, and there were frequent outbursts of resentment and hostility toward them. The cause of anti-Jewish sentiment was probably the antipathy often felt to those who have different customs. In the case of Jews, the resentment might have been aggravated because Jews maintained that their differences were ordained by God and, moreover, that their deity was not a local deity for them only but was creator and ruler of the whole universe. Thus their differentness represented an *ethnic superiority* to the Greeks. The human race seems barely able to endure differences under the best of circumstances; differences that come with a stamp of authority from a single deity require a forbearance that has not yet found a host. In addition, in lands under Roman domination, where the practice was to accept the religions of subject people,[6] Rome had granted Jews special exemptions to observe the Sabbath and other holidays, exemptions not shared by pagans and resented by them.[7]

An attempt by Jews to absorb Greek culture was manifested in various forms. In the literature of the first century B.C.E., Philo the Elder (fl. 100) composed an epic in Homeric hexameters, *On Jerusalem*, and a contemporary of his, Theodotus, wrote a poem on the rape of Dinah. At about the same time, a certain Ezekiel wrote tragedies (of which a portion of one, *Exodus*, survives) in iambic trimeter, one of the tragic rhythms. In Mesopotamia, at Dura-Europas, pagan art adorned the synagogues.

Elements of Jewish culture, through the medium of Christianity, were of course eventually to pervade the Western world. But until the advent of Christianity, Judaism seems to have made very little impact on pagan intellectual life. The story about how Aristotle once met a Jew, discussed various philosophical issues with him, and went away thinking that he had learned much more from the Jew than the Jew had learned from him is probably false.[8] The only attested reference to the Bible in classical literature is found in Longinus's *On the Sublime*,[9] perhaps the finest work of literary criticism that survives from antiquity, where, writing for a pagan audience, Longinus claims for Moses the same respect afforded Homer. He writes,

> In this way also the lawgiver of the Jews, a man who did not just happen, since he made room for the power of the divine and made it appear in accordance with its worthiness, says in the introduction to his Rules [*Nomoi* in Greek, that is, Pentateuch or Torah] "God said"—what?— "Let there be light, and there was; let there be earth, and there was."[10]

The definitive failure of Judaism to penetrate the greater pagan world lay in the future. At the turn of the millennium the optimism of the Hellenistic program of amalgamation still gave hope that reason could make the world happily uniform. But, if reason could unite, if it could show the shared commonness, it could also show where differences were foolish or harmful. After all, if my culture is different from yours, then any particular difference in my culture, vis-à-vis the same feature in your culture, is either better or worse. Nothing is perhaps more ordinary than a desire to cling to the habits and customs of one's own culture; because those habits and customs are so familiar, they seem nature itself. There exists, however, an alternative to cultural surrender or conquest: showing that one's culture is perfectly compatible with the great eternal truths that science and philosophy have discovered. The case for compatibility was the project of Philo of Alexandria (fl. 10 C.E.).

II. Philo of Alexandria

Philo may be called a Jewish Cicero. Like Cicero, he led a public life; in 39/40 C.E., he participated in an embassy to Emperor Gaius Caligula to plead the cause of Alexandrian Jews, who were in a dispute with Greeks over citizen rights. Like Cicero, he employed his eloquence in the service of philosophy and, like Cicero, was philosophically eclectic. At the same time, Philo was a serious, if not entirely orthodox,[11] Jew who found his starting principles in the Bible. Where those principles seemed at odds with rationally discovered truth, he found a happy expedient: metaphor and allegory. By interpreting metaphorically and allegorically passages that challenged reason, he could show a deeper meaning that was identical to the truths of philosophy. He could be a Jew and a philosopher too. He could embrace Judaism and still fly to the World of Being.

In discussing Genesis 1:26, where God makes mankind, Philo expresses both his religion and his Platonism with extraordinary eloquence:

> After all the rest, as I have said, Moses tells us that man was created after the image of God and after his likeness. Right well does he say this, for nothing earth-born is more like God than man. Let no one represent the likeness as one to a bodily form; for neither is God human in form, nor is the human body God-like. No, it is in respect of the Mind, the sovereign element of the soul, that the word "image" is used; for after the pattern of a single Mind, even the Mind of the Universe as an archetype, the mind of each of those who successively came into being was molded. It is in a fashion a god to him who carries and enshrines it as an object of reverence; for the human mind evidently occupies a position in men precisely answering to that which the great Ruler occupies in all the world. It is invisible while itself seeing all things, and while comprehending the substance of others, it is as to its own substance unperceived; and while it opens by arts and sciences roads branching in many directions, all of them great highways, it comes through land and sea investigating what either element contains. Again, when on soaring wing it has contemplated the atmosphere and all its phases, it is borne yet higher to the ether and the circuit of heaven, and is whirled round with

the dances of the planets and fixed stars, in accordance with the laws of perfect music, following that love of wisdom which guides its steps. And so, carrying its gaze beyond the confines of all substance discernible by sense, it comes to a point at which it reaches out after the intelligible world, and on descrying in that world sights of surpassing loveliness, even the patterns and the originals of the things of sense which it saw here, it is seized by a sober intoxication, like those filled with Corybantic frenzy, and is inspired, possessed by a longing far other than theirs and a nobler desire. Wafted by this to the topmost arch of the things perceptible to mind, it seems to be on its way to the Great King Himself; but, amid its longing to see Him, pure and untempered rays of concentrated light stream forth like a torrent, so that by its gleams the eye of understanding is dazzled.[12]

We notice at once how harmoniously and seamlessly Philo has combined his Genesis and his Plato. As Jerome, who three centuries later translated the Bible into Latin, joked, either "Plato philonizes or Philo platonizes."[13] Philo's use of the mystical language of the dialogues was to become a refrain in the Christian and Neoplatonist traditions. In the sentence following the quotation, Philo argues that because images do not always correspond to their patterns, Moses added the words "after the likeness" to "after the image" to show that God intended to make an accurate copy.[14] The additional sentence brings us back down to earth and to philology and makes it clear that Philo intended his hymn to reason as a purple patch in his discourse. The idea of the soul flying out of its human confines and glancing at the eternal ideas is found in Plato's *Phaedrus*, among other Platonic works, and is especially common in the Neoplatonists.[15] Philo's imagery deliberately links the Platonic ideas to the Bible.

The satisfying fullness of this biblical–Platonic mix was to affect the culture of the West deeply. Its single greatest influence was in showing intellectual Christians how to introduce the highly respectable philosophy of Plato into their new religion. This doubtlessly let Plato's doctrines resonate with educated people and allowed Augustine later to claim that the Platonists were better than the pagan gods.[16]

Perhaps an illustrative way to understand the success with which Philo brought the Bible and Greek philosophy together would be to examine what he wrote about the Sabbath, a subject at once central to Judaism and totally absent from Greek culture.[17] In the ancient world, there were three qualities that especially marked out Jews to their detractors: circumcision, the prohibition against eating pork, and the Sabbath.[18] Circumcision, "the subordination of beauty to cleanliness," seemed a barbaric mutilation of the body; the prohibition against pork seemed absurd, for, as Cicero wrote, the pig had no purpose other than to be eaten.[19] And observance of the Sabbath seemed to pagans a manifestation of the Jews' indolence. A nation that gave up one-seventh of its conscious life was reckoned able to accomplish little in comparison with other nations, especially if, as Tacitus, suggests, they magnified the restful seventh day by also giving up an entire sabbatical year to idleness.[20] An examination of Philo's views on the Sabbath—an exclusively biblical phenomenon—will conveniently represent the character of Philo's syncretism.

In his book on the Ten Commandments, Philo points out that while other nations celebrate a sacred day once a month as a feast for the start of the moon,[21] the Jewish nation observes a holy day continually after intervals of six days. The question arises of why the Jewish nation is so different. Philo says that the Creation story provides a "necessary cause." The words "necessary cause" are significant: the Jewish nation *cannot* but observe this special day, and the reason has to do with the making of the entire cosmos.

In *On the Creation*, Philo maintains that the creation story at the beginning of the Torah is an exordium intended both to give dignity to the long roll of commandments and to show how the specific laws of the Torah are in harmony with the entire created universe.[22] Philo summarizes the account of Creation thus:

> We are told that the world was made in six days and that on the seventh God ceased from His works and began to contemplate what had been so well created, and therefore He bade those who should live as citizens under this world-order follow God in this as in other matters.[23]

While pagan detractors of the Sabbath focused on the cessation from work, for Philo the key word associated with the day is *contemplate*, a term of the highest respect in philosophy, which gives a place of honor to contemplation. In the *Metaphysics* Aristotle had described the deity as contemplating himself contemplate, and in the *Ethics* he maintained that the greatest happiness to which a human being can aspire is a life of contemplation.[24] When Philo attributes contemplation to the Hebrew God, he is converting the God of Judaism into the God of Greek philosophy.

Though Philo makes it clear that he is discussing the holy seventh day of the Jewish nation, his metaphor suggests that God actually meant the Sabbath for all humanity. Philo says that God bid all who were about to live in this "polity" to follow God in this and other matters, and here *polity* refers to the world that has just been created and not just to the nation of Jews. The metaphor of referring to the whole of creation as a polity in which all people are citizens is a bold way of joining all humanity in a common brotherhood: we are all, so to speak, fellow citizens of a common city, of which God is the lawgiver. If *polity* referred only to the nation of the Jews, there would be a huge shift in the account from the universal story of creation to the story of a small state. In calling the world a single polity, Philo anticipates Marcus Aurelius by a century. Confirmation for this interpretation is found also in *On the Creation*, where Philo calls the seventh day the festival not of a single city but of the entire cosmos.[25] Here Philo seems to be recalling the *Panegyricus* of Isocrates,[26] where Isocrates had praised Athens because it did not hold "world's fairs" from time to time like other Greek states but was instead a perpetual world's fair. Philo outpraises Isocrates by expanding the metaphor to make the holy seventh day a festival for the whole cosmos, to which all human beings are sent by nature as spectators.[27]

Finally, in the definition of the day of rest we find a call to imitate God. Far from dwelling on the opportunity to devote the day to rest, Philo defines the Sabbath as a day for imitation of God by contemplation. Sabbath contemplation should deal with the outer world—its beauty and order[28]— and the inner world—one's own conduct.[29] Reflection on one's purity is to take place in the "council chamber" of one's soul. Surely the Socratic injunction that the unexamined life is not worth living is embodied in this weekly call to self-reflection. In the suggestion that one should admire nature and what makes for happiness, Philo marries the Greek intellectual tradition to the most central Jewish tradition.

The history of the Greek mind, as we have frequently observed, reflects a continuing debate on whether the contemplative or practical life is superior.[30] According to Philo, the concept of the holy seventh day is intimately connected to this debate:

> Have we not here a most admirable injunction full of power to urge us to every virtue and piety most of all? "Always follow God," it says; "find in that single six-day period in which, all-sufficient for his purpose, he created the world, a pattern of the time set apart to thee for activity. Find, too, in the seventh day the pattern of thy duty to study wisdom, that day in which we are told that he surveyed what he had wrought, and so learn to meditate thyself on the lessons of nature and all that in thy own life makes for happiness." Let us not then neglect this great archetype of the two best lives, the practical and the contemplative, but with that pattern ever before our eyes engrave in our hearts the clear image and stamp of them both, so making mortal nature, as far as may be, like the immortals by saying and doing what we ought.[31]

Thus Philo links the Hebrew Bible with this ancient controversy and to the advantage of the Bible, which not only advocates a combination of both activity and contemplation in the life of every person but also prescribes the proper proportion of each! In living actively for six days and contemplating for one, we will be imitating God. How different from the God of Aristotle and Plato or of the Stoics, a deity wholly contemplative, wholly theoretical, and not a jot practical.

Philo, when he turned his attention to numbers, was working in a philosophical tradition with much authoritative precedent. In the *Timaeus*, Plato had put forth the notion that the Craftsman made the heavenly bodies so that living creatures could learn number.[32] And through the work of Thales, credited with having first predicted an eclipse from computations, and the great Hellenistic astronomers like Hipparchus, mathematics had become the language of the skies. In Philo's environment, numerology—the investigation of the mystically hidden significance in numbers—was drawn into everyday life by the curious fact that in Greek and Hebrew notational systems, numbers were written by letters, and thus many words had numerical quantities associated with them.[33] Indeed, in our own times, there has been discussion of whether God makes secret predictions through numerical patterns hidden in the Bible.[34] Given, then, the Platonic–Pythagorean fascination with numbers, given the faith the schools put in the correspondence of numbers with the true nature of the universe, and given that the Sabbath day was known by a number,[35] it is not unexpected, perhaps, that Philo would dwell on the number seven.[36] For Philo, mankind and the heavens are linked by an understanding of number, and through abstract numbers, and especially through the number seven, humans can enjoy a glimpse of God:[37]

> For these reasons and many others besides seven is held in honor. But nothing so much assures its predominance as that through it is best given the revelation of the Father and Maker of all, for in it, as in a mirror, the mind has a vision of God as acting and creating the world and controlling all that is.[38]

If Philo can show that the number seven is special, then he can show that the division of time into seven days is not arbitrary but is harmonious with the nature of the universe and that a cosmic order pervades everything. Of course, the old question broached in Plato's *Euthyphro* arises here:[39] does God choose the number seven because the number seven is special, or is the number seven special because God chooses it? Philo skirts this issue, suggesting that seven itself is divine and hence God aims at spreading its divinity throughout creation. Through the holy seventh day, the divinity associated with seven enters into human life and extends the harmony between the cosmic order and humanity. Philo nowhere suggests that the benefits of the holy seventh day are reserved for the Jewish nation alone. Indeed, all his arguments tend toward the universality of the Sabbath.

Since in *On the Decalogue* his concern is to discuss only the seventh day, Philo does not discuss the significance of the *six* days of creation[40] but begins with a Pythagorean notion of seven's precedence:

> It is virgin among numbers, the essentially motherless, the closest bound to the initial Unit, the "idea" of the planets, just as the unit is of the sphere of the fixed stars, for from the Unit and Seven springs the incorporeal heaven which is the pattern of the visible.[41]

Here the Sabbath manifests the basic structure of God's creative process. Philo draws some of his views from the Pythagoreans and some from Plato's *Timaeus*. In the dialogue, Timaeus—portrayed as an Italian Pythagorean from Locri—said that the heavens consist of two revolving spheres. The outer sphere is of the fixed stars, and this is the sphere of the "same"—the Unit. The inner sphere contains the "wanderers," the planets, and is subdivided into seven concentric circles.[42] Philo stresses immediately that these celestial objects do not really wander—to do so would be a denial of God—since they move through eternity never swerving or altering their course.[43] In the passage just quoted, in claiming that "from the Unit and the Seven springs the incorporeal heaven which is the pattern of the visible," Philo Hebraizes his Platonism. The account says that God began by making the Unit and the Seven; next, God formed the Unit and the Seven into an *incorporeal* heaven, perhaps the idea or archetype of heaven; finally, God used this archetype as the pattern of the visible or corporeal heaven. What Philo proposes, then, is an extra step or two in the Platonic process, depending on which work of Plato we have in mind. If we refer to the Plato of the *Timaeus*, where the Demiurge first makes a pattern and then models the world on it, we find in Philo the one extra step of the incorporeal pattern based on the ideas of the Unit and the Seven. If we refer to the Plato of the *Republic*, where the corporeal world is fashioned after the model of the ideas, we find in Philo two extra steps: God, creator of the ideas, and the extra incorporeal layer of the Unit and the Seven. Perhaps the following chart will help clarify the differences:

Philo's Scheme	Plato's *Timaeus*	Plato's *Republic*
God	Demiurge	Incorporeal pattern of the heaven
↓	↓	↓
Unit and Seven	Incorporeal pattern of the heaven	Visible heaven
↓	↓	
Incorporeal pattern of the heaven	Visible heaven	
↓		
Visible heaven		

Thus, the gulf between God and the created universe is greater in Philo than it is in Plato, while at the same time there is a clear causal chain of creation.[44] Ever since Xenophanes, philosophy had stressed the distance between the divine and the human. Philo expands the difference within a basic Platonic pattern.

The Sabbath brings together, for Philo, the majesty of the heavens and the earth. It reflects the harmony of God's spirit as it marries form to matter. It shows the proper relationship of the lives of activity and contemplation. It focuses one's mind on self-reflection and reflection about nature and especially about philosophy, the greatest common possession of God and man. The Sabbath shows the wisdom of Greek mathematics, which exalts—with clear and sublime accuracy—the numerical superiority of seven, a number whose excellence is confirmed by human anatomy, the geographical structure of the earth, yea, by the revolutions of the celestial bodies and the composition of the most supreme fixed constellations.[45] Finally, the Sabbath allows Philo to bring together the secular science of the Greeks with the revealed truth of the Bible, a union that shows that there is one eternal inviolable truth for the whole cosmos.

In summing up the place of Philo in ancient philosophy, one might wonder at what audience he was aiming. On the one hand, perhaps he was attempting to be a proselyte for philosophy to Jews. Extremely well educated in philosophy, Philo might have wished to show his coreligionists that there was much in Greek philosophy of deep value. Of course, insofar as Jewish tradition for the most part rejected Greek philosophy— derogatorily referring to all philosophers as *Epikouroi*, after Epicurus, whose philosophy could be easily, even if wrongly, dismissed as merely pleasure-seeking and God-denying—Philo failed.[46] On the other hand, if he was attempting to render Jewish ideas acceptable to, even esteemed by, the pagan world, he also failed, for there is no direct evidence that he was ever read by a pagan.[47]

Though Philo failed to spread Greek philosophy to Jews and also failed in his mission to spread the truths of Judaism to the pagan world, he nevertheless uncovered notions that would be developed into full-scale doctrines in Christianity.[48] His insight was that the Platonic scheme was very like the account in Genesis and that, with only a few small modifications, like the extra layer of distance between God and the visible world,

Plato's view might be made entirely harmonious with the biblical story. The two accounts presented the same sort of divine participation in the creation of the world and hence, for Philo, showed the same truth. Thus he stands as an example of an enthusiastic attempt to reconcile the best philosophical and scientific views of his era with what he believed to be the truth of revelation. The same endeavor was taken up again in the Middle Ages in Islam, Judaism, and Christianity with the most established, most highly respected philosophy and science of *that* era—the science of Aristotle. The same endeavor continues today too as theologians and scientists continue to search for a reconciliation of the Bible and science in the most respected science of our day, such as in quantum physics, Big Bang cosmology, and evolutionary biology.[49]

Discussion Questions

1. In what ways could anti-Semitism be a response to the self-conscious separateness of Judaism? Given that philosophers similarly separated themselves, referring to themselves as the knowing "few" and to others as the unlearned "many," do you suppose that they stirred up the same sort of antagonism? Would a Jewish philosopher have been doubly annoying, claiming separateness on two counts? Is there any sort of separation that would not stir resentment and hostility?

2. What features of both Hellenism and Judaism, in addition to the one's polytheism and the other's monotheism, made integration difficult, if not impossible?

3. *Consilience* is the term used when evidence from one field in favor of a theory confirms evidence from another field in favor of the same theory. Both anatomical and genetic evidence, for example, independently confirm the evolutionary relationships between humans and chimpanzees. Can a similar consilience have given confidence to Philo that Plato and the Bible shared the same theory of the world's nature and origins? Is there any difference between consilience in science and consilience in philosophy and religion?

4. In what ways does Philo's treatment of the Sabbath—a concept wholly biblical—illustrate an attempt to reconcile philosophy and religion or reason and revelation?

5. Does the attempt to incorporate mathematics into an interpretation of the Sabbath render Philo's account more persuasive or less persuasive? How likely is it that a pagan would be persuaded of the truths of Judaism by Philo's account? How likely is it that a Jew would be persuaded of the truths of philosophy by Philo's account? What is there in the early centuries of the Christian era that made Philo credible?

Notes

1. Happily, it is unnecessary to include color, for though the ancients had as much ethnic prejudice as the rest of recorded peoples, there does not seem to have been prejudice based on color. See Frank M. Snowden, *Blacks in Antiquity: Ethiopians in the Greco-Roman Experience* (Cambridge, Mass.: The Belknap Press of Harvard University Press, 1970), 178–79. By the same author, see also *Before Color Prejudice: The Ancient View of Blacks* (Cambridge, Mass.: Harvard University Press, 1983).

2. There was a growing internalization of Hellenistic tendencies in the second-century Jewish aristocrats of Judaea. Tobias was attracted by the trappings of the Greeks, Jason the high priest established a gymnasium and founded Jerusalem-at-Antioch as a Greek city, and Menelaus, who succeeded Jason as high priest, went so far as to incite Antiochus Epiphanes to persecute the Jews who were hostile to the encroaching Hellenization. The increasing Hellenization is perhaps shown most vividly in the Greek names that Jews, even those destined to be high priest, were adopting.

3. The rabbis forbade attendance at the theatre (*Avodah Zarah* 18b).

4. Philo, *In Flaccum* 43.

5. Acts of the Apostle 1.6 mentions both Hebraioi and Hellenistai, and this has been interpreted as distinguishing those Jews who conducted religious services in Hebrew from those who conducted them in Greek.

6. Among Rome's few exceptions was the Egyptian worship of Isis, perhaps because of what the Romans regarded as licentious rituals (Edward Gibbon, *Decline and Fall of the Roman Empire*, Great Books of the Western World Edition, vol. 1, chap. 2 [Chicago: Encyclopaedia Britannica, 1952]). But a religious exemption granted to Jews and denied others living in the same regions would surely have aggravated resentments.

7. On pagan resentment of the Sabbath, see Peter Schäfer, *Judeophobia: Attitudes toward the Jews in the Ancient World* (Cambridge, Mass.: Harvard University Press, 1997), 82–92.

8. Josephus tells the story (*Apion*, 1.176–82), saying that it comes from the lost treatise *On Sleep* by Clearchus, a student of Aristotle's.

9. Still, like so much in classics, the genuineness is contested. Longinus does not quote the Septuagint quite exactly, and so he may be quoting from memory. In his note on the passage, D. A. Russell, *Longinus: On the Sublime* (Oxford: Oxford University Press, 1964), summarizes the controversy and concludes that the passage is authentic.

10. Longinus, *On the Sublime*, trans. with commentary by James A. Arieti and John M. Crossett (New York: Edwin Mellen Press, 1985), 9.9.

11. He writes that he often attended the theater (*On Drunkenness* 177), probably off limits for a very orthodox Jew.

12. Philo, *On the Creation*, trans. F. H. Colson and G. H. Whitaker (Cambridge, Mass.: Harvard University Press, 1929), 69–71. Subsequent translations of Philo are from the same edition.

13. Jerome, *De Viris Illustribus* 11.

14. Philo, *On the Creation* 68 ff.

15. On Neoplatonism, see pp. 332–37.

16. Augustine, *City of God* 2.7, 14.

17. Pagan culture divided time into days, months, and years. The *week*, with its seventh day of rest, is established in the first chapter of the Book of Genesis.

18. These are found conjoined in Horace (*Satire* 1.6), Juvenal (*Satire* 14.96–99), and Petronius (frag. 37). For an excellent anthology of pagan references to Jews, see M. Stern, *Greek and Latin Authors on Jews and Judaism* (Jerusalem: Israel Academy of Science and Humanities, 1974–1984).

19. Cicero, *On the Nature of the Gods* 2.160.

20. In Seneca's lost *On Superstition* as cited by Augustine (*City of God* 6.11); Tacitus *History* 5, 4:3; Juvenal *Satire* 14, 105 ff.

21. Philo, *On the Decalogue* 96. He may have in mind the Spartans, whom Herodotus (6.57) says make offerings to Apollo on the new moon and on the seventh day after the new month.

22. This idea, that there should be a harmony between the physical laws of the universe and proper human behavior, that physics and ethics should be in harmony, is a view fundamental to the spirit of the Hellenistic Age, as we saw in chapters 13 and 14, in connection with the philosophies of Epicureanism and Stoicism. In conformity with this spirit, Philo sees a harmony between physics—which for Philo is the story of Creation—and ethics—which is established in the laws of Moses. For a man of the Hellenistic Age, physics and ethics are simply different notes of a harmonious chord.

23. Philo, *On the Decalogue*, trans. F. H. Colson (Cambridge, Mass.: Harvard University Press, 1937), 97–98.

24. *Metaphysics* 1074 b26; *Ethics* 1177a12 ff.

25. Philo, *On the Creation* 89.

26. Isocrates, *Panegyricus* 46.

27. The same expanded metaphor is used by Longinus, possibly a Hellenized Jew, in *On the Sublime* (35.2). For a discussion of the metaphor in Longinus and of possible relations between Philo and Longinus, see James A. Arieti and John M. Crossett, *Longinus: On the Sublime* (New York: Edwin Mellen Press, 1985), 254–56.

28. Judaism's love for nature is shown in the prayers that are said on seeing a rainbow or lightning or on hearing thunder.

29. Philo, *On the Decalogue* 98.

30. See pp. 8–9, 285.

31. Philo, *On the Decalogue*, trans. F. H. Colson, 101–2.

32. Plato, *Timaeus* 47a. In *Interpreting Plato* (p. 32) I argue that the passage is meant as a parody of the Pythagorean fixation on numbers, but it is likely that Philo took the whole dialogue as straightforward.

33. For an account of the genesis of such numbers, see Georges Ifrah, *From One to Zero: A Universal History of Number*, trans. Lowell Bair (New York: Viking, 1985), 291–310. On the notational systems of Hebrew and Greek, see, in the same book, 251–74.

34. D. Witztum, E. Rips, and Y. Rosenberg, "Equidistant Letter Sequences in the Book of Genesis," *Statistical Science* 9 (1994): 429–38.

35. In Hebrew most day names are indicated by number (First Day, Second Day, and so forth). Only the seventh day has a name—Rest (Sabbath). It is ironic that the names of the days of the week, a biblical concept, are now named in European languages after pagan deities—Norse and classical (that is, *Thursday* for the god Thor, *Sunday* for the Sun, *Mardi* [in French] for Mars, *Venerdi* [in Italian] for Venus, and so forth).

36. Philo had a predecessor in allegorizing the Bible and in discussing the significance of the number seven—a certain Aristobulus, an Alexandrian Jew, perhaps of the second century B.C.E., who may have written a commentary on the Pentateuch that is quoted very often by Eusebius and other Christian writers. See W. D. Davies and L. Finkelstein, eds., *The Cambridge History of Judaism: Volume Two: The Hellenistic Age* (Cambridge: Cambridge University Press, 1989), 389–91.

37. The abstract quality of numbers is perhaps what first attracted them to the Platonists. While numbers themselves have no concrete existence—one cannot weigh, touch, feel, smell, or see a number—the world is arranged into things that can be counted. Hence, for one looking for an incorporeal pattern of material reality, numbers seem to supply the goal. Computations with numbers yield precise and equal results for all who do them. Their objective validity puts them in a class outside the nebulous fields of law and ethics and gives a hint of what clarity about everything must be like for God. Indeed, it is when we engage in mathematical computation that we are most like God: after all, if God multiplies two numbers, will he not arrive at the same product as we? If he engages in a grisly long division, will he not find the same quotient?

Perhaps God might solve a problem instantaneously while we might labor over it—but the solution will be the same. Stephen Hawking, though surely not at all influenced by Philo, nevertheless equates understanding modern physics with knowing the mind of God in *A Brief History of Time: From the Big Bang to Black Holes* (Toronto: Bantam Books, 1988), 175.

38. Philo, *On the Decalogue* 105.

39. Plato, *Euthyphro* 10b.

40. Philo discusses the significance of six at length in *Allegorical Interpretation of Genesis II, III* 2–4.

41. Philo, *On the Decalogue* 102.

42. Plato, *Timaeus* 36 c–d.

43. Philo, *On the Decalogue* 103. Since Philo can never allow any chaos in the universe, he is critical of vocabulary that suggests any suspension of divine authority. I find very provocative the suggestion by Philo that in calling the planets "wanderers" we are attributing to them our human weaknesses. The suggestion, perhaps borrowed from Plato's *Laws* (821C–D), is that we ought to model our behavior on the heavens and not blaspheme them by sharing our faults with them. Similarly, Cicero writes, "I believe that the immortal gods implanted souls in human bodies to provide overseers for the earth who would contemplate the heavenly order and imitate it in the constancy and moderation of their lives" (*On Old Age* 77). For Cicero, as for Philo, gazing on the heavens and the cosmos is a way of enabling us to understand the hierarchy of things and our dual obligation to it—to study the divine order above as a means of enabling us to govern the human order below idealistically and compassionately.

44. On how Philo emphasizes the distance between man and God in his analysis of the creation of man in Genesis 1:26, see James A. Arieti, "Man and God in Philo: Philo's Interpretation of Genesis 1:26," *Lyceum* 4 (1992): 1–18.

45. For the wonders of the number seven, see Philo, *On the Decalogue* 102 ff. and *On the Creation of the World*, where he devotes some forty paragraphs (paras. 89–128) to this number! His excursus ends with a veritable hymn of praise to the number (*On the Creation of the World* 128).

46. According to the *Encyclopedia Judaica* (entry under "Epicureanism"), *Epicurean* became "a byword for 'deviance'—ranging from disrespect to atheism—in Philo, Josephus, and rabbinism alike" (Jerusalem: Keter Publishing, 1972), 6.817.

47. E. Goodenough, *The Politics of Philo Judaeus with a General Bibliography of Philo* (New Haven, Conn.: Yale University Press, 1938), 250, and A. D. Nock, "The Loeb Philo," *The Classical Review* 75 (1943): 77–78, argue that no pagans knew the work of Philo. H. A. Wolfson, *Philo: Foundations of Religious Philosophy in Judaism, Christianity, and Islam* (Cambridge, Mass.: Harvard University Press, 1947), 158, believes that he finds echoes of Philo in various works. James A. Arieti and John M. Crossett (New York: Edwin Mellen Press, 1985), have suggested that Philo is the unnamed philosopher in the last chapter of Longinus's *On the Sublime*, but they have also suggested that Longinus was perhaps a Hellenized Jew.

48. For example, Philo's understanding of Genesis 1.26, where God says, "Let us make man in our image," wherein he finds the image to be the *logos*, is adopted by nearly all the Church fathers. Among those who see man's rationality as God's image are Clement of Alexandria, Origen, Basil, Gregory of Nazienza, Cyril of Alexandria, and Eusebius. For a discussion of this verse, see James A. Arieti, "Man and God in Philo: Philo's Interpretation of Genesis 1:26," *Lyceum* 4 (1992): 1–18, and the references cited.

49. See James A. Arieti and Patrick A. Wilson, *The Scientific and the Divine* (Lanham, Md.: Rowman & Littlefield, 2003), 250–301.

Select Bibliography

Web resource: www.torreys.org/bible/philopag.html.

Berchman, Robert M. *From Philo to Origen: Middle Platonism in Transition*. Chico, Calif.: Scholars Press, 1984.

Davies, W. D., and L. Finkelstein, eds. *The Cambridge History of Judaism: Volume Two: The Hellenistic Age*. Cambridge: Cambridge University Press, 1989.

Wolfson, H. A. *Philo: Foundations of Religious Philosophy in Judaism, Christianity, and Islam*. Cambridge, Mass.: Harvard University Press, 1947.

CHAPTER **17**

The War for the Ancient Soul

I. The War of Politics and Philosophy

From their debut in the ancient world, philosophy and its practitioners appeared strange. The strangeness might have surfaced as the relatively innocuous propensity of Thales to fall into wells or as Xenophanes' mildly vexatious carping that athletes were more esteemed than thinkers. But as philosophers became involved with the chief men of the city, the feelings people had about them evolved into anger, and that anger was translated into hostile action. Athens charged Anaxagoras, the adviser of Pericles, with impiety for the suggestion that the sun was a rock and banished him. In the next generation, Athens executed Socrates, perhaps for his association with Alcibiades, perhaps because his fellow citizens felt threatened by his pesky dialectic. Three generations later, an ominous charge of impiety against Aristotle, perhaps motivated by anger at the philosopher's association with Alexander, frightened the philosophical giant into fleeing Athens.

Roman antipathy toward rhetoric and philosophy dates back to the second century B.C.E, when, after conquering Greece, the Roman Republic had to confront the overwhelming genius of Greek culture. The poet Horace (65 B.C.E.–8 C.E.) would later say about this cultural conundrum that "Greece conquered her conqueror Rome."[1] Greece's cultural victory did not come without fierce resistance, first and fiercely from Marcus Porcius Cato (234–149). Cato despised all Greek influences on Rome: in luxury, in literature, in sex. He so hated everything Greek that he even urged his sons to avoid Greek medicine, by far the best in the classical world.[2] When Greece sent philosophers as ambassadors to Rome, Cato argued that they should be expelled lest their views corrupt the populace. Well into the imperial period, Roman satirists continued to mock "Greek decadence" and to despise its influence over pure ancient Italian traditions.[3] Philosophy was included in this mockery: Trimalchio, a comic figure in Petronius's *Satyricon*, declares, with ostentatious pride in the accomplishment, "I never listened to a philosopher."[4]

Rome gradually and grudgingly accepted rhetoric and rhetoric teachers as well as philosophy and philosophers. Nevertheless, the two disciplines—

often blended and confused—were intermittently suspect under the empire, for political conspiracy often flourished under the cloak of rhetoric and philosophy. Paradoxically, the emperor Vespasian (reigned 69–79 C.E.)—who first endowed chairs for professors of rhetoric in both Greek and Latin[5]—became the first emperor in the century to banish a class of intellectuals, rhetoricians. And—also paradoxically—it was a philosopher named Mucianius who persuaded the emperor to banish philosophers.[6] It is clear that rhetoricians and philosophers crept back into the city, for a few years later (93 C.E.) Domitian (reigned 81–96) again banished both groups from Rome and all of Italy.[7]

Romans, of course, prided themselves on their *practical* wisdom. In the *Aeneid*, the great epic that links Rome's origins with the Greek conquest of Troy, Virgil sings the glory that is to be Rome and delineates how its greatness will differ from that of Greece:

> Others will more gently hammer out the breathing bronze,
> I grant, and draw living faces from marble,
> plead causes better, and describe with rods
> the course of the heavens and explain the rising stars;
> remember, Roman, these will be your arts:
> to rule the nations with your empire, to impose the way of peace,
> to spare those whom you defeat, and to crush the proud.[8]

313

While the Greeks are better artists and better scholars, the job of Rome is to rule the world. To be sure, Cicero showed how Greek philosophy could make one a brilliant orator, and, indeed, some Romans were interested in philosophy for its service to action. Hence, for as long as they practiced paganism—a religion that did not demand knotty metaphysical reasoning about the divine—Roman philosophers concentrated on ethics, the most practical branch of philosophy.[9]

Hellenistic schools of philosophy—Cynics, Stoics, and Epicureans—did not lend themselves to this Roman interest in civic duty, for they taught that it was best to avoid politics. Perhaps these schools were imitating the Socrates of Plato's *Apology*, who claimed that until his trial he had never been in a courtroom, even as a juryman, and described the risks to any ethical man who engaged in politics.[10] Zeno, the founder of Stoicism, explained how politics should take place in the era of the world-state, and the later Stoics distinguished between true monarchy, which is in accordance with nature, and tyranny, which is not. They debated whether it is morally right to kill a tyrant (concluding that it is).[11] Eventually, as discussed earlier,[12] an accommodation was made between Stoicism and politics, as Stoics did their duty and served the state.

Yet philosophers who pursued a life of virtue and embraced a vision of the sage as the exemplar of human conduct and wisdom could scarcely look on tyrannical savages like Caligula and Nero without deep disgust, and unless these philosophers were perfectly skilled at disguising their contempt, they were not likely to avoid the ire of these mad rulers. In fact, perhaps because dissimulation does not come naturally to philosophers, the list of martyrs to philosophy is quite lengthy.[13]

II. Cultural Decline and Its Explanations

314

In the first century after the disintegration of the Republic, there was a sense that greatness lay in the past and that a time of sterility had set in. Intellectuals were asking why cultural genius had declined. Romans in particular were asking why eloquence, the main expression of the life of the mind, had taken wing and flown away. A glimpse at the ancients' own attempts to explain the decline provides a window onto the intellectual climate of their period. There were three basic theories to explain the decline: the ordinary course of nature, the political situation, and moral corruption.

According to the natural theory of cultural decline, decay comes about either as a consequence of growing old—the lot of all living creatures and hence, by analogy, of societies—or as a period of deterioration in a natural and continuing cycle of growth and decay. A sense of natural decay appears with the dawn of literature, occurring as early as Nestor's reminiscences in the *Iliad* and Homer's own awareness that later generations are inferior even to those that appeared degenerate to Nestor. Concerning eloquence, Cicero remarks that the oratorical period of Roman greatness had reached its height and predicted that "it now seems about to grow old and, in a little while, to come to nothing," for, he says, "such decay is natural to almost all things."[14] The historian Velleius Paterculus (19 B.C.E.–30 C.E.) asks why the genius in each art flourishes in groups within specific and small periods of time. While admitting he has no certain explanation, he offers a psychological variation of the theory of natural decay: 1) genius is nourished by competition; 2) such competitive striving leads to perfection; 3) to stay at the peak of perfection is difficult, and what does not go forward naturally goes back; 4) when we despair of surpassing or equaling, we lose our zeal; 5) as a result, we abandon the pursuit and seek new fields; and 6) such fickleness is a hindrance to perfection.[15] Pliny the Elder (23–79) foresees an earth exhausted of its resources as a result of avarice; he adds, with full sense of Stoic doctrine, that his age is moving toward the inevitable conflagration and gives as evidence that men are now universally smaller than their fathers. In praising Vespasian as a patron of the arts and sciences, Pliny laments that the patronage is of little avail: no new work is being done in science, and even what was known about the past is being forgotten because "men's character has grown old."[16]

The political theory of cultural decline—that political repression destroyed the greatness to be found in Cicero and his contemporaries—is not fully developed until the time of Tacitus, who wrote at the end of the first century C.E. Because of the close connection between politics and oratory, the political theory is primarily an explanation of oratorical decline. The political causes had to be proposed gingerly, as the tyrants who ruled in the early empire would not brook criticism. Tacitus, in his *Dialogus*,[17] has one of his characters maintain that there had been a cultural decline in general, especially in oratory, and that it had begun during the reign of Augustus. He develops the theory that political repression destroyed the kind of oratorical greatness to be found in the time of Cicero.[18] Petronius, writing cautiously during the reign of Nero (54–68), veils his political explanation of cultural decline. He says that the orators of his day confine the "practice" of freedom to declamations, that is, artificially rhetorical exercises in eloquence. The charge itself is made in a declamation, as the speaker parodies the declaimers who extol "freedom"—a word loaded with political associations in the first century[19]—in unrealistic conceits. He cites examples of the unrealistic topics assigned to students—pirates in chains, tyrants ordering sons to cut off their fathers' heads, oracles requiring the sacrifice of three or more virgins to avert a plague—but only the topic of freedom is stressed and parodied. From this fact, and from an oblique allusion to Nero's slaying of his mother, we can perhaps infer a political theory of decline.[20]

Toward the end of the first century C.E., when it became relatively safe to criticize an earlier dynasty of emperors, writers again took up the causes of cultural decline as embodied in a decline in oratory. But now they sought an explanation in moral terms. Pliny the Younger (61–112) offered as a date for the commencement of decline the reign of Nero, and he described the decline in terms of excess, the characteristic that marked all the vices prevalent in the century.[21] The vices were examples of what we today call "conspicuous consumption"; that is, they were public, and their practitioners seemed almost to require an applauding audience. Petronius blames the decline on the universal base desire for money to spend on luxurious excess.[22]

Longinus, the literary critic and author of *On the Sublime*, who was most likely writing during the reign of Nero, finds the causes of cultural decline to be internal to the human psyche. The first century and the peace that Roman imperial rule brought to Europe enabled the educated classes to acquire great wealth, a wealth they used to pursue pleasure:

> The love of material things (of which we are all now insatiably sick) and the love of pleasure drive us into slavery—rather (as one might say), they plunge us—men, lives, and all—down into an abyss: though love of money is a disease that makes for pettiness, love of pleasure is one that makes men most ignoble. Indeed, I am not able to discover by reasoning how those of us who over-esteem limitless wealth and make it into a divinity can avoid admitting into our souls the vices that naturally follow it. Extravagance, you see, accompanies immoderate and uncurtailed wealth. . . . And if anyone should allow offspring bred of this wealth to come to maturity, they swiftly implant inexorable despots in our souls— contumely and lawlessness and shameless impudence. Thus it is necessary for these things to happen and for humanity no longer to gaze openly at the cosmos nor for there to be any speech and writing made for later fame, but it is necessary for such vices little by little to accomplish their end in the cycle of corruption in our lives, and for the greatness of our souls to dwindle and wither away and become what no one

will emulate, when mortal man wonders utterly at his own bloated parts and neglects to develop what is deathless. You see, no one who in making a judgment has accepted a bribe may still come to be a free and sound judge of what is justifiable and fine. . . . Whenever bribes determine our lives, and . . . the purchasing of profit from every source at the price of our souls—each man made captive and prisoner from the love of material things—would we, in such a plague-stricken corruption of life believe that there still remains any kind of free and unbribable judge to decide what works are great and will come down through the ages and that this judge will not be out-electioneered by the craving for gain? But perhaps for such as us it is better to be governed than to be free, since such acquisitiveness, if let entirely loose, as if from prison, against its neighbors, would burn up the world with its vices. And, on the whole, I said that ease was the expending the natures bred nowadays—an ease in which all of us (except a few) live out our lives, without struggling or undertaking anything except for the sake of praise and pleasure and not for the benefit derived from emulation and a worthy esteem.[23]

In Longinus we see a despair for the state of his world. The schools of philosophy were unable to fortify citizens with the ability to resist external pleasures, and, as a result, the competitive desire to be best for the sake of lasting glory no longer stirred men to attempt great things. This is the corruption that he identified as the cause of cultural decline.[24]

Into this gloom arrived Christianity, a new phenomenon in the first century. While the story of early Christianity lies outside the scope of this book, the relationship of Christianity to many of these issues is an important chapter in the philosophy of the ancient world.

III. The City on a Hill

In the *Apology*, Plato has Socrates describe his mission: "I do nothing but go about persuading you all, old and young alike, not to take thought for your persons or your properties, but first and chiefly to care about the greatest improvement of the soul. I tell you that virtue is not given by money, but that from virtue come money and every other good of man, public as well as private."[25] The work of Socrates and of the schools that traced their ancestry to his mind could affect only that rare soul inspired by reason. Most human beings appear to need incentives greater than the idea that virtue itself *is* all of happiness. Unlike the rare Stoic, most people do not believe that they would be happy on the rack, even if they were consummately virtuous.

For souls lost in the vast tyranny of the Roman Empire, a new religion arose that blended Judaism with the Hellenistic mystery religions, secret cults offering happiness in the next world.[26] A splendid reward awaited those willing to believe that Jesus of Nazareth was the *messiah*—a figure that had been hinted at in certain passages of the Hebrew Bible and whose qualities were developed during the period of the Second Temple.[27] The messiah would destroy the crushing dominion of pagan rulers and reign over a revivified Israel, to which all exiled Jews would return. For believing that Jesus was the messiah people would receive a permanent abode in the Kingdom of Heaven.

Pagan philosophy taught that man is a political animal who fulfills his nature in service to the state. The greatest glory achievable was that expressed in Pericles' Funeral Oration—an anonymous, collective esteem from having served a state worth dying for. No individual is named in the Oration, and the glory is not personal. As for the immortality of the private soul, Plato told various tales about an afterlife in which only the philosopher's soul was really well off. Epicurus preached that there was no immortality for anyone, for the atoms that constituted soul would, on the body's death, be recycled into other things. Stoics claimed that souls would be reabsorbed into a cosmic fire. None of these outcomes offered an electrifying hope. But Christianity, like the mystery religions, offered the promise of a permanent splendid individual reward for all those who had suffered on earth. "The last will be first." Here was a message that made suffering sufferable. To obtain this happy futurity, all one needed was faith.

Faith—the belief that miraculous principles and occurrences are true—was not a pagan philosophical virtue. Cicero, describing himself as an Academic, said that while Academics do believe that there is a truth, they hold so rigorous a set of criteria for it that the number of propositions they admit as true is very small. The Academics were perhaps unusually rigorous, but all the schools were united on the need for sound logical argument. The beliefs of Christianity—that Jesus is literally the son of God, that he died and was resurrected, that through his sacrificial suffering heaven was opened to human beings—defied logical proof.

At the same time, early Christianity had a number of traits in common with the philosophical schools. First was the astounding similarity of the phenomenon of conversion. There is very little separating the experiences of Peter and Andrew as they put down their fishing nets when Jesus calls to them, "Follow me and I shall make you fishers of men"[28] or of Paul as he suddenly adopts Christianity while traveling to Damascus from the experiences of Polemon at the lecture of Xenocrates, as he plucks the leaves from his laurel wreath and becomes a Platonist, and of Zeno at the bookseller's, when he instantly follows Crates.[29] In addition, just as the schools of philosophy agreed that a happy life consisted of virtuous activity and scorned wealth and urged improvement of the soul, so Christians followed Jesus, who preached, "If you will be perfect, go and sell what you have, and give to the poor, and you shall have treasure in heaven."[30]

Despite the compatibility of Christian ethics with the ethics of the philosophical schools, no pagan philosopher was drawn to the new religion. Since the tradition of philosophy was well established in the ancient world, one question confronting Christians was how to deal with it. Should philosophy be ignored or embraced? The question was made more tortuous because, as we have seen, the dividing line between philosophy and religion was perilously thin: what is Platonism—a religion or a philosophy? Aristotle and Cleanthes wrote hymns. Because of this overlapping quality, the ancient philosophical schools served, if only in a faint way, as churches, and conversions could be made to them. Plato was a successful convert; Alcibiades was a failure. Moreover, the philosophical schools offered, along with an explanation of nature, a way of life: we may recall, for example, the Pythagorean withdrawal into ascetic solitude and practices. In a word like *contemplation* (Greek *theoria*) we may observe the overlapping of philosophy and religion: is contemplation, even in Aristotle, merely an intellectual and biological phenomenon or a transcendent and religious one? And when Christians took a word like *metanoia*, which to the Greek philosophers means a "changing of one's mind, an afterthought, a sober second thought," and used it to mean "repentance," we again see an overlapping of meanings. Moreover, Christianity and philosophy both had famous martyrs.

Stoicism was exalted for the most austere and refined character—but perhaps therein lay its weakness. For Stoicism made no allowance for human weakness, a weakness that people wish to feel is justified and forgivable. Stoics accepted the Platonic notion that the soul was a bit of life carrying a dead body and that death was the release of the soul from its prison.[31] Christianity, with its doctrine of the resurrection of the body, seemed somehow more congenial than Stoicism, with its belief in the soul's reabsorption into the cosmic process. Perhaps the difference between Stoics and Christians on the question of suicide is revealing. Stoics sanctioned suicide: for them it was the ultimate form of adaptation to nature; to commit suicide lay in the power of a person, and by it he showed that he could defeat the dead body that weighed down his living soul. To a Christian, suicide looked like desperation and was a mortal sin. A Christian saw life after death as dependent on judgment, on personal judgment from a personal God. To a Stoic, the universe was a machine that would crush him unless he adapted to it but that would not reward him for adaptation except by crushing him—and even then adaptation itself might be the acceptance of being crushed.

IV. Christianity and Philosophy

The classical world developed two basic traditions of religion. One was philosophic—that embodied in Platonism, Pythagoreanism, Stoicism, and Epicureanism, where a rational explanation of phenomena was sought and found. In understanding the rational explanation, those who devoted their minds to philosophy thought that they had transcended the phenomena to the abstract concepts. This process of understanding and transcendence was called *contemplation*. The second religious tradition was a mixture of ecstatic transcendence and of observances, such as self-castration and magical transformations, that often appeared to those outside the cults as gross superstitious and ritualistic practices.[32] Christianity succeeded, in part, because it eventually appealed to both traditions. Christianity met its first success with the superstitious, to whom it offered the ecstasy of the cults without the grossness and barbarism. Success with philosophic minds came later and after a good deal of struggle. To convert this sort of mind, Christians had to become philosophers.

One can, perhaps, see the beginnings of such an effort in Paul. His own conversion he attributed to a miracle; his attempts to convert others are philosophical, as portrayed in his speech to the Athenians, recorded in Acts.[33] The most conspicuous attempt at Hellenizing Hebraic concepts is the opening of the Gospel of John, where the word *logos* is used to define the nature of Jesus Christ.[34]

The task of reaching the philosophical mind was, however, by no means sought by all Christians. Tertullian (155–222), one of the first major non-Gospel Christian writers, asked, "What has Athens to do with Jerusalem"—what have philosophy and Greek culture to do with revelation? His answer was a resounding "Nothing." For him, philosophers were charlatans, hucksters of wisdom and eloquence, and the ideas of philosophers, including Aristotle, were a source of heresy.[35] Reading any pagan literature was corrupting. As a lawyer and a rhetorician educated in the classics, Tertullian used the powerful tools of pagan thought to attack pagan thought and to extirpate everything pagan. To support his case, Tertullian could quote the Gospel of Matthew, where Jesus says, "I thank you, O Father, Lord of Heaven and Earth, because you have hidden these things from the wise and intelligent and have revealed them to infants."[36]

But to reject pagan literature and philosophy was to reject education altogether. And this rejection implied a denial both of the grand declaration in Genesis that human beings were fashioned in God's image and of the idea that the chief component of the image is reason (*logos*). Ultimately Christian intellectuals spent a good deal of energy arguing for the proposition that it was philosophically respectable to be Christian. Minucius Felix and Basil of Caesarea are representative of attempts to do so.

V. The Christian Dance with Philosophy: Minucius Felix and Basil of Caesarea

A. MINUCIUS FELIX (FL. 200–240)

Nothing is known about Minucius Felix apart from his *Octavius*, a short pamphlet in the form of Cicero's philosophical works. Cicero cast his works as dialogues, not Platonic dialectical examinations, but genteel conversations that begin with a sketchy mise-en-scène followed by a monologue or series of contrasting lectures. There is no verbal wrestling;

instead each interlocutor gives a solo set-piece gymnastic performance. The form suited the Roman legalistic mentality more closely than did the Socratic dialogue.

In the opening scene of the *Octavius*, three men, two of them lawyers, walk on a beach skipping stones on the water. They pass a statue of Serapis, the Egyptian god of healing, miracles, and the underworld, to whom the pagan lawyer Caecilius throws a kiss. When Octavius, a Christian lawyer, objects to the casual and impious salutation, the dialogue commences. Minucius is present as judge, and, by the end, the pagan lawyer is converted to Christianity. What is quite remarkable is that the Christian lawyer convinces the pagan lawyer by using pagan arguments and terms.

Caecilius, who makes the case for paganism, argues that since what we can know about the gods is obscure, we are best off not investigating them but accepting what our parents have told us. Then, employing the Epicurean physics of atomism, he tries to demolish the Christian belief in resurrection. Though professing to argue Socratic positions, all the arguments are far from Socratic. First he argues, contrary to Socrates, that might makes right: Roman gods must be powerful because they enabled Romans to rule the world. Caecilius then applies to the gods Socrates' remark, "The things above do not concern us"—a remark that Socrates had applied instead to the impossible quest for unchanging knowledge about this material and fluid world. At the end of his speech, Caecilius beams with pride and is ready to take the prize even before his opponent has uttered a word. Minucius, the referee, must remind him of the rules of debate.

The Christian lawyer replies with a classical oration. Beginning with a description of man as a creature endowed with reason, he states his agreement with the Delphic maxim "know thyself" that Caecilius had cited. But where Caecilius had used the maxim as an excuse for ignoring divine matters, Octavius insists that to understand ourselves, we must understand divinity. He follows the insight of both Plato and the Book of Genesis: humans were made in God's image; to understand them, we must seek to understand the model, God. To prove his point, he paraphrases, not Scripture but (!) Cicero's *On Laws*:

> Things are so coherent, so closely combined and interconnected that, without careful investigation of the nature of the deity, you cannot

know that of man; just as you cannot manage civic affairs successfully without some knowledge of the wider world-society of men; all the more that our distinction from the beasts is this, that their downward earth-bound gaze is fixed only on their food: we, with countenance erect and heavenly gaze, endowed with speech and reason, enabling us to recognize, perceive, and imitate God, neither may nor can ignore the heavenly sheen which thrusts itself upon our eyes and senses; for it is next to sacrilege to seek upon the ground that which you ought to find on high.[37]

All the works Octavius cites in his argument for Christianity are pagan, and the name *Jesus* does not appear once in the dialogue. Here pagan philosophy defeats paganism and supports Christianity.[38]

Octavius assembles a Who's Who of ancient philosophy to his side. Thales is invoked as proclaiming that God formed all things from water. Anaximenes, Anaxagoras, Democritus, even Epicurus (!) are called one by one to testify to the presence of a single force in the universe. The poets Homer and Hesiod, who, as Herodotus said, gave the Greeks their gods, are summoned as witnesses for monotheism. Concluding his appeals to authority, he forges ahead with the argument from design: the world is so lovely that there must be a governing divine rationality. Octavius cannot, of course, transform *all* the ancients into monotheists, and where he cannot, he resorts to the expedient of Plato in the *Republic*, who banished Homer's epics and other unsuitable writings. Like Plato, he argues that literature must be chosen for its truth in heaven, not on earth.

Octavius next turns his moral eye on Rome herself, which Caecilius had claimed was made great by the support of her gods. The Christian points out that the same gods who showed their strength and power in helping Rome showed their weakness and uselessness in helping Rome's enemies (since, as he says, Rome and her enemies worshiped the same gods). Roman history itself, he continues, was far from a source of pride. Rome's founder, Romulus, killed his own brother and orchestrated the rape of the Sabine women, many of whom were married. Christians, he says, have a greater claim to moral excellence than do pagans with their gorgeous temples. True divinity, he says, rests in the spirit, not in the wealthy accoutrements of gardens and columned buildings.

323

Where Caecilius had ended his speech with a lavish but hypocritical praise of Socrates, Octavius ends with a scourging condemnation of the philosopher, who is mocked for his superstitious belief in his *daimon*—that voice mentioned in the *Apology* as warning him against certain actions.[39]

In a brief epilogue, Minucius Felix expresses his admiration for Octavius's speech, and Caecilius registers his agreement by declaring his conversion to Christianity.

Minucius Felix's work reflects the debates concerning philosophy and religion that were taking place in intellectual circles during the third century. The philosophical traditions of the ancient world were being summoned as evidence to help bring about conversions like those of Polemon and Plato and Zeno to the new religion. No doubt this work was influential in enhancing the stature of Christianity, and when Constantine legalized the religion early in the fourth century, the empire was ready to accept a faith that no longer seemed strange. In the fourth century, when Christian emperors ruled and had the power to extirpate every trace of Greek and Roman philosophy, the challenge for Christians was how to preserve anything of value in the vanquished pagan heritage. Basil of Caesarea (in Cappadocia, as distinct from Caesarea in Judaea[40]) took up the challenge.

B. BASIL OF CAESAREA (330–379)

Basil, one of the three Cappadocian fathers of the Greek Orthodox Church, wrote a sermon explaining to young men how they could benefit from Greek literature and philosophy. This sermon, "Letter to Young Men," classical in form, is suffused with classical learning and ornamented with classical allusions. Reviewing the panoply of pagan writers, it separates those that should be retained from those that should be discarded. As a bee flits from flower to flower, extracting the nectar that will make good honey, so, says Basil, a young Christian reader should flit from pagan work to pagan work, extracting the nectar of ideas. A wise reader, like a discerning bee, should be choosy about which flowers to settle on and how much to draw from each flower.

To show the relationship of paganism and Christianity, Basil uses the image of a tree that produces both fruit and foliage. Fruit is more important than foliage, for human beings can live on fruit but not on foliage. Still, a tree that produced only fruit without foliage would be a barren tree. For Basil the foliage is ancient culture and classical wisdom; the fruit is truth. As the foliage enhances the beauty of the fruit, so classical culture enhances the beauty of truth. The distinction, then, is between accident and essence, between style and substance. It is the same distinction Milton makes in the invocation to book 7 of *Paradise Lost*, where he defends using a classical form—the epic—to express the Christian story of Adam's fall.[41]

What Basil has in mind is clear from his discussion of Olympic athletes. These athletes, says Basil, spend a great many hours sweating in the gymnasia, enduring hard physical exercise. Finally, when the day of contest arrives, they strip, undergo all hardships, and receive—if they win—a mere crown of olive or laurel leaves. What humility, what modesty, he exclaims. Of course, a pagan Olympic victor valued nothing more highly than a laurel wreath, which represented resplendent glory, and when he returned as a champion to his native city, he was celebrated with abundant praise, afforded the best seats at civic festivals, and fed lavish dinners at public expense. But under Basil's optimistic eye, this thoroughly pagan ritual was transformed into the Christian virtue of humility.

Basil closes his essay by placing himself squarely in the Platonic tradition. Like Socrates in the *Phaedo*, he maintains that the proper course of life is one that prepares us for death. The image of the body as a prison house confining a divine soul, where freedom for the soul is through death, is congenial to Christianity, with its focus on an afterlife in heaven. If the dim view of life on earth is true, then the glory and the beauty and the bright sunshine of this world are but empty phantoms, tawdry and worthless. Basil writes,

> We, my children, in no wise conceive this human life of ours to be an object of value in any respect, nor do we consider anything good at all, or so designate it, which makes its contribution to this life of ours only. Therefore neither renown of ancestry, nor strength of body, nor beauty, nor stature, nor honors bestowed by all mankind, nor kingship itself, nor other human attribute that one might mention, do we judge great, nay, we do not even consider them worth praying for, nor do we look with admiration upon those who possess them, but our hopes lead us forward to a more distant time, and everything we do is by way of preparation for the other life.[42]

In his essay, Basil rejects the delights of this world—perfumes, ornaments, fancy clothes. The body should be ignored, and even extreme good health is bad. Basil incorporated these views into his ascetic life and died at an early age from the severe conditions to which he subjected himself. By the example of his life and in his words, we witness a rejection of ancient humanistic values; instead, Basil erects the sole Christian value: salvation in the next world.

Basil foreshadows the Middle Ages by his outward forms and by his inner mood. Outwardly he retains the glitter, the analogies, the poetic splendor of the classics, just as will such authors as Dante, who populates his Hell with monsters from the Greek and Roman myths, but they are all ornamental trappings for a wholly Christian voyage to union with God. Inwardly, Basil's psychic mood is bleak and pessimistic. At the end of his sermon, he compares his readers to patients who have different degrees of illness. Those who are a little sick go to a physician. Those who are very sick call the physician to them. Those who are depressed, in a condition of melancholia, refuse to see the physician when he comes to their house. Depression was pervasive in Basil's age.[43] Basil expresses the hope that the sick people will not refuse to associate with those who are healthy. In his analogy, the healthy people are the great pagan authors, whose emphasis on reason and clarity and light can act like medicines on souls that are fevered from contending with the problems of this world and the next. The Middle Ages will also be a period of anxiety and despair, a period fed by isolation, poverty, disease, religious fanaticism and superstition, deadly foreign enemies, and a steady, pervasive terror of nature and supernature. Through the darkness of these fears, the light of faith showed the faint outlines of a happy afterlife. When faith becomes a cardinal virtue, along with its brothers hope and charity, we are no longer in the ancient world; we have entered the Middle Ages.

Discussion Questions

1. During both the latter part of the Republic and the empire, Rome found it prudent to banish philosophers. In the earlier banishment, philosophy was despised as something foreign, something odiously Greek. In the later period, philosophy was seen as subversive to the imperial will. Try to devise

some persuasive arguments for banishing philosophy in either era. How would you answer those arguments?

2. In the early centuries of the Christian era there seems to have been a deeply felt sense that culture had declined and was continuing to decline. What does it mean for an entire *culture* to decline? Would you agree with the assessment that culture had declined since the fourth century B.C.E., the century when the great schools of philosophy had been founded?

3. Of the various theories of cultural decline discussed in the text, which seems to have the greatest applicability to today, and why?

4. While Christianity appealed to many people in its early centuries, one group to which it did not appeal was philosophers. Looking back historically, this fact might at first seem an anomaly since in terms of regulating life in this world by means of ethical principles, the Christians and the philosophical schools differed very little. What reasons—political, social, or intellectual—might account for the gulf between Christianity and philosophy? Some Christians, such as Tertullian, were hostile to philosophy. Which side, philosophers or Christians, had the stronger case for rejecting the other?

5. How fairly does Octavius represent the consilience of philosophy and Christianity? Does he do as good a job as Philo had done for the consilience of Judaism and Plato? If *you* had been a pagan like Caecilius, would you, on the basis of what you had heard, have converted?

6. Has Basil succeeded in his quest to justify a classical education for a Christian young man? Does he ever seem to "make the worse argument the better" in the manner alleged of the sophists? Or has he actually succeeded in translating pagan practices and beliefs into Christian ones?

Notes

1. Horace, *Epistles* 2.1.156: *Graecia capta ferum victorem cepit.*
2. Plutarch, *Life of Cato the Elder* 23.
3. See, for example, the invective of Juvenal (fl. 100 [?]) against Greeks in *Satire* 3.58–125.
4. Petronius, *Satyricon* 71.12.
5. Suetonius, *Vespasian* 18.
6. Dio Cassius 55.13.1–2.
7. Suetonius, *Domitian* 10.3; Dio Cassius 67.13.3.
8. Virgil, *Aeneid* 6.847–853.
9. When Christianity arose as a major intellectual force and brought with it a host of metaphysical challenges, Christian philosophers arose to deal with them. By the Middle Ages, logic and metaphysics—not ethics—are the focus of Christian philosophy.
10. Plato, *Apology* 17d and 33a.
11. So says Cicero, *On Moral Duties* 3.19.

12. See p. 266.

13. It includes Julius Canus, Rectus, Seneca, Thrasea Paetus. and others. See Chester G. Starr, *Civilization and the Caesars: The Intellectual Revolution in the Roman Empire* (New York: Norton, 1965), 135–41. Epictetus, *Discourses* 1.29.57, actually encourages philosophical martyrdom (trans. George Long [Cambridge, Mass.: Harvard University Press, 1925]):

> Therefore when the tyrant threatens and calls me, I say, Whom do you threaten? If he says, I will put you in chains, I say, You threaten my hands and my feet. If he says, I will cut off your head, I reply, You threaten my head. If he says, I will throw you into prison, I say, You threaten the whole of this poor body. If he threatens me with banishment, I say the same. Does he then not threaten you at all? If I feel that all these things do not concern me, he does not threaten me at all; but if I fear any of them, it is I whom he threatens. Whom then do I fear? the master of what? The master of things which are in my own power? There is no such master. Do I fear the master of things which are not in my power? And what are these things to me?

14. Cicero, *Tusculan Disputations* 2.1.5.

15. Velleius Paterculus, *Roman History* 1.16–18.

16. Pliny the Elder, *Natural History* 33.1.3, 7.16.73, 2.5.18.

17. This was written after 80 C.E.; the fictive date of the setting is 75 C.E.

18. Tacitus, *Dialogus* 38.

19. See Chaim Wirszubski, *LIBERTAS as a Political Idea at Rome during the Later Republic and Early Principate* (Cambridge: Cambridge University Press, 1960).

20. Political decline showed itself also in the inability of the ordinary citizen to engage in meaningful political activity at any level. For a discussion of this matter, see Starr, *Civilization and the Caesars*, 112–13.

21. Pliny the Younger, *Epistles* 2.14.9 ff.

22. Petronius, *Satyricon* 88.

23. Longinus, *On the Sublime*, chap. 44.

24. On the empire's "rampant materialism" see Starr, *Civilization and the Caesars*, 273. Concerning this materialism, Starr quotes the piquant observation of Gregory the Great: "There was long life and health, material prosperity, growth of population, and the tranquility of daily peace, yet while the world was still flourishing in itself, in their hearts it had already withered."

25. Plato, *Apology* 30b.

26. For more information on these cults, see W. F. Jackson Knight, *Elysion: On Ancient Greek and Roman Beliefs concerning a Life after Death* (New York: Barnes & Noble Books, 1970), 74–79; see also Walter Burkert, *Ancient Mystery Cults* (Cambridge, Mass.: Harvard University Press, 1987).

27. See Hyam Maccoby, *Revolution in Judaea: Jesus and the Jewish Resistance* (New York: Taplinger Publishing, 1980), 75–76. The rest of the chapter (pp. 77–82) deals with the differences between Jewish and Christian notions of the messiah.

28. Matthew 4:19.

29. See Maccoby, *Revolution in Judaea*, 182. On Polemon see pp. 168–69 and on Zeno see pp. 263–64.

30. Matthew 19:21.

31. This Stoic view is attributed to Marcus Aurelius in A. D. Nock, *Conversion* (Oxford: Clarendon Press, 1933), 248. The reference to Plato is *Phaedo* 81–84.

32. An interesting example of this sort of religious experience may be seen in Catullus's poem *Attis* (Poem 63). Catullus describes a young man who falls under the spell of the great mother-goddess Cybele, an oriental deity, and in a frenzy of excitement castrates himself, the sign of joining her worship. The Romans, as children of Venus, could scarcely sanction such conduct. In the *Golden Ass* of Apuleius, we see a picture of the eunuch priests of Isis portrayed, though, to be sure, with genuine religious feeling, as a nevertheless morbid and rapacious lot.

33. Acts 17:16–34.

34. For a discussion of this matter, see Alexander Altmann, "*Homo Imago Dei* in Jewish and Christian Theology," *Journal of Religion* 48 (1968): 235–59, and W. J. Burghardt, *The Image of God in Man According to Cyril of Alexandria* (Washington, D.C.: Catholic University of America Press, 1957). See also page 310, n48.

35. Tertullian, *Apology* 46. Though one can find abuse hurled on philosophers throughout the work of Tertullian, he is particularly dramatic in *de Praescriptione* 7.

36. Matthew 11:25.

37. Minucius Felix, *Octavius* 17.2, trans. G. H. Rendall (Cambridge, Mass.: Harvard University Press, 1931). The passage quoted is from Cicero, *On Laws* 1.9.26.

38. It is perhaps interesting to observe that in the Middle Ages, al Ghazali will apply a similar approach, when in *On the Incoherence of the Philosophers* he seeks to prove the correctness of Islam by showing that philosophy itself shows the folly of philosophy.

39. See pp. 135–36.

40. This, the less famous Caesarea, indicates for the contemporary reader how widely the intellectual debate had dispersed.

41. Milton puts it thus:

> Descend from Heav'n Urania, by that name
> If rightly thou art call'd, whose Voice divine
> Following, above th' Olympian Hill I soare,
> Above the flight of Pegasean wing.
> The meaning, not the Name I call: for thou
> Nor of the Muses nine, nor on the top
> Of old Olympus dwell'st, but Heav'nlie borne,
> Before the Hills appeerd, or Fountain flow'd,
> Thou with Eternal wisdom didst converse,
> Wisdom thy Sister, and with her didst play
> In presence of th' Almightie Father, pleas'd
> With thy Celestial Song. . .

42. *To Young Men, On How They Might Derive Profit from Pagan Literature* 2.1–2, trans. R. J. Deferrari and M. R. P. McGuire (Cambridge, Mass.: Harvard University Press, 1970).

43. In *Pagan and Christian in an Age of Anxiety: Some Aspects of Religious Experience from Marcus Aurelius to Constantine* (New York: Norton, 1965), E. R. Dodds takes up this subject in detail.

Select Bibliography

Dodds, E. R. *Pagan and Christian in an Age of Anxiety: Some Aspects of Religious Experience from Marcus Aurelius to Constantine.* Cambridge: Cambridge University Press, 1965.

Starr, Chester, G. *Civilization and the Caesars: The Intellectual Revolution in the Roman Empire.* New York: Norton, 1965.

Wirszubski, Chaim. *LIBERTAS as a Political Idea at Rome during the Later Republic and Early Principate.* Cambridge: Cambridge University Press, 1960.

THE CHRISTIAN DANCE WITH PHILOSOPHY

Fedwick, Paul Jonathan, ed. *Basil of Caesarea: Christian, Humanist, Ascetic.* Toronto: Pontifical Institute of Medieval Studies, 1981.

Gregg, R. C. *Consolation Philosophy: Greek and Christian Paideia in Basil and the Two Gregories.* Patristic Monograph Series 3. Cambridge, Mass.: Philadelphia Patristic Foundation, 1975.

Meredith, Anthony. *The Cappadocians.* Crestwood, N.Y.: St. Vladimir's Seminary Press, 1996.

Rousseau, Philip. *Basil of Caesarea.* Transformation of the Classical Heritage 20. Berkeley: University of California Press, 1994.

CHAPTER 18

Philosophy at the End of Antiquity

I. Neoplatonism

The belief that it is necessary to reconcile opposed views of the world emerged deep in antiquity and continues to the present day. One of the greatest unmet challenges to modern physicists, for example, is the unification of quantum mechanics with the theory of relativity. The remarkable success of both theories in explaining physical phenomena makes the need for unification all the more pressing. Hence physicists suppose either that both theories are special cases of some underlying or more general theory or that they are somehow complementary. Showing that they are harmonious and can be reconciled is the holy grail of contemporary theoretical physics.

In antiquity there was a similar desire, the desire to reconcile the system of Plato, with its heavy emphasis on a transcendent realm of Being apprehended by mind alone, and the system of Aristotle, with its emphasis on the dynamic and changing world apprehended by the senses. If the theories of Plato and Aristotle could be blended or reconciled, the transcendent and the immanent could be brought together and all problems solved. There would be a "theory of everything," of the physical and spiritual realms, and mere humans would have a means of carrying their souls aloft to that latter realm. Underlying this grand hope lay the problematic premise that each of these thinkers was putting forth the truth in a complete whole, a whole that had to be accepted in its entirety. The eclecticism of antiquity did not simply take the best pieces of various thoughts and put them together; it was instead a syncretism that sought *synthesis*. Perhaps the analogy with quantum mechanics and relativity is applicable here too: because the parts of each system seem harmoniously to constitute a whole, each theory has to be accepted in its entirety, and a blending would need to show that the two self-contained theories do not contradict one another or at least that the difficulties in one system are resolved by the other. The most successful and well-known attempt to reconcile Aristotle and Plato was that of Plotinus (204–270), the person chiefly responsible for devising the system known as Neoplatonism.

The work of Plotinus survives principally in the *Enneads*, a collection of essays published after his death by his student Porphyry (232–305).

Though Plotinus never mentions Christianity, the religion shares so many ideas with Neoplatonism that its attraction to intellectualizing Christians like Augustine is easy to fathom.[1] Neoplatonism did not return the compliment, however, and some Neoplatonist philosophers wrote refutations of Christianity, for there were certain fundamental Christian beliefs—the salvation of an individual soul, God as a personal deity, God as creator of the universe in time, and the claim of revelation—that members of the philosophical school could not tolerate.

II. Plotinus (205–270)

Were it not for Plotinus's energetic disciple Porphyry, who edited the work of his master some three decades after he died, we would neither know any details of the life of Plotinus, nor would we have the work known as *Enneads*. This work, the name of which comes from the Greek word for *nine* (*ennea*), is a collection of fifty-four treatises that Porphyry organized into groups of nine because he subscribed to the Pythagorean notion that nine, as the square of three, is a perfect number. The mystical thinking manifested in the title is pervasive in Plotinus's system of Neoplatonism. If Porphyry had not edited the work, it would undoubtedly have been even less clear than it is, as we learn from Porphyry's description of his teacher's work patterns:

> When Plotinus had written anything he could never bear to go over it twice; even to read it through once was too much for him, as his eyesight did not serve him well for reading. In writing he did not form letters with any regard to appearance or divide his syllables correctly, and he paid no attention to spelling. He was wholly concerned with thought; and, which surprised us all, he went on in this way right up to the end. He worked out his train of thought from beginning to end in his own mind, and then, when he wrote it down, since he had it all set in order in his mind, he wrote as continuously as if he were copying from a book.[2]

Plotinus, born in Egypt, turned to philosophy when he was twenty-eight.[3] (One can only wonder whether he felt it a calamity that he had missed by only one year the auspicious age of twenty-seven—the magical cube of the magic number three.) Seeking a good teacher of philosophy, he wandered from one to another until at length he found a certain Ammonius Saccas,[4] who had been a Christian before turning to philosophy. Saccas was the teacher also of Origen, who became a Church father and, though in some respects excessively zealous,[5] was one of the most capable of the Christian Platonists of Alexandria. After eleven years of study with Ammonius, Plotinus joined an expedition of the Roman emperor to Persia, not for the purpose of gaining military glory but to learn about Eastern philosophy. His attempt at learning Eastern thought was brief, however, and he returned to Rome in 244, where he established his own school of philosophy.

Porphyry reports that Plotinus, while reluctant to talk about himself, nevertheless occasionally dropped hints about his life. He was eccentric from boyhood. He continued to demand breast feeding until he was eight, when he was shamed by a companion into stopping.[6] Porphyry opens his life of Plotinus with a dramatic revelation of his Plato-inspired eccentricities:

> Plotinus, the philosopher of our times, seemed ashamed of being in a body. As a result of this state of mind he never could bear to talk about his race or his parents or his native country. And he objected so strongly to sitting to a painter or sculptor that he said to Aemilius, who was urging him to allow a portrait of himself to be made, "Why really, is it not enough to have to carry the image in which nature has encased us, without your requesting me to agree to leave behind me a longer-lasting image of the image, as if it was something genuinely worth looking at?"[7]

Plotinus directly confronted the set of problems that began with Xenophanes and Parmenides of how a perfect deity—who, since both change and matter imply imperfection, must be both nonphysical and unchanging—could change the world. Although Aristotle's conception of God as Prime Mover equated knower and known by identifying the Prime Mover as thought thinking about itself, this concept explains the effects of God on the world only in terms of desire, a notion hard to defend when referring to things incapable of desiring.

Plotinus proposes a solution to the problem of interaction between immaterial and material entities in his theory of emanation. He posits as a first principle a deity so transcendent, so beyond being, so beyond anything in our experience or imagination as to be wholly ineffable, that is, wholly incapable of articulation. Such a deity cannot be known except by a "way of removing," by which every attribute that can be thought is removed until only God alone is left. Any attribute that *can* be conceived is too limiting—and if a word for an attribute exists, the attribute can be conceived. Whereas Aristotle allows a *distinction* between the deity as thinker and the deity as thought—even though this thinker and its thought are as inseparable as the concave and convex surfaces of a lens—Plotinus holds that the unity of the absolute ultimate One is so pure as to be utterly without internal distinctions.

The unity of Plotinus's deity recalls the unity of Parmenides' world but differs chiefly in the theory of emanation. The emanation from the One is the Divine Intelligence, from which emanates the General Soul. From the General Soul emanates everything else, including matter. The first three—the One, the Divine Intelligence, and the General Soul—constitute an ordered "trinity" of descending hierarchical value.[8] We might compare emanation to the light that shines from a torch with an incandescent bulb: it illuminates what it shines on without itself being diminished. Thus the torch "emanates" light, and the light affects everything within its range, but the torch itself is unaffected by what it illuminates.[9] The emanations occur continuously, without beginning or end and without being willed by the One. As Plotinus puts it, "What is full must overflow, what is mature must beget."[10] Emanation thus provides for continuous creation.

As emanations become more distant from the One, Plotinus speaks of a "descent." Thus the Divine Intelligence is a falling away or descent from the transcendent One. Matter, as the level or emanation lowest and farthest away from the One, is in that sense evil, although even it is good and beautiful insofar as it is a reflection of the intelligible world. Plotinus's doctrine of emanation thus undergirds his attempt to reconcile the seemingly contrary notions of immanence and transcendence on the one hand and good and evil on the other.

The theory of emanation presents a deity that answers many of the requirements of philosophy: the deity is unchanging and therefore has no will (for a will suggests choice, and choice suggests change). It is not dependent on anything, yet everything is dependent on it. It is knowledge, goodness, and everything else, but not in any definable way, and it is all these things as both cause and result. If this description makes no sense—and perhaps it doesn't—it is because such a deity is beyond comprehension. It is simultaneously immanent and transcendent. It is unmoved and yet is the agent of cause in everything else.

Another problem that Neoplatonism addresses concerns the central promise of religion, namely, the means by which humans might come into contact with the divine. Because many of the writings of Neoplatonism deal with this subject, one might say that Neoplatonism is as much a religion as a philosophical doctrine. Given the basic Neoplatonist principle that matter is bad and spirit good (to put it plainly), the intellectual challenge to human beings is to liberate the soul from its imprisoning body—its matter. Various ways of separating the soul from its body and from bodily things had long been a topic. In the *Phaedo*, for example, Plato's Socrates defined philosophy as a preparation for death. When a mind was engaged in philosophy, Socrates said, it escaped its earthly concerns and dwelled, as it were, in the region of ideas. Socrates also suggested a literal escape from the body through bodily death, at which point a philosophic soul took up residence in the world of the spirit. In the *Republic*, Plato had Socrates divide the soul into three parts, the appetitive and spirited parts—linked quite firmly to the body—and the intellectual part—freest from the body.[11]

In Neoplatonism, soul is a wholly spiritual entity independent of the body. By a process known as *theurgy* [from the Greek *theos*, "god," and *ergon*, "work"]—a program of disciplining through ethical and intellectual purification—soul can return to its source. In a Neoplatonist theurgy a soul travels through five stages of purifying ascent, 1) purification, 2) illumination, 3) union, 4) mystic union, until 5) it achieves apotheosis as it apprehends the absolute One. "Ecstasy" is the escape of a soul from its prison-body by these stages. The escape is what is meaningful, not the time when the body and soul are joined together. When a soul has returned to the source from which it emanated, it is reabsorbed into the cosmic universal soul, and the soul's individual qualities, acquired when it was dressed in a body, are lost. This is its supreme happiness, this, its salvation: to be merged into the universal soul.

In its religious doctrine of mystical union, Neoplatonism asserts the fundamental identity of the incorporeal soul with the trinity of the One, the Divine Intelligence, and the General Soul. The matter that one's body comprises is not one's essence; one's essence is one's soul, and that soul is ultimately the same as universal soul.[12] The means by which one achieves this union of individual and universal soul is contemplation. The further one goes in contemplation of the One, the further one is removed from material existence.

This mystic union is much more easily spoken of than achieved. While some people experience an ecstatic exhilaration from intense contemplative activity, this form of ecstasy is perhaps the rarest and most difficult to obtain. Yet there is something unsatisfying to most people, at least to those in whom the Greek ideal of individuality is deeply rooted, about salvation into a universal soul, that is, reabsorption into a cosmic psychic soup, where the soup is not even a vegetable soup where one might be a pea or carrot, but an undifferentiated consommé where perfect unified sameness prevails. This loss of identity seems to compromise whatever rewards attend the arduous five stages of ascent.

The greatest difficulty for Neoplatonism, as for dualistic systems generally, is the connection—or the breaking of the connection, as the case may be—between the spiritual and the physical. The Neoplatonist conceptions of emanation and ecstasy suffer from the same shortcoming. Despite fine rhetoric about breaking or transcending the connection to the physical, the process is unproved by any persuasive argument or empirical observation. The whole edifice rests on foundations that are simply asserted, even if poetically, and depend on the willingness of the adherent to suspend disbelief.

III. Christian Philosophy

Christian philosophy, accepting many of the attractive features of Neoplatonism, would address the shortcomings of the philosophy in a way that would be emotionally and intellectually appealing. The phrase "emotionally and intellectually appealing" does not, however, mean "demonstratively proven" by means of rigorous syllogistic arguments from unassailable premises. Indeed, part of the appeal of Christianity, for such thinkers as Augustine, was that it did *not* claim to offer demonstrative proofs.

Augustine applauds the humility of Catholicism because it calls for *belief* in matters that *cannot be demonstrated*, that is, matters that cannot be known in Aristotle's strong sense of knowledge through syllogistic proof. Other religions, such as Manichaeism, claimed to have knowledge on various subjects even without the requisite demonstrations.[13] For Augustine, the Catholic Church was more intellectually respectable than the Manichaean sect expressly because the Church was honest in its more modest intellectual claims.

IV. Augustine (354–430)

Aurelius Augustine paints a portrait of his early life for us in his *Confessions*. Since this autobiographical work was written for publication, that is, with the intention that its contents be publicly known, and since its author was a highly trained and skilled rhetorician, we can assume that he created the image of himself that he wanted his readers to have and that he did so for a particular purpose. This purpose was to make himself a sympathetic model for people spiritually adrift so that they could follow his example and commit themselves fully to a Christian life. The work is successful because readers can sympathize with his anguished confusion and spiritual wandering and because the sins he reveals—needlessly purloining pears or cheating at school games—are the kind of sins that all but the most impeccably prim and proper will find familiar. Augustine's references to his victims are too cursory to arouse much sympathy for them—a nameless mistress whom he threw off, even though she had borne him a son, as he began an abortive two-year wait for a ten-year-old fiancé to grow of marriageable age; a second mistress, whom he acquired at the beginning of the two-year wait to satisfy his sexual appetites but whom he quietly forgot when he adopted a celibate Christianity at the climactic moment of his religious conversion. Despite this particular lapse, the *Confessions* is a fascinating description of one man's spiritual explorations and of the general intellectual climate in the late fourth century.

Since the early life of Augustine was punctuated by several conversion experiences, it might be helpful to use them to organize this brief account of his place in ancient philosophy. The *Confessions* chronicles Augustine's conversions to philosophy, to Manichaeism, to Neoplatonism, and his last, to Christianity, which occurs at roughly the chronological midpoint of his life. He spent the rest of his life refining, adjusting, and even retracting some of his religious views as he argued against and persecuted those whom he believed to be heretics.[14]

A. AUGUSTINE'S CONVERSION TO PHILOSOPHY

Like Basil, who argued that as bees flit from flower to flower gathering nectar, so Christians should go from pagan masterpiece to pagan masterpiece gathering wisdom, Augustine saw pagan philosophy as a great source of learning. Less poetically than Basil, Augustine compares the truths of pagan philosophy to the objects of gold and silver that the Children of Israel stole from their Egyptian captors as they embarked on the Exodus from Egypt. The Egyptians had not created the gold and silver for themselves, says Augustine, but "dug the precious metals out of the mines of God's providence that are everywhere scattered abroad" and used the gold and silver "perversely and unlawfully to prostitute to the worship of devils."[15]

Perhaps Augustine felt kindly toward philosophy because he credited it with having started him at the age of nineteen on a path toward goodness. He reports how he was deeply moved by the content of the *Hortensius*, which Cicero wrote expressly to inspire philosophical conversions:

> The *Hortensius* changed my feelings. It altered my prayers, Lord, to be towards you yourself. It gave me different values and priorities. Suddenly every vain hope became empty to me, and I longed for the immortality of wisdom with an incredible ardour in my heart. I began to rise up to return to you. For I did not read the book for a sharpening of my style. . . . I was impressed not by the book's refining effect on my style and literary expression but by the content. My God, how I burned with longing to leave earthly things and fly back to you. I did not know what you were doing with me. For "with you is wisdom" (Job 12:13, 16). "Love of wisdom" is the meaning of the Greek word *philosophia*. This book kindled my love for it.[16]

From Cicero, Augustine turned to Aristotle, and he was so taken with the *Categories* that he believed, like the wisely-foolish second-year student of philosophy, that he knew everything.[17] While he soon realized that the *Categories* did not provide full wisdom, he employs Aristotelian concepts in his later thinking on such theological subjects as the Trinity, where he uses the categories of *substance* and *relation* to defend the identity of God the Father and God the Son.[18]

B. AUGUSTINE'S MANICHAEAN PERIOD

As a young man, Augustine was attracted to the sect known as Manichaeism, after its Persian founder Mani (216–276). Though it was a syncretistic religion made up of elements of Christianity, Buddhism, Taoism, and Zoroastrianism, it consciously rejected the Hebrew Bible. Manichaeism claimed that there is a perpetual war between the powers of God, as represented by light, goodness, and spirituality, and Satan, as represented by darkness, evil, and materiality. People, because they are composed of matter, are infused with evil but, because they also possess a bit of divine light, are also infused with some good. As a result, human beings are at war with themselves. For Manichaeans, it is this presence of evil matter and not the Christian doctrine of the Fall that accounts for the presence of evil in the world. The religion was initially attractive to Augustine because it seemed to free an all-good God from responsibility for evil. The religion may also have offered the young Augustine an explanation of his own carnal cravings, an explanation that liberated him from the guilty responsibility for sinning:[19] he could blame his matter, his flesh, from the evil of which he *could* not escape.

Eventually Augustine found Manichaeism inadequate, for it could not stand under the light of philosophical analysis. First, it demanded belief in absurd notions, such as that a fig tree weeps when its leaves are picked.[20] Worse, it claimed knowledge of matters where, because it lacked demonstrative arguments, it could assert only belief,[21] and, for the philosophical Augustine, unjustified claims of knowledge undermined intellectual validity. Finally, the religion collapsed in self-contradiction, reason's most inflexible standard. Augustine takes as conclusive the argument of his friend Nebridius:

> For me, Lord, there was a sufficient refutation of those deceived deceivers and those word-spinners with nothing to say (for it was not your

word which sounded out from them). It was enough to state the argument which used to be put forward by Nebridius long before at Carthage, an argument which struck us dumb when we heard it: The Manichees postulate a race of darkness in opposition to you. What could that have done to you, if you had refused to fight against it? If they were to reply that you would have suffered injury, that would make you open to violation and destruction. But if nothing could harm you, that removes any ground of combat, and indeed for combat under such conditions that some portion of you, one of your members, or an offspring of your very substance, is mingled with hostile powers and with natures not created by you, and is corrupted by them so changed for the worse that it is altered from beatitude to misery and needs help to deliver and purify it. They say this is the soul, enslaved, contaminated and corrupt, to which aid is brought by your word, free, pure, and intact; and yet your word is itself corruptible, because it is of one and the same substance as the soul. Thus if they say that you, whatever you are (that is your substance in virtue of which you have your being), are incorruptible, the entire story becomes false and execrable. But if corruptible, then without further discussion the very proposition is false and to be abominated.[22]

C. AUGUSTINE'S NEOPLATONIST PERIOD

Neoplatonism represented for Augustine the cutting-edge philosophy, and he was drawn to its many attractive features. The doctrine of a perfect One emanating goodness, with emanations that become less perfect as they extend farther from their source, could account for a perfect God and for an imperfect universe.

As he reports in *Confessions*, his Neoplatonist studies helped him develop a solution to the problem of evil. The problem arises from trying to reconcile the assumptions that God is perfectly good and completely powerful and all-knowing with the apparent presence of evil in the world. A Neoplatonist would say that everything emanated from the One is good but that as the emanations extend farther from their source, they become less good until they extend so far away as to become material; hence what appears evil appears so because of the contrast with the good that is closer to the source of goodness. But even these emanations are actually good, just less so. Augustine's solution to the problem of evil is very similar: he defines evil as the absence of good. Thus, instead of saying that any particular thing is *evil*, we should say that it is *less good*. Insofar as a thing partakes of any being, it possesses some good. Evil is an absence of good, or *not-good*. Not-good does not exist for, as Parmenides maintained, non-Being is not. Thus everything that is is good—good to some degree. In this way, God's perfect goodness is preserved: he has created only good; what appears evil is simply what is less good, and the totality of higher goods and lower goods is better than a world in which there would be uniform pure goodness. Uniform perfect goodness, in fact, would be a Parmenidean One and would preclude the existence of our world.

In this philosophy, where the whole universe could be understood as a unity with gradations more imperfect as they extend farther from the Source, Augustine saw a way of rejecting the Manichaean dualism of spirit and matter. But Neoplatonism could take Augustine only so far. In the end, no philosophy could provide him with the complete satisfaction of Christianity. The doctrines central to Christianity—the divinity of Jesus, that he is both very man and very God simultaneously, that through his sacrifice all humanity might enjoy redemption, that Jesus died and was resurrected—must all be held by *faith*, a belief in the reality of the miraculous that cannot be demonstrated by argument. Augustine ultimately chose to accept the authoritative claims of his religion rather than to demand the strong proofs of philosophy or to live with the doubt that philosophers must often accept in the absence of conclusive demonstrative arguments.

D. AUGUSTINE'S CHRISTIAN PHILOSOPHY

The distinction between Augustine's philosophy and theology is not so clear as one might desire. Once Augustine fully embraced the Catholic faith, he accepted the teachings of that faith as true. But as a person trained in philosophy and convinced of its value, he wished to affirm those teachings by rational arguments, and so he set out to provide the best arguments he could. In this way, he might be compared to a person who is trying to solve a labyrinth in which he knows the starting and ending places and must find the most expeditious path from start to finish. For Augustine, the starting place was the truth of logical premises; the ending place was Catholic doctrine, and the puzzle was to develop a convincing argument that led persuasively from starting place to ending place. Augustine's task was no different from that of, say, a literary critic who commences his puzzle solving with a text and the principle that a novelist has a literary effect as the goal of every metaphor or narrative device that he uses. The critic's job is to make a plausible case that the text achieves its intended effect. The problem for both Augustine and the literary critic is to make his case without twisting the bounds of plausibility.

For example, Augustine holds that Adam's disobedience to God's single commandment—eating the forbidden fruit in the Garden of Eden—is responsible for the sinfulness of subsequent human beings. According to Augustine, though it was Eve who was deceived by the serpent, Adam sinned because his wish not to be separated from his partner was greater than his wish to obey God.[23] Hence, because of his carnal cravings for Eve, Adam's will was already corrupt. The sin brought death into the world as its punishment, and the punishment, says Augustine, was fair because obedience "is the mother and guardian of all other virtues in a rational creature."[24] For one to obey his own will instead of God's will is calamitous. After the sin, continues Augustine, Adam covered his genital organs because he realized that they were no longer subject to his will,[25] and this independence of his body from his will was the visible sign of a severely diminished self. The sinfulness of Adam has been inherited by all his progeny forever, and mankind cannot avoid this heavy burden of sinfulness except through the grace—the undeserved gift—of God. As there is not any kind of demonstrative argument for this view, the justice of the inheritability of Adam's sinfulness must be accepted as an article of faith.

It was on this point that Augustine engaged in a pivotal controversy with his contemporary Pelagius (355–425), a monk from Britain. Pelagius denied the inevitable sinfulness of man and argued that mankind has a natural ability to reject evil and seek goodness. Because Pelagius denied the doctrine of original sin and the consequent need for baptism, he would allow virtuous pagans into Heaven because of their good actions and good characters. Augustine opposed these views vigorously as contrary to the Church's teachings. Augustine was posthumously successful in his campaign in 431, when Pelagianism was declared a heresy at the Council of Ephesus.

In the debate with Pelagius, we can see that Augustine had a clear ending place in view—the affirmation of the doctrine of original sin by a persuasive argument. To achieve this affirmation, he wove together relevant biblical passages, facts about sexual urges, and a Neoplatonist disdain for the material world. The doctrine, of course, depended on the literal truth of the story of Adam, a truth that could be held only by faith. Perhaps Augustine could claim that ultimately all premises are held by faith—since, by definition, a premise is not itself supported by argument—and that philosophy requires only a consistent set of noncontradictory arguments. Nevertheless, the premises of philosophy and those of theology are not the same, for those of philosophy devolve into a few assumptions of logic, while those of theology rest on the assumption that revelation is both revealed by God and true.

Among other doctrines that Augustine labors to explain is that of the Trinity. His reflections show the influence of Aristotle's *Categories*, which he had read in youth:

344

> He [that is, God] is, however, without doubt, a substance, or, if it be better so to call it, an essence, which the Greeks call *ousia*. For as wisdom is so called from the being wise, and knowledge from knowing; so from being comes that which we call essence. And who is there that is, more than He who said to His servant Moses, "I am that I am;" and, "Thus shall thou say unto the children of Israel, He who is hath sent me unto you?" But other things that are called essences or substances admit of accidents, whereby a change, whether great or small, is produced in them. But there can be no accident of this kind in respect to God; and therefore He who is God is the only unchangeable substance or essence, to whom certainly *being* itself, whence comes the name of essence, most especially and most truly belongs. For that which is changed does not retain its own being; and that which can be changed, although it be not actually changed, is able not to be that which it had been; and hence that which not only is not changed, but also cannot at all be changed, alone falls most truly, without difficulty or hesitation, under the category of *being*.[26]

Ultimately, Augustine concludes that Aristotle's categories are unable to provide a demonstrative argument, and so the Trinity must be held as an article of faith. To understand why the holy spirit is not begotten and how the holy spirit proceeds from the father and the son, Augustine says, one must await heaven.[27] Obviously, this conclusion, too, is in the realm of religious faith, not philosophy.

E. CONCLUSIONS ABOUT AUGUSTINE

Augustine's influence on the history of Christianity cannot be overestimated. Some of his views, such as the effect of Adam's sin on all subsequent generations of humanity, were affirmed and attacked in Church controversies for centuries and later significantly influenced the founders of the Protestant Reformation. The story of Augustine's life remains on course syllabi in colleges and universities, where it continues to evoke the sympathy of readers who identify with the confused and distraught young protagonist, and it succeeds in rousing those readers to root for his conversion, so that when Augustine prays, "Give me chastity, but not yet," the reader too wants to beseech God—for Augustine, at least— "Give *him* chastity *now!*"

Augustine's works can be said to do for theology—the application of reason (that is, *logos*) to God (that is, *theos*)—what Plato's dialogues did for philosophy: kindle in their readers a passionate desire to take up the arguments and debate them. In the case of Augustine, he may perhaps be blamed for at least some of the violence that these debates stirred up, for at a certain point in his life he changed from his view that Christianity ought to prevail by her persuasiveness and not by coercion and instead became convinced that it was better to compel orthodoxy than to consign souls to an eternity of damnation.[28] And he was perhaps the first to incite a Roman emperor to take up arms against heretics, even though he sometimes asked that heretics be spared execution.[29]

345

V. Boethius (475–524)

Manlius Boethius, the last of the ancient martyrs of philosophy, endeavored, like Cicero, to blend the active and contemplative lives. From his elevation to consul in 510 until his imprisonment in 523, he helped manage the empire under Emperor Theodoric. Despite his commitment to public affairs, Boethius was a fruitful scholar whose scholarly works were among the most influential the world has known. His treatise on music was the standard text on the subject for a millennium; his translation of Aristotle's logical works was perhaps the founding document of medieval philosophy; and his literary masterpiece, the *Consolation of Philosophy*, a work translated both by Alfred the Great and Elizabeth I, was among the most widely read books of the Middle Ages, influencing, among many others, Dante and Chaucer.

One can observe Boethius's Neoplatonism in his theological work *On the Trinity* as well as in the *Consolation*. The concept of the Trinity perhaps lends itself to Neoplatonist analysis. Neoplatonism had undertaken to formulate a plausible explanation of the seemingly impossible—how something could be eternal and unchanging and also be responsible for a continuing process of creation, which appears to be a type of change. Boethius, with a similar Neoplatonist daring, undertook to explain how things that were three could also be one. According to his formulation, God, as One, admits of no composition but is a simple entity not consisting of parts. He is a single essence. This single essence, however, has three faces, or masks, or "persons." The first, the "Father," is not generated; the second, the "Son," is "posterior" or "after" the Father, not in time but in logic. To understand what this means, consider a syllogism. In a syllogism, the major premise is logically (but not temporally) "prior" to the minor premise. For example, in the syllogism, "All men are mortal; Socrates is a man; therefore Socrates is mortal," the major premise "all men are mortal" does not occur *before* the particular claim that Socrates is a man but underlies it or "precedes" it in the order of thought. In the same way, says Boethius, "God the Father" is prior to "God the Son" not in time but in order of thought. And this holds also for the third person, "God the Holy Spirit." Thus the three persons are equally eternal, and the term "begotten," when used of the Son, is a metaphor for logical posteriority. Arguing the case further, Boethius observes that the ways in which things can be the same or different are in genus, species, or number. To use Boethius's examples, a horse and a man are the same because they share the same genus—animal; Cato and Cicero are the same in species, man; and Tully and Cicero are the same in number, each being one. Since the persons of the Trinity do not differ in genus, species, or number, they are the same in essence. Perhaps a rough parallel would be where we call a single individual a *student*, a *freshman*, and a *pupil of freshman English*—where the essence of the individual is the same, but the "persons" are logically ordered: being a student is logically prior to being a freshman, and being a freshman is logically prior to being enrolled in freshman English.

Neoplatonist thinking is reflected also in Boethius's *Consolation of Philosophy*. At the beginning of this lovely book, the formerly flourishing Boethius laments his sorry state as he waits in prison for execution. In his own account of the charges against him, Boethius reports that in supporting the Senate he was accused of treason.[30] In a figurative sense, he is experiencing the imprisonment of his earthbound values and private pains. The allegorical figure Lady Philosophy appears in his cell and commences to restore him to equanimity by a refresher course of ancient philosophy, recalling to him the true nature of fortune; the falsity of the glamorous goods of honor, wealth, and pleasure; the true human happiness of virtue and wisdom; the doctrine that God is not responsible for what appears to be evil; the nature of God as simple unity; the proof that there is no randomness in the universe; and finally the demonstration that since God resides in a timeless present, there is no contradiction at all between human free will and divine foreknowledge. If at the beginning of the work Boethius has wallowed in self-pity for his private woes, by the end he has forgotten himself entirely as his spirit soars into a realm where the profoundest divine mysteries are revealed. He and his attentive reader alike achieve consolation for any earthly woes by completely forgetting them. *Consolation of Philosophy*, one of the glories of ancient literature, provides a practical model of the Neoplatonist program of moving the soul step by step to contemplation of the divine.

In the climactic book of the *Consolation*, Lady Philosophy and Boethius discuss the question of whether God's omniscience, which includes foreknowledge, is compatible with human free will. If God is perfect in every possible respect, must he not have perfect, complete knowledge of everything that has happened, is happening, and will happen? But if God knows what will happen, how then can the will be free? For example, if God knows that a person will be shopping for shoes next Wednesday at 3:00 P.M., how could it be possible for the person to be doing

347

anything else? If it is not possible for the person to be doing anything else, how can his will be free?

Obviously, the simplest solution to the dilemma would be either to deny that God's omniscience extends to the future—a limitation of God's power that is inconsistent with Boethius's view of God as the highest imaginable good, that is, a deity without any limit whatsoever—or to deny human free will—a solution that demolishes any possibility of human morality and also questions the moral rightness of God in punishing sin or rewarding virtuous behavior.

Boethius's solution posits the existence of "eternity." While human beings live in time, where events succeed one another in a linear fashion, one after the other, God dwells in eternity, gazing on all time as a simultaneous present. For God, past, present, and future merge into a single point. Thus, though an action seems future to us, it is always in the present to God, for future, present, and past are one in God's vision. By positing this type of eternity, Boethius finds a consistent solution to the problem of free will and divine omniscience: the will is free because humans choose their own course of action in the temporal world; that same will is foreknown from God's vantage point in eternity.[31]

When Boethius was a young man setting out on a career in philosophy, his ambition was to translate all the works of Aristotle and Plato and then to reconcile their differences. One of the problems on which Plato and Aristotle seemed most divided concerned the question of the Platonic Forms, or Universals, whether they have an independent existence—a notion suggested in the Platonic dialogues—or whether they exist only as common elements *in* particular objects without a separate existence. Boethius, in his commentary on Aristotle's *Categories*, suggests that he himself was unable to make up his mind on this subject. After presenting an argument that the incorporeal universals of genera and species subsist only in things grasped by the senses, in other words, in particulars, he concludes,

> But Plato held not only that genera, species, and the others are thought of as universals but also that they subsist apart from bodies. Aristotle, on the other hand, held that they are thought of as incorporeal and universal but subsist in sensibles. I have not deemed it fitting to judge between

these views, for that belongs to a deeper philosophy. We have followed closely Aristotle's view, not because we especially agree with it, but because this book was written to accompany the *Categories* of which Aristotle is the author.[32]

Boethius, alas, was executed while only in his forties, before he had had an opportunity to do much more than translate Aristotle's logical works, and before he had come to a conclusion on the question of universals, which remained a favorite topic of debate in the medieval schools of philosophy.

At the darkest moment in his life, cast in prison, his life's work at an end, Boethius turned his mind to philosophy. Because in *Consolation of Philosophy* he did not invoke religion, some have doubted that he was a Christian. Indeed, Samuel Johnson thought it strange that in the crisis Boethius was "more a philosopher than a Christian" (*magis philosophus quam Christianus*).[33] Yet to read the book in this way is to miss Boethius's marriage of philosophy and religion. When we, and Lady Philosophy, first encounter Boethius in his prison cell, he is wholly focused on his own sorrows. But as he thinks about philosophy in ever more abstract terms, ending with a glimpse of eternity itself, Boethius completes a Platonic ascent to the World of Being; in effect, he gives up his worldly concerns and sorrows. In reflecting on the sublimest questions of philosophy, Boethius transcends his misery and finds God. Perhaps, then, Boethius began his philosophical labors with Aristotle because he was saving the more spiritual Plato for dessert—and in this way the *Consolation of Philosophy* reflects what was to have been his life's philosophical program.

349

VI. Heresy and the End of Ancient Philosophy

From the third century on, many of the best minds were devoted to strengthening the newly legal and triumphant Church. The current "best" philosophy was Neoplatonism, a set of views that had given an intellectual stamp of authority to mystic leaps to the world of Being, the realm of God. Neoplatonism claimed knowledge not only of a process by which the divine interacts continuously with the human and material worlds but also of a process by which human souls can move up the ladder of perfection to the Absolute. This sort of transformation or metamorphosis, which could change souls into something better, was thought by later proponents to suggest a means for metamorphosing matter as well and thus encouraged a belief in magic. But minds that turned their attention to *such* transformations had abandoned philosophy.

Injurious as well to a rational exploration of the world was the Christian dread of heresy. The word *heresy* is derived from the Greek verb meaning *to choose* and indicates to Orthodox Christians the choice of rejecting an obedient acceptance of the dogmatic true teachings of the Church in favor of willfully independent and unsanctioned false views. To those demanding religious submission, heresy is a form of vanity and rebelliousness. To observers outside the faith, however, the various heresies may not appear less compelling than the orthodox views.

The Arian heresy, for example, named for Arius (fl. 320), taught that before creating everything else, God created a Son, who was neither equal nor coeternal with the Father. According to Arian, Jesus was a supernatural creature not quite human and not quite divine. At the Council of Nicaea in 325, Arianism was condemned, and the dogma that the Father and the Son were exactly the same was affirmed. This teaching was to be accepted as a *mystery*, that is, a truth not understandable in rational terms.

The Sabellian heresy, named for Sabellius (fl. 235), advanced the doctrine that God is one indivisible substance who has three fundamental activities, or modes—Father (creator and lawgiver), Son (redeemer), and Holy Spirit (the maker of life and the divine presence in humans). This conception of the Trinity was rejected in favor of a single mode.

The Pelagian heresy discussed earlier, which Augustine opposed, rejected the concept of an original sin inherited from Adam. The Donatist heresy insisted that the validity of a sacrament depends on the personal virtue of the priest administering it. The Montanist heresy held that once a Christian fell from grace he could never be redeemed. The Ebionite heresy held that one ought to follow the Mosaic laws and that Jesus was merely a miracle-performing prophet. These are only a few from the long list of heresies against which many of the best thinkers devoted their efforts. Augustine, for example, spent his life fighting the Donatists and the

Pelagians. In the end, he came to the conclusion that force should be used to coerce orthodoxy.

Earlier in the history of thought, when the followers of Pythagoras suspended inquiring into new areas and subscribed fully to whatever had been the master's teaching—even if such devotion meant departing from rationality—it had spelled the end of their school as a significant force in philosophy. The same was bound to occur in the West when the most important decisions of life were to be made on the basis of religious authority and any independent thought might result in a charge of heresy and a sentence of execution—a sentence celebrated as a defense of the faith and a glory to the humble executioners. Before fully embracing Catholicism, Augustine had written several books on philosophical subjects, including one on beauty, but these have not survived. What has survived is his enormous corpus rejecting heresy; this fact is in itself evidence of what was valued in the intellectual world of late antiquity.

The cultural ambience of the period further undermined rationalism. In art, a mystic transformation was converting (or metamorphosing) pagan symbols into Christian ones. For example, images of birds became symbols of the soul's flight to a spiritual realm; the famous Roman baths, where citizens once had gone to gossip about politics or to engage in sports, became baptisteries where souls could be cleansed of their sins; images of Orpheus and his lyre were converted into a symbol of the crucifix, perhaps because of the resemblance of strings stretched on a frame to Jesus stretched on the cross. In music, Boethius's treatise reigned, with its threefold division: music of the spheres (the music the heavenly bodies were believed to make as they move around the earth); human music, which, echoing the language of Plato's dialogue *Phaedo*, is an attunement of body and soul and of the other oppositional elements of human beings (like the moist and dry, hot and cold, and so on); and, at the lowest level, the music generated by musical instruments that we hear with our ears. The lower music, of course, ought to be aimed at moving us to the higher levels, until we experience a mystic union with the divine. In architecture, the noblest edifice now was the church, to be built with soaring arches and domes that direct the eye upward toward heaven, again in the service of leading a soul toward God. In short, artis-

351

tic culture now aimed at a mystic intuitive merging with the divine, not at logical proofs of propositions.

As men aimed their souls toward God and contemplated the divine nature, they were confronted with a grave dilemma: if, on the one hand, the divine is utterly transcendent and unlimited, then it is unknowable; if, on the other hand, it is knowable, then it is limited, definable, and hence not divine. Christian theologians maintained that God's attributes are transcendent and that God is omnipotent, omniscient—perfect in every respect. Such reasoning presented knotty problems of reconciling these attributes of God with his participation in human life. For example, the idea that God can be both merciful and just requires that God act in contradictory ways. For mercy involves *not* giving a guilty person a just punishment; in other words, mercy requires a forbearance from doing what is just; hence God cannot logically be both just and merciful simultaneously. Another example would be the attribution of all credit for any human good actions to God while assigning the entire blame to humans for their bad actions. In the end, theologians resolved most such difficulties as Augustine did, by denying the possibility of rational analysis of spiritual matters and by affirming instead the acceptance of the Church's authority.

Classical antiquity began with Achilles' discovery of guilt, a discovery that took the moral good out of collective public opinion and placed it in individual consciences. Later, rejecting the relativism that sprang from making the individual the measure of all, Plato used Parmenides' gift of logic and Pythagoras's discovery of the universal forms of mathematics to make God the measure. Aristotle refined the tools of thinking and used them to construct a rational view of metaphysics, physics, biology, and human beings. The Stoics and Epicureans turned their efforts to establishing the rules for human happiness given the physical world in which we humans live. Philo and the Christian thinkers attempted to reconcile the principles of metaphysics, especially Plato's, with the description of God in the Bible. To do for Aristotle what Philo and Augustine had largely accomplished for Plato was to be a task for the high Middle Ages.

In the twelfth century, when this effort was taken up in earnest in the West by the method known as *scholasticism*—an argumentative method of investigation based on the assumption that God created the world to embody rational principles—the enterprise was full of peril. The teachings of Thomas Aquinas, the greatest Christian synthesizer of Christian faith and Aristotelian reason, were for a while declared heretical, and anyone holding them was excommunicated.[34] And in the centuries that followed, the Church continued to keep a watchful eye on philosophy and science.

VII. Concluding Remarks

Philosophy, said Aristotle, is the activity by which we obtain knowledge of truth.[35] The word *philosophy* is a compound, the first part of which, *philo-*, indicates a love; the second part of which, *-sophy*, indicates the object of the love, here "knowledge." According to the ancients, knowledge is an apprehension of things and their causes that is sure and safe and not to be faulted by any argument.[36] And truth is the unchanging, universal, and eternal nature of things.

It was not long before the original discoverers of philosophy realized that they had come upon the greatest good available to human beings. Philosophy enabled human beings to understand the heavens, to transform ugly rocks into beautiful shapes, to diminish the fear of nature by converting the caprice of winds and storms and earthquakes to fundamental laws, and to direct human life toward goodness, truth, and immortality. Under the exacting gaze of philosophy, specious goods like money, honors, sensual pleasure, and power revealed their emptiness. It lay within the power of philosophy to turn human beings into virtual gods.

To ancient thinkers, the world appeared to be such as it is *so that* human beings could take up philosophy. Plato, for example, maintained that human anatomy is designed for this very purpose. Here he describes how intestines are lengthy and coiled for the sake of philosophy:

> In order that the mortal race not perish without fulfilling its end— intending to provide against this, the god made what is called the lower belly, to be a receptacle for the superfluous meat and drink, and formed the convolution of the bowels [that is, the intestines], so that food might be prevented from passing quickly through and compelling the body to require more food, thus producing insatiable gluttony and making the

353

whole race an enemy to philosophy and culture, and rebellious against the divinest element within us.[37]

Galen (129–199), a medical writer educated in the schools of philosophy, elaborates Plato's insight by contrasting humans with the animals that have straight intestines:

> All animals whose intestines are not coiled but extend straight from the stomach to the fundament are greedy, gluttonous, and forever engaged in taking nourishment, like the plants.[38]

Cicero wrote that since man alone can appreciate the heavenly bodies, they must have been created especially for him:

> The courses of the sun and moon and stars are an essential part of the fabric of the universe, but they also present a marvelous spectacle to Man. This is the sight of which we can never tire, beautiful beyond words, and a supreme example both of wisdom and of art. Man alone has measured out the courses of the stars and knows their times and their seasons, their changes and variety. If Man alone knows this, we must infer that it was for Man's sake that they were made.[39]

These affectionate tributes are characteristic of Western philosophy throughout the ancient period. Though philosophy had its enemies in antiquity—within both tyrannies and democracies—many of whom were deadly, and though these enemies might kill individual philosophers, they could not kill the philosophical spirit. When Thales first awoke to the power of rational thought, he lit a light whose flame was never wholly extinguished, even in the dark moments when Rome's collapse seemed to herald a world of barbarism and stupidity. Once philosophy set up house in the very core of human beings, it could not be evicted.

Following the example of Plato, who from time to time ended a dialogue with a myth, let us conclude this exploration of philosophy in the ancient world with a few mythological words from the Roman poet Ovid. Here, in his *Metamorphosis*, he tells how, after the gods had finished making the other animals, they turned to humans:

A living creature of finer stuff than these, more capable of lofty thought, one who could have dominion over all the rest, was lacking yet. Then man was born: whether the god who made all else, designing a more perfect world, made man of his own divine substance, or whether the new earth, but lately drawn away from heavenly ether, retained still some elements of its kindred sky—that earth which the son of Iapetus mixed with fresh, running water, and moulded into the form of the all controlling gods. And, though all other animals are prone, and fix their gaze upon the earth, he gave to man an uplifted face and bade him stand erect and turn his eyes to heaven.[40]

Discussion Questions

1. As we have seen, there were parts of the systems of Aristotle and Plato that have stood the test of time and remain valuable for philosophy. At the same time, there were some speculative parts of those philosophies that in their inception were shakily confused. Neoplatonism aimed at taking on the weak points of each system, strengthening them by correcting their errors, and, after solving the problems of each system, reconciling them to create a perfect unity. If Plato and Aristotle had, so to speak, risen from the dead and seen what Plotinus produced, what would their reactions have been?

2. Neoplatonism has some features of a religion, some of a philosophy. What is the difference between the two? Is there a clear line of demarcation, or is the border fuzzy? Is one "more respectable" than the other? Is there a polite way of debating this question?

3. How well does Neoplatonism deal with the vexing problem of the connection between things material and things spiritual? Compared to Plato's theory of "participation" in the forms, is the theory of emanation sounder, less sound, or equally sound?

4. Is Augustine's conversion to philosophy essentially the same as the earlier conversions of Plato, Zeno, Polemon, and others? Or does Augustine's differ because it was inspired not by a charismatic figure but by a book? What difference is there, intellectually or emotionally, between inspiration by a person and inspiration from a book?

5. How satisfying is Augustine's solution of the problem of evil by defining evil as *nonbeing*? Does Augustine seem to have made a contribution to the problem, or does he seem to have finessed the whole matter by a clever

logical game? Either way, in terms of philosophical validity, does it matter, so long as Augustine presents a logically plausible solution?

6. If, as a Manichaean, Augustine could blame matter for his sinfulness and later, when he had embraced the doctrine of the Fall of Adam, could blame the inherited sin of Adam and the irresistible hold of sinfulness, is he equally free of responsibility for his sinfulness in either system? Is the Christian solution to the problem of evil—the Doctrine of the Fall—more satisfying than Manichaean dualism?

7. The doctrine of the Fall of Adam is a key principle in Christianity. Are there any philosophical arguments to support it? Or must it be taken as a first principle for which no argument is necessary? Is there a fundamental difference between the first principles of mathematics and philosophy on the one hand and those of religion on the other? If so, what is the difference?

8. Does Boethius's explanation of the concept of the Trinity on the basis of Neoplatonist distinctions satisfy the requirements of philosophy for being a valid argument?

9. Does Boethius's solution to the problem of God's foreknowledge and human free will strike you as plausible? Can you think of any mechanism by which the theory might be testable?

Notes

1. Augustine borrows long passages from the *Enneads*, for example, which he read in a Latin translation. See Augustine, *Confessions* 9.10, where he paraphrases Plotinus, *Enneads* 5.1.2, and Augustine, *On the Immortality of the Soul*, where he paraphrases Plotinus, *Enneads* 4.7.3.

2. Porphyry, *Life of Plotinus* 8.1–12, trans. A. H. Armstrong, in *Plotinus* (Cambridge, Mass.: Harvard University Press, 1966). Subsequent quotations to Porphyry and to Plotinus are from this translation.

3. Porphyry, *Life of Plotinus* 3.5.

4. Porphyry, *Life of Plotinus* 3.10.

5. In a burst of antipathy toward himself for his lustful thoughts, Origen adopted the teaching of Jesus' Sermon on the Mount and castrated himself or, as Edward Gibbon put it, "disarmed the tempter." Gibbon adds in a footnote, "Before the fame of Origen had excited envy and persecution, this extraordinary action was rather admired than censured. As it was his general practice to allegorize scripture, it seems unfortunate that, in this instance only, he should have adopted the literal sense" (*The Decline and Fall of the Roman Empire*, chap. 15).

6. Porphyry, *Life of Plotinus* 3.3.

7. Porphyry, *Life of Plotinus* 1.1.

8. Plotinus, *Enneads* 6.9.9, 5.1.3, 5.1.5–7.

9. The analogy is defective because in fact the torch would be affected, at least at the quantum level, by the photons it emits.

10. Plotinus, *Enneads* 5.4.1, 5.1.6, 5.2.1.

11. One form of separation from the body is *ecstasy*, a word that signifies literally "a standing outside of." Philo (*Who Is the Heir?* 249 ff.) distinguishes four kinds of ecstasy—a classification that in itself is suggestive of

how seriously he took attempts to separate one's soul from one's body while living. For the literary critic Longinus, ecstasy can be brought about by speeches and writings that are sublimely beautiful. In his discussion of ecstasy, Philo says that the best of the four kinds is an inspired state of being possessed and is a kind of madness as well, the kind prophets make use of. This desire to feel one's mind as a thing separate from the body (or at least to imagine that one is feeling it so) is probably responsible for the human interest in seeking the sensation of ebriety or a "high." This feeling may be obtained most immediately and harmfully with alcohol or other mind-altering drugs, a fact that explains their ubiquity. Today we also believe that it may be obtained by vigorous athletic exercise, religious frenzy, discovery, or the beauty in nature, music, literature, and art.

12. For Aristotle, by contrast, a person's intellect is the core part of his soul, but a human being is nevertheless a composite of form and matter, soul and body. In the particular composite, a person achieves individuality. The Neoplatonists follow the Stoics in identifying a person with his soul and considering the body only so much excess baggage. The Aristotelian and Stoic conceptions of happiness also differ. Although for Aristotle the core of human happiness is an activity of the soul in accordance with virtue, he acknowledges (*Ethics* 1099b1–10) that good birth, health, a sufficiency of wealth, and good appearance are required as well. The Stoics disagree, teaching that a good man can be happy "even on the rack." In other words, they wholly dismiss the need for external goods. The constant theme of the spiritual philosophies and heaven-aiming religions is disdain for the body and things physical; nevertheless, human nature seems to rebel against such asceticism and asserts, in agreement with Aristotle, its composite character.

13. See Augustine, *Confessions* 6.5.

14. Augustine rivaled Balzac in his output. Augustine himself calculated (Letter 224) that he had written more than two hundred and thirty tractates. Just one of these, the *City of God*, runs almost eleven hundred pages in the Penguin addition. In addition, there are preserved well over two hundred letters, many of prodigious length, as well as sermons, which often contain interpretations of Scripture. There are very many excellent works on Augustine. One will find fine bibliographies in Allan D. Fitzgerald, *Augustine through the Ages: An Encyclopedia* (Grand Rapids, Mich.: William B. Eerdmans, 1999), and the older W. W. Battenhouse, *A Companion to the Study of Augustine* (Grand Rapids, Mich.: Baker Book House, 1979). Peter Brown's biography, *Augustine of Hippo: A Biography* (Berkeley: University of California Press, 1967), is still the standard.

15. Augustine, *On Christian Doctrine*, trans. J. F. Shaw (Edinburgh: T. & T. Clark, 1892), 75–76.

16. Augustine, *Confessions* 3.4 (7), trans. Henry Chadwick (Oxford: Oxford University Press, 1991). Subsequent quotations from *Confessions* are from this translation.

17. Augustine, *Confessions* 4.16 (28–29).

18. This is particularly the case in books 5 to 7 of *On the Trinity*. See also the quotation on p. 344.

19. On Manichaean attitudes toward sexuality, see the very interesting account in Peter Brown, *The Body and Society: Men, Women, and Sexual Renunciation in Early Christianity* (New York: Columbia University Press, 1988), 198–201.

20. Augustine, *Confessions* 3.10.

21. Augustine, *Confessions* 6.5.

22. Augustine, *Confessions* 7.2(3).

23. Augustine, *City of God* 14.11.

24. Augustine, *City of God* 14.12.

25. Augustine, *City of God* 14.17.

26. Augustine, *On the Trinity* 5.3, trans. A. W. Haddan; rev. W. G. T. Shedd, in *Nicene and Post-Nicene Fathers*, ed. P. Schaff, vol. 3 (Peabody, Mass.: Hendrickson Publishers, 1994).

27. Augustine, *On the Trinity* 15.25.

28. These views are found, in the order discussed, in Augustine, *Letters* 93 and 204. See also Brown, 336. On Augustine as "the patron of repression" see Garry Wills's biography *Saint Augustine* (New York: Penguin Books, 1999), 102–4. Under the Christian emperors Valentinian and Theodosius, heresy was declared a capital crime.

29. Augustine, *Letters* 103, 133.

30. Boethius, *Consolation of Philosophy* Book 1, Prose 4.

31. For a sympathetic discussion of the Augustinian–Boethian conception of eternity as an immutable, atemporal duration, see Eleonore Stump and Norman Kretzmann, "Eternity," *Journal of Philosophy* 78 (1981): 429–58.

32. Boethius, *Second Commentary on Porphyry's Isagoge* 36–37, in *Five Texts on the Mediaeval Problem of Universals: Porphyry, Boethius, Abelard, Duns Scotus, Ockham*, trans. Paul V. Spade (Indianapolis: Hackett Publishing, 1994).

33. G. B. Hill, *James Boswell's Life of Johnson* (New York: Harper and Brothers, n.d.), vol. 2, 146.

34. In 1277 Pope John XXI had the bishop of Paris declare a number of Thomas's views heretical, including such views as that angels lacked bodies.

35. Aristotle, *Metaphysics* 993b20.

36. The part of the definition of knowledge as a safe and sure apprehension is from Philo, *On the Preliminary Studies* 144 ff.; the part about causes from Aristotle, *Metaphysics* 992a24.

37. Plato, *Timaeus*, trans. Benjamin Jowett (Oxford: Oxford University Press, 1953), 73a.

38. Galen, *On the Usefulness of the Parts of the Body*, trans. Margaret Tallmadge May (Ithaca, N.Y.: Cornell University Press, 1968), I.241.

39. Cicero, *The Nature of the Gods*, trans. Horace C. P. McGregor (London: Penguin Books, 1972), 1.40.

40. Ovid, *Metamorphoses*, trans. Frank Justius Miller (Cambridge, Mass.: Harvard University Press, 1968), 1.78–86.

Select Bibliography

NEOPLATONISM

358

Gerson, Lloyd P. *Plotinus*. The Arguments of Philosophers Series. London: Routledge, 1998.
Rist, John M. *Plotinus: The Road to Reality*. Cambridge: Cambridge University Press, 1967.
Wallis, R. T. *Neoplatonism*. London: Duckworth, 1995.

AUGUSTINE

Web resource: http://ccat.sas.upenn.edu/jod/twayne/twaynebib.html.
Brown, Peter. *Augustine of Hippo*. London: Faber and Faber/University of California Press, 1967.
Cochrane, Charles Norris. *Christianity and Classical Culture*. Oxford: Oxford University Press, 1942.
Gilson, Etienne. *The Christian Philosophy of Saint Augustine*. New York: Knopf, 1960.
Portalie, Eugene. *A Guide to the Thought of Saint Augustine*. Chicago: Regnery, 1960.

BOETHIUS

Gibson, M.T., ed. *Boethius: His Life, Thought and Influence*. Oxford: Blackwell, 1981.
Reiss, Edmund. *Boethius*. Boston: Twayne Publishers, 1982.

This glossary attempts to bring together the material most relevant to the main lines of ancient philosophy. In some cases, the definitions are not wholly accurate for all periods. For example, very early philosophers, whose language is often impossible to distinguish from myth, appear to have regarded the human and natural orders as identical and moral rules to apply over both the human and physical realms—and so the general philosophical sense of *law* that appears below may not apply to these thinkers. The reader will understand that each of the entries that follow could receive a detailed book-length treatment.

Art   Art is form imposed on a medium with the primary intention of instructing or pleasing or both. Many artifacts, whose purpose is primarily functional and utilitarian—bridges and industrial machines, for example—may, insofar as they give pleasures to their viewers, also be regarded as works of art. Ancient critics gave the highest praise to works of art that instruct as well as amuse—a point noted in Horace's *Ars Poetica*. Art's instruction is in human nature, that is, in humans' understanding of themselves and their relationships both with external nature and with other human beings.

Beauty   Beauty is the pleasing form imposed on a medium, whether the medium be words, sounds, or matter. Beyond this bald minimum definition, there is much disagreement, and ancients from Plato to Augustine wrote entire works on the subject. Among the many matters of debate are whether beauty is different from the good, whether beauty is in activities or in things motionless, whether it is in causes as well as in effects, whether the recognition of beauty is relative to human beings or whether things are beautiful in themselves, whether one form (such as the circular) is the most perfectly beautiful form, and how beauty and desire are related.

Being   Being is the vexing subject that underlies metaphysics. The question of whether being is unitary, eternal, and unchanging—as Parmenides seems to have maintained—or whether there are different kinds of being has concerned philosophers from Presocratics to moderns. Some thinkers equate being with existence, while others maintain that things come into and go out of existence whereas being itself can never be destroyed or created. Whether being underlies the things that exist or inheres in them or is otherwise related to them is a matter of serious debate, as is the question of whether incorporeal substances such as ideas have any kind of being at all.

Cause   For Aristotle, there are four causes, and these are discussed in detail in the text. For Herodotus, the main term for *cause* (*aitia*) refers to human "responsibility," and it seems always to amount to the desire, whim, aim, or impulse of an individual human being, beyond which it is not necessary to inquire further.

Chance   Chance is an outcome that is accidental, that is, not essential to an activity in itself, and it happens for the least part. An example of chance involves a person who goes into his garden to dig a hole to plant a tree and finds a buried treasure since finding treasure is not part of the activity included in planting trees and finding treasure when planting trees hardly ever happens. It is able to be appreciated by creatures such as human beings that can engage in deliberation. Aside from Epicurus, with his teaching of a spontaneous "swerve" in atoms, the ancients did not believe that there were events that happened spontaneously, and so *chance* refers to an unanticipated concurrence of events.

Contradiction   A pair of statements, one of which is the denial of the other. Necessarily, one of these statements is true and one false. The pair of statements "God exists" and "God does not exist" is a contradiction. Here one of the statements must be true and one false. Which is true and which is false may be debated, but so long as "God" is taken as a definite thing with a meaning, one of the components of the contradiction will be true, the other false. The pair of statements "The elephant is pink" and "The elephant is gray" does not constitute a contradiction because neither statement is a denial of the other. An *affirmation* is the part of a contradiction that affirms. In the previous example, "God exists" is the affirmation. A *denial* is the part of a contradiction that denies. In the example, "God does not exist" is the denial.

Convention   *Convention* comes from the Latin word meaning *to come together*. It indicates a prearranged agreement to act in a certain way, even when any given individual has no personal conviction that such action is appropriate. For example, members of a certain fraternity may be expected to shake hands in a certain way on particular occasions. Because human beings become so habituated to their environment (with its conventions) that everything in it seems to be natural, they sometimes have difficulty distinguishing its natural and conventional features. The ancients discussed this matter in the fifth century B.C.E., in what is known as the debate about custom and convention (*nomos* and *physis*).

Cosmos   *Cosmos* is the term for an ordered whole. It is also the word for *universe*, a whole that for the ancients includes the earth, the sun, the moon, the planets, and the comets, of which orderliness is an inherent feature. For Aristotle and all other ancient thinkers except for the atomists, the universe is finite.

Definition   Definition is the act of giving boundaries to meaning. An etymological analysis will clarify the idea. The root is the Latin word *finis*, boundary. As when drawing boundaries, a minimum of several points are necessary, so in constructing definitions a certain minimum are necessary. Hence one-word definitions are useless; they are not definitions but synonyms. For a definition there must be a formula for the essence of the object being defined or a statement of a thing's genus and its differentia.

361

Desire   Desire, occurring only in animals, is a movement toward a pleasure or other perceived good (or a movement away from a pain or other perceived evil) that is stirred by perception, imagination, or thought. It occurs only in animals since only they can conceive of pleasures and pains and only they have the necessary mental faculties. An individual can desire only what he does not have. When one thinks he desires what he already has, what he actually wants is to keep it, and a desire to keep it means "to have it in the future"; since "having it in the future" is something that he does not presently have, the apparent difficulty is resolved. Desires come in various kinds, among which is *eros*, which originally indicates a sexual desire but by metaphor comes to refer to other urges; hatred, which is a desire for the destruction of the object hated; love, which is a desire for the good of the object of love; the appetites; and so forth.

Dialectic   A technique of question-and-answer in which the participants debate some issue that is (to them) vitally important. Dialectic rests on the assumptions that 1) truth exists; 2) truth is the agreement of two human beings following the rules of reason; 3) inconsistency, that is, contradiction, is the surest sign available that the conclusion reached is not true; and 4) both people must be willing to "stay at their posts" and argue until consistency is reached. When consistency is achieved, the participants enjoy the certainty and the calmness of soul that results from it.

Form   Form is the relationship of the parts to the whole; it exists when a *medium* has been so arranged as to be repeatedly recognizable. Whether the form itself has an existence apart from the medium and the mind is a metaphysical question not yet settled. For Plato, form had separable existence and was, in truth, the only real existence since media were all transient. For Aristotle, the form had no existence apart from the medium, except in the mind of human beings. The Latin word *forma* means "shape" and "beauty," as does the Greek equivalent *morphê* (as in the English word *metamorphosis*): the association of form and proportion with beauty is characteristic of classic art.

Free Will   Free will is the exercise of choice, whether exercised on trivia—such as strawberry or chocolate ice cream—or on central *moral* matters—such as to kill, to commit suicide, to defy the gods, to seek perfect self-sufficiency. Whether it actually exists is a subject of much debate. Most great works of art in the Western world assume that it does: thus the gods give Achilles the choice between a short glorious life or a long undistinguished life; they allow Aeneas to decide between staying in Libya with Dido or continuing to Italy; in Christian art, they offer Dante an education that, both as pilgrim and as poet, he is free to reject or misunderstand. Readers who wish to understand such works must make the same assumption.

Generalization   A generalization, from the Latin *genus*, meaning "birth" or "origin," refers to statements about classes or kinds of things, that is, to objects, persons, propositions, and so on, that have by nature an essential similarity in the relationship of their parts to the whole. Thus we may speak of the genus "animal," the species "human being," and then individual humans like Socrates or Marie Curie. Generalizations are statements about either the species or the genus; that is, assertions or propositions that hold true for every member of the class. In ordinary usage, generalizations need not be absolutely true so long as they are true for the most part. Our phrases "in general" and "generally" and "generally speaking" indicate that the proposition that follows is true for the most part. Most arguments about generalizations occur because those who make them have insufficient evidence. The logical conundrum implicit in total skepticism of generalizations is contained in the proposition "All generalizations are false, including this one."

Good   *Good* has four related meanings: 1) existent, that is, a thing exists rather than does not exist; 2) efficient, that is, a thing works or functions, either as a part or as a whole; 3) esthetically pleasing; and 4) morally right. The word may be used in any or all of these senses; context alone will tell. With respect to the second definition, the function of a thing will be good insofar as it contributes to the other three sorts of good; an instrument of torture might be efficient, but it would not be good as it did not contribute to moral existence or aesthetic pleasure. Here the goodness of the torture machine could be called good only in itself or from the point of view of the user but not from the point of view of mankind.

Human Being   A human being is the one creature who attempts to define his nature, who—at least in the Western world—thinks of himself as being uniquely different from other animals. Many definitions have been propounded, for example, a human being is a rational animal, a human being is a political animal, a human being is the animal who laughs, and a human being is the animal who makes tools. As yet, no satisfactory, uncontroversial definition has been found. The work of anthropologists, from the Greeks on, has constantly uncovered tribes that pose problems for the various definitions offered. The Greeks invented the concept of human being, at least as it is conceived of in the Western world. Other characteristics of a human being according to Western thought include the following: adherence to the idea and the ideal of reason, belief in the family as the natural social unit, acceptance of responsibility for one's actions, and an attitude of sustained and critical doubt, even of these characteristics.

Hypothesis   A statement that either denies or affirms and is immediately taken as true when used as a premise. A synonym for *hypothesis* is *assumption*.

Imitation   Imitation, or *mimesis*, is the process of making a likeness that resembles an original. Aristotle distinguished three kinds of imitation: things as they were or are, things as they were said to seem or to be, and things as they ought to be. The last—the paradigm—he says, ought to excel. The paradigm is not the model that the artist imitates but the imitation itself. Ancient thinkers generally believed that human beings are imitative by nature, though their works of imitation—poetry, painting, sculpture—come from technique. Some ancient critics, like Dionysius of Halicarnassus, believed that artistic imitation is conducted according to theories, a view that left open the question of why not all successful works of art have been made in accordance with theories.

Language   Language is the system of gestures, sounds, and sometimes letters by which human beings express meaning to each other. Its usual parts are words. The relationship of words is, in Western languages, called *grammar* or *syntax*. Words refer to actions (verbs), to things (nouns and pronouns), to qualities (adjectives and adverbs), to relationships (prepositions and conjunctions), and to attitudes (interjections). All words are vocal representations of actions, things, qualities, relationships, and attitudes. At least in Western languages, verbs seem to be the earliest words. To what degree the vocal sounds or their written forms express the nature of what they intend to represent is the subject of much debate. Two schools predominate: those who believe that the meaning of a word is fixed by the nature of things and those who believe that words are the result of convention. Nothing is known about the origin of language, and both views lead to difficulties. The earliest study of language is Plato's paradoxical dialogue the *Cratylus*.

Law   Order underlies all notions of law, and the various ancient words that are used to translate our word *law* cover different manifestations of the concept. The Greek *nomos*, perhaps best translated as *rule*, is used of both man-made conventions and "unwritten laws" and generally refers to the order in human society, both the social order and the moral order. Sometimes *diké (justice)* is used as a synonym; sometimes *themis* (literally, *something laid down* or *established*) is used, though *themis* sometimes refers to the natural order, sometimes to the divine order. For a *law* of nature, *physis* (*nature*) is sometimes used alone, *horé* (*hour*) and *kairos* (*critical moment*) are sometimes used in the sense of the right time, and *metron* (measure) is used in the sense of the right measure. The ancients did not always observe these distinctions, and they frequently employed the terms metaphorically. Thus *justice* is sometimes used of the physical world. Human law is traditionally seen as an imitation of divine law; even when it is not considered an imitation of divine law, it is held to be generally valid enough to allow for choice. The branch of philosophy called *metaphysics* tends to deal with natural law. The Romans, who were preoccupied with the legal process, used *ius* and *lex* as synonyms for law. They divided *ius* into *ius civile*—the various regulations distinct and different for individual states—and into what was called either *ius commune* (the shared law) or *ius gentium* (law of nations), which, established by natural reason (*naturalis ratio*), is the same for all humankind. *Lex* includes the particular rules that are be covered by *ius* but unlike *ius* does not seem to have been used in the larger, broadly conceptual sense.

Logos *Logos* refers to the chief quality that, in ancient thought, separates human beings from other animals—the faculty of reasoning with its concomitant of speech. In paganism this is a quality shared with the gods; in religions rooted in the Bible, it reflects the image of God, according to which human beings were created. In the ancient tradition, it takes two forms, speech and reason (in Latin, *oratio* and *ratio*), which are connected organically as they affect civic duty. Isocrates observes that we use the same *logos* in reasoning with ourselves as we use in persuading others. It is this dual nature of *logos*—internal and external—that causes modern readers difficulty in conceiving and translating the Greek word.

Metaphysics *Metaphysics* is a term variously used. In general, it refers to the study of being as being (that is, existence considered in itself, apart from the existence or mode of existence of particular things). For example, animals, rocks, and ideas all have some form of being; metaphysics is the branch of philosophy that deals with being by itself, without dealing with the things having being. Among the many questions with which metaphysics deals are whether only substances evident to the senses exist; whether principles are universal or individual; whether the objects of mathematics, such as points and lines, are substances and, if so, what kind. To people with no interest in philosophy, these sorts of questions seem pointless and are parodied as, for example, investigation into the number of angels who can dance on the point of a needle; to philosophers, these questions are fundamental to human understanding and worthy of study in their own right.

Mind   *Mind* is one of several words used to designate human awareness; synonymous terms are *brain, heart, sense, intelligence, intellect, psyche, spirit,* and *soul.* These may be arranged in an order based on their physical or natural reality: for example, brain and heart are physical organs; sense and intelligence are functions of physical organs; spirit and soul are, generally, nonphysical and supernatural. The word *mind* is the most neutral and comprehensive of these terms. It can be used for the total awareness either of an individual or of a group, as when we speak of "the Greek mind."

Morality   The word *morality* is from the Latin word for *custom* (*mos*) and is equivalent in meaning and etymology to the word *ethics.* Both words refer generally to the way things are done in a society and, by extension, to the way they should be done, on the grounds that successful practices of the past ought not to be disregarded. Attempts to find a universal morality have proceeded both deductively, as in the *Nicomachean Ethics* of Aristotle, and inductively, as in the work of anthropologists. In our age it is sometimes said that art is *amoral,* that is, outside the prescriptive and normative grounds of social conduct. Moralists from Plato on have argued, however, that all human actions, including art, are necessarily social and therefore moral. Contemporary morality often regards actions as good or bad insofar as they affect individuals, and the effect on society at large is ignored. A similar phenomenon occurred during Hellenistic times, a fact that is perhaps suggestive of parallels between that age and ours.

Nature   Nature is what art imitates, what science analyzes. Most uses of nature can be resolved into one of these three propositions: 1) nature is whatever happens, 2) nature is the statistical majority, or 3) nature is what ought to be. The famous line in *Hamlet*—that art holds a mirror up to nature—rests on the assumption that nature has reality and form; contemporary relativistic notions assume that reality consists of a series of imposed viewpoints the sum total of which will, at any given time, constitute reality, and this totality increases with each new scientific theory or observation, with each new artistic vision. Human nature is that part of nature in which we find the operations of the human psyche—reason, free will, emotion, thought. When Stoics speak of a "life according to nature," they often mean "according to human nature," that is, "in accordance with reason."

Necessity   Necessity, the impossibility of things to be other than they are, takes two forms in the West. In its religious form, it is called *predestination*, the view that the gods or God have determined everything that happens and, in consequence, that human beings have no free will. Logically, rigorous predestination is unanswerable, except by Samuel Johnson's observation that all argument is for it, all experience against it. In its secular form, it is called *determinism* and is the view that a series of natural causes has brought about what happens in the world. One contemporary form of determinism is behavioral psychology, which explains behavior in mechanical terms of stimulus and response.

Paradox   A paradox (from the Greek for what goes against a *doxa*, a common opinion about what is true) is a proposition that *seems* to be a contradiction but that, on complete understanding, turns out to be consistent. For example, the claim that in art "less is more" appears to be a contradiction. But when the claim is understood to mean that "less paint is more effect," it becomes a paradox. Paradoxes exist in compact form, such as the oxymoron ("jumbo shrimp"), and in longer statements, as in the saying of Heraclitus, "the way up is the way down," or that of Jesus, "the first will be last."

367

Persuasion   Persuasion is the process of inducing a desired response in other individuals. In general, though there are many forms of persuasion, including torture, bribery, extortion, and threats, the term refers to inducing the response by *logos*. In rhetoric, the *logos* generally takes the form of an appeal to the emotions; in philosophy it takes the form of argument. Civilized society allows both forms. Since it is easier to give a semblance of truth rather than formulate a comprehensible and consistent argument, rhetoric has enjoyed a greater success than philosophy. In antiquity hundreds of manuals were written to teach the arts of persuasion by rhetorical means. For Plato, however, such rhetoric was the enemy of philosophy; for Aristotle, rhetoric was a subject of philosophical inquiry and could serve philosophy. It is perhaps ironic therefore that the dialogues of Plato are emotionally inspirational on account of their rhetoric, while the surviving works of Aristotle, rhetorically dull, are far less stirring.

Plausibility In philosophy, plausibility refers to the logical coherence and persuasiveness of an argument; in rhetoric, to the apparent soundness of a set of claims. One of the objections to rhetoric is that the propositions in a speech may *appear* valid because of deception, either through manipulations of logic or through a misrepresentation of evidence. To the many—a group that is often spoken of derogatively by ancient philosophers but that never includes the speakers—the distinction between the plausibility of rhetoric and that of philosophy was often lost. In Rome, philosophers and rhetoricians were sometimes confounded and suffered a shared banishment.

Principle A principle (from the Latin word meaning "first" or "beginning") is a generalized observation of nature used as a starting point or assumption or premise or axiom for the purpose of logical argumentation (*starting point, assumption, premise,* and *axiom* are synonyms of *principle*). Thus the statement "If equals are added to equals, the results are equal" is a principle in mathematics; the statement that of two given explanations for a set of phenomena, both of which are adequate, the simpler is likely to be the right one is a principle of science. It is possible to lay down principles that are not based on nature; such principles lead to arguments that can be perfectly valid but that may not have true conclusions. No logical system has yet been found for determining the truth of principles. We must rely on experience and observation.

Psyche *Psyche* is a Greek word that means, etymologically, *breath*; it is equivalent to the Hebrew *ruach*, which is generally translated "soul." In Homer, the psyche seems to be a kind of wraithlike image of the living man; later, in Plato, it becomes the conscious and sentient center of human beings, the awareness of itself and its environment that attempts both to adapt to the environment and to change it, presumably in accordance with some conception or idea of what is better. The word *psyche* is one of the roots of the word *psychology*, that is, the *logos*, rationale, science, or study of the psyche. Roughly equivalent terms are *mind* and *soul* and sometimes—erroneously—*personality*. These are distinguished from "brain," that part of the body that is subject to scientific investigation. Mind tends to be treated as reason or intellect; soul—at least in Christianity—is considered to be that infusion of divine being, of God, made at the birth of each human being. Its nature is variously considered as a particle of God's essence; as an innate set of ideas by nature predisposed toward right reason, truth, and virtue, though hindered by the matter of flesh and original sin; and as the yearning of the individual for union with the oneness of perfection.

Purpose　Purpose refers to end of an action, seen before the beginning and used as a reason for choosing to begin. To have a purpose presupposes an ability to see the relationship between the parts and the whole and to understand the sequence of acts, spatial and temporal, that will result in the whole. Purposes may be either immediate or ultimate; an immediate purpose is any part that, in the eyes of the agent, marks some kind of dividing point in the action. Immediate purposes are sometimes called "mediate ends" or "mediate goals."

Rhetoric　Rhetoric is the use of language to work on the emotions. One starts with certain aims and intentions, certain ideas, and then seeks ways to make them persuasive. The set of techniques for doing so leaves the user of rhetoric open to the charge of insincerity, of a lack of organic connection with his subject and position—hence the sustained attack by Plato on rhetoric. Because the art of rhetoric arose from the practice of making speeches, of oratory, it reached its height in antiquity, and the best book on the subject is still Aristotle's.

Science　Science consists of 1) the observation of natural phenomena in order to express causal relationships or the relationships of the parts to the whole in a formula or law, an activity called theory, and 2) the application of theoretical formulae to the needs and desires of human life. Pure theory occurs in mathematics, where the subject matter is at best platonically connected with matter, or in those parts of physics, chemistry, and so on that most closely approach mathematics. Elsewhere scientists may use experiments on actual matter as a means to theory; so long as the aim is a formula, they are engaged in what is called "pure research," that is, knowledge without a specific utilitarian end in view. Traditionally, science was a species of the genus philosophy and was called "natural philosophy" as distinct from the investigation of human and divine conduct called "normal philosophy." In Greco-Roman antiquity, the distinction was not clearly observed; the Greek word *technê* (English "technique") and the Latin word *ars* (English "art") covered both.

Theology Theology, a Greek word coined by Plato, refers to the rational analysis of the order of God, the gods, or the divine. Whether theology is possible is itself the subject of much debate: if the divine be utterly transcendent, then it is unknowable; if it be knowable, then it is limited, definable, and hence not divine. Although notions of limited deity are current in many religions, Western theologians tend to make the deity's attributes (for example, omnipotence, omniscience) utterly transcendent. Such reasoning presents insoluble problems in reconciling free will and predestination. The debate has been intensified in Christianity, where monotheism has led to a concentration of omni-attributes; polytheistic antiquity was aware of the problem insofar as issues were framed in terms of philosophic monotheism.

Theory Theory, from the Greek word meaning "to see," refers to the activity of the mind when it understands the relationship between the parts and the whole. In ancient Greece, especially in Aristotle, theory referred to the activity of the mind as it investigated metaphysics and the nature of divine being, that which "thinks about thinking," a view that held throughout the Middle Ages and early Renaissance. Theory is to be distinguished from *vision*, a Latin word also etymologically connected with the verb *to see*. A vision is an apprehension of the relationship between the parts and the whole but not one ready to be worked out in analytical and rational terms.

Thesis An undemonstrable statement that is used as a premise in a syllogism or investigation. Aristotle suggests that a thesis may be either a definition or a hypothesis when these are to be applied to the question at hand. For example, the definition of a monkey need not be investigated if we are endeavoring to learn about the endocrine system of monkeys. We take as a thesis (sometimes also called a *posit*) what a monkey is. It is not necessary for an investigator to work out a definition of *monkey* in order to investigate the hormonal system.

A page number in boldface indicates that a passage is quoted. Foreign terms are noted only where they are translated and discussed.

About the Author

James A. Arieti is the Graves H. Thompson Professor of Classics at Hampden-Sydney College, where he has taught since 1978. He received his B.A. from Grinnell College and Ph.D. from Stanford University and previously has taught at Stanford University, The Pennsylvania State University, and Cornell College. He is the author of six other books, *The Dating of Longinus, Love Can Be Found, Longinus's On the Sublime: Translation and Commentary, Interpreting Plato: The Dialogues as Drama, Discourses on the First Book of Herodotus*, and *The Scientific and the Divine: Conflict and Reconciliation from Ancient Greece to the Present*, as well as editor of four other books. Dr. Arieti has delivered more than sixty papers at professional conferences, colleges, and universities in North America and Europe and has published numerous articles on subjects that include Empedocles, Greek athletics, ancient medicine, Herodotus, Homer, Horace, Livy, Machiavelli, Philo, Plato, and the Septuagint.

About the Illustrator

David M. Gibson, received his B.F.A and M.F.A from the San Francisco Art Institute and is a painter and pastelist who maintains studios in Saratoga Springs, New York, and Montreal, Quebec. He has exhibited his work widely in the United States and in Canada